The Art of Leadership

GEORGE MANNING
Northern Kentucky University

KENT CURTIS
Northern Kentucky University

Boston   Burr Ridge, IL   Dubuque, IA   Madison, WI   New York   San Francisco   St. Louis
Bangkok   Bogotá   Caracas   Kuala Lumpur   Lisbon   London   Madrid   Mexico City
Milan   Montreal   New Delhi   Santiago   Seoul   Singapore   Sydney   Taipei   Toronto

McGraw-Hill Higher Education

A Division of The **McGraw-Hill** *Companies*

THE ART OF LEADERSHIP

Published by McGraw-Hill/Irwin, a business unit of The McGraw-Hill Companies, Inc., 1221 Avenue of the Americas, New York, NY, 10020. Copyright © 2003 by The McGraw-Hill Companies, Inc. All rights reserved. No part of this publication may be reproduced or distributed in any form or by any means, or stored in a database or retrieval system, without the prior written consent of The McGraw-Hill Companies, Inc., including, but not limited to, in any network or other electronic storage or transmission, or broadcast for distance learning.

Some ancillaries, including electronic and print components, may not be available to customers outside the United States.

This book is printed on acid-free paper.

2 3 4 5 6 7 8 9 0 QPD/QPD 0 9 8 7 6 5 4 3

ISBN 0-07-252789-7

Publisher: *John E. Biernat*
Senior sponsoring editor: *Andy Winston*
Editorial coordinator: *Sara E. Ramos*
Senior marketing manager: *Ellen Cleary*
Producer, Media technology: *Jennifer Becka*
Project manager: *Natalie Ruffatto*
Senior production supervisor: *Michael R. McCormick*
Coordinator freelance design: *Mary L. Christianson*
Senior supplement producer: *Susan Lombardi*
Senior digital content specialist: *Brian Nacik*
Cover freelance designer: *Maureen McCutcheon*
Cover illustration: *© Nip Rogers*
Typeface: *10.5/12 Times Roman*
Compositor: *Carlisle Communications, Ltd.*
Printer: *Quebecor World Dubuque Inc.*

Library of Congress Cataloging-in-Publication Data
Manning, George, 1943–
    The art of leadership / George Manning, Kent Curtis.
      p. cm.
    Includes index.
    ISBN 0-07-252789-7 (alk. paper)
    1. Leadership. I. Curtis, Kent, 1939- II. Title.
BF637.L4 .M36 2003
158'.4—dc21   2002070995

www.mhhe.com

Dedication

We dedicate this book to our families:

Nancy and Page, Larry, and Heather

Mary and Lisa, Denise, and Craig

Contents in Brief

Contents

Preface

The Art of Leadership is an applied book that combines behavior theory with business practice. Each unit teaches central concepts and skills in an important area of leadership development. The book is made more valuable and the impact greater by the self-evaluation questionnaires and practical exercises that are used for personal development and class involvement. *The Art of Leadership* is more than a textbook; it is a "learning" book that actively involves the reader in the learning process.

The Art of Leadership teaches concepts, principles, and skills of leadership in a way that is appropriate for both new and experienced leaders, as well as for the everyday person who must influence others to get things done. Our goal is for you to use this book to develop your full potential as a leader and to *become the kind of leader you always wanted to have.*

Central Ideas of This Book

This book is based on two ideas. The first is that leadership will take place to the extent the leader cares about the work to be done. Equally important, the leader must care about people. Neither of these qualities is sufficient without the other, and neither can be false. People know when the leader cares. When the leader is committed to the task and is concerned about people, these qualities serve as magnets and motivators to followers, and their potential for achievement becomes enormous.

The second premise of the book is that leadership is an art that can be developed through mastery of nine key areas of success. The successful leader must possess knowledge and skills in the following areas: understanding leadership variables, the power of vision, the importance of ethics, the empowerment of people, leadership principles, understanding people, effective delegation, developing others, and performance management.

Who Should Read This Book?

The Art of Leadership is written for students in leadership development and other management-related courses, such as leadership principles, contemporary leadership, and managerial skills. The material is appropriate for use at the university level as well as in corporate university programs. It is ideally suited for undergraduate degree-completion students and corporate education, where there is an emphasis on developing leadership competency.

The level of material is appropriate for both emerging and experienced leaders. Emerging leaders can use this book to prepare themselves to meet the demands of being a leader. Having a vision of what should be done, effectively using authority, motivating people to perform at their best, and solving tough personnel problems—discussed in Parts 2, 4, 6, and 9—are challenges all leaders must face.

Experienced leaders can use this book to address workplace issues, taking leadership skills to new levels of effectiveness. Matching leadership style with the needs of followers, leading by values and ethical principles, raising employee morale, delegating work effectively, and helping people through change—discussed in Parts 1, 3, 5, 7, and 8—are important areas for leaders to address.

By understanding leadership and its challenges, appreciating the importance of caring leadership, and developing the skills required for effective leadership, readers will (1) be more effective at work, (2) gain knowledge and skills, and (3) have the ability to lead others when the opportunity occurs.

Approach and Style of the Book

The difference between most other leadership texts and *The Art of Leadership* can be compared to the difference between a lecture and a seminar. Although both are good educational vehicles, the lecture is better for conveying large amounts of information, while the seminar is better for developing skills and attitudes. A good lecture is interesting and builds knowledge, while a good seminar is stimulating and builds competency. Without sacrificing either theoretical foundation or important content, *The Art of Leadership* emphasizes the interactive, seminar approach to learning.

The writing style is personal and conversational, with minimal professional jargon. True-life examples clarify points under consideration. Concepts are supported by facts and figures, as well as by stories and anecdotes that are meaningful and easy to remember. Each unit includes learning activities to bridge the gap between theory and on-the-job practice. Our goal has been to include material that is interesting to read, practical to use, and personalized to the reader's own concerns.

Supplemental Information and Instructional Aids

An *Instructor's Guide* is available to accompany this text. Contents include:

- Study quizzes—to test for understanding.
- Discussion questions—to personalize the subject.
- PowerPoint transparencies—to enhance lectures.
- Notes and anecdotes—for class discussion.
- Suggested films and videos—for additional learning.
- An extensive bibliography—for book reports and term papers.
- Suggested articles—for related reading.
- Interactive questionnaires and exercises—for experiential learning.

The emphasis is on using cases and applications to complement the text, increase interest, and personalize the subject.

How to Use This Book

The Art of Leadership integrates current knowledge, skill development, and personal insight about leadership. It can be used as a textbook for teaching others, a workbook for personal development, and a deskbook for ready reference in the area of leadership. The material is arranged in a logical sequence for learning. The best approach is to *interact* with the material. Read the narrative, complete the questionnaires, examine the interpretations, and review the principles and techniques. Then ask: How does this apply to me? How can I use this concept or information to improve my leadership effectiveness? Then *take action*.

To increase interest and improve overall learning, try the following:

1. Use the Learning Points and Reflection Points included in each part of the book to focus your reading, improve comprehension, and increase retention of the material.

2. Share questionnaires and exercises with family, friends, and co-workers, especially those who are interested in leadership development. In that way, you can make tangible use of what you learn and may even help others.

3. Think of the best leader you have ever had. What qualities did this individual possess? In what ways did he or she demonstrate the art of leadership? Use the material in this book to develop your own leadership effectiveness.

4. Write in the book. Follow the advice of Yale professor William Phelps: "Books are for use, not for show; you should own no book that you are afraid to mark up." You may want to use two markers to highlight information—one for personal development and one to help others. Use the margins, underline, write your own ideas: Personalize the material.

Good luck in your learning!

We want your suggestions. If you have questions or see a way to improve this book, please write. Thank you.

George Manning
Kent Curtis
Northern Kentucky University, Highland Heights, Kentucky 41099
E-mail: manningg@nku.edu
         curtisk@nku.edu

Acknowledgments

The last words written in a book are the acknowledgments, and they are placed in the beginning, as they should be.

Special thanks goes to Mary Curtis for her tireless efforts in researching, editing and preparing the multiple manuscript revisions for publication.

We are especially grateful to those whose work has helped shape and guide our ideas. Many of these prominent thinkers are mentioned in this book. Although the others are too numerous to list, we are no less indebted to them for their contributions to the field.

Appreciation also goes to the following colleagues and supporters who have provided substantive help in manuscript review and research:

Mark Berry, Delta Airlines

Melanie Bingham, Perfetti-Van Melle, USA

Bruce K. Blaylock, Radford University

Timothy Burt, University of Durham (England)

Mike Campbell, American Electric Power

Bob Caplon, IBM

Ruth Cash-Smith, Ottawa University

Dennis Chandler, Measured Progress

Mary Deville, Pulaski Technical College

Jeanne Dexter, Southwestern College

A. Charles Drubel, Muskingum College

Kerry Gillihan, Cardinal Hill Healthcare System

Sharon Glazer, San Jose State University

Ronald Green, Johnson & Johnson

Dan Gregorie, Choicecare/Humana

David M. Hall, Saginaw Valley State University

William R. Harbour, Longwood College

Loretta Harper, University of Utah

Larry Hitch, Ford Motor Company

Jill Isaacs, Western & Southern Financial Group

Dan Keefe, Great American Insurance Companies

Anne Kilpatrick, Medical University of South Carolina

Michael Koshuta, Purdue University North Central

Cathy Kramer, Association for Quality and Participation

David Krings, Hamilton County Government

Niaz Latif, Purdue University

Charles Leffler, North Carolina State University

Bill Lindsay, Northern Kentucky University

Steve Martin, The Huber Company

Barbara Mathews, Baptist Healthcare System

Steve McMillen, Hillenbrand Industries

Laban Miller, Cardinal Hill Healthcare System

Joe Ohren, Eastern Michigan University

Joe Petrick, Wright State University

Paul Quealy, Cincinnati Milacron

David Richeson, Mannesmann-Stabilus, USA

Tony Ross, Delta Airlines

Joseph C. Santora, Essex County College

Margaret Sassler, Unbound Consulting

Kraig Schell, Angelo State University

Vince Schulte, Northern Kentucky University

Angel Scott, University of Durham (England)

Art Shriberg, Xavier University

Betty Jo Sproull, Ohio Valley Medical Center

Terri Stewart, Just the Basics

Marius Van Melle, Van Melle, Inc.

Claus Von Zychlin, TriHealth

Jeff Walter, Great American Insurance Companies

John L. Waltman, Eastern Michigan University

Beverly Watts, Kentucky Commission on Human Rights

Angela Woodward, Leadership Kentucky

Jim Youngquist, University of Georgia

With deep appreciation, we would like to thank the talented and dedicated book publishing team of McGraw-Hill/Irwin: Publisher – John E. Biernat; senior sponsoring editor – Andy Winston; editorial coordinator – Sara E. Ramos; senior marketing manager – Ellen Cleary; project manager – Natalie Ruffatto; copy editor – Alice Jaggard; senior production supervisor – Michael R. McCormick; coordinator freelance design – Mary L. Christianson; producer, media technology – Jennifer Becka; senior supplement producer – Susan Lombardi; and senior digital content specialist – Brian Nacik. Each of you have made the writing of this book enjoyable and the quality of the book immeasurably better.

Most of all, we would like to thank our wives, Nancy and Mary, for their love, encouragement, and never-ending support.

About the Authors

George Manning is professor of psychology at Northern Kentucky University. He is a consultant to business, industry, and government, serving clients such as AT&T, General Electric, IBM, the United Auto Workers, Young Presidents' Organization, and the National Institutes of Health. He lectures on economic and social issues, including quality of work life, workforce values, and business ethics. He maintains an active program of research and writing in organizational psychology. His current studies and interests include the changing meaning of work and coping skills for personal and social change.

Kent Curtis is professor and coordinator of leadership and organizational studies at Northern Kentucky University. He recently examined the collegiate tutorial system as a visiting Fellow at the University of Durham in England. He has designed numerous employee and management development programs and has served as a consultant to business, industry, and government, with such clients as Texas Medical Center, Wendy's International, and American Electric Power. His current research includes developing the leader as an effective teacher, employee empowerment, process management, and distance learning.

The Art of Leadership

art (ärt), noun. 1. Skill acquired by experience or study. 2. a system of rules to facilitate performance; the use of skill and imagination in applying such rules (the art of building, the art of persuasion). 3. endeavor requiring special knowledge and ability (fine arts, practical arts). 4. the product or result of artistic faculty (body of work).

leadership (lēd-er-ship), noun. 1. Showing the way or direction; the course of action. 2. influencing or causing to follow by words and deeds. 3. guiding the behavior of others through ideas, strength, or heroic feats. 4. the position or function of one who leads (the king led his people). 5. the ability to lead (she displayed leadership skill).

Introduction: Setting the Stage

ALL OVER THE WORLD in corporations and government agencies, there are millions of executives who imagine their place on the organization chart has given them a body of followers. And of course it hasn't. It has given them subordinates. Whether the subordinates become followers depends on whether the executives act like leaders.

—John Gardner

Learning Points

In the Introduction, you will discover the answers to these questions:
- What is leadership, and why is it important?
- Where do leaders learn to lead, and what do people want in a leader?
- What are the satisfactions and frustrations of leadership?
- What are the elements of caring leadership?

Leadership is a concept that is both current and timeless. In one form or another, the leadership process has been central to human interaction since the dawn of society. Excellence in leadership requires the ability to attract capable people, motivate them to put forth their best efforts, and solve problems that arise. These are difficult tasks, which helps explain why effective leadership is rare and why we respect those who excel.

To personalize the subject, consider these questions: Have you ever been the victim of a poor leader? How do you feel about the good leaders you have known? If you have experienced both types of leaders, you know firsthand the importance of good leadership. No other factor is more important for work morale and job performance.

There are millions of people who know what it is like to work for a boss who

- Takes all the credit for work done by others.
- Is selfish and rude.
- Makes mistakes and blames others.
- Is tyrannical and cruel.
- Cares only about self-preservation.
- Is threatened by competence.
- Is dishonest and unfair.

All these examples are real, all these factors diminish people's lives at work, and none is necessary. We are convinced that the weakest link in business and industry today is leadership. It is not technology; it is not tools or equipment; it is not facilities; it is not the skills of employees; it is not systems and procedures. It is leadership.[1]

What Is Leadership?

Leadership is social influence. It means leaving a mark. It is initiating and guiding, and the result is change. The product is a new character or direction that otherwise would never be. By their **ideas** and **deeds,** leaders show the way and influence the behavior of others.[2]

To understand the importance of ideas, consider the legend of King Arthur, who led the Knights of the Round Table with his vision of chivalry:

My teacher Merlyn, who always remembered things that haven't happened better than things that have, told me once that a few hundred years from now it will be discovered that the world is round—round like the table at which we sat with such high hope and noble purpose. If you do what I ask, perhaps people will remember how we of Camelot went questing for right and honor and justice. Perhaps one day men will sit around this world as we did once at our table, and go questing once more . . . for right . . . honor . . . and justice.[3]

To understand the importance of deeds, consider the storyteller Homer's account of Achilles, who led Greek warriors by his heroic feats:

So saying, he plunged once more into the fight and man after man fell before his sword and before his spear. He raged among the Trojans like a whirlwind that drives the flames this way and that when there is a forest fire along the dry slopes of the mountains.[4]

History holds countless examples of ideas and acts that have determined human destiny. Consider the events put in motion and the impact on the world when 56 leaders signed the Declaration of Independence, a Unanimous Declaration of the Thirteen United States of America, in Congress July 4, 1776.[5]

The Importance of Leadership

Upon every wave of political history has been a Caesar, an Elizabeth, a Napoleon, or a Saladin. In every lull, leadership has been absent. Consider the period of approximately A.D. 800 to 1000:

Europe lapsed into utter decentralization, and lost for centuries the administrative unity that the reign of Charlemagne promised. A heavy blow was dealt at the slowly developing culture that the eighth century produced. It was not without justice that the ninth and tenth centuries have been called the "the Dark Ages." The internal history of continental Europe became a dismal record of tiresome local feuds and private wars.[6]

Leadership is important not only in government, but in other areas of life as well. Social conscience and conduct have been influenced by reformers such as Martin Luther King and Susan B. Anthony:

Susan B. Anthony was a passionate advocate, who saw "the vote" as the symbol of women's emancipation and independence as well as the indispensable condition of a true government. In her old age, although still voteless, she declared, "The world has never witnessed a greater revolution than in the status of women during the past half century."[7]

The fates of nations have been determined by military figures such as Alexander the Great and Joan of Arc:

Alexander the Great opened a new era in the history of the world and, by his life's work, determined its development for many centuries. The permanent result of his life was the development of Greek civilization into a civilization that was worldwide.[8]

Civilization has been shaped by philosophers such as John Stuart Mill and Adam Smith:

John Stuart Mill was one of England's greatest philosophers, hardly surpassed by thinkers of the highest order. Mill taught that a popular representative government (democracy) inevitably makes for progress.[9]

The initiative of leaders has a formative place in history. At times their eloquence, like Churchill's, may be worth a thousand regiments; their skill, like Napoleon's, may win battles and establish states. If they are teachers or prophets, like Mohammed, wise in insight, their words may inspire good deeds.[10]

Three Types of Leaders

There are many ways to lead, and indeed, we are influenced by some people even centuries after they are gone. Some leaders are **teachers,** committed to being rule breakers and value creators; some are **heroes,** devoted to great causes and noble works; and some are **rulers,** motivated principally to dominate others and exercise power. Consider how the ideas and deeds of the teachers, heroes, and rulers in Table I–1 have influenced the world.

Table I–1
Types of Leaders in History

Teacher	Hero	Ruler
Aquinas	Columbus	Alexander
Aristotle	Curie	Charlemagne
Augustine	da Vinci	Elizabeth I
Buddha	Darwin	Frederick II
Confucius	Edison	Genghis Khan
Jesus	Einstein	Hitler
Lao-tzu	Ford	Isabella I
Luther	Galileo	Julius Caesar
Marx	Gutenberg	Louis XIV
Moses	Hippocrates	Mao Tse-tung
Mohammed	Michelangelo	Napoleon
Paul	Newton	Ramses II
Plato	Pasteur	Saladin
Rumi	Shakespeare	Washington
Socrates	Watt	Yoritomo

How Many Leaders Are There?

Are we led by a few, or are there many who lead? Words such as *emperor, king,* and *chief* differentiated rulers from others in earlier times. There were few powerful positions, books were rare, and mass education was unknown. Today information is everywhere, ideas are free, and self-expression is encouraged. It is a different world, as evidenced by the fifty-sixth edition of *Who's Who in America, 2002,* which contains entries for more than 125,000 people. Each of these individuals, by ideas or deeds, has influenced the lives of others; each has been a teacher, hero, or ruler.

There is a changing perception of who can be a leader today. The response is heard over and over: Everyone can be a leader. Leadership is shifting from an autocratic, hierarchical model toward an empowering, participatory model. The new definition recognizes the potential and unique contributions of everyone. As former secretary of labor Robert Reich says, "Everyone has a leader inside." No longer is leadership viewed as a combination of charisma and expertise possessed only by a few people at the top of an organizational pyramid. Today it is viewed as the challenge and responsibility of every individual with potential to make a difference.[11]

Consider the example of Rosa Parks, whose courage helped determine the course of civil rights in American society:

It was December 1, 1955, when a white passenger aboard a Montgomery, Alabama, bus asked Rosa Parks to yield her seat. Her refusal to move to the back of the bus ended in her arrest, but began the non-violent protest movement for civil rights in the United States. A year-long boycott of the Montgomery bus system, led by Martin Luther King, forced the issue of the South's Jim Crow laws to the forefront of America's consciousness. The Supreme Court's 1956 decision to declare segregation laws unconstitutional signaled a victory for Parks, of whom King said "she had been tracked down by the Zeitgeist—the spirit of time."[12]

In meaningful ways, leadership is provided by the multitude of people who influence their families, friends, work groups, and organizations. These leaders are parents, supervisors, officers, and other leadership figures. Think of your own experiences. Have you not at some time provided leadership to others, either by your ideas or by the example you set?

How Qualities of the Individual and Environmental Factors Influence the Leadership Process

The leadership scholar James MacGregor Burns once called leadership one of the most observed and least understood phenomena on earth. One of the questions frequently asked is, Which is more important—the individual or the environment? In his book *Leadership,* Burns concludes that leadership is fired in the forge of both personal ambition and social opportunity.[13]

Qualities of the Individual

Historically, leadership has been attributed to the individual. This view is sometimes called the great man theory. Reflecting this view, the Scottish philosopher and historian Thomas Carlyle believed that among the undistinguished masses are people of light and learning, individuals superior in power, courage, and understanding. Carlyle saw the history of the human race as the biographies of these leaders, its great men and women: "Their moral character may be something less than perfect; their courage may not be the essential ingredient; yet they are superior. They are followed, admired, and obeyed to the point of worship."[14]

Ralph M. Stogdill, one of the most distinguished scholars on leadership, has found certain traits of the individual that correlate positively with leadership:

The leader is characterized by: a strong drive for responsibility and task completion; vigor and persistence in pursuit of goals; venturesomeness and originality in problem-solving; drive to exercise initiative in social situations; self-confidence and sense of personal identity; willingness to accept consequences of decision and action; readiness to absorb interpersonal stress; willingness to tolerate frustration and delay; ability to influence other persons' behavior; and capacity to structure social interaction systems to the purpose at hand.

It can be concluded that the cluster of characteristics listed above differentiate leaders from followers, effective from ineffective leaders, and higher echelon from lower echelon leaders. In other words, different strata of leaders and followers can be described in terms of the extent to which they exhibit these characteristics. These characteristics considered individually hold little diagnostic or predictive significance. In combination, it would appear that they interact to generate personality dynamics advantageous to the person seeking the responsibilities of leadership.[15]

Environmental Factors

More recently, leadership has been viewed as an acquired competency, the product of many forces, not the least of which are environment and circumstance. In this sense, leadership is seen as a social phenomenon, not an individual trait. This school of thought helps explain why leaders who are successful in one situation (for example, building a bridge) may not be successful in another (such as directing a play or a research team).[16] The same individual may exert leadership in one time and place and not in another. Stogdill explains:

It should be noted that to a large extent our conceptions of characteristics of leadership are cultur-ally determined. The ancient Egyptians attributed three qualities of divinity to their king. They said of him, "Authoritative utterance is in thy mouth, perception is in thy heart, and thy tongue is the shrine of justice." This statement would suggest that the Egyptians were demanding of their leader the qualities of authority, discrimination, and just behavior.

An analysis of Greek concepts of leadership, as exemplified by different leaders in Homer's *Iliad,* showed four aspects were valued: (1) justice and judgment—Agamemnon; (2) wisdom and counsel—Nestor; (3) shrewdness and cunning—Odysseus; and (4) valor and action—Achilles. All of these qualities were admired by the Greeks. Shrewdness and cunning are not as highly regarded in our contemporary society as they once were (although justice, judgment, wisdom, valor, and action remain in high esteem).[17]

The patterns of behavior regarded as acceptable in leaders differ from time to time and from one culture to another; thus, the establishment of educational institutions and curricula to impart and reinforce knowledge, skills, and attitudes deemed to be important by a society or group.[18]

Probably the most convincing support for leadership as a social phenomenon is the fact that throughout history male leaders have outnumbered female leaders to a significant degree. Even the definition of the word leader is a social phenomenon. Consider the case of "President" Edith Wilson, leader in all but name during the incapacitating illness of her husband, President Woodrow Wilson. It is Woodrow, however, whom history credits as leader, as president, even during the period of his inability to govern. Public recognition of Mrs. Wilson's influence would not have been in line with the norms of the times.

Interaction between the Individual and the Environment

Evidence shows that both the qualities of the person *and* environmental factors are important elements in the leadership equation. Leadership results from the inextri-cable interaction between the two. Findings from sociobiological studies of other animal species support this view. For example, biologist Richard Borowsky has discovered spontaneous growth among male fish. Young males remain small and sexually underdeveloped until the adult population in the group is reduced. Then, size and sexual maturation accelerate dramatically. Clearly, biological and sociological systems are closely related.[19]

Similar signs of sudden maturation are found in human beings. Leaders may emerge spontaneously in social crises after filling essentially anonymous roles for years. Consider the transformation of Poland's Lech Walesa from shipyard worker to national labor leader during the 1980s. Some people seem to have innate abilities that unfold under certain conditions—external circumstances and internal qualities interact to create a sudden and dramatic spurt of performance.

Where Leaders Learn to Lead and What People Want in a Leader

In the most extensive study ever done on leadership, the U.S. Chamber of Commerce sought to answer two questions: (1) Where do leaders learn to lead? and (2) What do people want in a leader?[20]

The number one place people say they learn to lead is from **experience.** They are thrown in the water and expected to sink or swim. Ask yourself how much of your leadership approach and skill you have learned from experience.

The second most cited place people learn to lead is from **examples** or models. They watch Bill or Jill lead and it seems to work out, so they do the same. They watch Sarah or Sam lead and it doesn't work out, so they resolve never to use those methods or techniques. Who have been your models or examples in the practice of leadership?

The third most cited place people say they learn to lead is from **books and school.** Formal education, learning seminars, and professional reading can provide valuable information and insight. What book, theory, or class has helped in the development of your leadership skills?

Even more interesting, especially for leaders, is to know what people want in a leader. Desired qualities change across culture and time, but what people say they want most in American society is **integrity.** When people are asked to define *integrity,* the word they mention most frequently is *honesty.* The leader with integrity always tells the truth as he or she believes it to be. Think about the best leader you have ever had; she or he probably had integrity. First and foremost, people want a leader they can trust. Ask yourself whether you have a reputation for integrity.

The second most cited quality people want in a leader is **job knowledge.** This quality ranges from knowing what direction to take (abstract visioning) to knowing how to solve problems (practical ability). Again, think about the best leader you have ever had; it is likely that this person had a purpose, a plan, and the skill to succeed. Moreover, truly great leaders keep job knowledge current. They know what it takes to be effective in the leadership position—they are good but not complacent, and they continually strive to improve. How do you currently rate on the job knowledge scale?

The third most cited quality people want in a leader can be summarized as **people-building skills.** This quality includes the ability to assemble and develop a winning team, and it involves a variety of important skills: performance planning, performance coaching, and correction of poor performance; effective delegation; effective discipline; and the ability to motivate. People want an empowering leader who will be a mentor and developer of others. Do you have the interest, ability, and patience required to motivate and develop others?[21]

**Exercise I–1
Personalizing
Leadership**

1. Where have you learned your leadership skills? Describe each pertinent learning area.

   ■ Personal experience _____

   _____

   _____

   _____

   ■ Examples or models _____

   _____

   _____

   _____

   ■ Books and school _____

   _____

   _____

   _____

2. Do you possess the qualities people want in a leader? Support your response.

   ■ Integrity (honesty)—resulting in trust

   _____

   _____

   _____

   _____

   _____

   ■ Job knowledge—resulting in confidence

   _____

   _____

   _____

   _____

   _____

   ■ People-building skills—resulting in motivation and teamwork

   _____

   _____

   _____

   _____

   _____

Satisfactions and Frustrations of Leaders

Approximately 1 out of every 10 people in the American workplace is classified as a supervisor, administrator, or manager.[22] Management author Andrew DuBrin identifies seven satisfactions and seven frustrations that individuals in leadership roles typically experience. If you are a leader, make note of the ones that relate to you.

Satisfactions of Leaders

1. *A feeling of power and prestige.* Being a leader typically grants one power and a sense of importance.
2. *A chance to help others.* A leader works directly with people, often teaching them job skills, serving as a mentor and an advisor.
3. *High income.* Leaders, in general, receive higher pay than nonleaders, and executive leaders typically earn substantial incomes.
4. *Respect and status.* A leader is typically respected by group members and enjoys a higher status than people who are not occupying leadership roles.
5. *Opportunities for advancement.* Once one becomes a leader, advancement opportunities usually increase.
6. *A feeling of being in a position of knowledge.* A leader typically receives more information than do nonleaders.
7. *An opportunity to control money and other resources.* A leader is typically in the position of determining budgets and authorizing expenses.

Frustrations of Leaders

1. *Too much uncompensated worktime.* People in leadership positions typically work longer hours than nonleaders. During periods of high demand, working hours can surge to 80 hours per week and more.
2. *Too many problems.* A leader is subject to the universe of problems involving people and things. The leader is expected to address problems and get them solved.
3. *Not enough authority to carry out responsibility.* People in leadership positions may be held responsible for outcomes over which they have little control.
4. *Loneliness.* The higher one rises as a leader, the more lonely it can be. Leadership limits the number of people in whom one can confide.
5. *Too many problems involving people.* A frustration facing a leader is the number of people problems requiring action. The more employees one has, the more problems one is likely to face.
6. *Organizational politics.* The leader must engage in political byplay from three directions: below, sideways, and above. Although tactics such as forming alliances and coalitions are a necessary part of a leader's role, it can be particularly frustrating if people purposefully work against each other within an organization.
7. *The pursuit of conflicting goals.* A major challenge facing leaders is navigating among conflicting goals. The central issue of such dilemmas is attempting to grant others the authority to act independently, yet still get them aligned and pulling together for a common purpose.[23]

At this time, do the satisfactions of leadership outweigh the frustrations you may have, or is the opposite the case? Consider the pros and cons of your leadership position.

Caring Leadership

Whether one leads by word or deed; whether a leader is teacher, hero, or ruler; whether leadership is inborn or formed; no matter where one learns to lead; no matter the arena where leadership occurs; no matter the level of satisfaction or frustration a leader may feel; there is an essential ingredient necessary for success. The leader must *care*. Only when the leader cares will others care. Only when the leader cares will there be focus and energy for the work to be done.

There are two aspects of caring leadership: First is **commitment to a task;** second, and equally important, is **concern for people.** Theodore Roosevelt captures the spirit of the caring leader with a task to achieve:

> The credit goes to the man
> who is actually in the arena,
> whose face is marred with
> sweat and dust and blood;
> who strives valiantly;
> who errs and comes short again and
> again; who knows the great
> enthusiasms, the great devotions,
> and spends himself in a worthy
> cause; who at the best knows
> the triumph of high achievement;
> and who, if he fails,
> at least fails while daring greatly.
> Far better it is to dare mighty things,
> to win glorious triumphs,
> even though checkered by failure,
> than to take rank with those cold and timid souls
> who live in the gray twilight that knows not
> victory nor defeat.[24]

With fervor and eloquence, Roosevelt blasts a life of ease and advocates a strenuous life of engagement and meaning. For the caring leader, this means personal commitment to accomplish a goal. The goal may be a one-time endeavor or a life's work. The goal may be a tangible product, such as the creation of a business, or it may be an idea or a cause, such as stamping out tyranny. In any case, the leader's commitment becomes contagious, igniting the emotions of all who are present.

Caring leadership also means caring about people. The caring leader is unselfish, ready and eager to hear the other person's story. The caring leader will dedicate her- or himself in service to others. Concern for others results in loyalty to the leader and dedication to the leader's goals.[25] Jan Carlzon, former chairman and CEO of Scandinavian Airlines, explains the importance of caring leadership in the work setting: "In my experience, I have learned there are two great motivators in life. One is fear. The other is love. You can manage people by fear, but if you do, it will diminish both them and you. The path to success begins in the heart."[26]

James Autry, former CEO of the Meredith Corporation, reminds us that caring leadership must come from the heart, from within, not from policy books. Sharing the wisdom of years of experience in his wonderful volume *Love and Profit,* Autry states, "If you don't truly care about people, you should get out of leadership; it will save a lot of people a lot of trouble and maybe even a heart attack." He captures the spirit of the caring leader in a poem entitled "Threads."[27]

Threads

Sometimes you just connect, like that,
no big thing maybe, but something beyond
the usual business stuff. It comes and goes
quickly so you have to pay attention,
a change in the eyes when you ask about
the family,
a pain flickering behind the statistics about
a boy and a girl in school, or about seeing them
every other Sunday.
An older guy talks about his bride,
a little affection after 25 years.
The hot-eyed achiever laughs before you want
him to.
Someone tells you about his wife's job
or why she quit working to stay home.
An old joker needs another laugh on the way
to retirement.
A woman says she spends a lot of her salary on
an au pair and a good one is hard to find but
worth it because there is nothing more important
than the baby.
Listen. In every office you hear the threads of
love and joy and fear and guilt, the cries for
celebration and reassurance, and somehow you
know that connecting those threads is what you
are supposed to do
and business takes care of itself.

Both commitment to a goal and concern for others must be present for caring leadership to occur. Without commitment there is no passion, and without concern there is no loyalty. Caring leadership cannot be legislated, and it cannot be an act. It is either present or not. When the leader cares, others become focused and energized. It is at this point that direction and momentum develop and great achievements are made.

Leadership in the Work Setting

Leadership is a vital factor influencing the success of the work group and the organization. Think of problems that can occur in any work setting: low morale, high turnover, communication breakdown, lack of teamwork, performance problems, quality problems, unethical behavior, and lack of pride. Now think of the ability required of those individuals whose responsibility it is to solve these and a multitude of other work-related problems. Leadership is an important and difficult task, and it is the cornerstone of organizational success.

Management author John Kotter describes the need for effective leadership at work, saying that too many organizations are overmanaged and underled. Too much emphasis on order and control, and not enough emphasis on motivation and creativity can reduce vitality and lead to failure. What is needed is development of leadership capacity at all levels of responsibility. With good selection, training, and encouragement, many more people can play valuable leadership roles.[28]

The question is often asked—What is the difference between leadership and management? These are terms that are often used interchangeably. Management involves four functions or processes: planning, organizing, directing, and controlling, all of which are essential for organizational success. The term *leadership* is popularly used to describe what takes place in the first three of these functions—**establishing a direction** (planning), **aligning people and resources** (organizing), and **energizing people to accomplish results** (directing). These processes require insight, decisiveness, courage, strength, resolve, diplomacy, and other important leadership qualities to be successful.[29]

Another way to describe the difference between management and leadership is to say that management denotes formal authority and accountability is delegated, while leadership is the ability to influence the activity or behavior of people. Successful organizations have excellent management and great leadership.

The political theorist Karl Marx observed that the manner in which a society does its work shapes most of the other things the society believes and does. This belief only adds to the importance of leadership in the work setting. Principles and practices on the job are repeated and have impact in the home and larger community.

Nine Key Areas of Leadership

The successful leader must master the art of leadership, with its nine key areas for success. If people cannot decide which course of action to take or if they are not making satisfactory progress along a chosen path, breakdown occurs. Breakdown can be traced to deficiency in one or more of these areas:

Leadership variables

The power of vision

The importance of ethics

The empowerment of people

Leadership principles

Understanding people

Multiplying effectiveness

Developing others

Performance management

Each of these key areas is discussed in the following pages. Also included are principles and techniques to improve leadership effectiveness, along with questionnaires and learning exercises for personalizing the concepts.

Introduction Summary

After reading the Introduction, you should know the following key concepts, principles, and terms. Fill in the blanks from memory, or copy the answers listed below.

Leadership is social influence. By (a) _____ and _____, leaders light the path and influence the behavior of people. Types of leaders include (b) _____, _____, and _____. Two basic factors that influence the leadership process are (c) _____, and _____. People learn to lead primarily from (d) _____, _____, and _____. The three qualities people want most in a leader are (e) _____, _____, and _____. Satisfactions of being a leader include (f) _____, _____, and _____; frustrations of being a leader include (g) _____, _____, and

_____. The two essential elements of caring leadership are
(h) _____, and _____. Leadership, in essence, is
(i) _____, _____, and _____.

Answer Key for Introduction Summary

a. **ideas, deeds,** page 2

b. **teachers, heroes, rulers,** page 3

c. **qualities of the individual, environmental factors,** pages 4, 5

d. **experience, examples, books and school,** page 6

e. **integrity, job knowledge, people-building skills,** page 6

f. (any three) **a feeling of power and prestige, a chance to help others, high income, respect and status, opportunities for advancement, a feeling of being in the know, an opportunity to control money and other resources,** page 9

g. (any three) **too much uncompensated work time, too many problems, not enough authority to carry out responsibility, loneliness, too many problems involving people, organizational politics, the pursuit of conflicting goals,** page 9

h. **commitment to a task, concern for people,** page 10

i. **establishing a direction, aligning people and resources, energizing people to accomplish results,** page 12

Part 1 Leadership Variables

1. **The Leadership Equation**
2. **Leadership Qualities**
3. **Characteristics of Followers**
4. **Situational Factors**

IT IS NOT THE RACE that makes the civilization, it is the civilization that makes the people: geographical, economic, and political circumstances create a culture, and the culture creates a human type. The Englishman does not so much make English civilization as it makes him; and he carries it wherever he goes. When he dresses for dinner in Timbuktu, it is not that he is creating his civilization there anew, but that he acknowledges even there its mastery over his soul.

—Will and Ariel Durant
The Lessons of History, 1968

Learning Points

In Part One, you will discover the answers to these questions:
• What are the variables that determine leadership effectiveness?
• Do you possess the 10 qualities that distinguish a leader?
• How susceptible are you to leadership influence? What is your level of interpersonal trust?
• In which situations are you likely to lead? What is your natural kind of intelligence?

The Leadership Equation

For years, researchers have been trying to answer the questions, What does it take to be a successful leader? and What is the most effective leadership style? Early studies were based on two main theories—**trait theory,** focusing on qualities of the leader, and **behavior theory,** focusing on leadership actions.

Leadership Trait Theory

Sir Francis Galton is credited with being one of the earliest leadership theorists, mentioning the trait approach to leadership for the first time in his book *Hereditary Genius,* published in 1869. In keeping with the general thinking of the period, Galton believed that leadership qualities were genetic characteristics of a family. Qualities such as courage and wisdom were passed on—from family member to family member, from generation to generation.[1]

The trait theory of leadership makes the assumption that distinctive physical and psychological characteristics account for leadership effectiveness. Traits such as height, attractiveness, intelligence, self-reliance, and creativity have been studied, and lists abound, from *The Leadership Traits of the U.S. Marine Corps* to the *Leadership Principles of the U.S. Army.* Almost always included in these and other lists of important leadership traits are (1) basic **intelligence,** (2) clear and strong **values,** and (3) high level of personal **energy.**[2]

One of the most widely reported studies of leadership traits was conducted by Edwin Gheselli, who evaluated over 300 managers from 90 different businesses in the United States. Gheselli identified six traits as being important for effective leadership:

1. *Need for achievement*— seeking responsibility; working hard to succeed.
2. *Intelligence*—using good judgment; having good reasoning and thinking capacity.
3. *Decisiveness*—making difficult decisions without undue hesitation.
4. *Self-confidence*—having a positive self-image as a capable and effective person.
5. *Initiative*—being a self-starter; getting jobs done with minimal supervision.
6. *Supervisory ability*—getting the job done through others.[3]

To personalize the concept of trait theory, evaluate yourself (or a leader you know) on Ghiselli's six traits for leadership effectiveness.

**Exercise 1–1
Six Traits of
Leadership**

Rate yourself (or a leader you know) on the following six traits for leadership effectiveness by circling a number from 1 to 10 (1 is low; 10 is high).

1. Need for achievement

| 1 | 2 | 3 | 4 | 5 | 6 | 7 | 8 | 9 | 10 |

2. Intelligence

| 1 | 2 | 3 | 4 | 5 | 6 | 7 | 8 | 9 | 10 |

3. Decisiveness

| 1 | 2 | 3 | 4 | 5 | 6 | 7 | 8 | 9 | 10 |

4. Self-confidence

| 1 | 2 | 3 | 4 | 5 | 6 | 7 | 8 | 9 | 10 |

5. Initiative

| 1 | 2 | 3 | 4 | 5 | 6 | 7 | 8 | 9 | 10 |

6. Supervisory ability

| 1 | 2 | 3 | 4 | 5 | 6 | 7 | 8 | 9 | 10 |

Scoring and Interpretation:

Add all the circled numbers to find the overall trait score: _____

High	**Individual Trait Score**	**Overall Trait Score**	**Evaluation**
↑	9–10	54–60	Outstanding
	7–8	42–53	Very good
↓	5–6	30–41	Good
Low	4 and below	6–29	Needs improvement

Leadership Behavior Theory

During the 1930s, a growing emphasis on behaviorism in psychology moved leadership researchers in the direction of the study of leadership behavior versus leadership traits. A classic study of leadership behavior was conducted by **Kurt Lewin** and his associates in 1939. These researchers trained graduate assistants in behaviors indicative of three leadership styles: **autocratic, democratic,** and **laissez-faire.** The autocratic style was characterized by the tight control of group activities and decisions made by the leader. The democratic style emphasized group participation and majority rule. The laissez-faire leadership style involved very low levels of any kind of activity by the leader. The results indicated that the democratic style of leadership was more beneficial for group performance than the other styles. The importance of the study was that it emphasized the impact of the behavior of the leader on the performance of followers.[4]

By the 1940s, most research on leadership changed focus from leadership traits to leadership behaviors. Behavioral leadership theories assume that there are distinctive actions that effective leaders take. In 1945 **Ralph Stogdill** and others at Ohio State University developed an assessment instrument known as the Leader Behavior Description Questionnaire (LBDQ).[5] Respondents to the questionnaire described their leaders' behaviors toward them in terms of two dimensions:

1. **Initiating structure**—the extent to which leaders take action to define the relationship between themselves and their staff, as well as the role that they expect each staff member to assume. Leaders who score high on initiating structure establish well-defined channels of communication and ways of getting the job done. Five assessment items measuring initiating structure are as follows:

   a. Try out your own new ideas in the work group.

   b. Encourage the slow-working people in the group to work harder.

   c. Emphasize meeting deadlines.

   d. Meet with the group at regularly scheduled times.

   e. See to it that people in the group are working up to capacity.

2. **Showing consideration**—the extent to which leaders take action to develop trust, respect, support, and friendship with subordinates. Leaders who score high on showing consideration typically are helpful, trusting, and respectful, and have warm relationships with staff members. Five questionnaire items that measure showing consideration are as follows:

   a. Be helpful to people in the work group.

   b. Treat all people in the group as your equal.

   c. Be willing to make changes.

   d. Back up what people under you do.

   e. Do little things to make it pleasant to be a member of the group.

At about the same time the Ohio State studies were being conducted, the University of Michigan's Survey Research Center started leadership studies under the direction of Rensis Likert.[6] The Michigan studies identified two similar dimensions of leadership behavior:

1. *Job-centered*—same as initiating structure.

2. *Employee-centered*—same as showing consideration.

Different combinations of the two dimensions result in four leadership styles, as shown in Figure 1–1.

Figure 1–1
Ohio State University and
University of Michigan
Models of Leadership

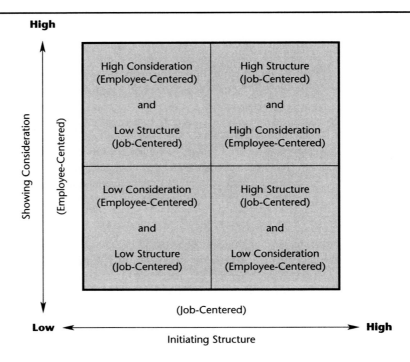

To personalize leadership behavior theory, evaluate yourself (or a leader you know) on two dimensions of leadership effectiveness—concern for production and concern for people. Note that concern for production is analogous to the terms job–centered and initiating structure, while concern for people is analogous to the terms employee–centered and showing consideration.

**Exercise 1–2
Two Dimensions
of Leadership**

Rate yourself (or a leader you know) on the two dimensions of leadership effectiveness indicated in the graph below. Then mark the point where *concern for people* and *concern for production* intersect.

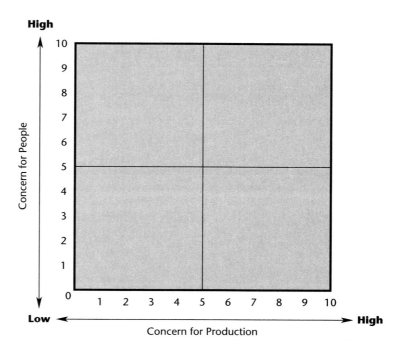

Scoring and Interpretation:

The higher the score on both axes, the higher the expectation for overall leadership effectiveness. To find the overall score, multiply the scores for the two dimensions. The best possible score is 100 (10 × 10).

   The ideal leader is a caring leader who focuses on job tasks and results, and is simultaneously concerned with the welfare of employees.

Leadership Contingency Theory

Both the trait theory and the behavioral theory of leadership were attempts to identify the one best leader and the one best style for all situations. By the late 1960s, it became apparent that there is no such universal answer. Leadership **contingency theory** holds that the most appropriate leadership qualities and actions vary from situation to situation. Effectiveness depends on leader, follower, and situational factors.[7]

Matching Qualities of Leaders, Characteristics of Followers, and the Nature of the Situation

Over 15,000 books and articles have been written about the elements that contribute to leadership effectiveness. The usual conclusion is that the answer depends on leader, follower, and situational variables. A leader in a bank and a leader on the farm will need different interests, values, and skills. Experienced followers and new followers will have different leadership needs. Situational factors include the job being performed, the culture of the workplace, and the urgency of the task.

No single element explains why leadership takes place. Leadership results when the ideas and deeds of the leader match the needs and expectations of the followers in a particular situation. As Woodrow Wilson once said, "The ear of the leader must ring with the voices of the people. Together they rise to the challenge of the day."

The relationship between General George Patton, the U.S. Third Army, and the demands of World War II resulted in leadership; however, the same General Patton probably would not have much influence on the membership and goals of a PTA meeting today. Even if there were agreement about goals, disagreement over style probably would interfere with the leadership process. Similarly, the relationship between Cesar Chavez, California's migrant farm workers, and the economic conditions of the 1960s resulted in leadership, but Chavez probably would not have much success as the board chairman of a Fortune 500 company today.

Modern examples of matching qualities of the leader, characteristics of followers, and the nature of the situation include Lech Walesa, the Polish labor and political leader, and Nelson Mandela, the first black president of South Africa. A negative example, but one of historic significance, is that of Adolf Hitler, the German people, and the period 1919 to 1945:

Hitler generated his power through the skillful use of suggestion, collective hypnosis, and every kind of subconscious motivation that the crowd was predisposed to unleash. In this way, the people sought out Hitler just as much as Hitler sought them out. Rather than saying that Hitler manipulated the people as an artist molds clay, certain traits in Hitler gave him the opportunity to appeal to the psychological condition of the people.

Seen in this light, Hitler was not the great beginner, but merely the executor of the people's wishes. He was able to feel the character and direction of the people and to make them more conscious of it, thereby generating power that he was able to exploit. This is not due to his personal strength alone. Isolated from his crowd, Hitler would be with reduced potency.

Hitler had many personal weaknesses, but as one who sensed the character and direction of the group, he became the embodiment of power. No doubt his strength came through his claiming for himself what actually was the condition and achievement of many.[8]

Ultimately, the leader, the followers, and the situation must match for leadership to take place. One without the other two, and two without the third, will abort the leadership process.[9]

Transformational Leadership

Some people have an extraordinary ability to inspire others and bring forth loyalty. A person who has such a personality is said to have charisma. The German sociologist Max Weber states in his *Theory of Social and Economic Organization:* "The term 'charisma' applies to a certain quality that causes one to be set apart from ordinary people and to be treated as endowed with superhuman, or at least exceptional, powers or qualities. In this sense, charisma is a gift or power of leadership."

The psychologist David McClelland describes the nature of charismatic leadership:

We set out to find exactly, by experiment, what kinds of thoughts the members of an audience had when exposed to a charismatic leader. They were apparently strengthened and uplifted by the experience; they felt more powerful, rather than less powerful or submissive. This suggests that the traditional way of explaining the influence of leaders has not been entirely correct. The leader does not cause followers to submit and go along by intimidation and force. In fact, the leader is influential by strengthening and inspiring the audience. The personality of the leader arouses confidence in followers, and the followers feel better able to accomplish whatever goals they share with the leader.[10]

In every walk of life, an individual with charisma may emerge. When this happens, the person is recognized as a leader. See, for example, the account by Willie Davis, all-pro lineman for the Green Bay Packers, which shows how Vince Lombardi exercised tremendous influence in the field of sports because of his charismatic

He Made Me Feel Important

Willie Davis

Football is a game of emotion, and what the old man excels at is motivation. I maintain that there are two driving forces in football; one is anger and the other is fear, and he capitalized on both of them. Either he got us so mad we wanted to prove something to him, or we were fearful of being singled out as the one guy who didn't do the job.

In the first place, he worked so hard that I always felt the old man was really putting more into the game on a day-to-day basis than I was. I felt obligated to put something extra into it on Sunday; I had to, just to be even with him. Another thing was the way he made you a believer. He told you what the other team was going to do, and he told you what you had to do to beat them, and invariably he was right. He made us believe that all we had to do was follow his theories on how to get ready for each game and we'd win.

Probably the best job I can remember of him motivating us was when we played the Los Angeles Rams the next-to-last game of 1967. We had already clinched our divisional title, and the game didn't mean anything to us, and he was worried about us just going through the motions. Before the game, he was trembling like a leaf. I could see his leg shaking. "I wish I didn't have to ask you boys to go out there today and do this job," he said. "I wish I could go out and do it myself. Boy, this is one game I'd really like to be playing in. This is a game that you're playing for your pride."

How about the day we beat the Rams 6–3 in Milwaukee in 1965? We'd broken a two-game losing streak, and we were all kind of happy and clowning around, and he came in and you saw his face and you knew nothing was funny anymore. He kicked a bench and hurt his foot, and he had to take something out on somebody, so he started challenging us. "Nobody wants to pay the price," he said. "I'm the only one here who's willing to pay the price. You guys don't care. You don't want to win."

We were stunned. Nobody knew what to do, and finally Forrest Gregg stood up and said, "My God, I want to win," and then somebody else said, "Yeah, I want to win," and pretty soon there were forty guys standing, all shouting, "I want to win." If we had played any football team in the world during the next two hours, we'd have beaten them by ten touchdowns. The old man had us feeling so ashamed and angry. That was his greatest asset—his ability to motivate people.[11]

personality. Men played their hearts out for Lombardi. Their goal was to please him, to be equal to their understanding of his values and goals.

The example of Lombardi shows how an individual can generate the respect and following of others through personal charisma. According to Willie Davis, how did Lombardi do this?

- First, he *cared.* No one was more committed to achieving the goal and winning the game.
- Second, he *worked hard.* No one worked harder and more diligently to prepare.
- Third, he *knew the right answers.* He knew the game of football, he knew the teams, and he had a plan to succeed.
- Fourth, he *believed.* He believed in himself and his players, and that made them believers as well.
- Fifth, he *kept the bar high.* He had uncompromising standards that raised the pride of his team as they rose to the challenge.
- Sixth, he *knew people.* He knew how to motivate each of his players, each in his own way.

In his book *Leadership,* James MacGregor Burns states that the term *charisma* has taken on a number of different but overlapping meanings: leaders' magical qualities; an emotional bond between the leader and the led; dependence on a powerful figure by the masses; assumptions that a leader is omniscient and virtuous; and simply popular support for a leader that verges on love.[12]

The term **transformational leadership** can be used to describe the leadership of individuals such as Vince Lombardi. These leaders use optimism, charm, intelligence, and a myriad of other personal qualities to raise aspirations and transform individuals and organizations into new levels of high performance[13]

In contrast to transactional leaders, who emphasize exchanging one thing for another, such as jobs for votes and rewards for favors, transformational leaders engage the full person of the follower. The result is elevation of the potential of followers and achievement beyond previous expectations.[14]

Leadership Qualities

Certain qualities belong potentially to everyone, but leaders possess these qualities to an exceptional degree. The following is a discussion of 10 qualities that mark a leader and help influence the leadership process—vision, ability, enthusiasm, stability, concern for others, self-confidence, persistence, vitality, charisma, and integrity.[15]

■ **Vision.** *The first requirement for a leader is a strong sense of purpose.* A vision of what could and should be is a basic force that enables the leader to recognize what must be done and to do it. Vision inspires others and causes the leader to accept the duties of leadership, whether pleasant or unpleasant. A sense of vision is especially powerful when it embodies a common cause—overcoming tyranny, stamping out hunger, or improving the human condition. The statesman Adlai Stevenson wrote: "I want somebody on that hilltop or its equivalent who can be thinking and looking far ahead, and who can prod me into doing the things that it would be easier not to do. Don't try to think of things that are politically shrewd. Try to think of the next generation."[16]

Native Americans believe that the leader should look to the seventh generation when making decisions today, and this will ensure that a vision is sound and just. Antoïne de Saint-Exupéry once commented on the imaginative nature of vision, saying, "A rock pile ceases to be a rock pile the moment a single man contemplates it, bearing within him the image of a cathedral."[17]

Examples of leadership vision and its power can be seen in computer pioneer Steve Jobs, who foresaw a computer on every desktop and in every home, and in business entrepreneur Bill Gates, who asked the optimistic and compelling question, Where do you want to go today? Jobs of Apple and Gates of Microsoft have altered business and society in irreversible ways.

If you are the leader of a work group or an organization, you should ask, Do I have a plan? What is my vision of what this department or organization should be?

■ **Ability.** *The leader must know the job—or invite loss of respect.* It helps if the leader has done the job before and done it well. Employees seldom respect the individual who constantly must rely on others when making decisions, giving guidance, or solving problems. Although employees usually show a great deal of patience with a new leader, they will lose faith in someone who fails to gain an understanding of the job within a reasonable period of time. Also, the leader must keep job knowledge current. Failure to keep up leads to lack of confidence and loss of employee support. Finally, a leader must have a keen mind to understand information, formulate strategies, and make correct decisions.

Leaders should ask, How competent am I? Am I current in my field? Do I set an example and serve as a resource for my employees because I keep job knowledge current? Mentally, are my perceptions accurate, is my memory good, are my judgments sound?

■ **Enthusiasm.** *Genuine enthusiasm is an important trait of a good leader.* Enthusiasm is a form of persuasiveness that causes others to become interested and willing to accept what the leader is attempting to accomplish. Enthusiasm, like other human emotions—laughter, joy, happiness—is contagious. Enthusiasm shown by a leader generates enthusiasm in followers. As Harry Truman once said, "The successful man has enthusiasm. Good work is never done in cold blood; heat is needed to forge anything. Every great achievement is the story of a flaming heart."[18]

If you are a leader, you must ask, Do I care personally and deeply about what I am doing? Do I show this to my employees? Does my enthusiasm ignite others to take action?

■ **Stability.** *The leader must understand her or his own world and how it relates to the world of others.* One cannot solve the equation of others when preoccupied with the equation of self. Empathy for employees cannot be developed if the leader is emotionally involved with personal problems. Problems with alcohol, problems with money, and problems with relationships are fertile fields for emotional instability. A display of emotional instability places the leader in a precarious position with regard to employees, because they will question the leader's objectivity and judgment. Leaving personal problems at home allows the leader to think more clearly and to perform more effectively on the job. One can see the consequences of loss of stability with examples ranging from the fall of Alexander the Great to the fall of Captain Queeg in *The Caine Mutiny.*

The leader must ask, Do I possess objectivity? Do I convey stability to my employees? Do they trust that personal problems will not interfere with my judgment?

■ **Concern for others.** *At the heart of caring leadership is concern for others.* The leader must not look down on others or treat them as machines—replaceable and interchangeable. The leader must be sincerely and deeply concerned about the welfare of people. The character of caring stands in clear contrast to the character of bullying. The caring leader never belittles, diminishes, or tears people down. The leader must also possess humility and selflessness to the extent that, whenever possible, others' interests are considered first. Concern for others requires patience and listening, and the result is trust, the bedrock of loyalty. Loyalty to followers generates loyalty to the leader; and when tasks become truly difficult, loyalty carries the day.

Leaders must question, Do I truly care about my employees as people, or do I view them more as tools to meet my goals? Do I ever demean people, or do I always lift them up? If I value my employees, do they know it?

■ **Self-confidence.** *Confidence in one's ability gives the leader inner strength to overcome difficult tasks.* People quickly sense a leader's self-confidence, and this quality results in increased commitment and performance. If, on the other hand, leaders lack self-confidence, people may question their authority and may even disobey orders. Researchers at the Center for Creative Leadership have found that successful leaders remain calm and confident even during intense situations. By demonstrating grace under pressure, they inspire those around them to stay calm and act intelligently. According to football quarterback Roger Staubach, the key to self-confidence is how hard the leader works: "Confidence comes from hours, days, weeks, and years of preparation and dedication. When I'm in the last two minutes of a December playoff game, I'm drawing confidence from windsprints I did the previous March. It's just a circle: work and confidence."[19]

A leader must ask, What is my self-confidence level? Do I show confidence in my actions? Have I done the homework and preparation needed to build self-confidence?

■ **Persistence.** *The leader must have drive and determination to stick with difficult tasks until they are completed.* According to Niccolò Machiavelli, "There is nothing more difficult to take in hand, more perilous to conduct, or more uncertain as to success, than to take the lead in the introduction of a new order of things."[20] Israeli prime minister Golda Meir referred to the quality of persistence when she said, "Nothing in life just happens. It isn't enough to just believe in something. You have to have the perseverance to meet obstacles and overcome them, to struggle." Leaders from Walt Disney to Ray Kroc, founder of McDonald's, have shown the importance of persistence for business success, and military leaders from Ulysses Grant to George Patton have proved its importance on the battlefield. However, no better example exists to show the importance of fierce resolve as a leadership quality than that of Winston Churchill. Historians agree that this leader, with his bulldog will, was a determining element in the success of the Allied nations in defeating the Axis powers in World War II. In the face of impossible odds and seemingly certain defeat, Churchill rallied his people. Simply, he would not give in; he would not give up.[21]

If you are the leader, ask, Do I have self-drive and unflagging persistence to overcome adversity even when others lose their strength and their will?

■ **Vitality.** *Even if the spirit is willing, strength and stamina are needed to fulfill the tasks of leadership.* Effective leaders are typically described as electric, vigorous, active, and full of life, no matter how old they are or if they are physically disabled. Consider Franklin Roosevelt, who had polio, and Helen Keller, who was blind. It is interesting to note that at one point in recent history, the American president Ronald Reagan, the Roman Catholic Pope John Paul II, and the Ayatollah Khomeini of Iran were all over 70 years of age—and more vital than many people half their age. At all ages, leaders require tremendous energy and stamina to achieve success. The caring leader must have health and vigor to pursue his or her goals. Physical checkups and physical fitness are commonsense acts.

Leaders must ask, Am I fit for the tasks of leadership? Do I have sufficient energy? Am I doing everything I can to keep physically strong?

■ **Charisma.** *Charisma is a special personal quality that generates others' interest and causes them to follow.* Napoleon once said, "Great leaders are optimists and merchants of hope." Optimism, a sense of adventure, and commitment to a cause are traits found in charismatic leaders. These are qualities that unleash the potential of others and bring forth their energies. Charisma is difficult to define, but the result is admiration, enthusiasm, and the loyalty of followers. Charismatic leaders in history include Julius Caesar, Charlemagne, and Elizabeth I.

As a leader, ask yourself, Do I possess a positive outlook and commitment in my demeanor that transforms followers to new levels of performance as well as personal loyalty to me?

■ **Integrity.** *The most important quality of leadership is integrity, understood as honesty, strength of character, and courage.* Without integrity there is no trust, the number one element in the leader–follower equation. Integrity leads to trust, and trust leads to respect, loyalty, and ultimately, action. It is trust coming from integrity that is needed for leading people from the boardroom, to the shop floor, to the battlefield.[22] A model of integrity was George Washington, about whom it was written:

Endowed by nature with a sound judgment, and an accurate discriminating mind, he was guided by an unvarying sense of moral right, which would tolerate the employment only of those means that would bear the most rigid examination, by a fairness of intention which neither sought nor required disguise, and by a purity of virtue which was not only untainted but unsuspected.[23]

As a leader, ask, Do my people trust me? Do they know that I seek the truth and I am true to my word? Do they see that I possess strength of character and the courage of my convictions?

How do you rate on the 10 qualities of leadership: vision, ability, enthusiasm, stability, concern for others, self-confidence, persistence, vitality, charisma, and integrity? Do you have the qualities that inspire others to follow? The following exercise will help you evaluate yourself (or a leader you know).

**Exercise 2–1
Ten Leadership
Qualities—How Do
You Rate?**

Evaluate yourself (or a leader you know) on the following leadership qualities by circling a number from 1 to 10 (1 is low; 10 is high.)

1. **Vision:** a sense of what could and should be done

   1   2   3   4   5   6   7   8   9   10

2. **Ability:** job knowledge and expertise to achieve results

   1   2   3   4   5   6   7   8   9   10

3. **Enthusiasm:** personal commitment that invigorates and motivates people

   1   2   3   4   5   6   7   8   9   10

4. **Stability:** emotional adjustment and objectivity

   1   2   3   4   5   6   7   8   9   10

5. **Concern for others:** service to followers and interest in their welfare

   1   2   3   4   5   6   7   8   9   10

6. **Self-confidence:** inner strength that comes from preparation and competence

   1   2   3   4   5   6   7   8   9   10

7. **Persistence:** determination to see tough tasks through to completion

   1   2   3   4   5   6   7   8   9   10

8. **Vitality:** strength and stamina

   1   2   3   4   5   6   7   8   9   10

9. **Charisma:** magnetic ability to attract people and cause them to follow

   1   2   3   4   5   6   7   8   9   10

10. **Integrity:** honesty, strength of character, and courage that generates trust

   1   2   3   4   5   6   7   8   9   10

Scoring and Interpretation:

Add all the circled numbers to find the overall score: _____

Score	Evaluation
100–90	Excellent; exceptional
89–80	High; very good
79–70	Average; needs improvement
69–60	Low; much work needed
59 and below	Deficient; poor

Characteristics of Followers

UNIT

3

Two characteristics of followers that influence the leadership process are **respect for authority** and **interpersonal trust.** People who respect authority figures and have a trusting nature are led more easily than people who disregard authorities and are suspicious of others. (Exercise 3–1, at the end of this unit, evaluates susceptibility to follow, based on the trust you have in others.)

A general decline is evident in the level of trust employees have in leadership personnel in American society. The tendency to withhold trust and be self-guarded can be traced to a number of factors: (1) breakdown of the traditional family structure; (2) decline of a wide range of social structures, such as schools, churches, and neighborhoods; (3) lack of shared values and a sense of community as the society has focused on individual advantage and self-absorption; and, perhaps most importantly, (4) case after case in which highly visible and influential leadership figures are discovered putting self-interest over the public good—clear evidence that too many leaders violate the trust that they have been given.[24]

Attitudes toward authority have been changing in Western society, and effective leadership today requires adjustment to the ideas and expectations of a new generation of followers. In the past, the leader in the work setting typically was a taskmaster who ruled with a strong arm and forced employees to obey or face the consequences. If employees failed to show respect or follow orders, they were threatened with dismissal or other punishment. Over the years, employees have developed defenses to protect themselves. They have organized unions to represent their interests, and labor legislation has been created to protect workers from arbitrary firing or mistreatment. In addition, management has learned that people who feel oppressed usually respond in negative ways—slowing down production, producing poor-quality work, and being uncooperative.[25]

Today's effective leaders do not use the power tactics of the past. Modern managers find that the practice of threatening employees is usually counterproductive. Instead, they view their task as one of motivating employees to do their best. In adopting this approach, leaders function as facilitators and teachers as opposed to enforcers and disciplinarians, believing that trust and respect should be earned, not demanded.[26]

The Importance of Trust

Management author Michael Crom writes about building trust in the workplace. He identifies six principles of trust for leadership effectiveness:

   1. *Deal openly with everyone.* Hidden agendas will erode people's trust in you, while also showing that you don't trust them.

2. *Consider all points of view.* See situations from the other person's perspective. Show that, although you may not agree, you do respect the views of others.

3. *Keep promises.* Never say you will do one thing and then do another. If you can't do what you have promised, explain why; don't try to hide the fact that you couldn't keep your word.

4. *Give responsibility.* As a leader, you have bottom-line expectations. Explain your expectations to employees; then let them use their talent, education, and experience to achieve results.

5. *Listen to understand.* Situations may arise that at first appear as though someone is untrustworthy. Missed deadlines, unreasonable expenses, and deviations from standard practices are examples. By simply asking what is happening instead of assuming the worst, you will build a trusting relationship.

6. *Care about people.* This principle will have a major impact on how people react to you and to situations. If they know you care about them, they will be honest with you and will do all they can to meet your expectations.[27]

**Exercise 3–1
Interpersonal Trust
Scale** [28]

The following is a survey of a number of work and social issues. Respond to each item on the basis of your own experience and judgment in dealing with people. Many views are represented in this survey. You may find yourself agreeing strongly with some of the statements, disagreeing with others, and perhaps undecided about others. Whether you agree or disagree with any statement, you can be sure that many people feel the same as you do. Circle the response that shows the extent to which you agree or disagree with each statement.

1. The best way to handle people is to tell them what they want to hear.
   a. Strongly disagree
   b. Disagree
   c. Undecided
   d. Agree
   e. Strongly agree

2. It is hard to get ahead without cutting corners here and there.
   a. Strongly disagree
   b. Disagree
   c. Undecided
   d. Agree
   e. Strongly agree

3. Anyone who completely trusts someone else is asking for trouble.
   a. Strongly disagree
   b. Disagree
   c. Undecided
   d. Agree
   e. Strongly agree

4. When you ask someone to do something for you, it is best to give the real reasons for the request rather than giving reasons that might carry more weight.
   a. Strongly disagree
   b. Disagree
   c. Undecided
   d. Agree
   e. Strongly agree

5. It is safest to assume that all people have a vicious streak and that it will come out when they are given a chance to use it.
   a. Strongly disagree
   b. Disagree
   c. Undecided
   d. Agree
   e. Strongly agree

6. One should take action only when sure it is morally right.
   a. Strongly disagree
   b. Disagree
   c. Undecided
   d. Agree
   e. Strongly agree

7. Most people are basically good and kind.
   a. Strongly disagree
   b. Disagree
   c. Undecided

    d. Agree

    e. Strongly agree

8. There is no valid reason for lying to someone else.

    a. Strongly disagree

    b. Disagree

    c. Undecided

    d. Agree

    e. Strongly agree

9. Most people forget more easily the death of their father than the loss of their property.

    a. Strongly disagree

    b. Disagree

    c. Undecided

    d. Agree

    e. Strongly agree

10. Generally speaking, people won't work hard unless they are forced to do so.

    a. Strongly disagree

    b. Disagree

    c. Undecided

    d. Agree

    e. Strongly agree

Scoring:

Complete Steps 1 and 2:

Step 1:

In the following key, circle the score that corresponds to your answer for each item of the questionnaire:

1. a. 5	2. a. 5	3. a. 5	4. a. 1	5. a. 5
b. 4	b. 4	b. 4	b. 2	b. 4
c. 3	c. 3	c. 3	c. 3	c. 3
d. 2	d. 2	d. 2	d. 4	d. 2
e. 1	e. 1	e. 1	e. 5	e. 1
6. a. 1	7. a. 1	8. a. 1	9. a. 5	10. a. 5
b. 2	b. 2	b. 2	b. 4	b. 4
c. 3	c. 3	c. 3	c. 3	c. 3
d. 4	d. 4	d. 4	d. 2	d. 2
e. 5	e. 5	e. 5	e. 1	e. 1

Step 2:

Add your scores; then divide the total by 10:

Total score _____ ÷ 10 = _____

Interpretation:

Scores on the Interpersonal Trust Scale, which range from 1.0 to 5.0 (see Figure 3–1), show your tendency to trust people. Typically, the higher the score on the scale, the more trust you have in the inherent decency of others. A high score may also reflect susceptibility to suggestion from others. The lower the score on the scale, the less trusting you would be expected to be of others. A low score may also reflect a tendency to manipulate others in accomplishing goals.

Figure 3–1
Interpersonal Trust Scale

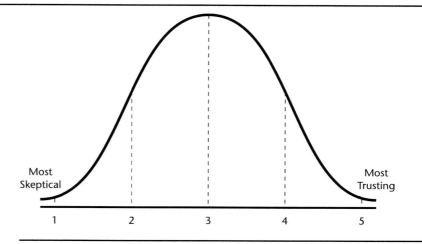

Score	Characteristics
1.0–2.0	This person believes that most people seek personal advantage, even at the expense of others; thus, the best course of action is self-protection. The 1.0–2.0 individual may manipulate others in interpersonal relations and avoid making personal commitments. Such a person is often difficult to lead.
2.0–3.0	This person is generally suspicious of the motives of others and tends toward skepticism and self-reliance rather than seeking assistance or direction. The 2.0–3.0 individual will usually act independently, rather than ask for help or delegate, believing the best way to get something done is to do it oneself.
3.0–4.0	This person has confidence in the basic decency of others, combined with an evaluation of the merits of the situation. The 3.0–4.0 individual will usually trust others temporarily, yet reserve final judgment.
4.0–5.0	This person believes that people are essentially good and therefore readily trusts others. Such a person may not look below the surface of things. The 4.0–5.0 individual is easily persuaded and should be encouraged to look at all sides of an argument before making a decision.

Review your interpersonal trust scores. What is your tendency? Do you lean toward suspicion and self-reliance? Do you tend to be trusting and suggestible? Or are you, like most people, somewhere in the middle? Given your level of trust, are you typically easy or difficult to lead?

Situational Factors

In addition to qualities of the leader and characteristics of followers, many situational factors influence the leadership process. The following is a discussion of important situational factors including the size of the organization, the social and psychological climate, patterns of employment, and the type, place, and purpose of work performed. Also included is a discussion of leader-follower compatibility.

■ **Size of the organization.** Studies show that the size of an organization demands a certain type of leadership skill. A small organization needs a leader who is both a salesperson and a production manager. Outside the organization, the leader is the organization's chief advocate, personally meeting with clients and winning their loyalty. On the inside, the leader organizes the work, assigns tasks, coaches employees, and evaluates progress. In contrast, the leader of a large organization devotes efforts primarily to the organization's public image and its investment and growth plans. Leaders of large organizations think in broad terms about the community and the marketplace, considering how the organization can be placed best in both.[29]

■ **Social and psychological climate.** Social and psychological factors such as confusion, anxiety, and despair can also influence the leadership process. Consider pre–World War II Germany, where a great depression and the inactivity of the people seemed intolerable:

The streets of German towns were full of millions of unemployed waiting for the dole, which was scarcely sufficient to provide for the indispensable needs of daily life. These observations were common to everyone who lived in Germany during the years preceding Hitler's advent to power. The lack of such an important educational factor as compulsory military service on the one hand, and the plague of unemployment on the other, produced their inevitable consequences in the slope of a deplorable moral relaxation and in a not less deplorable decrease of patriotism. In these circumstances that were ripe for leadership, Adolf Hitler came to power.[30]

■ **Patterns of employment.** In his book *The Age of Unreason,* management author Charles Handy describes how contemporary patterns of work are changing in fundamental ways. He describes the "shamrock" organization, in which there are three workforces supporting an organization, but only one leaf of the shamrock is permanent and full-time; the other two are (1) part-time or temporary or both, and (2) independent workers and contractors who form alliances with the organization to perform specified tasks. Handy describes how the seemingly unusual work assignments of our day—working at home, flextime, independent contractors, networks of professionals, associations, virtual offices and companies, and the like—are part of a new pattern of work that adds to the challenge of leadership.[31]

■ **Type, place, and purpose of work.** The type of work to be done is an important factor in the leadership process. Leadership studies show that, in general, when the work to be done is clear-cut, routine, or monotonous, a nondirective and supportive approach is best. If work duties are defined loosely, a directive and task orientation is needed until roles, responsibilities, and relationships are clarified.[32]

Also important is the context of place and purpose. Where is the setting, and what is the goal? Is the place the farm, the factory, or the lab? Is the purpose selling or serving? Is the task shipbuilding or singing? What is the challenge—starting a business or minding the store? All these factors of the situation have tremendous influence on who will light the path and how bright it will be.

Different Kinds of Intelligence

Different leadership situations require different kinds of intelligence. Once Henry Ford was asked who should lead the band. His answer was, "The one with rhythm." Exercise 4–1, based on the work of Keith Rogers, Robert Sternberg, and Howard Gardner, measures multiple intelligences. It can be used to answer the questions, What kind of intelligence do you possess? In which situations are you likely to lead, and in which are you likely to follow? What is your natural leadership strength?

For each statement, indicate your most accurate response by placing a checkmark in the appropriate space. Think about your knowledge, beliefs, preferences, behaviors, and experiences. Decide quickly and move on. There is no right or wrong, no good or bad, no expected or desirable response. Focus on the way you really are, not on the way someone else may think you ought to be.

	Rarely	Occasionally	Sometimes	Usually	Almost Always
	1	2	3	4	5
1. I am careful about the direct and implied meanings of the words I choose.	_____	_____	_____	_____	_____
2. I appreciate a wide variety of music.	_____	_____	_____	_____	_____
3. People come to me when they need help with math problems or any other calculations.	_____	_____	_____	_____	_____
4. In my mind, I can visualize clear, precise, sharp images.	_____	_____	_____	_____	_____
5. I am physically well coordinated.	_____	_____	_____	_____	_____
6. I understand why I believe and behave the way I do.	_____	_____	_____	_____	_____
7. I understand the moods, temperaments, values, and intentions of others.	_____	_____	_____	_____	_____
8. I confidently express myself well in words, written or spoken.	_____	_____	_____	_____	_____
9. I understand the basic precepts of music, such as harmony, chords, and keys.	_____	_____	_____	_____	_____
10. When I have a problem, I use a logical, analytical, step-by-step process to arrive at a solution.	_____	_____	_____	_____	_____
11. I have a good sense of direction.	_____	_____	_____	_____	_____
12. I have skill in handling objects such as scissors, balls, hammers, scalpels, paintbrushes, knitting needles, and pliers.	_____	_____	_____	_____	_____
13. My self-understanding helps me make wise decisions for my life.	_____	_____	_____	_____	_____
14. I am able to influence other individuals to believe and/or behave in response to my own beliefs, preferences, and desires.	_____	_____	_____	_____	_____
15. I am grammatically accurate.	_____	_____	_____	_____	_____
16. I like to compose or create music.	_____	_____	_____	_____	_____
17. I am rigorous and skeptical in accepting facts, reasons, and principles.	_____	_____	_____	_____	_____
18. I am good at putting together jigsaw puzzles, and reading instructions, patterns, or blueprints.	_____	_____	_____	_____	_____
19. I excel in physical activities such as dance, sports, or games.	_____	_____	_____	_____	_____

	Rarely	Occasionally	Sometimes	Usually	Almost Always
	1	2	3	4	5
20. My ability to understand my own emotions helps me decide whether or how to be involved in certain situations.	_____	_____	_____	_____	_____
21. I would like to be involved in the helping professions, such as teaching, therapy, or counseling, or to do work such as political or religious leadership.	_____	_____	_____	_____	_____
22. I am able to use spoken or written words to influence or persuade others.	_____	_____	_____	_____	_____
23. I enjoy performing music, such as singing or playing a musical instrument for an audience.	_____	_____	_____	_____	_____
24. I require scientific explanations of physical realities.	_____	_____	_____	_____	_____
25. I can read maps easily and accurately.	_____	_____	_____	_____	_____
26. I work well with my hands, as would an electrician, plumber, tailor, mechanic, carpenter, or assembler.	_____	_____	_____	_____	_____
27. I am aware of the complexity of my own feelings, emotions, and beliefs in various circumstances.	_____	_____	_____	_____	_____
28. I am able to work as an effective intermediary in helping other individuals and groups solve their problems.	_____	_____	_____	_____	_____
29. I am sensitive to the sounds, rhythms, inflections, and meters of words, especially as found in poetry.	_____	_____	_____	_____	_____
30. I have a good sense of musical rhythm.	_____	_____	_____	_____	_____
31. I would like to do the work of people such as chemists, engineers, physicists, astronomers, or mathematicians.	_____	_____	_____	_____	_____
32. I am able to produce graphic depictions of the spatial world, as in drawing, painting, sculpting, drafting, or mapmaking.	_____	_____	_____	_____	_____
33. I relieve stress or find fulfillment in physical activities.	_____	_____	_____	_____	_____
34. My inner self is my ultimate source of strength and renewal.	_____	_____	_____	_____	_____
35. I understand what motivates others even when they are trying to hide their motivations.	_____	_____	_____	_____	_____

	Rarely	Occasionally	Sometimes	Usually	Almost Always
	1	2	3	4	5
36. I enjoy reading frequently and widely.	_____	_____	_____	_____	_____
37. I have a good sense of musical pitch.	_____	_____	_____	_____	_____
38. I find satisfaction in dealing with numbers.	_____	_____	_____	_____	_____
39. I like the hands-on approach to learning, when I can experience personally the objects that I'm learning about.	_____	_____	_____	_____	_____
40. I have quick and accurate physical reflexes and responses.	_____	_____	_____	_____	_____
41. I am confident in my own opinions and am not easily swayed by others.	_____	_____	_____	_____	_____
42. I am comfortable and confident with groups of people.	_____	_____	_____	_____	_____
43. I use writing as a vital method of communication.	_____	_____	_____	_____	_____
44. I am affected both emotionally and intellectually by music.	_____	_____	_____	_____	_____
45. I prefer questions that have definite right and wrong answers.	_____	_____	_____	_____	_____
46. I can accurately estimate distances and other measurements.	_____	_____	_____	_____	_____
47. I have accurate aim when throwing balls or in archery, shooting, golf, and the like.	_____	_____	_____	_____	_____
48. My feelings, beliefs, attitudes, and emotions are my own responsibility.	_____	_____	_____	_____	_____
49. I have a large circle of close associates.	_____	_____	_____	_____	_____

Scoring:

In the Scoring Matrix on the next page, the numbers in the boxes represent the statement numbers in the preceding survey. You made a rating judgment for each statement. Now place the numbers that correspond to your ratings in the numbered boxes. Then add the columns, and write the totals at the bottom to determine your score for each of the seven intelligence categories.

Once you have calculated your total score for each kind of intelligence, consult the section "Interpretation" to determine the intensity level that corresponds to each total score. Record that number in the final section of the Scoring Matrix.

Scoring Matrix

Verbal-Linguistic	Musical-Rhythmic	Logical-Mathematical	Visual-Spatial	Bodily-Kinesthetic	Intrapersonal	Interpersonal
1	2	3	4	5	6	7
8	9	10	11	12	13	14
15	16	17	18	19	20	21
22	23	24	25	26	27	28
29	30	31	32	33	34	35
36	37	38	39	40	41	42
43	44	45	46	47	48	49
Total						
Intensity of knowledge, beliefs, preferences, behaviors, and experiences: (3) equals low, (2) equals moderate, and (1) equals high						

Interpretation:

To some degree, everyone possesses all seven kinds of intelligence, and all can be enhanced. We are each a unique blend, however, and we differ in the degree to which we prefer and have competence to use each of the intelligences. Presented below are interpretations for the total scores for each kind of intelligence. Intensity levels range from (3) low, to (2) moderate, to (1) high.

Score	Intensity of Knowledge, Beliefs, Preferences, Behaviors, and Experiences
7–15	*Tertiary preference (3): Low intensity. You tend to avoid activities in this area.* This intelligence area is not one of your strengths. In most circumstances, you lack confidence and will go out of your way to avoid situations involving extensive exercise of this intelligence. Unless you are unusually motivated, gaining expertise would be frustrating and would likely require great effort. Keep in mind, however, that all intelligences, including this one, can be enhanced throughout your lifetime.
16–26	*Secondary preference (2): Moderate intensity. You tend to be comfortable with activities in this area.* You could take or leave the application of this intelligence. Although you accept it, you do not necessarily prefer to use it. On the other hand, you would not typically avoid using it. This may be because you have not developed your ability, or because you have a moderate preference for using this intelligence. Gaining expertise in this area would be satisfying, but would require attention and effort.
27–35	*Primary preference (1): High intensity. You tend to prefer activities in this area.* You enjoy using this intelligence. You are excited and challenged by it, perhaps even fascinated. Given the opportunity, you will usually select it. Everyone knows you love it. Your competence is relatively high if you have had opportunities to develop it. Becoming an expert in this area would be rewarding and fulfilling, and would probably require little effort compared with the effort required for intelligence in a moderate or low area of preference.

The following are the specific characteristics of each of the seven kinds of intelligence:

1. If you have *verbal-linguistic intelligence,* you have highly developed auditory skills, enjoy reading and writing, like to play word games, and have a good memory for names, dates, and places. You like to tell stories, and you are good at getting your point across. You learn best by seeing, saying, and hearing words. People whose dominant intelligence is in the verbal-linguistic area include poets, authors, speakers, attorneys, politicians, lecturers, and teachers.

2. If you have *musical-rhythmic intelligence,* you are sensitive to the sounds in your environment, enjoy music, and prefer listening to music when you study or read. You appreciate pitch and rhythm. You probably like singing to yourself. You learn best through melody and music. Musical intelligence is obviously demonstrated by singers, conductors, and composers, but also by those who enjoy, understand, and use various elements of music.

3. If you have *logical-mathematical intelligence,* you like to work with numbers, ask questions, perform experiments, and explore patterns and relationships. You enjoy doing activities in sequential order and find it satisfying to solve problems using logical reasoning. You learn best by classifying information, engaging in abstract thinking, and looking for basic principles. People with well-developed logical-mathematical abilities include mathematicians, biologists, geologists, engineers, physicists, researchers, and other scientists.

4. If you have *visual-spatial intelligence,* you feel at home with the visual arts. You enjoy thinking in images and pictures. You are likely to engage in imagining things, sensing changes, and working through mazes and puzzles. You probably like to draw, build, design, and create things. You learn best by looking at pictures and slides, watching videos or movies, and visualizing. People with well-developed visual-spatial abilities are found in professions such as sculpting, painting, surgery, and engineering.

5. If you have *bodily-kinesthetic intelligence,* you process knowledge through bodily sensations and use your body in skilled ways. You have good balance and coordination, and you are good with your hands. You need opportunities to move and act things out. You tend to respond best in situations that provide physical activities and hands-on learning experiences, and you are able to manipulate objects with finesse. People who have highly developed bodily-kinesthetic abilities include carpenters, repair persons, soldiers, mechanics, dancers, gymnasts, swimmers, and other athletes.

6. If you have *intrapersonal intelligence,* you are a creative and independent thinker. You like to reflect on ideas. You possess independence, self-confidence, and determination, and are highly motivated. You are comfortable focusing inward on thoughts and feelings, following personal instincts, and pursuing goals that are often original. You may respond with strong opinions when controversial topics are discussed. You learn best by engaging in independent study rather than working on group projects. Pacing your own work is important to you. People with intrapersonal abilities include both philosophers and entrepreneurs.

7. If you have *interpersonal intelligence,* you enjoy being with people, like talking with others, have many friends, and engage in social activities. You have the ability to understand people, and people often come to you for help. You learn best by relating, sharing, and participating in cooperative group environments. People with strong interpersonal abilities are found in sales, consulting, community organizing, counseling, teaching, or one of the other helping professions.

The different categories of intelligence should not be thought of in a rigid or deterministic way. Intelligence is not a singular entity. It is complex and multidimensional. You may find that you have strengths in several different areas. When needs for leadership arise in your areas of strength, you can capitalize on these aptitudes for success.

The concept of multiple intelligences is relevant to successful leadership. Leadership effectiveness is in direct proportion to strength of commitment; commitment comes from passion; and passion comes from within the person.

A person's passion for a task must be real, and it must flow naturally. True passion can come only from the basic nature and talent of the individual. Although there are many models and ways to describe and express human talent, the idea that there are seven kinds of intelligence is interesting and useful. The force of an idea or action is greatly determined by the style of intelligence of the leader.

Styles of Leading

An important factor in the leadership process is leader–follower compatibility based on styles of leading. Exercise 4–2 is designed to evaluate your preferred style of leading—directive, participative, or free-rein.[34]

**Exercise 4–2
What Is Your
Leadership Style?**

Answer the following questions, keeping in mind what you have done, or think you would do, in the situations described.

		Yes	No
1.	Do you enjoy the authority leadership brings?	___	___
2.	Generally, do you think it is worth the time and effort for a supervisor to explain the reasons for a decision or policy before putting the policy into effect?	___	___
3.	Do you tend to prefer the planning functions of leadership, as opposed to working directly with your employees?	___	___
4.	A stranger comes into your work area, and you know the person is a new employee. Would you first ask, "What is your name?" rather than introduce yourself?	___	___
5.	Do you keep employees up-to-date on a regular basis on developments affecting the work group?	___	___
6.	Do you find that in giving out assignments, you tend to state the goals, leaving the methods up to your employees?	___	___
7.	Do you think leaders should keep aloof from employees, because in the long run familiarity breeds lessened respect?	___	___
8.	It comes time to decide about a company event. You have heard that the majority prefer to have it on Wednesday, but you are pretty sure Thursday would be better for all concerned. Would you put the question to a vote rather than make the decision yourself?	___	___
9.	If you had your way, would you make communication sessions employee-initiated, with personal consultations held only at their request?	___	___
10.	Do you favor the use of audits and performance evaluations as a way of keeping work standards high?	___	___
11.	Do you feel that you should be friendly with employees?	___	___
12.	After considerable time, you determine the answer to a tough problem. You pass along the solution to your employees, who poke it full of holes. Would you be annoyed that the problem is still unsolved, rather than become upset with the employees?	___	___
13.	Do you agree that one of the best ways to avoid problems of discipline is to provide adequate punishment for violation of rules?	___	___
14.	Your way of handling a situation is being criticized by your employees. Would you try to sell your viewpoint, rather than make it clear that, as supervisor, your decisions are final?	___	___
15.	Do you generally leave it up to your employees to contact you, as far as informal, day-to-day communications are concerned?	___	___
16.	Do you feel that everyone in your work group should have a certain amount of personal loyalty to you?	___	___
17.	Do you favor the practice of using task force teams and committees, rather than making decisions alone?	___	___
18.	Some experts say that difference of opinion within a work group is healthy; others say it indicates basic flaws in the management process. Do you agree with the first view?	___	___

Scoring:

In the Scoring Matrix below, place a checkmark next to each question you answered *yes*. Add the checkmarks for each column to find the totals for the leadership styles you prefer.

Scoring Matrix

Directive	Participative	Free-Rein
1. _____	2. _____	3. _____
4. _____	5. _____	6. _____
7. _____	8. _____	9. _____
10. _____	11. _____	12. _____
13. _____	14. _____	15. _____
16. _____	17. _____	18. _____
Total _____	Total _____	Total _____

Interpretation:

Your highest score indicates your most preferred style of leading. A description of each style is presented in Figure 4–1.

Figure 4–1   Continuum of Leadership Styles[35]

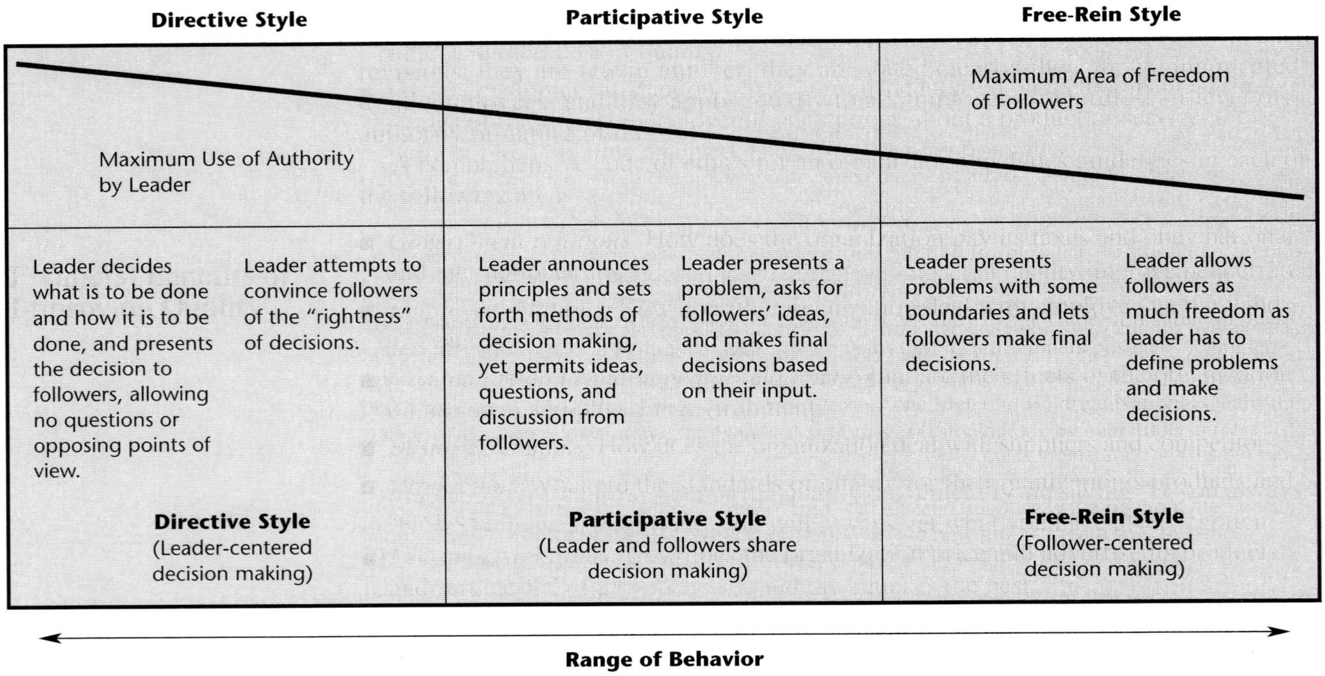

Directive Style		Participative Style		Free-Rein Style	
Maximum Use of Authority by Leader				Maximum Area of Freedom of Followers	
Leader decides what is to be done and how it is to be done, and presents the decision to followers, allowing no questions or opposing points of view.	Leader attempts to convince followers of the "rightness" of decisions.	Leader announces principles and sets forth methods of decision making, yet permits ideas, questions, and discussion from followers.	Leader presents a problem, asks for followers' ideas, and makes final decisions based on their input.	Leader presents problems with some boundaries and lets followers make final decisions.	Leader allows followers as much freedom as leader has to define problems and make decisions.
Directive Style (Leader-centered decision making)		**Participative Style** (Leader and followers share decision making)		**Free-Rein Style** (Follower-centered decision making)	

Range of Behavior

Figure 4–2 shows the different emphases in the use of power for the three styles of leadership.

Figure 4–2
Emphasis in the Use of Power[36]

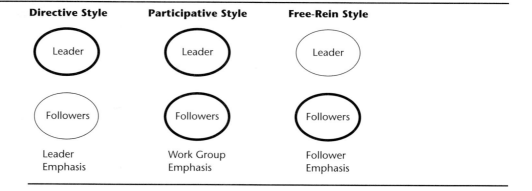

According to the ideas of Hollander, Vroom and Yetton, Tannenbaum and Schmidt, Hersey and Blanchard, Daniel Goleman, and others, there are five points to remember about styles of leading:[37]

1. Styles of leading are influenced by experience. People develop preferred styles by modeling others, going through formal training, and learning from personal experience.

2. An individual usually prefers the same style of leading and of following. Confusion results when this matching of styles is not the case. General George Patton was a directive leader and a free-rein follower, causing mixed signals and much controversy in his relations with commanders and subordinates.

3. Leaders have been successful along all points of the continuum: Elizabeth I was directive in her style; Thomas Jefferson chose participative leadership; Dwight Eisenhower preferred the free-rein style. It is interesting to contrast Italian political philosopher Nicollò Machiavelli (1469–1527), who advocated being directive to the point of believing that the ends justify the means, to sixth-century B.C. Chinese philosopher Lao-tzu, who prescribed nondirective leadership to the point of believing in total selflessness.

4. There is no universally effective style of leading. Sometimes it is best for the leader to tell employees what to do; sometimes it is best for leaders and subordinates to make decisions together; and sometimes it is best for employees to direct themselves. The best style of leadership depends on qualities of the leader, characteristics of the followers, and the nature of the situation.

Increasingly, the American workplace is becoming faster paced, more culturally diverse, and more global in nature. See Table 4–1, which shows a general shift from directive (command and control) to free-rein (relationship management) focus of leadership, and a shift from a hierarchy to a community nature of business culture, as innovative products, quick reaction time, and individual initiative are requirements for success.

Table 4–1
The Changing Character of Business Culture and Changing Focus of Effective Leadership[38]

	Directive		
Decade	**Nature of Business Culture**		**Focus of Leadership**
Pre-1950	Hierarchy		Command and control
1950s	Organization		Supervision
1960s	Systems		Administration
1970s	Strategy		Management
1980s	Innovation		Entrepreneurship
1990s	Diversity		Team building
Post-2000	Community		Relationship management
	Free rein		

5. If styles of leading and styles of following conflict, extra patience and communication are needed, especially in the following areas:

- *Decision making.* Directive leaders may be upset by free-rein followers who insist on challenging decisions and behaving independently. These leaders must remember that free-rein followers usually do their best work on special assignments and independent projects. They respond best to individual treatment and personal freedom.

- *Goal setting.* Directive followers may be upset by free-rein leaders who provide few details on how to do a job. These leaders must remember that directive followers usually do their best work when job duties are spelled out and direct orders are given.

- *Communication.* Participative followers usually are upset by leaders who fail to have staff meetings, ignore the open door policy, and show little concern for people's feelings. These leaders must remember that participative followers want open communication and active involvement in the decision-making process. They usually perform well on task forces, committees, and other work teams.

To understand the importance of leader–follower compatibility, consider your own experience. Have you ever had a leader who missed the mark in meeting your needs? Do you, yourself, have the range to meet the needs of all three styles—directive, participative, and free-rein?

Leadership Effectiveness Today

Considering qualities of leaders, characteristics of followers, and the nature of the situation, what form of leadership meets the preference of most leaders, the needs of most followers, and the requirements of most situations today? Business leader and author Robert Townsend answers:

As for the best leaders, the people do not notice their existence. The next best, the people fear. And the next, the people hate. When the best leader's work is done, the people say, "We did it ourselves."[39]

One is made to think of the leadership practices of good parents and good teachers in this regard. Essentially, good leaders develop followers to become good leaders. For this approach to work, the leader must embrace democratic ideals, followers must be both motivated and capable, and the situation must allow sufficient time for discussion and consensus. Not all leaders do, not all followers are, and not every situation does. The requirements for effective leadership change from leader to leader, follower to follower, and situation to situation.

Because there is no universal formula for success, leadership is more **art** than science and more skill than knowledge. Above all, leadership is difficult. In "No Easy Task," management author and educator Douglas McGregor, originator of the terms *theory X* and *theory Y,* describes how difficult leadership can be.

No Easy Task

Douglas McGregor

I believed (before becoming President of Antioch College) that a leader could operate successfully as a kind of advisor to his organization; I thought I could avoid being a "boss." Unconsciously, I suspect, I hoped to duck the unpleasant necessity of making difficult decisions, of taking the responsibility for one course of action among many uncertain alternatives, of making mistakes and taking the consequences. I thought that maybe I could operate so that everyone would like me—that "good human relations" would eliminate all discord and argument.

I couldn't have been more wrong. It took a couple of years, but I finally began to realize that a leader cannot avoid the exercise of authority any more than he can avoid responsibility for what happens to his organization. In fact, it is a major function of the leader to take on his own shoulders the responsibility for resolving the uncertainties that are always involved in important decisions. Moreover, since no important decision ever pleases everyone in an organization, the leader must also absorb the displeasure, and sometimes the severe hostility, of those who would have taken a different course.[40]

The role of the leader in today's high-tech, fast-paced, and ever-changing workplace is increasingly difficult. In dealing with a wide variety of employees along a full range of skills, the leader must add new demands to traditional duties (see Table 4–2):

Table 4–2
Leadship Duties and Demands

Traditional Duties	New Demands
1. Give orders.	1. Empower people.
2. Implement plans.	2. Generate ideas.
3. Manage individuals.	3. Coach teams.
4. Do things right.	4. Do the right things.
5. Organize work.	5. Develop people.

The effective leader today must be a director *and* motivator, implementer *and* innovator, mentor *and* team builder, expert *and* moral force, organizer *and* developer of people. These are great challenges that bring both satisfaction and appreciation for caring leaders who are willing and able to meet them.

Part One Summary

After reading Part One, you should know the following key concepts, principles, and terms. Fill in the blanks from memory, or copy the answers listed below.

Historically, the study of leadership has emphasized (a) ＿＿＿＿＿＿ theory, focusing on qualities of the leader, and (b) ＿＿＿＿＿＿ theory, focusing on leadership actions. Almost always included as important leadership traits are (c) ＿＿＿＿＿＿, ＿＿＿＿＿＿, and ＿＿＿＿＿＿. Leadership behavior theory has included styles of leadership—(d) ＿＿＿＿＿＿, ＿＿＿＿＿＿, and ＿＿＿＿＿＿—studied by (e) ＿＿＿＿＿＿, and others, as well as dimensions of leadership—(f) ＿＿＿＿＿＿, and ＿＿＿＿＿＿—studied by (g) ＿＿＿＿＿＿, and others. Leadership (h) ＿＿＿＿＿＿ theory holds that the most effective leadership qualities and actions vary from situation to situation, depending on qualities of leaders, characteristics of followers, and the nature of the situation. The term (i) ＿＿＿＿＿＿ is used to describe the elevation of the performance of followers beyond previous expectations. Qualities that mark a leader include (j) ＿＿＿＿＿＿, ＿＿＿＿＿＿, ＿＿＿＿＿＿, ＿＿＿＿＿＿, ＿＿＿＿＿＿, and ＿＿＿＿＿＿. Characteristics of followers that influence the leadership process are (k) ＿＿＿＿＿＿, and ＿＿＿＿＿＿. Principles for developing trust in the workplace include (l) ＿＿＿＿＿＿, ＿＿＿＿＿＿, ＿＿＿＿＿＿, and ＿＿＿＿＿＿. Many situational factors influence the leadership process, including (m) ＿＿＿＿＿＿, ＿＿＿＿＿＿, ＿＿＿＿＿＿, and ＿＿＿＿＿＿. There is no universal formula for leadership success, so what is effective can change, case by case. Thus, leadership is more (n) ＿＿＿＿＿＿ than science.

Answer Key for Part One Summary

a. **trait,** page 16

b. **behavior,** page 16

c. **intelligence, values, energy,** page 16

d. **autocratic, democratic, laissez-faire,** page 19

e. **Kurt Lewin,** page 19

f. **initiating structure, showing consideration,** page 19

g. **Ralph Stogdill,** page 19

h. **contingency,** page 23

i. **transformational leadership,** page 25

j. (any six) **vision, ability, enthusiasm, stability, concern for others, self-confidence, persistence, vitality, charisma, integrity,** pages 26–28

k. **respect for authority, interpersonal trust,** page 30

l. (any four) **deal openly with everyone, consider all points of view, keep promises, give responsibility, listen to understand, care about people,** pages 30–31

m. **size of the organization; social and psychological climate; patterns of employment; type, place, and purpose of work performed,** pages 36–37

n. **art,** page 50

Reflection Points—personal thoughts on the leadership equation, leadership qualities, characteristics of followers, and situational factors

Complete the following questions and activities to personalize the content of Part One. Space is provided for writing your thoughts.

■ How do you rate on leadership traits—need for achievement, intelligence, decisiveness, self-confidence, initiative, and supervisory ability? Which are high? Which are low? Describe a situation where you have demonstrated these traits.

_____

_____

■ Critique the idea that leadership success requires effectiveness on two dimensions: (1) initiating structure—focus on the task and concern for production—as well as (2) showing consideration—employee support and concern for people. Evaluate an actual leader's effectiveness using these two dimensions.

_____

_____

■ Describe an incident or time when the qualities of the leader, the characteristics of followers, and the nature of the situation matched and leadership occurred. What took place, who was involved, and what were the results?

_____

_____

■ Consider the qualities that mark a leader—vision, ability, enthusiasm, stability, concern for others, self-confidence, persistence, vitality, charisma, and integrity. On the basis of these 10 qualities, discuss the best leader you have ever had.

_____

_____

■ How susceptible to leadership are you? Are you basically a trusting person or a suspicious person when it comes to following others?

_____

_____

■ What is your natural intelligence strength? When and where have you provided leadership based on your preferred intelligence area(s)?

_____

_____

■ What is your preferred leadership style? Is your style effective with the employees you have and the challenges you face?

_____

_____

■ Have you ever clashed with a supervisor over leadership style? Discuss dynamics and results.

_____

_____

Action Assignment

As a bridge between learning and doing, complete the following action assignment.

1. What is the most important idea you have learned in Part One?

2. How can you apply what you have learned? What will you do, with whom, where, when, and, most important, why?

Part 2 The Power of Vision

5. The Importance of Vision
6. The Motive to Lead
7. Organizational Climate

MOMENTUM COMES FROM HAVING A CLEAR VISION of what the organization ought to be, from a well-thought-out strategy to achieve that vision, and from carefully conceived and communicated directions and plans that let everyone participate and be accountable in achieving these plans. Momentum is vital and palpable. It is the feeling among a group of people that their lives and work are intertwined and moving toward a recognizable and legitimate goal.

—Max DePree
Leadership Is an Art

Learning Points

In Part Two, you will discover the answers to these questions:
- What is the role of vision for leadership success? How does a leader create and implement a powerful vision?
- Why would you want to be a leader? What would be your purpose for assuming the tasks of leadership?
- How can a leader develop an organizational climate that attracts and keeps good people?

The Importance of Vision

Management author Peter Drucker once said, "The best way to predict the future is to create it." Most leaders agree with this statement completely. The leader wants to make a difference and strives to create a thing that never was before. This thing, this difference, constitutes a **vision.**

The most important function of a leader is to develop a clear and compelling picture of the future, and to secure commitment to that ideal. Consider the words of Henry Ford as he communicated his vision to make a car for the masses: "I will build a motor car for the great multitude . . . constructed of the best materials, by the best men to be hired, after the simplest designs that modern engineering can devise . . . so low in price that no man making a good salary will be unable to own one and enjoy with his family the blessing of hours of pleasure in God's great open spaces."[1]

Ford's leadership success began with a vision. To this, he added a **strategy** to succeed. Three great ideas that gave his vision life were (1) the moving assembly line; (2) paying workers not as little as possible but as much as was fair; and (3) vertical integration, which made Ford's River Rouge plant a marvel of the industrial world.[2]

In addition to developing a vision and a strategy to succeed, the leader must have intensity and **stamina** to see these through. As CEO at Johnson & Johnson, James Burke estimated that he spent 40 percent of his time communicating and reinforcing the company's vision. Much is said about the vision of leaders and about their creative strategies. However, the incredible energy they display as they face repeated challenges and even failures must not be overlooked. Leaders typically have substantial vitality, and they manage to transmit this energy to others. This is a force born out of deep convictions and passion for the work or goal. Such leaders breathe life into their organizations; hence the term *animator* is used to describe the leader.[3]

Examples of Powerful Visions

Consider the strong and all-embracing vision of Johnson & Johnson that has helped thousands of employees throughout the world understand that their first obligation is to the customer: "We believe our first obligation is to the doctors, nurses, and patients; to mothers and all others who use our products and services."[4]

Consider the moving vision of Collis Huntington, founder of Newport News Shipbuilding and Dry Dock Company in 1886:

We shall build good ships here.
At a profit—if we can;
At a loss—if we must.
But always good ships.

What is the role of vision in helping organizations succeed? As Figure 5–1 shows, success begins with a clear, compelling vision, a picture in the minds of the members of the organization of how things should and could be. Without vision, there is confusion. Also required are other important ingredients: skills, incentives, resources, and an action plan.

Figure 5–1
Organizational Success[5]

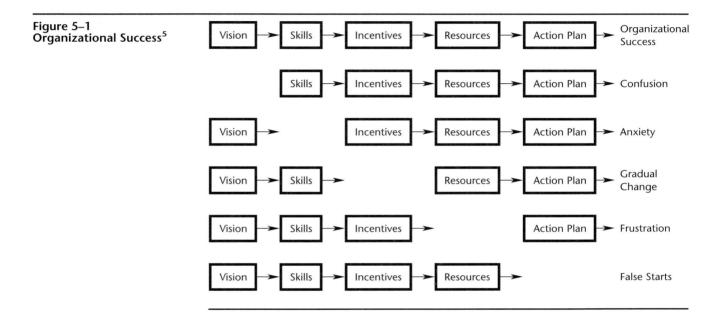

Vision as an Ideal

The word *vision* evokes pictures in the mind. It suggests a future orientation, implies a standard of excellence or virtuous condition, and has the quality of uniqueness. These are the elements that give life and strength to vision. Vision is an ideal image of what could and should be. The leader must ask three questions to test his or her vision: (1) Is this the right direction? (2) Are these the right goals? (3) Is this the right time? Then, the leader must share this vision and have it supported. Turn to the next page and read and feel the power of the words of Martin Luther King, Jr., as he delivered his vision of civil rights before the Lincoln Memorial on August 28, 1963.[6]

Leader as Visionary and Motivator of People

Management author Warren Bennis states that leaders must be clearly focused on a positive and future-focused goal or vision. Clarity of purpose provides guidance for making decisions about time and resources. Also required is constancy of effort. Passion and authority come to leaders who clearly know where they are going and have dedication to succeed. When leaders have passion and authority, others are inspired to follow.[7]

I Have a Dream

Martin Luther King, Jr.

So I say to you, my friends, that even though we must face the difficulties of today and tomorrow, I still have a dream. It is a dream deeply rooted in the American dream that one day this nation will rise up and live out the true meaning of its creed—we hold these truths to be self-evident, that all men are created equal.

I have a dream that one day on the red hills of Georgia, sons of former slaves and sons of former slaveowners will be able to sit down together at the table of brotherhood.

I have a dream that one day, even the state of Mississippi, a state sweltering with the heat of injustice, sweltering with the heat of oppression, will be transformed into an oasis of freedom and justice.

I have a dream my four little children will one day live in a nation where they will not be judged by the color of their skin, but by content of their character. I have a dream today!

I have a dream that one day, down in Alabama, with its vicious racists, with its governor having his lips dripping with the words of interposition and nullification, that one day, right there in Alabama, little black boys and little black girls will be able to join hands with little white boys and little white girls as sisters and brothers. I have a dream today!

I have a dream that one day every valley shall be exalted, every hill and mountain shall be made low, the rough places shall be made plain, and the crooked places shall be made straight and the glory of the Lord will be revealed and all flesh shall see it together.

So let freedom ring from the prodigious hilltops of New Hampshire.

Let freedom ring from the mighty mountains of New York.

Let freedom ring from the heightening Alleghenies of Pennsylvania.

Let freedom ring from the snow-capped Rockies of Colorado.

Let freedom ring from the curvaceous slopes of California,

But not only that.

Let freedom ring from Stone Mountain of Georgia.

Let freedom ring from Lookout Mountain of Tennessee.

Let freedom ring from every hill and molehill of Mississippi, from every mountainside, let freedom ring.

And when we allow freedom to ring, when we let it ring from every village and hamlet, from every state and city, we will be able to speed up that day when all of God's children—black men and white men, Jews and Gentiles, Catholics and Protestants—will be able to join hands and to sing in the words of the old Negro spiritual, "Free at last, free at last; thank God Almighty, we are free at last."

In a major study of leadership effectiveness, the Forum Corporation reports on the characteristics of successful leaders at middle to senior levels of responsibility. The study identifies three leadership qualities that are needed for steering organizations through periods of change:

1. *Taking personal responsibility for initiating change.* A major function of the leader is to manage attention. The leader must be personally involved and committed to make a difference. Absolute identity with one's cause is the first condition of successful leadership.

2. *Creating a vision and strategy for the organization.* The vision and strategy must be leader-initiated, shared and supported by followers, comprehensive and detailed, and above all, worth doing. The leader must create a vision that is uplifting and inspiring to others.

3. *Trusting and supporting others.* The leader must treat people with respect and dignity, expecting the best in effort and personal responsibility, and showing sincere appreciation for work performed. The leader combines individual incentive with group success as an important empowerment principle.[8]

Key findings of the Forum study are summarized as follows:

- *Leadership is important from the boardroom to the shop floor.* In a sense, the leadership chain is as strong as its weakest link. Without effective leadership at every level of responsibility, frontline employees and, ultimately, customers are bound to suffer.

- *Positions and titles have little or no relationship to leadership performance.* People are often skeptical of authority figures. New leaders have to earn the trust and respect of subordinates; otherwise, people will resist their efforts to lead. Indeed, workers with strong leadership skills can inspire their peers as well as any chief executive could.

- *Without leadership, organizations falter in times of change.* This situation is analogous to that of a car without an engine or a ship without a rudder. The organization will be dormant, or a terrible crash will occur as the group goes in the wrong direction.

- *Organizational leadership involves interdependence more than individualism.* The genius stroke of the independent contributor is important, but more important for organizational leadership are relationship skills, such as demonstrating concern for members of the work group, recognizing other peoples' contributions, and building enthusiasm about projects and assignments.

- *Leaders inspire others to take on the tasks of leadership.* Giving others the power and encouragement to make decisions frees the leader from the role of controller, liberating critical time and energy for charting and shaping the overall future of the organization.

- *Leadership is contextual.* Effective leadership requires an understanding of the forces and events that have shaped an industry, a company, or a work group; an assessment of organizational strengths, weaknesses, opportunities, and threats; and the development of a plan to meet current and future challenges. Understanding, assessment, and plans are specific to the organization and its environment.[9]

Leadership Effectiveness

The following questionnaire can be used to evaluate your leadership effectiveness (or the effectiveness of a leader you know).

The following 20 practices cluster into four distinct areas that correlate positively with leadership effectiveness. Using a scale from 1 to 10 (1 is low; 10 is high), evaluate yourself (or a leader you know) on each practice in the following four areas.

Getting the Facts

The effective leader gains insight into the realities of the world and into him- or herself. This process includes getting the facts and interpreting conditions affecting the group. Rate each item separately (from 1 to 10).

1. Determining the facts by seeking information from as many sources as possible—library, field, lab, and so on. _____
2. Learning the challenges facing the group, including internal strengths and weaknesses, as well as external opportunities and threats for meeting these challenges. _____
3. Knowing the capabilities and motivations of the individuals in the group. _____
4. Analyzing how well the members of the group work together. _____
5. Knowing the leader's own capabilities and motivations. _____

Add your ratings and divide by 5 for an overall score on *getting the facts.* Circle that score on the scale below.

| 1 | 2 | 3 | 4 | 5 | 6 | 7 | 8 | 9 | 10 |

Creating a Vision

The effective leader develops a vision and a strategy to give meaning to the group's work, thus providing purpose and clarity of direction. Rate each item separately (from 1 to 10).

1. Standing up for what is important, including basic principles or core values. _____
2. Involving the right people in developing the group's vision and strategy. _____
3. Creating a clear and positive picture of the future of the group. _____
4. Developing a strategy for the success of the group, including clarity of individual and group assignments. _____
5. Adjusting plans and actions as necessary based on changing conditions. _____

Add your ratings and divide by 5 for an overall score on *creating a vision.* Circle that score on the scale below.

| 1 | 2 | 3 | 4 | 5 | 6 | 7 | 8 | 9 | 10 |

Motivating People

The effective leader is a motivator, possessing the ability to mobilize individuals with different ideas, skills, and values to achieve a common mission. Rate each item separately (from 1 to 10).

1. Appealing to people's hearts and minds to accomplish a worthy endeavor. _____
2. Communicating clearly the high standards and performance results expected from others. _____
3. Demonstrating concern for members of the group. _____
4. Showing confidence in the abilities of others. _____
5. Letting people know how they are progressing toward the group's goals, including giving recognition when milestones are reached. _____

Add your ratings and divide by 5 for an overall score on *motivating people.* Circle that score on the scale below.

| 1 | 2 | 3 | 4 | 5 | 6 | 7 | 8 | 9 | 10 |

Empowering Others

The effective leader has the ability to increase effectiveness by sharing power, thus igniting the energy and liberating the talent of the group. Rate each item separately (from 1 to 10).

1. Recognizing the contributions of others, for example, through performance awards, letters of commendation, and personal appreciation._____

2. Promoting the development of people's abilities, by providing training and challenging assignments._____

3. Enabling others to feel and act like leaders._____

4. Stimulating others' thinking and creativity by soliciting suggestions and ideas._____

5. Building enthusiasm about projects and assignments, especially through personal involvement._____

Add your ratings and divide by 5 for an overall score on *empowering others.* Circle that score on the scale below.

1	2	3	4	5	6	7	8	9	10

Scoring and Interpretation:

Add the overall scores for all four areas to determine your leadership effectiveness.

Total Score	Evaluation
37–40	Excellent; your leadership effectiveness is outstanding.
28–36	Very good; your effectiveness as a leader is high.
17–27	Average; you are neither high nor low in your overall leadership effectiveness.
8–16	Below average; your effectiveness as a leader is low.
4–7	Failing; much work is needed to improve.

A useful exercise is for the leader to compare his or her self-evaluation on the leadership assessment with the evaluations of constituents or colleagues. Points of agreement and disagreement can be explored, and actions can be taken to improve as needed.

The Concept of Visioning

The concept of visioning as it is used in organizations today is credited to Ronald Lippitt, who, as early as 1949, began referring to "images of potential" rather than to "problems" as starting points for change.[11] Management author Stephen Covey identifies certain process, content, and application principles that have been found to be effective in creating a vision.

Visioning Process Principles

1. *Initiate and provide constant vigilance by leaders.* It is the proper role of leadership to begin the process, to discuss and articulate the basis for developing a vision, and to start drafting a document. This effort begins the top-down portion of the visioning process.

2. *Be challenging, yet realistic.* Set the mark high, but stay in touch with reality. A vision should stretch the abilities of the organization, but not destroy its members.

3. *Seek significant early involvement by other members of the organization.* This aspect includes discussing, writing, and rewriting the vision. In this joint-effort phase, senior leaders, in effect, say, "We've begun—but we need your input. Your involvement is essential."

4. *Encourage widespread review and comment.* Include as many people as possible. This bottom-up period of review invites critical analysis. Here, leaders are saying, "We've worked hard on this and like it—but what do you think? Give us your ideas. We want this to belong to everyone." Be open and show appreciation for suggestions. Incorporate modifications and the best thinking of all respondents. Involvement fosters commitment.

5. *Keep communications flowing.* Don't assume everyone knows what is going on. Report on progress for developing the vision. Give acknowledgment and appreciation, and report on the adoption of elements of the vision—agreement on purpose, broad goals, core values, stakeholders, strategic initiatives, and so on. Provide feedback as achievements are made toward attaining goals.

6. *Allow time for the process to work.* People need time to think about and adjust to change, even positive change. The development of a vision may take longer than people expect. Top leaders may spend weeks on the original draft, months on the involvement and feedback process, and a year or more to finish the product.

7. *Demonstrate commitment, follow-through, and concurrent action by leaders.* Leaders must make reality match rhetoric. Any sincere effort to put words into action will lend credibility and will reinforce the actual attainment of the vision.

8. *Maintain harmony of subunits.* The content of the vision statements for subunits (such as divisions, plants, departments, and work teams) should be in harmony with the overall vision of the organization.[12]

Visioning Content Principles

Key elements of an overall vision or strategic plan typically include:

1. *Central purpose or mission (reason for existence).* This is a clear, compelling statement of purpose that provides focus and direction. It is the organization's answer to the question, Why do we exist?

2. *Broad goals to achieve the mission (enduring intentions to act).* These are process or functional accomplishments that must be met to achieve the mission.

3. *Core values to measure the rightness and wrongness of behavior (hills worth dying on).* Sometimes called operating principles, core values such as truth, trust, and respect define the moral tone or character of the organization.

4. *Stakeholders and what the attainment of the vision will mean to them (the human element).* These are the people who will be affected by what the organization does or does not do.

5. *Analysis of the organization and its environment, including internal strengths and weaknesses, as well as external opportunities and threats.* This is a **SWOT assessment** of current conditions that must be both thorough and objective. Information that is unknown and facts that are denied will hinder and can even destroy an organization.

6. *Strategic initiatives (sometimes called critical success factors).* These are short-term, intermediate, and long-term objectives necessary to achieve the goals and mission. They may be person- or group-specific, or may involve all members of the organization. They are strategic, measurable, action-oriented, realistic, and timely, with dates or numbers to measure accomplishment.

7. *Tactical plans and specific assignments (projects and activities) to support strategic initiatives, broad goals, and the attainment of the mission.* These projects and activities serve as guides in performance planning for units and members of the organization, and constitute the plan of work.

Elements 1 through 4 provide *general direction* for the organization. Adding elements 5 and 6 involves *strategic planning.* This gives definition to the vision and focuses people and resources on specific objectives that can be measured. Element 7, *tactical planning,* refers to projects and activities designed to implement strategy, the plays that drive the game to success. Tactical planning results in group- and person-specific assignments and concrete actions.[13]

An important element in the visioning process is the SWOT analysis. A major goal is to identify core competencies in the form of special *strengths* that the organization has or does exceptionally well. These can become sources of competitive advantage. Core competencies may be found in efficient manufacturing technologies, special product knowledge or expertise, or unique distribution systems, among many other possibilities. Another goal is to identify *opportunities* in the environment that the organization can act upon. Examples include new technologies, strategic alliances, and possible new markets for products and services. See Figure 5–2.

Visioning Application Principles

1. *Honor and live the vision as the organization's constitution.* The values and principles of the vision, not the personal style of individuals, should govern organizational culture and behavior.

2. *Encourage new-member understanding and commitment through early introduction.* Those not involved in the development process can identify with the vision from the first association: "This is what we are all about; if you can embrace this

---

Figure 5–2
SWOT Analysis of Organizational Strengths and Weaknesses and Environmental Opportunities and Threats[14]

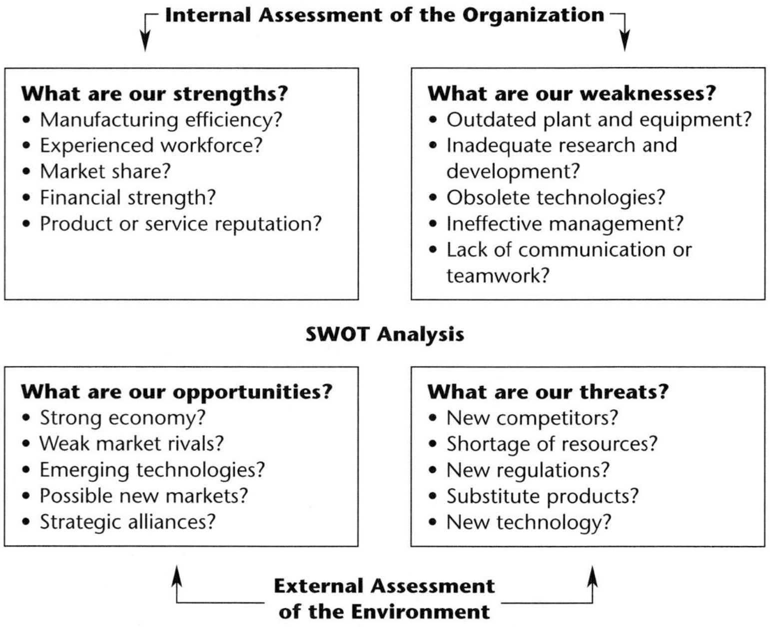

⌐ **Internal Assessment of the Organization** ⌐

What are our strengths?
- Manufacturing efficiency?
- Experienced workforce?
- Market share?
- Financial strength?
- Product or service reputation?

What are our weaknesses?
- Outdated plant and equipment?
- Inadequate research and development?
- Obsolete technologies?
- Ineffective management?
- Lack of communication or teamwork?

SWOT Analysis

What are our opportunities?
- Strong economy?
- Weak market rivals?
- Emerging technologies?
- Possible new markets?
- Strategic alliances?

What are our threats?
- New competitors?
- Shortage of resources?
- New regulations?
- Substitute products?
- New technology?

External Assessment of the Environment

mission and these values as your own, then we may join together." The vision should be the centerpiece of the orientation program for all new members.

3. *Make it constantly visible.* Express constancy of purpose through a written statement. The vision should be publicized to customers, employees, suppliers, owners—everyone.

4. *Create integrity through alignment and congruency.* Use the vision as a leadership tool and decision-making guide; as a checkpoint to test alignment of strategy, structures, systems, and member behavior; and as a means to track progress.

5. *Review the vision periodically, revising as appropriate to reflect changing conditions.* Even the U.S. Constitution has been amended over the long term. View the vision as a program with people as the programmers.[15]

The process of creating a vision must be tailored to each organization to be most effective. The process, content, and application principles are guidelines to achieve the required objective—agreement on direction and commitment to succeed.

Why Create a Vision?

Peter Drucker explains the importance of having a vision:

Because the modern organization is composed of specialists, each with his or her own narrow area of expertise, its purpose must be crystal clear. The organization must be single-minded, or its members will become confused. They will follow their own specialty rather than apply it to the common task. They will each define "results" in terms of their own specialty and impose its values on the organization. Only a focused and shared vision will hold an organization together and enable it to produce. Without agreement on purpose and values, the organization will soon lose credibility and, with it, its ability to attract the very people it needs to perform.[16]

Management authors James Collins and Jerry Porras report on the business benefits of having a vision. They asked a sample of CEOs from Fortune 500 and INC 100 companies to identify "visionary" organizations. For the 20 companies most frequently selected, they "invested" one dollar in stock in 1926 or whenever the firm was first listed. They found that, as a group, these visionary companies performed 55 times better than the general market. They also compared visionary companies with nonvisionary counterparts—companies that started at the same time—such as Motorola and Zenith, and Disney and Columbia. Again, vision-driven companies proved more successful, performing 8 times better than their competitors.[17]

Occupying center stage in explaining the importance of vision is author and educator Joel Barker. Barker's ideas are drawn primarily from three individuals—Frederick Polak, Benjamin Singer, and Viktor Frankl.[18]

Historian Frederick Polak asked the question, Is a nation's positive image of its future the consequence of its success, or is a nation's success the consequence of its positive image of the future? He concluded that the fates of nations and civilizations have depended primarily on their visions for the future. He cites examples in history of ancient Greece, Rome, Spain, England, and America to support this thought. Polak makes three main points: (1) Significant vision precedes significant success; (2) a compelling image of the future is shared by leaders with their followers, and together they strive to make this vision a reality; and (3) a nation with vision is enabled, and a nation without vision is at risk.[19]

Psychologist Benjamin Singer showed how children's lives are similarly shaped by positive self-concepts and expectations for the future. Children without vision become powerless, feeling no control over their own futures. Children with vision are focused and energized, and these are strong and positive agents in a self-fulfilling prophecy. Adults should always take seriously a child's dreams of what he or she wants to be. The interest and support shown communicates the message that the child is worthy and his or her future is important.[20] Consider the power of vision for one child, somehow conveyed by her father:

I was fourteen years old the night my daddy died. He had holes in his shoes but two children out of college, one in college, another in divinity school, and a vision he was able to convey to me as he lay dying in an ambulance that I, a young black girl, could be and do anything; that race and gender are shadows; and that character, self-discipline, determination, attitude and service are the substance of life.[21]

Barker believes that what is true for nations and what is true for children is especially true for organizations, because organizations have the ideal size and complexity to put vision's power into practice.

The third individual who influenced Barker was Viktor Frankl, author of *Man's Search for Meaning,* based on his experiences in the Nazi death camps of World War II. Frankl believed that everyone needs a purpose or meaning in life, something important yet to be done. Often this can be attained in the experience and achievements of one's work. In Frankl's view, meaning that transcends the self and extends to people and ideals beyond the individual is meaning on its highest and most human plane. Just as an airplane is most like an airplane when it rises from the runway and flies, so are we most human when we seek meaning in our lives, and commit to a purpose or mission that transcends the self.[22]

Requirements for an Effective Vision

The requirements for an effective vision are as follows:[23]

■ *First, a vision must be developed by leaders, those individuals with strength and influence to establish direction and mobilize the organization.* Leadership is dreaming a dream and then making it come true. Leaders create clear and worthy images that motivate the organization, and then create a climate so that ideas are transformed into deeds. Leadership is commitment to purpose along with persistence to see it through. The leader's vision should appeal to a common good and be believed passionately. Of six characteristics common to peak performers, management author Charles Garfield describes as the most important commitment to a mission that motivates.[24]

■ *Second, a vision must be communicated to followers and must be supported by them.* Leaders have to let others see, hear, taste, touch, and feel their vision. A picture in the mind of the general is merely that until it is understood in the minds and adopted in the hearts of the soldiers. Only then will hands and feet be activated and the vision be implemented in fact. It may take leadership to articulate and give legitimacy to a vision, but it takes the strength of an empowered people to get things done. In this regard, the vision of leaders must be in harmony with the nature and needs of the people.[25]

■ *Third, a vision must be comprehensive and detailed, so that every member of the organization can understand his or her part in the whole.* Roles and responsibilities must be well understood if the vision is to be fulfilled. Each person must know what is expected and the rewards that will accrue when the vision is achieved. Put yourself in the shoes of the soldier, who, upon hearing the vision and seeing the battle plan of the general, can't help wondering, Yes, but what about me? A clear line of sight between personal effort and personal reward is a major determinant of the ultimate fulfillment of the vision.[26]

■ *Fourth, a vision must be uplifting and inspiring.* It must be worth the effort; it must be big enough. Relating to Frankl's message that every person needs meaning in life and something important yet to be done, the organization's vision must be meaningful and important for the members to do.[27] Psychologist Abraham Maslow once remarked, "If you purposefully choose to be less than you can be, then you are surely doomed to be unhappy."[28] The same is true for organizations; the members of an organization must seek to achieve the organization's fullest potential.

The Motive to Lead

UNIT 6

Someone must provide the spark for action; someone must provide energy and purpose for leadership to occur. There are three basic motives for leadership: (1) **power**—the desire to have influence, give orders, and have them carried out; (2) **achievement**—the need to create and build something of value; and (3) **affiliation**—a heartfelt interest in helping others.

To understand the role of social motives at work, imagine three supervisors given the task of building a house: (1) The power-oriented leader focuses on how to organize the production of the house. She feels comfortable being in charge and enjoys being recognized as the powerful figure who causes the house to be produced. (2) The achievement-oriented leader obtains satisfaction from creating the house. Building a sound structure and completing the task on time is rewarding. (3) The affiliation leader enjoys working with his crew. He is concerned with human relations and strives to create a spirit of teamwork. Also, he is pleased to think of how much the home will mean to the family who lives in it.

Why would you want to be a leader? What would be your purpose for assuming the challenge of leadership? Do your job and personal life allow the expression of your social motives?

The questionnaire in Exercise 6–1 will help you answer these questions. Remember these three important points about the scores on the questionnaire:

■ Although it is normal for everyone to have some of each social motive, a person usually will prefer one or two over the others. Preference depends on the values (power, achievement, or affiliation) promoted by one's culture and on personal traits and experiences.

■ People exert leadership to satisfy one or a combination of these three motives. All leadership can be said to be motivated by power, achievement, or affiliation.

■ As either leader or follower, a person will be most happy and productive in a situation that allows the expression of personal social motives. If an individual's work precludes this, morale and productivity can be expected to go down.

**Exercise 6–1
Social Motives in
the Work Setting**[29]

This questionnaire consists of 12 statements. There are no right or wrong answers. For each statement, indicate which of the three alternatives—a., b., or c.—is most preferred by or most important to you by placing a 3 next to that choice. Place a 2 by your second choice and a 1 by the choice that is least preferred by or least important to you. Do not debate too long over any one statement. Your first reaction is desired.

1. In a work situation, I want to

_____ a. be in charge.

_____ b. give assistance to my co-workers.

_____ c. come up with new ideas.

2. If I have ultimate responsibility for a project, I

_____ a. depend on my own expertise to accomplish tasks.

_____ b. delegate work and oversee progress.

_____ c. use teamwork to accomplish tasks.

3. My co-workers see me as

_____ a. a competent person.

_____ b. a considerate person.

_____ c. a forceful person.

4. When I disagree with a decision, I

_____ a. voice my disapproval immediately.

_____ b. take into consideration other peoples' feelings and circumstances.

_____ c. suggest alternatives based on logic.

5. In a group discussion,

_____ a. I encourage others to express themselves.

_____ b. I will change my view only if a better one is suggested.

_____ c. my ideas generally prevail.

6. In a labor–management dispute, I would

_____ a. keep human relations smooth.

_____ b. maintain a position of strength.

_____ c. work for a compromise.

7. I am most satisfied with my job when I

_____ a. see progress being made.

_____ b. have a strong voice in determining policy.

_____ c. work with others to achieve results.

8. When disagreements arise, I usually

_____ a. yield a point to avoid conflict.

_____ b. stick to my guns.

_____ c. use reasoning to seek the best solution.

9. As a leader, I would

_____ a. permit flexibility, as long as the job gets done.

_____ b. recognize that workers have good days and bad days.

_____ c. insist on compliance with my rules and directions.

10. As a member of the board of directors dealing with a problem, I would most likely

_____ a. try to get my ideas adopted.

_____ b. solicit ideas from all members.

_____ c. review the facts.

11. When hiring a new employee, I would

_____ a. expect future loyalty to me.

_____ b. hire the person who is technically best qualified.

_____ c. take into consideration future relations with co-workers.

12. I am most happy in my work if I

_____ a. am the decision maker.

_____ b. work with good friends and colleagues.

_____ c. make significant achievements.

Scoring:

Step 1:

Scoring is done across the page, from left to right. For each question, put your a., b., and c. scores in the appropriate columns. Note that a., b., and c. scores do not remain in the same columns. Continue until all scores are filled in; then total the columns. (The grand total for the three columns should be 72.)

Column 1	Column 2	Column 3
1. a._____	1. c._____	1. b._____
2. b._____	2. a._____	2. c._____
3. c._____	3. a._____	3. b._____
4. a._____	4. c._____	4. b._____
5. c._____	5. b._____	5. a._____
6. b._____	6. c._____	6. a._____
7. b._____	7. a._____	7. c._____
8. b._____	8. c._____	8. a._____
9. c._____	9. a._____	9. b._____
10. a._____	10. c._____	10. b._____
11. a._____	11. b._____	11. c._____
12. a._____	12. c._____	12. b._____
Total _____	Total _____	Total _____

Step 2:

Mark the total scores for each column in the appropriate places in Figure 6–1. Shade in the areas as shown in the example, Figure 6–2.

Interpretation:

A high score in column 1 indicates social motives that are power-oriented. A power-oriented person strives for leadership because of the authority it brings. This person's goal is to influence people and events. Historical examples are Winston Churchill and Elizabeth I, who are recognized as outstanding leaders because of their mastery of power politics. Strength, assertiveness, and dominance are characteristics of power-oriented leaders. Positions involving the expression of power are manager, supervisor, and political office-holder.

A high score in column 2 indicates achievement-oriented social motives. This type of leader wants to discover, create, and build. Marie Curie and Charles Kettering are good examples of achievement-oriented people, each succeeding in making valuable contributions to humankind in science and technology. Achievement-oriented leaders are described as successful, competent, skillful, and productive. Achievement-oriented people are often found in occupations such as science, business, and the arts.

A high score in column 3 indicates a strong concern for human welfare. Such individuals care about other people and desire to serve humanity. This type of leader is likely to have traits similar to those of Florence Nightingale and Albert Schweitzer in the field of medicine. Common characteristics of these leaders are helpfulness, unselfishness, and consideration of the condition and well-being of others. Occupations such as teaching and counseling allow the expression of this social motive.

Figure 6–1
Your Social Motives

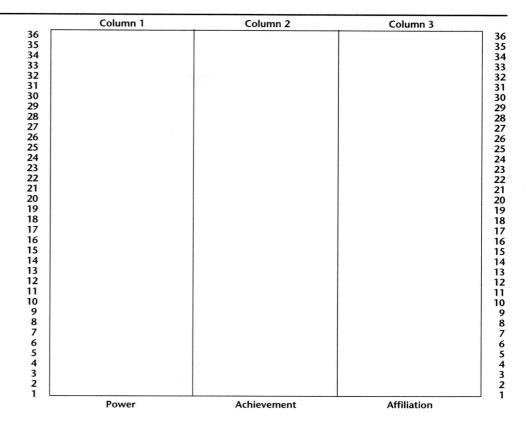

Figure 6–2
Example

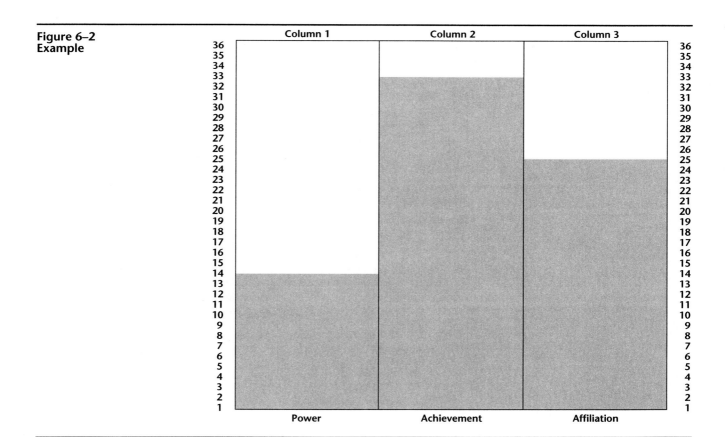

Organizational Climate

UNIT 7

E ven if an organization has a vision that is leader-initiated, member-supported, comprehensive and detailed, and worth doing, it must be sustained by a supportive organizational climate. Important dimensions of that climate include the **reward system, organizational clarity, standards of performance, warmth and support,** and **leadership practices.** An evaluation of these and other dimensions of an organization's climate can be used to determine whether that organization is exploitive, impoverished, supportive, or enlightened. Keep in mind the following points regarding an organization's climate:

■ An organization is only as strong as its weakest link. An individual may have an excellent nervous system, sound muscular system, and good respiratory system, but if the circulation system is poor, ultimately, the whole organism will fail. Similarly, an organization may be strong in performance standards, organizational clarity, and warmth and support, but if the reward system is poor, the entire organization will ultimately suffer.

■ Organizational climate is important because it supports the purpose and spirit of an organization. It directly influences both the quality of work and the quality of work life of members. Depending on the nature of the group or organization, even life-and-death consequences can result.

Consider an exploitive or impoverished hospital: People who can find employment elsewhere will probably leave, and these may be some of the best personnel. People who remain may spend more time complaining about working conditions and management practices than actually doing their work, with the result being unattended patients, poor housekeeping, and medical and clerical errors. Exploitive and impoverished hospitals experience unnecessary mistakes due to human factors—untrained, unqualified, and uncommitted workers.

Now consider an enlightened or supportive hospital, where standards of performance are high, leadership is effective, goals and responsibilities are clear, warmth and support prevail, and the reward system reinforces good work. Given a choice, where would you want to be treated, and where would you want to work? Which type of organization provides the best quality of health care and the best quality of work life?

■ Enlightened and supportive organizations represent good investments. Because of their reputations, they attract excellent personnel, who usually outperform their demoralized counterparts in exploitive and impoverished organizations.

■ Organizations are composed of interdependent groups. The success of the total organization depends on conditions in each of its subgroups. As such, every division and unit should develop an enlightened or supportive climate.

You can evaluate the climate of your organization by completing the questionnaire in Exercise 7–1.

Exercise 7–1
Organizational Climate
Questionnaire[30]

For each dimension of organizational climate, circle the number on the scale that represents conditions in your organization (1 is low; 20 is high).

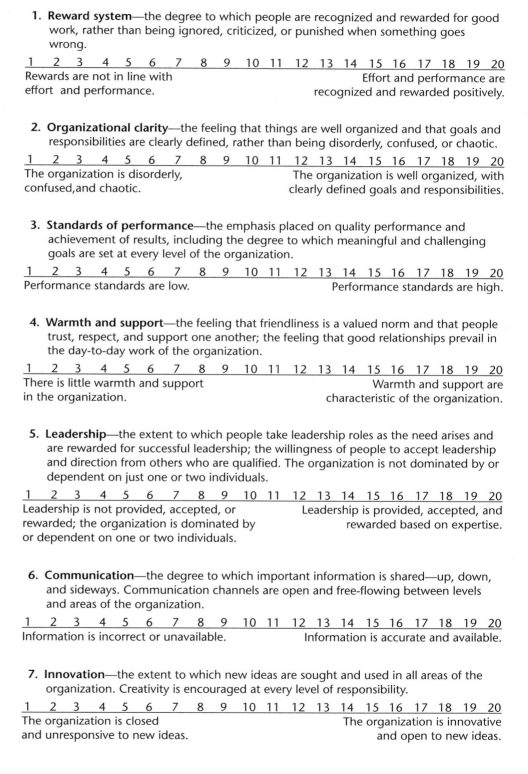

1. **Reward system**—the degree to which people are recognized and rewarded for good work, rather than being ignored, criticized, or punished when something goes wrong.

   1 2 3 4 5 6 7 8 9 10 11 12 13 14 15 16 17 18 19 20
   Rewards are not in line with   Effort and performance are
   effort and performance.   recognized and rewarded positively.

2. **Organizational clarity**—the feeling that things are well organized and that goals and responsibilities are clearly defined, rather than being disorderly, confused, or chaotic.

   1 2 3 4 5 6 7 8 9 10 11 12 13 14 15 16 17 18 19 20
   The organization is disorderly,   The organization is well organized, with
   confused,and chaotic.   clearly defined goals and responsibilities.

3. **Standards of performance**—the emphasis placed on quality performance and achievement of results, including the degree to which meaningful and challenging goals are set at every level of the organization.

   1 2 3 4 5 6 7 8 9 10 11 12 13 14 15 16 17 18 19 20
   Performance standards are low.   Performance standards are high.

4. **Warmth and support**—the feeling that friendliness is a valued norm and that people trust, respect, and support one another; the feeling that good relationships prevail in the day-to-day work of the organization.

   1 2 3 4 5 6 7 8 9 10 11 12 13 14 15 16 17 18 19 20
   There is little warmth and support   Warmth and support are
   in the organization.   characteristic of the organization.

5. **Leadership**—the extent to which people take leadership roles as the need arises and are rewarded for successful leadership; the willingness of people to accept leadership and direction from others who are qualified. The organization is not dominated by or dependent on just one or two individuals.

   1 2 3 4 5 6 7 8 9 10 11 12 13 14 15 16 17 18 19 20
   Leadership is not provided, accepted, or   Leadership is provided, accepted, and
   rewarded; the organization is dominated by   rewarded based on expertise.
   or dependent on one or two individuals.

6. **Communication**—the degree to which important information is shared—up, down, and sideways. Communication channels are open and free-flowing between levels and areas of the organization.

   1 2 3 4 5 6 7 8 9 10 11 12 13 14 15 16 17 18 19 20
   Information is incorrect or unavailable.   Information is accurate and available.

7. **Innovation**—the extent to which new ideas are sought and used in all areas of the organization. Creativity is encouraged at every level of responsibility.

   1 2 3 4 5 6 7 8 9 10 11 12 13 14 15 16 17 18 19 20
   The organization is closed   The organization is innovative
   and unresponsive to new ideas.   and open to new ideas.

8. **Feedback and controls**—the use of reporting, comparing, and correcting procedures, such as performance evaluations and financial audits. Controls are used for tracking progress and solving problems, as opposed to policing and punishment.

<u>1   2   3   4   5   6   7   8   9   10   11   12   13   14   15   16   17   18   19   20</u>
Controls are used for policing   Controls are used to provide
and punishment.   guidance and solve problems.

9. **Teamwork**—the amount of understanding, cooperation, and support demonstrated between different levels and groups in the organization.

<u>1   2   3   4   5   6   7   8   9   10   11   12   13   14   15   16   17   18   19   20</u>
Teamwork is low.   Teamwork is high.

10. **Involvement**—the extent to which responsibility for decision making is broadly shared in the organization. People are involved in decisions that affect them.

<u>1   2   3   4   5   6   7   8   9   10   11   12   13   14   15   16   17   18   19   20</u>
There is little participation   Participation in decision making is high.
in decision making.

Scoring:

Total the scores for all the dimensions; then divide by 10. Circle that number on the scale below.

Type of Organization

<u>1 2 3 4 5</u>   <u>6 7 8 9 10</u>   <u>11 12 13 14 15</u>   <u>16 17 18 19 20</u>
Exploitive   Impoverished   Supportive   Enlightened

Interpretation:

Results of this questionnaire can be used to reinforce strengths and improve weaknesses. High scores represent enlightened and supportive organizations. Low scores reflect exploitive and impoverished organizations.

Leaders and followers may have different views about the climate of a group or organization. People in upper levels of responsibility often evaluate conditions more favorably than do people in lower levels. See the example in Figure 7–1.

Figure 7–1
Extent to Which Leaders and Followers Agree on Organizational Conditions[31]

Behavior	Top Staff Self-Evaluation*	First-Line Supervisor Evaluation of Top Staff Behavior	First-Line Supervisor Self-Evaluation**	Employee Evaluation of First-Line Supervisor Behavior
Always tells subordinates in advance about changes that will affect them or their work	70%	27%	40%	22%
Nearly always tells subordinates	30% ⎬ 100%	36% ⎬ 63%	52% ⎬ 92%	25% ⎬ 47%
More often than not tells subordinates	—	18%	2%	13%
Occasionally tells subordinates	—	15%	5%	28%
Seldom tells subordinates	—	4%	1%	12%

*Top staff rated themselves 37% higher than they were rated by subordinates.
**First-line supervisors rated themselves 45% higher than they were rated by subordinates.

Patterns of Leadership

How do organizations become what they are? Who decides whether an organization will be enlightened, supportive, impoverished, or exploitive? Although members may have considerable influence, organizational climate is determined primarily by leaders. Those in charge establish the character and define norms of behaviors.

Management author Rensis Likert identifies four patterns of leadership that correspond to the four types of organizational climate. His conclusions are based on studies of thousands of leaders in widely different kinds of organizations, both inside and outside the United States. A description of each of the four patterns of leadership follows.[32]

Pattern I Leadership (Exploitive)

Exploitive leadership is autocratic and hierarchical, with virtually no participation by members. Leaders make decisions, and members are expected to comply without question. Leaders show little confidence or trust in others, and members do not feel free to discuss job-related problems with leaders. In a free social and economic order, Pattern I organizations rarely survive because people avoid them as much as possible. Where they do exist, they are characterized by a lack of loyalty and recurrent financial crises.

Pattern II Leadership (Impoverished)

Impoverished leadership makes some attempt to avoid being completely autocratic. Power remains at the top, but members are given occasional opportunities for participation in the decision-making process. Pattern II organizations fall into two categories that determine their relative success. Successful Pattern II organizations are benevolent autocracies in which leaders have genuine concern for the welfare of members. Failing

Pattern II organizations are autocracies that do not consider the interests or ideas of members. Some organizations are founded by autocratic but benevolent leaders, who achieve good results. Then, as time passes and new leaders assume power, the autocratic style of leadership is maintained, but benevolence is not, and the organization fails.

Pattern III Leadership (Supportive)

Supportive leadership shows a great deal of interest and confidence in members. Power resides in leaders, but there is good communication and participation throughout the organization. People understand the goals of the organization, and commitment to achieve them is widespread. Members feel free to discuss job-related problems with leaders. This leadership pattern involves broad member participation and involvement in decision-making activities.

Pattern IV Leadership (Enlightened)

Enlightened leadership delegates power to the logical focus of interest and concern for a problem. People at all levels of the organization have a high degree of freedom to initiate, coordinate, and execute plans to accomplish goals. Communication is open, honest, and uncensored. People are treated with trust rather than suspicion. Leaders ask for ideas and try to use others' suggestions. Pattern IV leadership results in high satisfaction and productivity. Absenteeism and turnover are low, strikes are nonexistent, and efficiency is high.

Likert describes the Pattern IV organization as follows:

A Pattern IV organization is made up of interlocking work groups with a high degree of group loyalty among the members and favorable attitudes among peers, supervisors, and subordinates.

Consideration for others and skill in problem solving and other group functions are present. These skills permit effective participation in decisions on common problems. Participation is used, for example, to establish objectives that are a satisfactory integration of the needs of all the members of the organization.

Members of the Pattern IV organization are highly motivated to achieve the organization's goals. High levels of reciprocal influence occur, and a high level of coordination is achieved in the organization.

Communication is efficient and effective. There is a flow from one part of the organization to another of all the relevant information important for each decision and action.

The leadership in the Pattern IV organization has developed an effective system for interaction, problem solving, and organizational achievement. This leadership is technically competent and maintains high performance goals.[33]

Four principles should be followed to develop an enlightened, Pattern IV organization:

1. **View human resources as the organization's greatest asset.**
2. **Treat every individual with understanding, dignity, warmth, and support.**
3. **Tap the constructive power of groups through visioning and team building.**
4. **Set high performance goals at every level of the organization.**[34]

Likert recommends that all organizations adopt the enlightened principles of Pattern IV leadership. He estimates that U.S. organizations, as a whole, are between Pattern II and Pattern III, and that a shift to Pattern IV would improve employee morale and productivity by 20 to 40 percent, or more.[35]

Research supports Likert's ideas. Study after study shows that when an organization moves to Pattern IV leadership, performance effectiveness improves, costs decrease, and gains occur in the overall satisfaction and health of the members of the organization. In addition, research findings show that Pattern IV leadership is applicable to every size and type of organization, including private businesses, not-for-profit organizations, and government agencies.[36]

How important are organizational climate and enlightened leadership practices? Management author John Hoerr states: "We are in a global economy. To have world-class quality and costs and the ability to assimilate new technology, an organization must have world-class ability to develop human capabilities. This can't be a drag on the system; it has to be a leading variable."[37]

Building Community in the Workplace

Thomas Carlisle, the Scottish philosopher, thought that each person wanted to be treated as a unique and valuable individual. He also believed we each have a simultaneous need to belong to something greater than self, something more than one alone can do or be. For many people, feelings of self-worth and transcendence to something greater than self occur in the experience of community.

The benefits of interrelationship can be found everywhere in nature. If a gardener places two plants close together, the roots commingle and improve the quality of the soil, thus helping both plants grow better than if they were separated. If a carpenter joins two boards together, they will hold much more weight than the total held by each alone.

In the human sphere, our challenge is to apply the creative cooperation we learn from nature in dealing with those around us. The essence of this is to value differences, build on each other's strengths, transcend individual limitations, and achieve the full potential of community.

Writer and educator John Gardner states, "We are a community-building species." He goes on to describe the conditions necessary to experience true community.[38]

■ *Shared vision.* A healthy community has a sense of where it should go, and what it might become. A positive and future-focused role image provides direction and motivation for its members.

■ *Wholeness incorporating diversity.* A group is less of a community if fragmentation or divisiveness exists—and if the rifts are deep, it is no community at all. We expect and value diversity, and there is dissent in the best of groups. But true community requires facing and resolving differences.

■ *Shared culture.* Success is enhanced when people have a shared culture, that is, shared norms of behavior and core values to live by. If a community is lucky, it has shared history and traditions as well. This is why developing communities must form symbols of group identity and generate stories to pass on core values, customs, and central purpose.

■ *Internal communications.* Members of a well-functioning community communicate freely with one another. There are regular occasions when people gather and share information. There are opportunities and means for people to get to know and understand what others need and want. Communication is uncensored and flows in all directions within the community.

■ *Consideration and trust.* A healthy community cares about its members and fosters an atmosphere of trust. People deal with one another humanely; they respect each other and value the integrity of each person.

■ *Maintenance and government.* A fully functioning community has provision for maintenance and governance. Roles, responsibilities, and decision-making processes are conducive to achieving tasks while maintaining a supportive group climate.

■ *Participation and shared leadership.* The healthy community encourages the involvement of all individuals in the pursuit of shared goals. All members have the opportunity to influence events and outcomes. The good community finds a productive balance between individual interests and group responsibilities as community tasks are accomplished.

■ *Development of younger members.* Opportunities for growth are numerous and varied for all members. Mature members ensure that younger members develop knowledge, skills, and attitudes that support continuation of the community's purpose and values.

■ *Affirmation.* A healthy community reaffirms itself continuously. It celebrates its beginnings, rewards its achievements, and takes pride in its challenges. In this way, community morale and confidence is developed.

■ *Links with outside groups.* There is a certain tension between the community's need to draw boundaries to accomplish its tasks and its need to have fruitful alliances with external groups and the larger community of which it is a part. A successful community masters both ends of this spectrum.

In *Productive Workplaces,* Marvin Weisbord writes that we hunger for community and are a great deal more productive when we find it. If we feed this hunger in ways that preserve individual dignity, opportunity for all, and mutual support, we will harness energy and productivity beyond imagining.[39]

In *A World Waiting to Be Born,* Scott Peck identifies the leader within a group or organization to be a potential obstacle to creating community. Specifically, no matter how deeply those at the bottom or middle desire it, community will be difficult to achieve if those at the top are resistant. Conversely, if the leaders are the kinds of people who want community, they can probably have it. They may have to work hard for it. It may require time and resources. But if leaders want to achieve a positive and healthy human environment, it can be done under almost any circumstances.[40]

In an article entitled "The Brave New World of Leadership Training," Jay Conger describes *building community* as the most important task facing leaders today. He views this as a special assignment that combines two basic leadership competencies—visioning and empowerment. Both of these are related since vision itself must be empowering. The vision's purpose is not only to achieve a meaningful strategic or company goal, but also to create a dedicated community of people.[41]

Part Two Summary

After reading Part Two, you should know the following key concepts, principles, and terms. Fill in the blanks from memory, or copy the answers listed below.

The most important function of a leader is to develop a clear, compelling (a) _____ and to secure commitment to that ideal. In addition, the leader must have a (b) _____ to succeed. Finally, the leader must have (c) _____ to see these through. These three items are the requirements for leadership success. Four distinct areas that correlate positively with leadership effectiveness are (d) _____, _____, _____, and _____. An effective vision must be (e) _____, _____, _____, and _____. The three motives for assuming leadership responsibility are (f) _____, _____, and _____. The climate of an organization includes the (g) _____, _____, _____, _____, and _____. The climate of an organization is determined primarily by the quality of leadership. Leaders in the best organizations follow four enlightened principles: (h) _____, _____, _____, and _____.

Answer Key for Part Two Summary

a. **vision,** page 56

b. **strategy,** page 56

c. **stamina,** page 56

d. **getting the facts, creating a vision, motivating people, empowering others,** pages 61–62

e. **leader-initiated, shared and supported by followers, comprehensive and detailed, uplifting and inspiring,** page 66

f. **power, achievement, affiliation,** page 67

g. (any five) **reward system, organizational clarity, standards of performance, warmth and support, leadership, communication, innovation, feedback and controls, teamwork, involvement,** pages 73–76

h. **view human resources as the organization's greatest asset; treat every individual with understanding, dignity, warmth, and support; tap the constructive power of groups through visioning and team building; set high performance goals at every level of the organization,** page 78

Reflection Points—personal thoughts on the importance of vision, the motive to lead, and organizational climate

Complete the following questions and activities to personalize the content of Part Two. Space is provided for writing your thoughts.

■ Describe the vision of a successful leader you have known; discuss the role of stamina in achieving that vision.

_____

_____

■ Have you ever taken responsibility for initiating change? Have you ever created a vision and a strategy for success? Discuss.

_____

_____

■ Evaluate a leader you know on the basis of four important practices—getting the facts, creating a vision, motivating people, and empowering others.

_____

_____

■ Critique the vision of an organization you know. Is the vision leader-initiated? Shared and supported? Comprehensive and detailed? Uplifting and inspiring?

_____

_____

■ Why would you want to be a leader—power, achievement, or affiliation? Does your work or personal life allow the expression of your social motives?

_____

_____

■ Evaluate the climate of an organization you know, including the reward system, organizational clarity, performance standards, warmth and support, leadership, and other dimensions. Discuss strengths and areas to improve.

Action Assignment

As a bridge between learning and doing, complete the following action assignment.

1. What is the most important idea you have learned in Part Two?

2. How can you apply what you have learned? What will you do, with whom, where, when, and, most important, why?

Part 3   The Importance of Ethics

8. **Leadership Ethics**
9. **The Role of Values**
10. **Ethics at Work**

UNTIL PHILOSOPHERS ARE KINGS, or the kings and princes of this world have the spirit and power of philosophy, and political greatness and wisdom meet in one, and those commoner natures who pursue either to the exclusion of the other are compelled to stand aside, cities will never have rest from their evils—no, nor the human race, as I believe—and then only will this our State have a possibility of life and behold the light of day.

—Plato (428–347 B.C.)
The Republic: An Ideal Commonwealth

Learning Points

In Part Three, you will discover the answers to these questions:
- What are the levels and stages of moral development?
- Why is leadership by values important? What values guide you in your leadership behavior?
- What is the role of the leader in setting the moral tone and ethical climate of the workplace?

Leadership Ethics

Leaders must understand the subject of ethics—what it is and why it is important. Ethics is the branch of philosophy concerned with the intent, means, and consequences of moral behavior. It is the study of **moral judgments** and **right and wrong conduct.** Some human judgments are factual (the earth is round); others are aesthetic (she is beautiful); and still others are moral (people should be honest and should not kill). Moral judgments are judgments about what is right and wrong, good and bad.[1] The Spanish writer Cervantes wrote about ethics in *Don Quixote:*

I know that the path of virtue is straight and narrow, and the road of vice broad and spacious. I know also that their ends and resting places are different; for those of vice, large and open, end in death; and those of virtue, narrow and intricate, end in life; and not in life that has an end, but in that which is eternal.[2]

The word *ethics* is derived from the Greek word *ethos,* referring to a person's fundamental orientation toward life. Originally, *ethos* meant "a dwelling place." For the philosopher Aristotle, *ethos* came to mean "an inner dwelling place," or what is now called "inner character." The Latin translation of *ethos* is "mos, moris," from which comes the English word *moral.* In Roman times, the emphasis shifted from internal character to overt behavior—acts, habits, and customs.[3]

In more recent times, ethics has been viewed as an overall human concern:

One of the chief problems is to determine what the basis of a moral code should be, to find out what one ought to do. Is right that which is the word of God given to man in the Ten Commandments? Is it what is revealed to us by conscience and intuition? Is it whatever will increase the sum of human happiness? Is it that which is the most reasonable thing to do? Is it whatever makes for the fullness and perfection of life? Above all, is there any absolute right, anything embedded, so to speak, in the nature of the universe, which should guide our actions? Or are right and wrong simply relative, dependent on time and place and cultural pattern, and changing with environment and circumstance? What, in short, is the basis of our moral values? These questions are of vital importance in a day when intellectual power threatens to outrun moral control and thus destroy humankind.[4]

Ethical questions are important in all areas of life—work and personal. Put yourself in the shoes of the individuals in Exercise 8–1.

**Exercise 8–1
Moral Dilemmas**

In each dilemma, what would you do? Place a checkmark by your response; then provide the rationale for your answer in the space provided.

1. *The citizen.* You are driving your car when you come upon the scene of an accident. One person will die without immediate medical care. You take the victim and speed to the hospital. The extra speed causes another accident, in which another person dies. How should you be judged? Was your act right because your motive was good, or was your act wrong because its consequences were bad?

   Check one: ☐ Right; motive was good   ☐ Wrong; consequences were bad   ☐ Alternative response

   Rationale: _____

   _____

   _____

   _____

2. *The salesperson.* You learn that your company is selling faulty equipment that could be dangerous. Your spouse needs medical treatment that costs a large percentage of your income. You have reason to believe that if you confront your employer, you will lose your job. What would you do?

   Check one: ☐ Confront employer   ☐ Avoid confrontation   ☐ Alternative response

   Rationale: _____

   _____

   _____

   _____

3. *The administrative assistant.* You are an executive administrative assistant who has been with the company for 20 years. You provide sole support for your family (boy, 12; girl, 10; mother, ailing). Your new boss, the company president, has made it clear to you that continued employment depends on occasional sexual favors. What would you do?

   Check one: ☐ Provide favors   ☐ Refuse to provide favors; risk losing job   ☐ Alternative response

   Rationale: _____

   _____

   _____

   _____

4. *The parent.* You have two daughters. One always complains when you send her on errands. The other doesn't like going either but usually goes without arguing. Typically, you send the daughter who does not complain more often than the one who does. Is this right or wrong?

   Check one: ☐ Right; Continue to send noncomplaining daughter   ☐ Wrong; send both daughters equally   ☐ Alternative response

   Rationale: _____

   _____

   _____

   _____

5. *The firefighter.* It is World War II, and you are a firefighter in a city in Germany that is under constant bombing. One day, after an especially heavy attack, you leave the bomb shelter to go to your fire station. On the way, you decide to see whether your family is safe. Although your home is quite distant, you go there first. Is this right or wrong?

Check one: ☐ Right; check   ☐ Wrong; go to fire   ☐ Alternative response
           family first   station first

Rationale: _____

            _____

            _____

            _____

6. *The friend.* You promise to keep your best friend's secret; then she tells you that her son is selling drugs and even has sold them at a nearby grade school. Your friend is upset but plans on taking no action. What would you do?

Check one: ☐ Notify   ☐ Keep friend's   ☐ Alternative response
           authorities   secret

Rationale: _____

            _____

            _____

            _____

7. *The supervisor.* Your company is reducing the workforce, and you must dismiss one of your engineers. You have narrowed the choices to T. J., an older employee who has been coasting for years, but who is capable of outstanding performance, and Morgan, a new employee who tries his best, but who almost certainly will never perform at the same level as T. J. Who would you let go?

Check one: ☐ T. J.   ☐ Morgan   ☐ Alternative response

Rationale: _____

            _____

            _____

            _____

These dilemmas show the range of ethical questions that people face and the consequences moral judgments can have. As a human being, you are constantly making decisions about what is the best or right action to take with family, friends, and colleagues. For leaders, the number and gravity of dilemmas are intensified because of the role and influence they have.

No Easy Subject

Ethics is a difficult subject, forcing people to think about moral issues with elusive answers. This is true now more than ever before. Consider the questions that people are being faced with today:

- *The conscious creation of new forms of life.* What are the benefits and penalties of creating new forms of life through recombinant genetics? Should people be cloned? If so, who should be cloned?

- *Exploration and the use of outer space.* Should people be exploring space? Are the huge financial sums spent on space exploration justified in view of the human misery on earth?

- *Nuclear energy.* What should be done with our knowledge about atomic energy? Should we build bombs that can destroy life, or should we apply this knowledge to human welfare? What should be done, and who is to decide?

- *Information technology.* Should everything that *can* be known *be* known by anybody anytime? Should children see the surface of Mars on a computer screen before they feel the surface of the earth—its rocks, sand, water, and grass— firsthand, with their own bodies? What should we do in response to the admonition not to become tools of our tools?

Aside from moral issues created by developments in science and technology, there are many ethical problems common to the workplace—issues of quality, safety, property, and human relationships. It is the task of the leader to understand and make judgments on these difficult subjects.[5]

The Roots of Ethics

Ethics has both religious and secular roots. Religious ethics is based on a theistic understanding of the world. What is real, true, and good is defined by God. Secular ethics is based on a scientific understanding of the world. Reality, truth, and goodness do not depend on the existence of a God. Both religious and secular ethics may endorse many common values, such as the preservation of life and the importance of the Golden Rule. The primary difference is how values are justified.

The Secular Tradition

Aristotle was one of the first and perhaps most influential of all people to shape the ethics of Western civilization from a secular orientation. He believed that every type of animal has a common essence or nature, and that human beings are essentially, or by nature, rational. He viewed rationality as the central and most significant trait distinguishing humankind from other creatures. Further, Aristotle taught that the good person is the one who lives most rationally and whose moral judgments and social conduct are born of contemplation and reason, in contrast to spontaneity and emotionality. Today, when we address a moral dilemma by saying, Let us use reason; let us use logic; let us think rationally about this, we are being ethical in the Aristotelian secular tradition.[6] Consider the short essay on the next page by the Englishman Bertrand Russell, a modern philosopher whose views were secular.

The Religious Tradition

All the world's religions make prescriptions for moral behavior. St. Augustine, for example, who generally is agreed to have had a greater influence on Western religious thought than any other writer outside of Biblical scripture, maintained that the naturally evil inclinations of humanity could be overcome only by divine grace. He believed that if we allow ourselves through faith to be drawn to God, we will overcome our basic immoral nature and eventually be reconciled in the city of God in heaven.[7]

What I Have Lived For

Bertrand Russell

Three passions, simple but overwhelmingly strong, have governed my life: the longing for love, the search for knowledge, and unbearable pity for the suffering of mankind. These passions, like great winds, have blown me hither and thither, in a wayward course, over a deep ocean of anguish, reaching to the very verge of despair.

I have sought love, first, because it brings ecstasy—ecstasy so great that I would often have sacrificed all the rest of life for a few hours of this joy. I have sought it, next, because it relieves loneliness—that terrible loneliness in which one in shivering consciousness, looks over the rim of the world into the cold, unfathomable, lifeless abyss. I have sought it, finally, because in the union of love I have seen, in a mystic miniature, the prefiguring vision of the heaven that saints and poets have imagined. This is what I sought, and though it might seem too good for human life, this is what—at last—I have found.

With equal passion I have sought knowledge. I have wished to understand the hearts of men. I have wished to know why the stars shine. A little of this, but not much, I have achieved.

Love and knowledge, so far as they were possible, led upward toward the heavens. But always pity brought me back to earth. Echoes of cries of pain reverberate in my heart. Children in famine, victims of torture by oppressors, helpless old people a hated burden to their sons, and the whole world of loneliness, poverty, and pain make a mockery of what human life should be. I long to alleviate the evil, but I cannot, and I too suffer.

This has been my life. I have found it worth living, and would gladly live it again if the chance were offered me.[8]

Another Christian philosopher, Thomas Aquinas, taught that all people are endowed with a natural desire to be good. He believed that this inclination could be dormant in an individual and could even be perverted. Nonetheless, he believed it to be present in all people and impossible to destroy. Aquinas taught that to resist God's pull is contrary to human nature and that if we allow ourselves to follow God, we will fulfill our nature and we will be purely good. Further, by acting out this goodness in our day-to-day lives, we will be moral and will experience the greatest meaning of which we are capable.[9]

The majority of people who have ever lived have been influenced by religions such as Christianity and individuals such as St. Augustine and Thomas Aquinas. Consider the words of Ben Franklin: "I believe that the soul of man is immortal and will be treated with justice in another life respecting its conduct in this."

Ethics, Humankind, and Other Animals

Whether based on religious belief or secular thought, ethics is a concern unique to humankind. People are the only creatures who combine emotion (feelings) with knowledge (information) and through abstract reasoning (thought) produce a moral conscience, or a sense of what should be.

Some ideas about right and wrong are of prehuman origin. Indeed, such social virtues as self-sacrifice, sympathy, and cooperation can be seen among many other species, such as elephants, porpoises, and lions. However, more than 40,000 years ago, the human race evolved into beings who could distinguish between what is and what ought to be, and it is this attribute that separates people from all other animals.[10]

In *The Origin of Species,* biologist and social philosopher Charles Darwin concludes of ethics, humankind, and other animals:

> I fully subscribe to the judgment of those writers who maintain that, of all the differences between man and the lower animals, the moral sense of conscience is by far the most important. It is summed up by that short but impervious word, ought, so full of high significance. It is the most noble of all attributes of man, leading him without a moment's hesitation to risk his life for the life of a fellow creature, or after due deliberation, impelled simply by the deep feeling of right or duty, to sacrifice it in some great cause.[11]

Moral Development

How is morality developed? The English philosopher John Locke viewed the newborn child as a tabula rasa, or blank tablet, on which a life script would be written. He believed that experience and learning would shape the content, structure, and direction of each person's life. In this sense, the ethics of the infant are amoral—that is, there is no concept of good and bad or right and wrong that is inborn.

After birth, babies soon discover that they are rewarded for certain things and punished for others. As a result of this early programming, they develop an understanding of what the adult world considers good and bad. Thus a social conscience is begun, and this becomes the foundation for future moral development.[12]

Through modeling and socialization, the older community passes on ethics to young people. The words and actions of parents, teachers, and older companions teach and reinforce morality before children develop their own critical faculties. Ben Franklin's advice to "teach children obedience first so that all other lessons will follow the easier" captures the spirit in which moral values are taught.[13]

On a societywide scale, the ethics of adults are similarly programmed. Swiss psychologist Jean Piaget writes that heteronomy (rules as sacred external laws laid down by authorities) is the unifying factor in adult societies, and that in every society there are leaders (governmental, religious, and educational) who believe in certain moral ideals, and who see their task to be one of imprinting these ideals on succeeding generations.[14]

Practically speaking, the three most important influences on character formation are:

- **Associations.** Family, friends, and role models help shape our future lives. The example and encouragement of some people may improve us, while that of others may pull us down.

- **Books.** The printed page and other media can poison us with wrong accounts and harmful thoughts, or can enlighten and lift up our lives with reason and spirit fundamental to a healthy person.

- **Self-concept.** We do what we do to be consistent with who we think we are. Our primary motivation is not self-preservation, but preservation of the symbolic self. Whoever considers him- or herself to be honest, brave, and worthy is likely to be so, as our outer lives are first decided in our inner hearts.

Consider the ABCs of your own character development:

1. *Associations.* Who in your life has influenced your character development?

_____

_____

_____

2. *Books.* What books, films, and other media have helped you become a better person?

_____

_____

_____

3. *Self-concept.* What image of yourself has shaped your values and guided your life?

_____

_____

_____

Levels of Morality

A person's level of morality is one of the most important dimensions of leadership, determining whether people will trust and respect the leader. Regardless of the code of ethics a society teaches and regardless of one's personal values, on what basis does the individual make ethical decisions? What motive, goal, or frame of reference does the person bring to moral dilemmas? There are many ideas on this question, but the work of social psychologist Lawrence Kohlberg occupies center stage.[15]

Kohlberg explains that each person makes ethical decisions according to three levels of moral development—**preconventional, conventional,** and **postconventional.** Table 8–1 describes these levels, defines two stages within each level, and presents examples of moral reasoning at each stage. As you read the chart, evaluate your own ethics. At which level do you usually operate? At which level would you want leaders to behave?

Different people go through the six stages of moral development at different rates, and some people never reach the principled morality of stages 5 and 6. Individuals who remain at lower levels of morality experience arrested developmental integrity. The egocentric orientation of stages 1 and 2 is most characteristic of preadolescent children, whereas the community-oriented morality of stages 3 and 4 is common in teenagers and most adults. The self-direction and high principles of stages 5 and 6 are characteristic of only 20 percent of the adult population, with only 5 to 10 percent of the population operating consistently at stage 6.[16]

The case and analysis that follow show how levels of morality influence human conduct in the face of moral dilemmas:

The Stolen Drug

In Europe, a woman was near death from a rare kind of cancer. There was one drug that the doctors thought might save her. It was a form of radium that a druggist in the same town had recently discovered. The drug was expensive to make, but the druggist was charging ten times what the drug cost him. He paid $200 for the radium and charged $2,000 for a small dose of the drug.

The sick woman's husband, Heinz, went to everyone he knew to borrow the money, but he could only get together about $1,000, which was half of what it cost. He told the druggist that his wife was dying and asked him to sell it cheaper, or let him pay later. But the druggist said, "No, I discovered the drug and I'm going to make money from it." Heinz became desperate and broke into the man's store to steal the drug for his wife.[17]

When confronted with the moral dilemma of either letting his wife die or stealing the drug, Heinz stole the drug. Was he right or wrong? Table 8–2 presents examples of moral reasoning Heinz may have used at each stage of moral development.

Table 8–1   **Levels, Stages, and Examples of Moral Development**[18]

Level of Moral Development	Stage of Moral Development	Example of Moral Reasoning at Each Stage
Level I Preconventional morality. The individual is aware of cultural prescriptions of right and wrong behavior. Response is based on two concerns: Will I be harmed (punishment)? Will I be helped (pleasure)?	**Stage 1** At this stage, physical consequences determine moral behavior. Avoidance of punishment and deference to power are characteristics of this stage.	I won't hit him because he may hit me back.
	Stage 2 Individual needs are the primary motives operating at this stage, and personal pleasure dictates the rightness or wrongness of behavior.	I will help her because she may help me in return.
Level II Conventional morality. Morality is characterized by group conformity and allegiance to authority. The individual acts in order to meet the expectations of others and to please those in charge.	**Stage 3** The approval of others is the major determinant of behavior at this stage, and the good person is viewed as the one who satisfies family, friends, and associates.	I will go along with you because I want you to like me.
	Stage 4 Compliance with authority and upholding social order are primary ethical concerns at this stage. Right conduct is doing one's duty, as defined by those in authority positions.	I will comply with the order because it is wrong to disobey.
Level III Postconventional morality. This is the most advanced level of moral development. At this level the individual is concerned with right and wrong conduct over and above self-interest, apart from the views of others, and without regard to authority figures. Ethical judgments are based on self-defined moral principles.	**Stage 5** Social ethics are based on rational analysis, community discussion, and mutual consent. There is tolerance for individual views, but when there is conflict between individual and group interests, the majority rules. This stage represents the "official" morality of the U.S. Constitution.	Although I disagree with his views, I will uphold his right to have them.
	Stage 6 At this stage, what is right and good is viewed as a matter of individual conscience, free choice, and personal responsibility for the consequences. Morality is seen as superseding the majority view or the prescriptions of authority; rather, it is based on personal conviction.	There is no external force that can compel me to do an act that I consider morally wrong.

Table 8–2   **Heinz's Reasoning: Should I Steal the Drug?**[19]

Moral Stage	Argument For	Argument Against
Stage 1: Orientation to punishment	It isn't wrong to take the drug. It is really worth only $200, and I probably won't get caught anyway.	It is wrong to take the drug. After all, it is worth $2,000. Besides, I would probably get caught and be punished.
Stage 2: Orientation to pleasure	If I don't want to lose my wife, I should take the drug. It is the only thing that will work.	I should not risk myself for my wife. If she dies, I can marry somebody else. It would be wrong for me to give up my well-being for her well-being.
Stage 3: Orientation to social approval	I have no choice. Stealing the drug is the only thing for a good husband to do. What would my family and friends say if I didn't try to save my wife?	I must not steal the drug. People won't blame me for not stealing the drug; it is not the kind of thing people would approve of.
Stage 4: Orientation to social order	When I got married, I vowed to protect my wife. I must steal the drug to live up to that promise. If husbands do not protect their wives, the family structure will disintegrate, and with it, our society.	Stealing is illegal. I have to obey the law, no matter what the circumstances. Imagine what society would be like if everybody broke the law.
Stage 5: Orientation to social rights and responsibilities	I should steal the drug. The law is unjust because it does not protect my wife's right to life. Therefore, I have no obligation to obey the law. I should steal the drug.	As a member of society, I have an obligation to respect the druggist's right to property. Therefore it would be wrong for me to steal the drug.
Stage 6: Orientation to ethical principles	The principle of the sanctity of life demands that I steal the drug, no matter what the consequences.	The principle of justice and the greatest good for the greatest number prevents me from stealing the drug, even for the good of my wife.

The following examples show the importance of levels of morality in history:

■ *Nazi death camps.* In April 1961, Adolf Eichmann, accused executioner of 5 million Jews in Nazi Germany during World War II, testified at his trial in Jerusalem:

> In actual fact, I was merely a little cog in the machinery that carried out the directives of the German Reich. It was really none of my business. Yet what is there to "admit"? I carried out my orders.[20]

Level II, stage 4 moral reasoning is reflected in Eichmann's statement.

■ *Civil disobedience.* In March 1922, Mohandas Gandhi, the Indian spiritual and political leader, addressed a British court with these words:

> Nonviolence is the first article of my faith. It is also the last article of my creed. But I had to make a choice. I had to either submit to a system that I considered had done irreparable harm to my country, or incur the risk . . . I am here, therefore, to invite and cheerfully submit to the highest penalty that can be inflicted upon me for what in law is a deliberate crime and what appears to me to be the highest duty of a citizen.[21]

Level III, stage 6 morality is seen in the life and teaching of Gandhi. With similar moral reasoning, Socrates refused to admit social wrong in his farewell address to the Athenian people. Instead, he drank the lethal hemlock, setting an example of moral heroism that has inspired Western civilization for over 2,000 years.

To personalize the subject of levels of morality, consider these questions: At what level of moral reasoning do you operate? Are you stage 1 or 2 (egocentric), 3 or 4 (community-oriented), or 5 or 6 (principled) in your response to ethical dilemmas at work, in your community, and in your personal life? Think of the leaders you respect. At what level of morality do they operate?

Virtue: The Nature of Level III, Stage 6 Morality

Moral evolution has followed a path from preconventional to postconventional ethics (level III, stage 6). Increasingly, people as individuals versus people as society have become the basis of moral judgments. The sentiment that just because the majority of a group or society judge an act to be right or wrong does not make it so reflects this orientation toward individual conscience (personal principles), as opposed to collective thought (community standards) or self-service (egocentric morality).[22]

At level III, stage 6 morality, a person's view of right and wrong depends on the meaning she or he attaches to personal existence, and that meaning is based on self-discovered and self-accepted values. This is the orientation of German writer Hermann Hesse's young Siddhartha, even after he had listened to the teachings of Buddha Gautama:

> "Do not be angry with me, O Illustrious One," said the young man. "I have not spoken to you thus to quarrel with you about words. You are right when you say that opinions mean little, but may I say one thing more? I did not doubt you for one moment. Not for one moment did I doubt that you were the Buddha, that you have reached the highest goal that so many thousands of Brahmins and Brahmins' sons are striving to reach.
>
> "You have done so by your own seeking, in your own way, through thought, through meditation, through knowledge, through enlightenment. You have learned nothing through teachings, and so I think, O Illustrious One, that nobody finds salvation through teachings. To nobody, O Illustrious One, can you communicate in words and teachings what happened to you in the hour of your enlightenment.
>
> "The teachings of the enlightened Buddha embrace much, they teach much—how to live righteously, how to avoid evil. But there is one thing that this clear, worthy instruction does not contain; it does not contain the secret of what the Illustrious One himself experienced—he alone among hundreds of thousands.

"That is what I thought and realized when I heard your teachings. That is why I am going on my way—not to seek another and better doctrine, for I know there is none, but to leave all doctrines and all teachers and to reach my goal alone—or die. But I will often remember this day, O Illustrious One, and this hour when my eyes beheld a holy man."[23]

Ethics and the Legal Department

The philosopher Lou Marinoff gives practical advice about leadership and moral dilemmas. "Everyone's ethical warning lights go off at different times," states Marinoff. "Although working will always involve compromises, it is important to know when an action may take you over a line you do not want to cross. In these situations, your conscience should guide you."

In the world of work, ethics is typically the purview of the legal department. But being legal may or may not mean being moral. Legality includes everything the law permits or doesn't expressly forbid. Morality is an even older idea, predating even legislated laws.

By all means, you should do what the people in the legal department advise to abide by the law, but you must never lose your own moral compass. If something makes you morally upset, so much so that you know what you are doing is clearly wrong, don't let legality alone appease you. The argument that I was only following orders won't absolve you if you make a moral error. Remember, every society has laws, but not all laws are just.

So what is a person to do? The best advice is to follow the dictum "nonharm to sentient beings." This is the basis of every professional code of ethics and every moral society. If your actions cause harm to others, they are immoral. Systems of morality and the laws of a society can get complicated, but if you live by this basic requirement, you will have a clear conscience.[24]

The Role of Values

In 1727 Benjamin Franklin formed the Junto, a forerunner of modern-day civic clubs. It was dominated by businessmen having goals of community fellowship and service. Character was a significant concern of that organization. Franklin's own value ideals included temperance, order, resoluteness, industry, sincerity, justice, moderation, cleanliness, and humility. Clearly, these are poles apart from current-day expressions such as "one-upmanship," "looking out for number one," and "assertiveness," which have captured considerable public following.[25]

Some organizations view values as a fundamental requirement for success. James Burke, former chairman of Johnson & Johnson, states that J&J's credo, first articulated in 1945, was responsible for the company's rapid action in taking Tylenol off the market after poisoning incidents in which seven people died. To support the importance of values, he cites a study of the financial performance of U.S. companies that have had written value statements for at least a generation. The net income of those companies increased by a factor of 23 during a period when the gross national product grew by a factor of 2.5.[26]

For many organizations, values are a social glue. Global enterprises requiring long-distance management may use values to provide structure and stability for people of diverse backgrounds in far-flung locations. Jack Welch, former CEO of General Electric, sees management values as a primary source of corporate identity, adding to a sense of cohesion among GE's highly diverse business units. Also, values can provide guidance for members who function as independent decision makers—for example, the factory team with the power to stop production if a core principle is violated.[27]

It should be noted that value statements can mask hypocrisy. If a company espouses quality in its written vision or promotional literature, but sacrifices it for short-term profits, cynicism will prevail among customers and employees. To be meaningful, values must enter into the daily practices of the organization. Values must reflect enduring commitments, not vague notions and empty platitudes. Thus, leaders who seek to manage through values must examine their own value systems, and put good intentions into concrete actions that others can witness.

An organization can have an abundance of values, but lack clarity and reinforcement of those that are the most important. A lack of agreement on core values that all members will live by will reduce the character and strength of the organization. Author Leon Wieseltier writes, "The contemporary problem in American society is not that people believe in too little, it is that they believe in too much. Too much of what too many people believe is too easily acquired and too thoughtlessly held." Wieseltier believes Americans are choking on identities. Not the lack of meaning, but the glibness of meaning is the trouble.[28]

How can an organization know if it needs to clarify or reinforce its values? Red flags are:

- Members lack clear understanding about how they should behave as they attempt to meet organizational goals.
- Different individuals and groups have fundamentally different value systems.
- Top leaders send mixed messages about what is important.
- Day-to-day life is disorganized, with the left hand and the right hand often working at cross-purposes.
- Members complain about the organization to neighbors, friends, and family.
- Like the person who has ears, but hears not, the organization has values, but does not practice them.

Management author Peter Drucker states:

Each organization has a value system that is influenced by its task. In every hospital in the world, health is the ultimate good. In every school in the world, learning is the ultimate good. In every business in the world, the production of goods and services that please the customer is the ultimate good. For an organization to perform at its highest level, its leader must believe that what the organization is doing is, in the last analysis, an important contribution to people and society, one that is needed or adds some value.[29]

In *A Business and Its Beliefs: The Ideas That Helped Build IBM,* Thomas Watson, Jr., explains the importance of values: (1) To survive and achieve success, an organization must have a sound set of values on which it premises all policies and actions; (2) the single most important factor in an organization's success is its leaders' faithful adherence to those values; and (3) if an organization is to meet the challenges of a changing world, it must be prepared to change everything about itself except its core values. The need is to be open to change in structure, tasks, technology, and people, but always guided by, and remaining true to, basic or core values.

Watson goes on to say that when IBM has been successful, it has been true to its three core values—respecting the individual, giving the best customer service possible, and performing every job with excellence. And when IBM has gone astray at times in its history, it is because it lost sight of—or deviated from—those three basic business values.[30]

Value Ideals and the Importance of Courage

Certain values are mentioned most often in the American workplace:

- **Honesty** in all dealings, as a foundation for all other values.
- **Respect** for others, as shown by consideration for their beliefs and needs.
- **Service** to others, guided by the principle of doing for others as you would have them do for you.
- **Excellence** in all work performed, reflecting the Greek ideal of excellence as a virtue, and resulting in both public admiration and personal pride.
- **Integrity,** having the courage to act and live by one's convictions.

When people define character, what they say is important, what they do is more important, but what they sacrifice for is most important. These are the layers of identity and character formation for individuals and groups. In its highest form, character is based on a value system that is known, cherished, stated, lived, and lived habitually. Caring to the point of personal sacrifice is the highest form of living by one's values.

Character and leading by values require **courage,** a superordinate quality of the person. Philosopher–psychologist Rollo May explains the importance of courage:

Courage is not a virtue or value among other personal values like love or fidelity. It is the foundation that underlies and gives reality to all other virtues and personal values. Without courage our love pales into mere dependency. Without courage our fidelity becomes conformism.

The word courage comes from the same stem as the French word coeur, meaning "heart." Thus just as one's heart, by pumping blood to one's arms, legs, and brain enables all the other physical organs to function, so does courage make possible all the psychological virtues. Without courage, other values wither away into mere facsimiles of virtue.

An assertion of the self, a commitment, is essential if the self is to have any reality. This is the distinction between human beings and the rest of nature. The acorn becomes an oak tree by means of automatic growth; no courage is necessary. The kitten similarly becomes a cat on the basis of instinct. Nature and being are identical in creatures like them. But a man or woman becomes fully human only by his or her choices and his or her commitment to them. People attain worth and dignity by the multitude of decisions they make from day-to-day. These decisions require courage.[31]

Many leadership situations are characterized by ambiguity, uncertainty, and even danger. The leader must be able to act in spite of these factors. Many decisions will require overcoming fear, gritting one's teeth, and doing what must be done. True leadership requires courage to act and live by one's convictions.

Honesty as a Leadership Value

The effective leader holds truth as a central value and foundation for all other values. This is a message as old as the Bible—"Know the truth and it will set you free."[32] It is the message of Shakespeare, who advised, ". . . this above all: to thine own self be true, and it must follow as the night the day, thou canst not then be false to any man."[33] And it is the message of successful leaders today. Herb Kelleher, former CEO of Southwest Airlines, was admired for both his business success and his basic honesty. When asked, "What is the secret to building a great organization; how do you create a culture of commitment?" Kelleher's answer was: "Be yourself."

The Bible, Shakespeare, and Kelleher agree that character begins with truth, that truth is inside the person, and that the leader must be true to his or her values. This is what Thomas Jefferson meant when he wrote: "In matters of style, swim with the currents; in matters of principle, stand like a rock. Character is what you are. It is different than reputation which is from other people. True character is in you."[34]

Full-Swing Values

There is a concept in ethics that can be used to assess the strength of one's values. It is especially important for people in leadership positions. This concept is **full-swing values.** Think about the sport of baseball, in which a full swing is needed to hit a home run. An arrested swing will result in less success—a triple, double, single, or foul ball. The same is true for questions of right and wrong, and good and bad: In ethical dilemmas, a values home run results only when one completes a full swing and does not suffer axiological arrest. Axiology is the branch of philosophy dealing with values, and ethics is applied axiology.[35]

A full swing comprises five points, from beginning through completion:[36]

- Point 1 is to *know* one's values.
- Point 2 is to *cherish* one's values.
- Point 3 is to *declare* one's values.
- Point 4 is to *act* on one's values.
- Point 5 is to *act habitually* on one's values.

Axiological arrest occurs when a person fails to complete all five points on the values swing. Consider the cases of Jim, Jane, Jack, Jill, and John, each facing an ethical dilemma (such as what to do about safety, what to do about taxes, what to do about Grandpa):

■ Jim knows what he values but has not examined other alternatives. His is an unthinking stance with little or no personal commitment. He hits a foul ball.

■ Jane knows what she values and cherishes this privately. She experiences self-satisfaction with her values. She hits a single.

■ Jack knows what he values, cherishes this personally, and declares his values. He hits a double.

■ Jill knows what she values, cherishes this personally, declares her values, and acts on her value system. She takes action and accepts the consequences. She hits a triple.

■ John knows what he values, cherishes this personally, declares his values, acts on them, and does this habitually. John shows maximum strength of values conviction.

See Table 9–1 for a depiction of the cases noted above. In dealing with their professional or personal ethical dilemmas, four of the five people experience axiological arrest at some point on the values swing. Only John hits a values home run.

Table 9–1
Full-Swing Values

Points on the Swing	Jim	Jane	Jack	Jill	John
Knows values	X	X	X	X	X
Cherishes values		X	X	X	X
Declares values			X	X	X
Acts on values				X	X
Acts habitually on values					X

To personalize the subject of values strength, evaluate your own values—freedom, responsibility, love, justice, and so forth. Consider an ethical dilemma—for example, discrimination according to gender, race, or religion—in which your values play a part. Ask yourself, Are your values full-swing, or do you experience axiological arrest? See Table 9–2.

Table 9–2
Personal Values Strength

Points on the Swing	Check (√) if appropriate
Do you know what you value?	_____
Do you cherish your values privately?	_____
Do you declare your values publicly?	_____
Do you act on your values and accept the consequences?	_____
Do you act habitually on your values and accept the consequences?	_____

In every field—science, art, government, business, service, religion—the highest level of leadership is full-swing. At this level of leadership, the leader is impelled to act because the act itself is deemed good, and for no other reason—not self-gain, aggrandizement, or public acclaim, but only because conscience dictates that the act is the right thing to do. The quality of doing the right thing for the right reason is called integrity, and it is possessed by all truly great leaders.

An ideal example of the importance of values and the power of full-swing leadership is that of Clara Barton, founder of the American Red Cross:

When the U.S. Civil War broke out in the 1860s, Clara Barton was working as a clerk in the U.S. Patent Office. Her compassion for soldiers on the battlefield drove her to get involved by organizing and undertaking supply deliveries to the front lines. Once there, she couldn't leave. She acted as a nurse to Union field surgeons, earning her the nickname "The Angel of the Battlefield." After the war, she heard about the International Red Cross while on a visit to Switzerland. It took her 13 years of lobbying Congress for funding before she was able to establish the American Red Cross in 1882. She ran the agency for 22 years, fulfilling the promise of a Red Cross that would serve Americans in war and peace.

Leadership and Values

Why is it important for an organization to have values, and what is the role of the leader in establishing and enforcing values? There are many ideas on these questions, but few are as influential as those of the philosopher Plato.

Plato answers these questions as he lays the groundwork for his book *The Republic.* He retells the myth of Gyges and the invisible ring: A young shepherd stumbles upon a magic ring that has the power to make the wearer invisible. Immediately, he takes advantage of the ring to do things he could never do before—eavesdrop, steal, trespass—and in a short time, he amasses wealth, kills the king, seduces the queen, and rules the land.

The moral of the story is that, given power without accountability, an individual may do terrible deeds that are harmful to others. People need the values of a just society and the oversight of wise leaders to govern their actions; otherwise, they may engage in selfish and destructive behavior.

Plato believed that, for the good of all individuals, a republic is needed, administered by philosopher–kings. The argument can be made that, in a similar way, every workplace needs high ethical values upheld by strong and caring leaders.

It must be recognized that a leader may have false or harmful values that are injurious to others. The examples of Hitler, Stalin, and many other tyrants in history can be cited. These cases only point more clearly to the need for caring leaders who are both good and strong.

People will forgive the leader who fails to manage by objectives, or is inefficient in the use of time, or fails to achieve the smoothest human relations; but they find it difficult to forgive the leader who is immoral and nonprincipled. Such a person lacks moral authority and is not trusted or respected. Even as important as vision is to leadership success, more important are values; because the values of the leader will determine the rightness and wrongness of all that he or she does.

What a leader says and does regarding values has enormous influence on others. More than any memo, directive, or brass band, the **actions** of the leader communicate. The leader's actions set the tone for people's behavior toward one another and for performance on the job. An effective leader accomplishes, through personal example, the building of individual commitment and group cooperation toward accomplishment of the task or mission. The leader who is honest, unselfish, and dedicated in his own actions helps the group succeed.[37]

It is safe to say that a leader's value system will be known. It won't be a secret because it will reveal itself in the policies and decisions she makes, the way she spends her time, and for what she sacrifices. In general, a leader's belief or value system will determine her success. The following are six values of caring leaders in every field and level of responsibility:

1. *Honesty*—knowing oneself and being honest in all dealings with others.
2. *Consideration*—doing unto others as you would have them do unto you.
3. *Responsibility*—taking the attitude that life is what you make it and choosing to make a difference.
4. *Persistence*—being determined; if at first you don't succeed, try, try again.
5. *Excellence*—living by the motto, Anything worth doing is worth doing well.
6. *Commitment*—viewing the great essentials of life as someone to love and something to do.[38]

Table 9–3 shows the relationship between what the leader says, what people hear, and the value or behavior this promotes.

Table 9–3
What You Do . . .
Is What You Get[39]

When the leader says . . .	the people hear . . .	and the value or behavior that is promoted is . . .
Let me know if you run into any problems.	I don't expect you to handle trouble alone.	Helpfulness
How can we improve the company?	I value your opinion.	Respect
You look like you need a break.	I care about your welfare.	Consideration
I'm sorry you weren't here.	You are important.	Self-worth
If that machine keeps breaking down, we'll order a new one.	You can count on me to get what you need to do your job.	Support
I really made a mistake on that one.	I admit it when I am wrong.	Honesty
How can you prevent that from happening again?	You are mature enough to correct your own errors.	Trust
Although your proposal was seen as too costly by top management, they were impressed. Keep up the good work.	I thought highly enough of the suggestion to send it upstairs.	Creativity

Because of the ability to influence moral behavior, the leader should address two questions: (1) What values or principles do I wish to promote? (2) Are my actions helping accomplish that goal? Exercise 9–1 can be used to clarify your values and evaluate whether your actions support your ideals.

Exercise 9–1
Workplace Values and
Leadership Actions

As a leader in the workplace, what values would you promote? What actions would you take to demonstrate and reinforce those values? List workplace values in column 1; list leadership actions that support those values in column 2.

Workplace Values	Leadership Actions
_____	_____
_____	_____
_____	_____
_____	_____
_____	_____
_____	_____
_____	_____
_____	_____
_____	_____
_____	_____

Discussion Questions:

What are the implications of your values and actions? Consider their influence on the quality of work and the quality of work life in your organization. What happens if values and actions are inconsistent or out of alignment?

_____

_____

_____

_____

_____

_____

_____

_____

_____

_____

_____

The workplace values listed in Table 9–4 were admired by Charles Schwab, legendary leader of Carnegie Steel Company over a century ago. Reading these values makes one realize that, like gravity, some things never change.

Table 9–4 **The Ten Commandments** **of Success**[40]		
	1. Work Hard.	*Hard work is the best investment a person can make.*
	2. Study Hard.	*Knowledge enables one to work more intelligently and effectively.*
	3. Have Initiative.	*Ruts often deepen into graves.*
	4. Love Your Work.	*Then you will find pleasure in mastering it.*
	5. Be Exact.	*Slipshod methods bring slipshod results.*
	6. Have the Spirit of Conquest.	*So you can successfully battle and overcome difficulties.*
	7. Cultivate Personality.	*Personality is to a person what fragrance is to the flower.*
	8. Help and Share with Others.	*The real test of greatness lies in giving opportunity to others.*
	9. Be Democratic.	*Unless you value people, you can never be a successful leader of them.*
	10. In All Things Do Your Best.	*Do your best and you will have everything;* *do less than your best and you will have done nothing.*

Personal Values

All aspects and institutions of society require leaders who are competent, caring, and value-based—committed to certain ideals and goals. A useful model and tool that addresses this issue is *The Study of Values* by Gordon Allport, Phillip Vernon, and Gardner Lindzey, based on Eduard Spranger's *Types of Men*. Complete Exercise 9–2 to discover your own value orientation.

**Exercise 9–2
Personal Values—What
Is Important to You?**[41]

Each of the following questions has six possible responses. Rank these responses by assigning a 6 to the one you prefer the most, a 5 to the next, and so on down to 1, the least preferred of the alternatives. Sometimes you may have trouble making choices, but there should be no ties; you should make a choice.

1. Which of the following branches of study do you consider most important?

   _____ a. philosophy

   _____ b. political science

   _____ c. psychology

   _____ d. theology

   _____ e. business

   _____ f. art

2. Which of the following qualities is most descriptive of you?

   _____ a. religious

   _____ b. unselfish

   _____ c. artistic

   _____ d. persuasive

   _____ e. practical

   _____ f. intelligent

3. Of the following famous people, who is most interesting to you?

   _____ a. Albert Einstein—discoverer of the theory of relativity

   _____ b. Henry Ford—automobile entrepreneur

   _____ c. Napoleon Bonaparte—political leader and military strategist

   _____ d. Martin Luther—-leader of the Protestant Reformation

   _____ e. Michelangelo—sculptor and painter

   _____ f. Albert Schweitzer—missionary and humanitarian

4. What kind of person do you prefer to be? One who

   _____ a. is industrious and economically self-sufficient

   _____ b. has leadership qualities and organizing ability

   _____ c. has spiritual or religious values

   _____ d. is philosophical and interested in knowledge

   _____ e. is compassionate and understanding toward others

   _____ f. has artistic sensitivity and skill

5. Which of the following is most interesting to you?

   _____ a. artistic experiences

   _____ b. thinking about life

   _____ c. accumulation of wealth

   _____ d. religious faith

   _____ e. leading others

   _____ f. helping others

6. In which of the following would you prefer to participate?

   _____ a. business venture

   _____ b. artistic performance

   _____ c. religious activity

   _____ d. project to help the poor

   _____ e. scientific study

   _____ f. political campaign

7. Which publication would you prefer to read?

_____ a. *History of the Arts*

_____ b. *Psychology Today*

_____ c. *Power Politics*

_____ d. *Scientific American*

_____ e. *Religions Today*

_____ f. *The Wall Street Journal*

8. In choosing a spouse, whom would you prefer? One who

_____ a. likes to help people

_____ b. is a leader in his or her field

_____ c. is practical and enterprising

_____ d. is artistically gifted

_____ e. has a deep spiritual belief

_____ f. is interested in philosophy and learning

9. Which activity do you consider more important for children?

_____ a. scouting

_____ b. junior achievement

_____ c. religious training

_____ d. creative arts

_____ e. student government

_____ f. science club

10. What should be the goal of government leaders?

_____ a. promoting creative and aesthetic interests

_____ b. establishing a position of power and respect in the world

_____ c. developing commerce and industry

_____ d. supporting education and learning

_____ e. providing a supportive climate for spiritual growth and development

_____ f. promoting the social welfare of citizens

11. Which of the following courses would you prefer to teach?

_____ a. anthropology

_____ b. religions of the world

_____ c. philosophy

_____ d. political science

_____ e. poetry

_____ f. business administration

12. What would you do if you had sufficient time and money?

_____ a. go on a retreat for spiritual renewal

_____ b. increase your money-making ability

_____ c. develop leadership skills

_____ d. help those who are disadvantaged

_____ e. study the fine arts, such as theater, music, and painting

_____ f. write an original essay, article, or book

13. Which courses would you promote if you were able to influence educational policies?

_____ a. political and governmental studies

_____ b. philosophy and science

_____ c. economics and occupational skills

_____ d. social problems and issues

_____ e. spiritual and religious studies

_____ f. music and art

14. Which of the following news items would be most interesting to you?
  _____ a. "Business Conditions Favorable"
  _____ b. "Relief Arrives for Poor"
  _____ c. "Religious Leaders Meet"
  _____ d. "President Addresses the Nation"
  _____ e. "What's New in the Arts"
  _____ f. "Scientific Breakthrough Revealed"

15. Which subjects would you prefer to discuss?
  _____ a. music, film, and theater
  _____ b. the meaning of human existence
  _____ c. spiritual experiences
  _____ d. wars in history
  _____ e. business opportunities
  _____ f. social conditions

16. What do you think the purpose should be for space exploration?
  _____ a. to unify people around the world
  _____ b. to gain knowledge of our universe
  _____ c. to reveal the beauty of our world
  _____ d. to discover answers to spiritual questions
  _____ e. to control world affairs
  _____ f. to develop trade and business opportunities

17. Which profession would you enter if all salaries were equal and you felt you had equal aptitude to succeed in any one of the six?
  _____ a. counseling
  _____ b. fine arts
  _____ c. science
  _____ d. politics
  _____ e. business
  _____ f. ministry

18. Whose life and works are most interesting to you?
  _____ a. Madame Curie—discoverer of radium
  _____ b. Katherine Graham—businesswoman
  _____ c. Margaret Thatcher—British prime minister
  _____ d. Mother Teresa—religious leader
  _____ e. Martha Graham—ballerina and choreographer
  _____ f. Harriet Beecher Stowe—author of *Uncle Tom's Cabin*

19. Which television program would you prefer to watch?
  _____ a. "Art Appreciation"
  _____ b. "Spiritual Values"
  _____ c. "Investment Opportunities"
  _____ d. "Marriage and the Family"
  _____ e. "Political Power and Social Persuasion"
  _____ f. "The Origins of Intelligence"

20. Which of the following positions would you like to have?
  _____ a. political leader
  _____ b. artist
  _____ c. teacher
  _____ d. theologian
  _____ e. writer
  _____ f. business entrepreneur

Scoring:

Step 1:

For each lettered response to each question, insert your score in the appropriate space in the following chart. Note that the letters are not always in the same column.

Example: a. _2_   b. _6_   c. _4_   d. _5_   e. _3_   f. _1_

	I	II	III	IV	V	VI
1.	a. _____	e. _____	f. _____	c. _____	b. _____	d. _____
2.	f. _____	e. _____	c. _____	b. _____	d. _____	a. _____
3.	a. _____	b. _____	e. _____	f. _____	c. _____	d. _____
4.	d. _____	a. _____	f. _____	e. _____	b. _____	c. _____
5.	b. _____	c. _____	a. _____	f. _____	e. _____	d. _____
6.	e. _____	a. _____	b. _____	d. _____	f. _____	c. _____
7.	d. _____	f. _____	a. _____	b. _____	c. _____	e. _____
8.	f. _____	c. _____	d. _____	a. _____	b. _____	e. _____
9.	f. _____	b. _____	d. _____	a. _____	e. _____	c. _____
10.	d. _____	c. _____	a. _____	f. _____	b. _____	e. _____
11.	c. _____	f. _____	e. _____	a. _____	d. _____	b. _____
12.	f. _____	b. _____	e. _____	d. _____	c. _____	a. _____
13.	b. _____	c. _____	f. _____	a. _____	d. _____	e. _____
14.	f. _____	a. _____	e. _____	b. _____	d. _____	c. _____
15.	b. _____	e. _____	a. _____	f. _____	d. _____	c. _____
16.	b. _____	f. _____	c. _____	a. _____	e. _____	d. _____
17.	c. _____	e. _____	b. _____	a. _____	d. _____	f. _____
18.	a. _____	b. _____	e. _____	f. _____	c. _____	d. _____
19.	f. _____	c. _____	a. _____	d. _____	e. _____	b. _____
20.	e. _____	f. _____	b. _____	c. _____	a. _____	d. _____
Totals	_____	_____	_____	_____	_____	_____

Step 2:

Add the scores for each column, and record the total in the appropriate space.

Step 3:

Mark the total for each personal value column in the appropriate place in Figure 9–1. Connect the scores with straight lines to form a profile of your overall value orientation. See the example in Figure 9–2.

Interpretation:

A description of each personal value follows:

Theoretical. The primary interest of the theoretical person is the discovery of truth. In the laboratory, field, and library, and in personal affairs as well, the purpose of the theoretical person is to know the truth above all other goals. In the pursuit of truth, the theoretical person prefers a cognitive approach, one that looks for identities and differences, as opposed to the beauty or utility of objects. This person's needs are to observe, reason, and understand. Because the theoretical person's values are empirical, critical, and rational, this person is an intellectual and frequently is a scientist or philosopher. Major concerns of such a person are to order and systematize knowledge and to understand the meaning of life.

**Figure 9–1
Your Personal Value
Orientation**

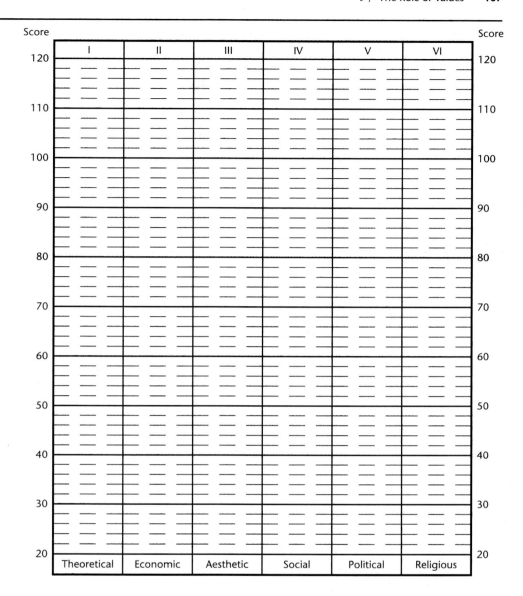

Economic. The economic person is interested in what is useful. Based originally on the satisfaction of bodily needs and self-preservation, the interest in usefulness extends to the practical affairs of the business world—the production and marketing of goods, and the accumulation of wealth. This type of person is enterprising and efficient, reflecting the stereotype of the average businessperson. Economic values sometimes come into conflict with other values. The economic person wants education to be practical and regards unapplied knowledge as wasteful. Great feats of engineering and application result from the demands economic people make on people in science. Economic values may conflict with aesthetic values, such as in the advertising and promotion of products and services, except when art meets commercial ends. In relationships with people, the economic person is more likely to be interested in surpassing others in wealth than in dominating them politically or in serving them socially.

**Figure 9–2
Example: Personal Value
Orientation**

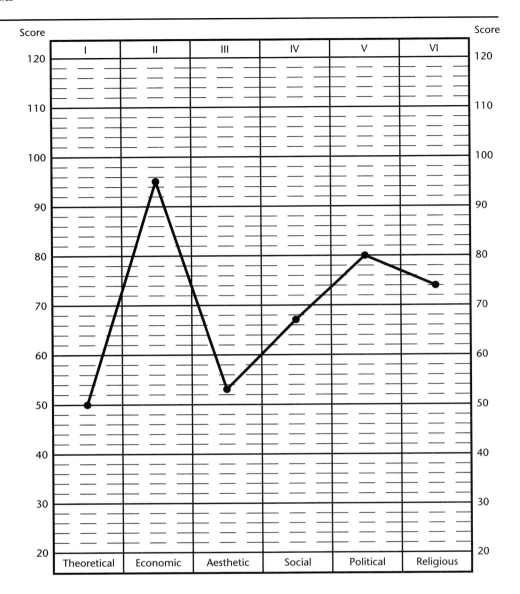

Score

	I	II	III	IV	V	VI

Theoretical | Economic | Aesthetic | Social | Political | Religious

Aesthetic. The aesthetic person finds highest satisfaction in form, harmony, and beauty. The value of each single experience is judged from the standpoint of grace, symmetry, and fitness. The aesthetic person regards life as a procession of events, with each impression to be enjoyed for its own sake. An aesthetic person may or may not be a creative artist; the aesthetic person finds chief interest in the artistic episodes of life. Unlike the theoretical person, the aesthetic person usually chooses, with the poet John Keats, to consider truth as equivalent to beauty, or agrees with H. L. Mencken, "To make a thing charming is a million times more important than to make it true." In the economic sphere, the aesthetic person often sees the process of manufacturing, advertising, and trade as a destruction of important aesthetic values. In social affairs, the aesthetic person may be said to be interested in people, but not necessarily in their welfare. The aesthetic person tends toward individualism, self-sufficiency, and idealism in personal relations.

Social. The highest value for this type of person is love. The altruistic or philanthropic aspect of love is the interest of the social person. Humanistic by nature, the social person prizes other people as ends in and of themselves, and not as tools or means to other goals. Therefore, the social person is kind, sympathetic, and helpful toward others. Such a person may find the economic and political values to be cold and inhumane. In contrast to the political type, the social person regards love instead of power as the most suitable form of human relationship. In purest form, social values are totally unselfish.

Political. The political person is interested in power and influence, although the person's activities may not fall within the narrow field of politics. Whatever the vocation, the political person seeks to be a *Machtmensch,* an individual who is powerful. Leaders in any field usually will have a high interest in power and status. Because competition and struggle play a large part in all of life—between the sexes, between groups, between nations, and between individuals—many philosophers have viewed power as the most universal and most fundamental of human motives. In certain people, however, the desire for direct expression of power is uppermost, and their primary values are social influence and the exercise of authority.

Religious. The highest value of this type of person is spiritual peace. A religious person may or may not belong to an organized religion; people are religious if they but seek to comprehend the cosmos as a whole and to relate themselves to its embracing totality. Religious people have as their goal the creation of the highest and most satisfying value experience. Some people who are religious focus on events, people, and experiences in this world; that is, they experience meaning in the affirmation of life and active participation therein. With zest and enthusiasm, they see something divine in every event. On the other hand, some religious people are transcendental mystics, seeking to unite themselves with a higher reality by withdrawing from life. This type is ascetic, and like the holy men of India, finds inner peace and unity through self-denial and meditation. In many individuals, the affirmation and negation of human existence alternate to yield the greatest value satisfaction.

In evaluating your personal values, remember the following points:

- All six values on the questionnaire are positive. The questions do not measure negative values, such as greed or violence.

- Culture influences personal values. Through the processes of imprinting, modeling, and socialization, people learn to place higher importance on some values over others. Thus, the prestige afforded the monarch, priest, businessperson, scientist, artist, and teacher depends on the values promoted by each society. In the Pygmy culture, for example, the male with the greatest social esteem usually is not the strongest, wealthiest, most spiritual, most artistic, or most intelligent; rather, he is the one who shares most generously. Consider American society: What are the primary values for people in the United States today? Are they the same for men and women? Do they reflect your personal values?

- By forcing choices among six personal values, the questionnaire provides an overall value orientation. This means that your lowest personal value may be more important to you than the highest personal value of another individual. Similarly, your highest may be less important to you than the lowest of another individual. The questionnaire measures the relative strength of six personal values, so that you obtain a picture of *your* overall value orientation, or an understanding of what is most important to you.

- Ideally, a person's life will allow maximum expression of personal values. This helps explain the achievements and satisfactions of "theoretical" Albert Einstein, "economic" John D. Rockefeller, "aesthetic" Leonardo da Vinci, "social" Jane Addams, "political" Elizabeth 1, and "religious" Martin Luther.

- Basic value systems are fairly firm by the time most people reach adulthood. Ideas about what is important are well established and are unlikely to change unless a significant emotional event takes place. For most people, few experiences are significant or emotional enough to disrupt basic values formed during childhood and adolescence. As a rule, if a person changes basic values during the adult years, it is only because a situation is experienced that previous values cannot resolve.[42]

- Different organizations reflect and endorse different values, and each organization's success depends on having people in it, especially leaders, who promote its value system. Some people may be ideally suited for *theoretical* organizations such as universities, *economic* organizations such as corporations, *aesthetic* organizations such as performing groups, *social* organizations such as human service agencies, *political* organizations such as political parties, or *religious* organizations such as churches, synagogues, and mosques. Mismatches can be stressful for both the individual and the organization. Examples include the social person who gives away the store, the individual who uses religious position for personal power, and the art curator whose priority is profit. Consider your own values. What type of organization, if any, would be most appropriate for you?

Remember, the personal values questionnaire does not measure other important factors, such as aptitude, personal interests, and individual temperament, nor does it measure levels of morality, a critical element in leadership and human relationships. Finally, remember that different values can actually enrich a group or organization. In this spirit, use the following thought as a guide: "Our errors and our controversies in the sphere of human relations often arise from looking on people as though they could be altogether bad, or altogether good."[43]

Ethics at Work

In his book *Management Tasks, Responsibility, Practices,* Peter Drucker suggests that once an organization reaches the size of 1,000 employees, work rules should be developed to maximize efficiency and serve as a guide for employee conduct. Such a code of conduct can be important in determining the nature, reputation, and success of the organization.[44] The best work rules meet the following criteria: They reflect the ethical ideals of the ownership, or, in the case of public organizations, the public trust; they are reviewed periodically for needed revisions; they are few in number; they are stated clearly; they are communicated to all employees; and they apply equally to all employees, regardless of level of authority or nature of duties.

A comprehensive code of ethics for an organization includes guidelines in each of the following areas:

- *Government relations.* How does the organization pay its taxes and obey national and international law?
- *Employee relations.* How does the organization deal with employee welfare and grievances?
- *Community and environmental relations.* What are the effects of the organization on its social and physical environment?
- *Business relations.* How does the organization deal with suppliers and competitors?
- *Production.* What are the standards of quality for the organization's products and services?
- *Consumer relations.* How does the organization price and advertise its products and services?

In his influential book *Vanguard Management,* James O'Toole identifies the key characteristics of ethical and successful organizations:

- They try to satisfy all their constituencies—customers, employees, owners, suppliers, dealers, special interest groups, communities, and governments. They subscribe to the utilitarian ideal, the greatest good for the greatest number.
- They are dedicated to high and broad purposes. Profit is viewed as an essential means to a higher end—human service and quality of life.
- They are committed to learning, investing enormous resources and effort to remaining current and responsive to change. They view employee growth and development as a critical foundation of business success.
- They try to be the best at whatever they do. Their performance standards rise continually. Excellence in product and service is an organizationwide commitment and source of pride.[45]

One of the most influential guidelines for ethics at work comes from Rotary International. Many generations of leaders from all areas of the world have been taught to test their actions against four basic questions:

1. **Is it the truth?**
2. **Is it fair to all concerned?**
3. **Will it build goodwill and better relationships?**
4. **Will it be beneficial to all concerned?**[46]

Ethical Climates of Organizations

In dealing with moral dilemmas regarding people, products, prices, and profits, organizations typically reflect one of three ethical climates: (1) profit maximizing; (2) trusteeship; or (3) quality of life management. Each climate provides different levels of organizational support for ethical decision making.[47]

Exercise 10–1 presents a description of each climate on 14 ethical dimensions. As you complete the exercise, you will see how different ethical climates influence moral judgments and result in different experiences for employees, customers, and citizens. As you read the descriptions, ask yourself what type of organization you respect; what type of organization you have; and what you can do to influence the ethics of your organization.

Exercise 10–1
Organizational Ethics[48]

Evaluate your organization by circling the appropriate description of the prevailing climate—profit maximizing, trusteeship, or quality of life management—for each of the 14 ethical dimensions listed in the first column.

Ethical Dimension	Profit Maximizing	Trusteeship	Quality of Life Management
1. Social definition of good	What is good for me is what counts.	What is good for my organization is what counts.	What is good for humankind is good for my organization and ultimately is best for me.
2. Democracy at work	I am a rugged individualist and will do as I please.	I am an individualist, but I recognize the value of employee participation in the decision-making process.	Democratic management is fundamental to a successful organization.
3. Attitude toward profit	I seek as much profit as the market will bear.	I want a substantial profit.	Profit is necessary, but not to the exclusion of other considerations that influence human welfare.
4. Attitude toward wealth	My wealth is more important than other people's feelings.	Money is important, but so are people.	Other people's needs are more important than my wealth.
5. Labor relations	Labor is a commodity to be bought and sold.	Labor has certain rights that must be recognized.	It is essential to preserve employee dignity, even if profit is reduced.
6. Consumer protection	Let the buyer beware.	Let us not cheat the customer.	Consumer welfare comes first; satisfaction is guaranteed.
7. Self-interest versus altruism	My interest comes first.	Self-interest and the interests of others are considered.	I will always do what is in the best interest of all concerned.
8. Employee relations	Employee personal problems must be left at home.	I recognize that employees have needs and goals beyond economics.	I employ the whole person and am concerned with achieving maximum employee welfare.
9. Management accountability	Management is accountable solely to the owners.	Accountability of management is to the owners, customers, employees, and suppliers.	Accountability of management is to owners, customers, employees, suppliers, and society in general.
10. Attitude toward technology	Progress is more important than people's feelings.	Technology is important, but so are people.	Human needs are more important than technology advances.
11. Minority relations	Minorities have their place in society, but not with me.	Some people are more important than others, and they should be treated accordingly.	Everyone—regardless of age, color, creed, or sex—should be treated equally.
12. Attitude toward government	Government is best when it stays out of my way.	Government is a necessary evil.	Business and government should work together to solve society's problems.
13. Human–environment interface	The environment exists for economic ends.	People should control and manipulate the environment.	People must preserve the environment for the highest quality of life.
14. Aesthetic values	Aesthetic values are a low priority.	Aesthetic values are ok, but not to the exclusion of economic needs.	Aesthetic values must be preserved, even if economic costs are increased.

Scoring:

Assign a score of 1 to each *profit maximizing* response, 2 to each *trusteeship* response, and 3 to each *quality of life management* response. Add the scores and enter the total here:

Interpretation:

The terms *profit maximizing, trusteeship,* and *quality of life management* correspond with Kohlberg's levels of morality—I, II, III. *Profit maximizing* reflects preconventional morality. In this case, the organization's focus is on self-gain and avoidance of punishment. *Trustee-ship* reflects conventional morality. The organization behaves to conform to the expectations of others and to satisfy higher authorities. *Quality of life management* reflects postconventional morality. Here, the ethical climate of the organization is to do what is right over and above self-interest and apart from the influence of others. With this climate, ethical conduct is based on the highest moral principles. Use your total score to determine your organization's overall climate and level of morality.

Scores	Level of Morality
14–23	Profit maximizing—level I, preconventional
24–32	Trusteeship—level II, conventional
33–42	Quality of life management—level III, postconventional

The following is an example of a *quality of life management—level III* company credo:

We will be honest and trustworthy in all our dealings. We will treat every individual with respect and dignity. We will follow the Golden Rule in all matters. We will strive for excellence in all work performed. We will obey the laws of our land in fact and in spirit. We will always do the right thing in every situation to the best of our abilities. If we fail in abiding by these principles, we will do whatever is needed to make amends.

The question may be asked, Won't quality of life management organizations fail in competition with rough-riding, profit maximizing organizations? Research does not bear this out. Data show a positive and significant relationship between the ethical climate of organizations and the level of profit. The higher the ethical climate, the higher the level of profit when computed over a period of years.[49]

Most people are attracted to what they consider good. In a free society, people are allowed to work where they choose, and employers are allowed to employ whom they wish. Individuals and organizations with good reputations attract each other and then, as one, focus on the achievement of common objectives. Parties outside the organization take note of this and elect such principled organizations over unprincipled organizations because they genuinely respect, trust, and like them. Employees want to work for them, other businesses want to deal with them, government officials want to support them, and customers want to buy from them. The bottom line is that reputation is important and goodness is valued.

The role of the leader is paramount in establishing the moral tone and ethical climate of the organization. With power to set policy and make decisions, the leader can create a place that attracts and rewards the best in both ethical conduct and business performance.

Part Three Summary

After reading Part Three, you should know the following key concepts, principles, and terms. Fill in the blanks from memory, or copy the answers listed below.

Ethics is the branch of philosophy concerned with (a) _____. The most important influences on character formation are (b) _____, _____, and _____. The three levels of moral development are (c) _____, _____, and _____, with the highest level being characteristic of only 20 percent of the adult population. Value ideals include (d) _____, _____, _____, _____, and _____. (e) _____ is the foundation that underlies and gives life to all other virtues and values. A concept in ethics that can be used to assess the strength of one's values is (f) _____. Fully ethical individuals know, cherish, declare, act on, and act habitually on their values. The leader's (g) _____ are critical in establishing the values and moral tone of an organization. One of the most influential codes of ethical conduct in the workplace is provided by Rotary International, which asks leaders to measure all actions against four questions: (h) _____, _____, _____, and _____.

Answer Key for Part Three Summary

a. **moral judgments and right and wrong conduct,** page 82

b. **associations, books, self-concept,** page 87

c. **preconventional, conventional, postconventional,** page 88

d. **honesty, respect, service, excellence, integrity,** page 93

e. **courage,** page 93

f. **full-swing values,** page 94

g. **actions,** page 96

h. **Is it the truth? Is it fair to all concerned? Will it build goodwill and better relationships? Will it be beneficial to all concerned?** page 113

Reflection Points—personal thoughts on leadership ethics, the role of values, and ethics at work

Complete the following questions and activities to personalize the content of Part Three. Space is provided for writing your thoughts.

■ Cite examples of the influence of leadership on the ethical behavior of an individual, work group, organization, or society. Use personal or historical examples.

_____

_____

■ Discuss levels of morality in the workplace today. Give examples of leadership actions that are preconventional, conventional, and postconventional.

_____

_____

■ What values are important to you? How strong is your value system? Do you exhibit full-swing values and courage of conviction in ethical dilemmas?

_____

_____

■ If you were the president of a company, what values would you promote? What values would guide you in dealing with people, products, prices, and profits?

_____

_____

■ Develop a code of ethics for an organization. The code should be between one and five pages in length. Present and defend this code of ethics before an audience of interested people.

_____

_____

■ Discuss organizations with differing ethical climates. What is it like to work in profit maximizing, trusteeship, and qualify of life management organizations?

_____

_____

Action Assignment

As a bridge between learning and doing, complete the following action assignment.

1. What is the most important idea you have learned in Part Three?

2. How can you apply what you have learned? What will you do, with whom, where, when, and, most important, why?

Part 4 The Empowerment of People

11. Leadership Authority
12. Empowerment in the Workplace
13. The Quality Imperative

LEADERSHIP IS SERVICE, not selfishness. The leader grows more and lasts longer by placing the well-being of all above the well-being of self. Through service to others, the leader becomes strong.

—Lao-tzu

Tao-te Ching, sixth century B.C.

Learning Points

In Part Four, you will discover the answers to these questions:
- What is your approach to leadership? Do you view leadership as a calling to serve?
- What practical steps can a leader take to empower others and develop a high-performance workplace?
- What are your beliefs and practices regarding quality in the workplace?

Leadership Authority

There are two views of leadership authority—*top-down* and *bottom-up*.[1] The top-down view holds that leadership authority is based on position in a social hierarchy, and that power flows from the highest level to the lowest. The classical organizational pyramid has frontline workers supporting managers and supervisors, who, in turn, support top-level executives. This pyramid of authority serves as the basis of most classical organizational structures. See Figure 11–1.

**Figure 11–1
Classical Organizational
Structure**

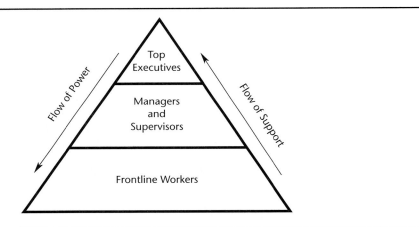

The top-down concept is well established, and it is the traditional view of leadership authority in the United States. The right of authority is derived from the right of private property, which is guaranteed in the Constitution. This guarantee gives owners of property the right to manage their affairs as they decide, as long as they do not violate the rights of others as determined by law. Owners may transfer power to a board of directors, which, in turn, may appoint top executives to manage the organization. These executives may delegate authority to managers and supervisors, who may empower employees to act in the interests of the organization. This transfer of authority is seen in Figure 11–2.

The bottom-up view of authority contends that power flows from below, because people can always reject a directive. By saying yes or no, the individual affirms or denies the authority of others. This view of authority was first described by Chester Barnard of AT&T. According to Barnard, people will accept an order if four conditions are met: (1) the person understands the order; (2) the person believes the order is consistent with the organization's goals; (3) the person believes the order is compatible with his or her interests; and (4) the person is mentally and physically able to comply with the order.[2]

**Figure 11–2
Classical Transfer
of Authority**[3]

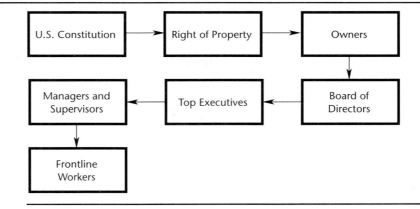

Effective leaders make certain that their directives fall within their subordinates' zones of acceptance. Otherwise, orders may be met with resistance and even hostility, as the following story shows:

An agent of the Textile Workers Union of America likes to tell the story of the occasion when a new manager appeared in the mill where he was working. The manager came into the weave room the day he arrived. He walked directly over to the agent and said, "Are you Belloc?" The agent acknowledged that he was. The manager said, "I am the new manager here. When I manage a mill, I run it. Do you understand?" The agent nodded, and then waved his hand. The workers, intently watching this encounter, shut down every loom in the room immediately. The agent turned to the manager and said, "All right, go ahead and run it."[4]

Both the top-down and the bottom-up views of authority have merit. By accepting employment, employees acknowledge the authority of owners and managers to make decisions and give orders, as well as their own duty to comply and obey. Also, the successful manager is the first to acknowledge the power of employees to achieve both their own and organizational goals. A manager can govern most effectively with the consent of those being governed. This condition shows the interdependence common to most leader–follower relationships.[5]

An approach to leadership that recognizes both the top-down and bottom-up views of authority, and that effectively addresses the interdependent nature of the leader–follower condition, is **servant leadership.**

Servant Leadership

Management author Robert Greenleaf states that servant leadership is a calling to serve. This calling begins with the feeling deep down inside that one cares about people and wants to help others. Then conscious choice causes one to aspire to lead. The great leader is a servant first, and that is the secret of his or her greatness.[6]

The servant leader is different from the individual who is motivated by selfish goals. Winston Churchill captured the spirit of servant leadership when he said, "What is the use of living if not to strive for noble causes and to make this muddled world a better place for those who will live in it after we are gone?"[7]

People do not trust the self-server whose primary thoughts are for personal gain. Trust is given to the leader who works for the common good and has the interests of others at heart. The servant leader is the one people will choose to follow, the one with whom they will prefer to work.[8]

Greenleaf coined the term *servant leadership* after reading *The Journey to the East,* by Herrmann Hesse. In this story, Leo, a cheerful and caring servant, supports a group of travelers on a long and difficult journey. His helpful ways keep the group's morale high and purpose clear. Years later, the storyteller comes upon a spiritual order and discovers that Leo is the group's highly respected leader. By serving the travelers unselfishly rather than trying to lead them for personal gain or prestige, Leo had helped ensure their survival and eventual success. This story represented a transformation in the meaning of leadership for Greenleaf. Servant leadership is not about personal ego or material rewards. It is about a true motivation to serve the interests of others.

A sure sign of servant leadership is the leader who stays in touch with the challenges and problems of others. One good way to do this is to get out of the executive suite and onto the shop floor, out of headquarters and into the field, out of the ivory tower and into the real world.

One company has an active reception area: pickup, delivery, walk-in customers, and in-coming calls. To give receptionists a little relief, and to stay in touch with real customers, real employees, real products, and real problems, each top executive is on a duty roster giving two hours a month at the reception desk . . . including the president.[9]

Access, Communication, and Support

The servant leader is committed to people, and this commitment is shown through **access, communication,** and **support:**

- *Access.* People need to have access to their leaders, to be able to read their faces, to see recognition of their own existence reflected in their leaders' eyes. Management by objectives and other rational techniques of management do not alter fundamental human needs. People need contact and support, and effective leaders at all levels of responsibility recognize this as one of their primary tasks. The age of computers, information technology, and e-mail does not change the importance of the human moment at work.

- *Communication.* The effective leader knows the value of communication. As long ago as 59 B.C., Julius Caesar kept people up-to-date with handwritten sheets and posters around Rome. Communication in today's organizations is frequently discussed, but not always delivered. The suggestion that leaders meet with their people on a regular basis is often greeted with the response that there is not enough time. But such meetings provide valuable opportunities to share information, lay out the work, anticipate problems, and gather momentum. They also serve to reinforce a sense of cooperative helpfulness and mutual support. Meetings can serve as an opportunity to close the communication loop and see if frontline people are receiving information and hearing the leader's message.

- *Support.* Even in routine operations, when there is no emergency or strategic crisis, people benefit from support in the form of feedback. As a rule, they do not get enough of it. One can ask people in almost any organization, "How do you know if you are doing a good job?" Ninety percent are likely to respond, "If I do something wrong, I'll hear about it." Too often this topic is discussed as if praise were the only answer; it is not. What people are saying is that they do not have sufficient discussion about performance and tangible support from their leaders to improve effectiveness. Successful leaders know that praise without support is an empty gesture.[10]

Servant leadership encourages trust, listening, and the ethical use of power and empowerment. A picture can be an excellent way to convey a concept. The servant leader uses the upside-down pyramid approach to leadership. See Figure 11–3.

Frontline workers are near the top of the pyramid. They are supported in their efforts by leaders below them. The implications are dramatic for day-to-day work. From this perspective, each person provides added value. The whole organization is devoted to satisfying the customer, and this is made possible through the support of caring leaders.[11]

Figure 11–3
The Upside-Down Pyramid
Approach to Leadership

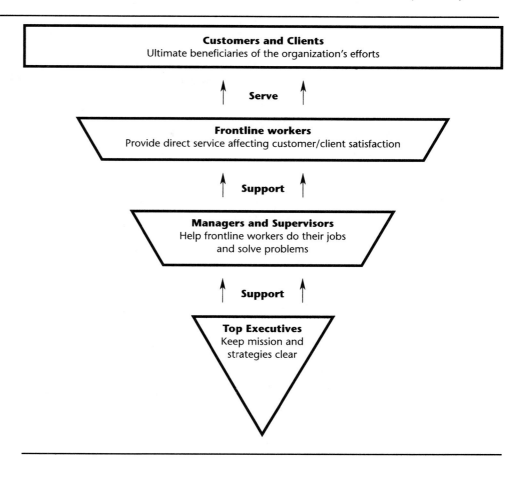

Max DePree, in his book *Leadership Is an Art,* describes the character of servant leadership:

The first responsibility of a leader is to define what can be. The last is to say thank you. In between the two, the leader must become a servant and a debtor. That sums up the progress of an artful leader.

In a day when so much energy seems to be spent on maintenance and manuals, on bureaucracy and meaningless quantification, to be a leader is to enjoy the special privileges of complexity, of ambiguity, of diversity. But to be a leader means, especially, having the opportunity to make a meaningful difference in the lives of those who permit leaders to lead.[12]

Can you think of a servant leader who embodies DePree's ideal? Consider her or his actions and impact on people. How do you fulfill this role?

Participative Leadership Philosophy

How do you tap the constructive power of people? How do you create both a humanistic and a productive workplace? The answer is through participative leadership. The process begins with involving people, which is necessary to achieve understanding, which is necessary to achieve commitment. It is important to know the views and consider the interests of all who are affected when decisions are made.

Paula Underwood Spencer, a Native American storyteller, tells how her tribe came to understand the importance of a single question: "Who speaks for wolf?"

AND SO IT WAS
>   that the People devised among themselves
>   a way of asking each other questions
>   whenever a decision was to be made
>   on a new place or a new way.
We sought to perceive the flow of energy through each new possibility,
>   and how much was enough,
>   and how much was too much.
UNTIL AT LAST
>   someone would rise
>   and ask the old, old question
>   to remind us of things
>   we do not yet see clearly enough to remember.
TELL ME NOW MY BROTHERS
TELL ME NOW MY SISTERS
WHO SPEAKS FOR WOLF?[13]

The effective leader today knows that all people have a voice and they seek to include the ideas of those who will be affected when a decision is made.

The triggering agent that facilitates both morale and performance is leadership, more particularly, the value system and style of behavior of those individuals with strength and influence to set direction, make policy, and decide issues. These are the powerful individuals, with or without title, we call leaders. The essential character of such leaders is **democratic,** and their mode of behavior is best described as open, inclusive, and participative. To develop an empowered workplace that leads to high-quality products and services, leaders must adopt the kind of leadership philosophy promoted by the Japanese Union of Scientists and Engineers:

No matter how much factories are mechanized, as long as there are people still working there, they should be treated as human individuals. Those companies that do not give due consideration to humanity will lose their best people sooner or later. There can be no excuse for disregarding individual personality, slighting a person's ability, regarding people as machinery, and discriminating against them. People spend much of their lifetime at their working place. It would be much more desirable to work in a pleasant place where humanity is paid due respect and where people feel their work has some real meaning. That is what quality practices aim to achieve. A mechanized factory still requires control by a workshop of people.[14]

Management authors Warren Bennis and Philip Slater identify the shift toward participative leadership as necessary if organizations are to survive under conditions of chronic change. They define participative leadership as democratic, not as permissiveness or laissez-faire, management. This type of management involves a system of beliefs and common values that govern behavior. These include:

- Full and free communication, regardless of rank and power.
- A reliance on consensus, rather than on traditional forms of coercion and compromise, to manage conflict.
- The idea that influence is based on technical competence and knowledge, rather than on the vagaries of personal whim or the prerogatives of power.
- An atmosphere that permits and even encourages emotional expression as well as task-oriented acts.
- A basically human bias, one that accepts the inevitability of conflict between the organization and the individual, but that is willing to cope with and mediate this conflict on rational grounds.[15]

Examples of work systems and techniques for employee participation in the United States and abroad can be arranged along a continuum, as shown in Figure 11–4. On the left part of this continuum, employees possess less power and are less involved in

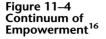

**Figure 11–4
Continuum of
Empowerment**[16]

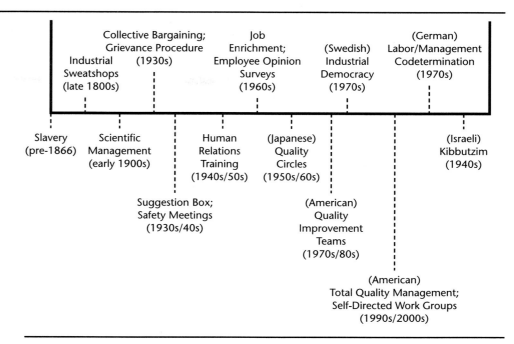

the decision-making process. Workers in industrial sweatshop systems exert less control over their work lives than do employees in industrial democracy systems.

Figure 11–4 explains much of the popularity and success of total quality management and other empowerment efforts. It shows quality improvement groups to the right of middle—satisfying needs for employee involvement, yet not so participative that owners and managers fear loss of power and ownership.

Participative leadership has been employed effectively by many supervisors and managers to build employee morale and achieve high performance. With roots in democratic ideals, participative leadership allows the leader to tap the constructive power of the group. In *Productive Workplaces,* Marvin Weisbord writes:

> The democratic process is the best procedure yet devised for promoting decision-making that is a part of all social living, and at the same time, safeguarding to each individual the conditions necessary for self-realization. The democratic process allows each individual to participate in making decisions that determine his or her conditions of life.[17]

The Leadership Position

Leadership is needed in all areas of society and at all levels of responsibility. Titles of leadership include *president, chief, captain, manager, director,* and *supervisor,* to name just a few. Both responsibility and power come with the office of leadership. The challenge is to meet the responsibility of the position without abusing its power.

An example of a leader using power effectively is Herb Kelleher, former CEO of Southwest Airlines. At one point in his career, he was recognized by *Business Week, Fortune,* and *The Wall Street Journal* as America's most effective executive. He states:

> I started to get involved in the day-to-day operations. I got to know people in a personal way, and that was very enjoyable for me. You'd go over to maintenance and talk about how the planes were running. You'd talk to the flight attendants and get involved in such discussions as what their uniforms ought to be.
>
> You have to treat your employees like customers. When you treat them right, then they will treat the customers right. This has been a powerful competitive weapon for us at Southwest Airlines. You've got to take the time to listen to people's ideas. If you just tell somebody *no,* that's an act of power and, in my opinion, an abuse of power. You don't want to constrain people in their thinking.[18]

Negative Consequences in the Use of Power

Abraham Lincoln once said, "Nearly everyone can stand adversity, but if you want to test a person's true character, give him power." And T. S. Eliot wrote, "Half of the harm that is done in this world is caused by people who have power and want to feel important. They do not mean to do harm; they are simply absorbed in the useless struggle to think well of themselves."

One interesting study reveals the tragic consequences of the negative use of power in the medical world. Researchers found a dramatic difference in performance results between intensive care units (ICUs) in which the staff unquestioningly followed the lead of an autocratic physician in charge and those ICUs that functioned as a team of colleagues, all of whom were free to make suggestions that might benefit the patient. The "obedient," power-oriented ICUs experienced higher staff turnover, lower efficiency, and twice the rate of patient deaths.[19]

The idea of using and not abusing the power that comes from leadership position is very old. The following quote is from Lao-tzu, the founder of Taoism, who was born in the village of Jhren, China, in 604 B.C.:

> I have three precious things which I hold fast and prize. The first is gentleness; the second is frugality; the third is humility, which keeps me from putting myself before others. Be gentle and you can be bold; be frugal and you can be liberal; avoid putting yourself before others and you can become a leader.[20]

Sources of Leadership Power

The successful leader masters the use of power to influence the behavior of others. Table 11–1 shows sources and types of power used by leaders: One is based in the leadership position; the second is based in the leader's personal qualities.

To personalize the concept of leadership power, complete Exercise 11–1.

**Table 11–1
Sources and Types of Power Used by Leaders**[21]

Power of the Position	Power of the Person
Based on what leaders can offer to others	Based on how leaders are viewed by others
Reward power is the capacity to offer something of value as a means of influencing others: "If you do what I ask, you will be rewarded."	*Expert power* is the capacity to influence others because of expertise—specialized knowledge or skill.
Coercive power is the capacity to punish as a means of influencing others: "If you don't do what I ask, you will be punished."	*Referent power* is the capacity to influence others because of their desire to identify with the leader.
Legitimate power is the capacity to influence others by virtue of formal authority or the rights of office: "Because I am the leader, you should do as I ask."	*Rational power* is the capacity to influence others because of well-developed reasoning and problem-solving ability.
Information power comes from having access to data and news of importance to others: "I have important information, so you should do as I ask."	*Charisma power* is the ability to motivate and inspire others to action by force of personality.

Exercise 11–1
What Type of Power Does Your Supervisor Use?[22]

Indicate how strongly you agree or disagree with the following statements as they describe your immediate supervisor. If you are not currently employed, evaluate a supervisor you have had in the past. For each statement, select the most appropriate response, using the following scale: 1 = strongly disagree; 2 = disagree; 3 = neither agree nor disagree; 4 = agree; 5 = strongly agree.

My supervisor:

1. _____ Rewards efforts and accomplishments.
2. _____ Uses fear and punishment to control behavior.
3. _____ Sees that recognition and appreciation are given.
4. _____ Makes life at work unbearable.
5. _____ Makes decisions about how things get done.
6. _____ Finds out things that are important to know.
7. _____ Keeps job knowledge current.
8. _____ Provides useful advice on how to do jobs more effectively.
9. _____ Has access to important information.
10. _____ Shares the benefit of his or her vast job knowledge.
11. _____ Makes people proud to work with him or her.
12. _____ Explains things so logically that people want to do them.
13. _____ Causes people to admire what he or she stands for.
14. _____ Shares a clear vision of what the future holds for the organization.
15. _____ Comes up with the facts needed to make a convincing case.
16. _____ Motivates and inspires others to action.

Scoring:

Power of the Position

1. Add the numbers assigned to statements 1 and 3. This is the *reward power* score.
   _____

2. Add the numbers assigned to statements 2 and 4. This is the *coercive power* score.
   _____

3. Add the numbers assigned to statements 5 and 7. This is the *legitimate power* score.
   _____

4. Add the numbers assigned to statements 6 and 9. This is the *information power* score.
   _____

Power of the Person

5. Add the numbers assigned to statements 8 and 10. This is the *expert power* score.
   _____

6. Add the numbers assigned to statements 11 and 13. This is the *referent power* score.
   _____

7. Add the numbers assigned to statements 12 and 15. This is the *rational power* score.
   _____

8. Add the numbers assigned to statements 14 and 16. This is the *charisma power* score.
   _____

Discussion:

The effective leader emphasizes the power of the person to accomplish goals. This involves maintaining knowledge and skill (expertise), having high moral character (referent power), demonstrating effective problem-solving ability (rational power), and motivating and inspiring people (charisma). The effective leader also uses the power of the position to reward efforts and accomplishments (rewards), make effective decisions (legitimacy), and keep people informed on important matters (information). The effective leader rarely if ever uses fear and punishment (coercion) as a form of power.

High scores for each type of power are 8, 9 and 10; low scores for each type of power are 2, 3 and 4.

Which type of power does your supervisor use—most to least? Which type of power do you use in your leadership role(s)?

Psychological Size and Two-Way Communication

Any person perceived as having influence over the freedom, success, or income of others, or who has the ability to make others appear ridiculous, incompetent, or weak, must guard against the abuse of **psychological size.** This concept has special relevance for people in authority positions. The individual who determines careers, decides wages, and makes job assignments has considerable power over others, and this power can influence the communication process.

Employees are in a weaker, less powerful position, dependent to some degree on the authority figure to protect them and watch out for their well-being. Some will deny this observation, but one has only to observe the typical work environment to see how differences in psychological size can affect relationships and determine the way things are done. Deference and paternalism are not uncommon.[23]

People in positions of authority are often surprised to discover that others may fear their power and inhibit behavior accordingly. A graphic representation of a leader with big psychological size and the one-way communication that can result is presented in Figure 11–5.

Figure 11–5
Abuse of Psychological Size

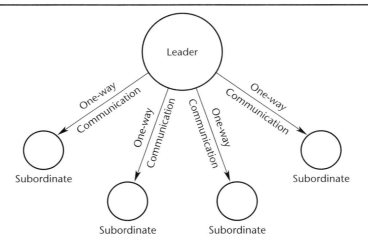

One-way communication presents three problems:

1. *People may be reluctant to say or do anything that might offend the powerful figure.* According to George Reedy in *The Twilight of the Presidency,* even people who had enjoyed two-way communication with Lyndon Johnson when he was in the Senate began to censure their behavior once he assumed the presidency. Because of his increased psychological size, a subtle shift from two-way dialogue to one-way communication developed.[24]

2. *People may become dependent on the leader to make all the decisions.* Unwilling to risk making a mistake and being criticized, people may fail to take initiative. The leader must then solve all the problems and make all the decisions. Dependency on the leader underuses the subordinates and overburdens the leader.

3. *People may become resentful of the leader.* The leader is seen as autocratic and arrogant, and this perception may cause anger, hostility, and even rebellion. Consider the case of the infamous Captain Queeg in the film classic *The Caine Mutiny.* The captain's abusive behavior eventually led to tragedy for everyone.

How can leaders avoid the abuse of psychological size and develop the two-way communication that is necessary for both employee morale and job performance? First, they must recognize the factors that contribute to psychological bigness:

High-status position.

Use of terminal statements so that no disagreement is possible.

Formal, distant manner.

Know-it-all, superior attitude.

Commanding physical appearance.

Power to make decisions.

Use of sarcasm and ridicule.

Job competence.

Cruel and punishing remarks.

Ability to express oneself.

Interrupting and shouting at others.

Public criticism.

Some of the items on this list are distinctly positive. For example, job competence and the ability to express oneself are desirable traits. Additionally, some of the factors causing psychological bigness are attributes of the person or the office, and it may be difficult or undesirable to change them. For example, neither a leader's commanding physical appearance nor the power to make decisions should be changed. Similarly, the status of the position is most likely an unchangeable factor. The seven remaining factors of psychological bigness on the list above, however, serve no purpose except to alienate people and result in one-way communication.

- Use of sarcasm and ridicule.
- Use of terminal statements, so that no disagreement is possible.
- Formal, distant manner.
- Cruel and punishing remarks.
- Know-it-all, superior attitude.
- Interrupting and shouting at others.
- Public criticism.

As a rule, leaders should avoid any behavior that demeans or intimidates another person. The solution is to equalize psychological size. A picture of the proper use of psychological size and good two-way communication is presented in Figure 11–6.

Figure 11–6
Effective Use of
Psychological Size

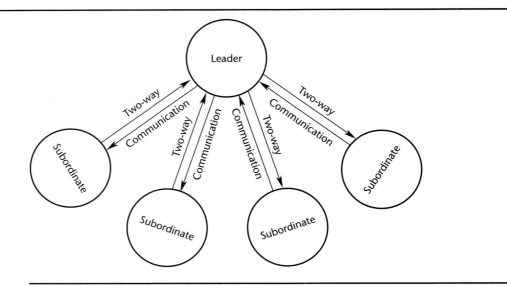

Many leaders mistakenly think that the best way to equalize psychological size is to reduce their own size. In doing so, however, they may reduce their size so much that respect is lost and cannot be regained. Few individuals have the ability to go from large psychological size to small psychological size and back again without losing effectiveness. Therefore, the most effective approach is not for leaders to reduce their own psychological size, but to raise the size of others.

The effective leader is a very big circle with a very big reputation, but he never gets in the way of the growth of others. The best way to raise psychological size is to show genuine interest in people. Through attention to others and sincere **listening,** the leader shows that others are important. A proven technique is to give people a project, some work to "grow into." This approach builds pride and commitment, and increases the productivity of the group as a whole.

Leaders should keep in mind three important points in developing two-way communication. First, model an honest and open style of communication. Be direct and sincere in speaking. Second, be patient. It takes time and trust to create dialogue between people, and too rapid a change from one style of operating to another may be interpreted as insincerity or may confuse people. Third, make a sincere effort to draw people out without constantly evaluating their remarks. This will be seen as a demonstration of respect and will help create true dialogue. The following guidelines can help accomplish this goal:[25]

- *Stop talking.* You cannot listen to others if you are talking. Shakespeare wrote, "Give every man thine ear, but few thy voice."[26] We each have two ears and one mouth, and we should use these in proportion.

- *Put the talker at ease.* Help the other person feel free to talk. Provide a supportive environment or atmosphere. Sit or stand in a relaxed manner.

- *Show the person that you want to listen.* Look and act interested. Don't read your mail while the other person is talking. Maintain eye contact.

- *Remove distractions.* Don't doodle on, tap, or shuffle papers. Shut down the computer. Hold telephone calls. Will it be quieter if you close the door?

- *Empathize with the person.* Try to put yourself in the other person's place to understand the speaker's point of view.

- *Be patient.* Allow time. Don't interrupt. Don't walk toward the door or walk away while the other person is talking. Some people take longer than others to make a point.

- *Hold your temper.* An emotional person may misinterpret a message or may say something unintended. If you are angry, cool off before responding. Take a walk, or try counting to 10.

- *Go easy on argument and criticism.* Being judgmental puts the speaker on the defensive and may result in a blowup, or it may cause the person to shut down. Listen to understand, rather than to make judgments.

- *Ask questions.* This response encourages the speaker and shows you are listening. It also helps develop additional points. Few actions demonstrate respect as much as asking others for their opinion.

- *Encourage clarification.* When the speaker touches on a point you want to know more about, simply repeat the statement as a question. This technique will allow clarification and elaboration.

- *Stop talking.* This is the first and last point, because all others depend on it. You cannot do a good job of listening while you are talking. As Shakespeare wrote, "Give thy thoughts no tongue."[27]

Overall, a leader's use of psychological bigness and overbearance is effective for only a short period of time. After a while, dissatisfaction causes employees to rebel or escape. Effective leaders at all levels of authority understand this human relations principle.

Lessons from Gandhi

What can we learn from Gandhi, the Indian spiritual and political leader? We can learn what Gandhi learned from his wife Kasturbi during 57 years of marriage. When they were married in their teens, as was the custom in India, the young bridegroom was full of strong opinions and recommendations for his young wife to implement. Her usual approach was to listen and smile, but then to proceed with her own methods and at her own pace.

Later in life, Gandhi reported that he had learned the power of civil disobedience and the importance of patience from his wife. From her, he had learned a lifelong leadership message—most people, in the final analysis, will do what they personally choose to do, and no amount of coaxing or force can overcome an idea or principle that is personally believed. Great leaders guide and inspire—not command and control.[28]

UNIT

12

Empowerment in the Workplace

In a report for the Brookings Institution, Steve Levine and Laura D'Andrea reviewed all major studies of empowerment in the workplace. Their findings: "If you sum it all up, employee participation has a positive impact on business success. It is almost never negative or neutral. Moreover, studies of employee-owned companies show that stock ownership alone doesn't motivate employees to work harder, while ownership combined with participation does."[29] As an old saying goes, "The person in the boat with you never bores a hole in it."

To diagnose the need for empowerment in a group or organization, answer the following questions:

- Do people seem uninterested in their work?
- Are absenteeism or turnover rates too high?
- Do people lack loyalty and team spirit?
- Is there a lack of communication among individuals and groups?
- Is there a low level of pride?
- Are costs too high as a result of waste and inefficiency?
- Does the quality of product or quality of service need to be improved?

If the answer is yes to any of these questions, then empowering people can help.

A great deal of empowerment in the workplace is generated by efforts to improve performance. As companies are forced to compete in an increasingly global economy, they are finding that the path to success is long and winding. On that path are many boulders and pebbles that must be cleared. It takes the strength of management to remove the boulders—build a new plant, create a new product, and the like. And it takes the attention and effort of employees to cast away the pebbles—solve problems with products and meet customer needs. Everyone must work together.

A story is told about a worker at a Ford plant many years ago who suggested a manufacturing improvement that saved the company hundreds of thousands of dollars. Henry Ford himself rewarded the employee and asked him when he had thought of the idea. "Years ago," the employee said. Asked by an incredulous Ford why he didn't say anything earlier, the employee replied, "Nobody asked me."[30]

Today, just as yesterday, the task of the leader is to unleash and channel the power of people. When he was asked, "What is your job?" General Electric's Jack Welch said: "I have three things to do. I have to choose the right people, allocate the right number of dollars, and transmit ideas from one group to another with the speed of light. I am really a communicator and facilitator for the work of others." The story of

Jack Welch is instructive for all leaders who seek to empower people and achieve success.[31]

As one of the most widely admired and studied CEOs of his time, Welch enriched not only GE's shareholders but also the shareholders of other companies around the globe. His total economic impact is impossible to calculate, but his leadership had staggering influence on GE's performance during his tenure in charge.

Welch began by changing GE's goal, which previously had been simply to grow faster than the economy. Welch gave GE a new mission: to be the world's most valuable company. As the centerpiece of the plan was his declaration that every GE business must be number 1 or number 2 in its industry.

Welch then concentrated on reforming the practices and culture that determined day by day how the company worked. He began by burning GE's blue books, five thick volumes of guidance for every GE manager. His message to GE's managers was, "You own these businesses. Take charge of them. Think for yourself. Get headquarters out of your hair. Fight the bureaucracy. Hate it. Kick it. Break it."

If employees were surprised by the words, they were more surprised by the actions that followed. Welch wiped out entire layers of bureaucratic management, and he launched the famous *workout process,* in which employees at all levels of an operation gathered for "town meetings" with their bosses and asked questions or made proposals about how the place could run better—80 percent requiring some kind of response then and there.

The multiday workout sessions took huge chunks of wasted money and time out of GE's processes, but their more important effect was to teach people that they had a right to speak up and be taken seriously; those who advanced good ideas were rewarded, as were those who implemented them.

The next natural step was to spread good ideas across the company. Doing this sounds logical and obvious—but it hadn't been done before. Then a more radical move followed: borrowing good ideas from other companies. Welch advocated this one personally to show it was actually OK, and today he states that what GE learned about asset management from Toyota or about quick market intelligence from Wal-Mart has been enormously important in the success of the company.

At least as important as these high-profile changes were Welch's behind-the-scenes people practices, which he says took more of his time than anything else. When a manager met with Welch, the exchange was candid, not scripted. There were arguments. There was shouting. The manager almost certainly had to stretch his mind and do new thinking on the spot. Afterward, Welch would dispatch a highly specific written summary of commitments the manager had made, and when Welch followed up later—also in writing—he would refer to the previous summary. He did this with relentless consistency with scores of managers.[32]

Principles of an Empowered Workplace

Robert Cole, influential author and educator, identifies five principles of leadership that empower people. Implicit in these principles is the assumption that broad participation in the decision-making process is necessary for success.

- **Trust in people.** Assume they will work to implement organizational goals if given a chance.

- **Invest in people.** View people as the organization's most important resource, which, if cultivated, will yield positive returns.

- **Recognize accomplishments.** Symbolic rewards are extremely important. Show people that they are valued.

- **Decentralize decision making.** Put responsibility for making decisions where the information is and as close to the customer as possible.

- **View work as a cooperative effort.** Model and reinforce the idea that by working together, people accomplish more.[33]

Characteristics of an Empowered Workplace

What is the character of an empowered workplace in contrast to one that is unempowered or out of control? In empowered organizations, people experience feelings of ownership. This ensures that they will do everything in their power to create success. Not only are their egos invested in the organization, but their abilities are as well. In the end, the result is victory for the person and the organization. See Table 12–1.

Table 12–1
Workplace Empowerment[34]

Processes	Unempowered	Out of Control	Empowered
Decision making	Check with leader on all decisions.	Check with nobody on decisions.	Check with those affected on decisions.
Performance planning	Leader writes performance plan and reviews with subordinates.	There is no performance plan.	Subordinate writes performance plan and reviews with leader.
Making policy	Leader decides policy.	People ignore policy.	Work with those responsible to develop policy.
Problem solving	Wait for "them" to fix problems.	Bypass "system" to work around problems.	Find out who "they" are and work together to fix problems.
Taking initiative	Never volunteer for anything—wait to be asked or assigned.	Many people work on the same thing without communicating.	Recognize what needs to be done; inform leader and others affected; start action to improve.
Defining roles	Roles and responsibilities are defined by leader.	Roles and responsibilities are conflicting and unclear.	Work together to define roles and responsibilities.
Setting standards	Perform to standards determined by others.	There is no concern with standards.	Work together to determine standards of employee effectiveness.

The Importance of Communication

An essential element of an empowered workplace is good communication. One of the best ways to achieve effective communication is to recognize where most people prefer to get information, as opposed to where they actually receive it. Table 12–2 shows various types of communication and ranks them, both as actual and as preferred information sources.

Table 12–2
Where People Go for Information[35]

Actual Rank	Source	Major Source for employees	Preferred Rank
1	Immediate supervisor	55.1%	1
2	Grapevine	39.8	15
3	Policy handbook and other written information	32.0	4
4	Bulletin board(s)	31.5	9
5	Small group meetings	28.1	2
6	Regular, general member publication	27.9	6
7	Annual business report	24.6	7
8	Regular, local member publication	20.2	8
9	Mass meetings	15.9	11
10	Union	13.2	13
11	Orientation program	12.5	5
12	Top executives	11.7	3
13	Audiovisual programs	10.2	12
14	Mass media	9.7	14
15	Upward communication programs	9.0	10

The actual and preferred rankings of where people go for information show that people want accurate, timely, and complete information, and that their most preferred sources are the **immediate supervisor, small group meetings, top executives, policy handbook, orientation programs,** and **member newsletters.**

The High-Performance Workplace

What practical steps can a leader take to develop a high-performance workplace? Management authors Eric Harvey and Alexander Lucia have identified 144 time-tested ways to increase leader effectiveness. Presented in Table 12–3 are 20 of the best. An effective approach is to review these 20 and pick 5 to implement. By concentrating on five, the leader can make a measurable difference in the morale and job performance of workers.

Table 12–3   Practical Tips for Developing a High-Performance Workplace[36]

1. *Adopt an orientation to action and results.* Focus on results-oriented processes and outcomes that add value to the organization, rather than on staying busy with activities and events that merely consume time.

2. *Recognize and reward those who make improvements to products, processes, and services.* Remember: What gets celebrated gets repeated.

3. *Be customer-driven.* Build customer satisfaction by underpromising, overdelivering, and following up to be sure customers are satisfied. Solicit input on how your products and services can be improved.

4. *Maintain a commitment to self-development.* Become a continuous learning machine. Set a personal goal to learn something new about your job, your organization, or your professional discipline every week.

5. *Make timely and value-driven decisions.* Involve those who must implement decisions in the decision-making process. Consider the ideas and opinions of those who do the work, because they frequently have a great deal to contribute. In addition, they'll be more likely to support decisions they help make.

6. *Be flexible.* Understand and appreciate that others may not do things exactly as you would do them. Be open-minded—you might discover their way is even better than yours.

7. *Coach others to succeed.* Pay attention to "middle stars." Avoid the trap of focusing only on the "super stars" (those with exceptional performance) and the "fallen stars" (those with significant performance problems). Most people shine somewhere in the middle.

8. *Schedule a short meeting with each of your direct reports once every two or three weeks.* Discuss their work in progress, provide feedback on how they are doing, and ask how you and others can contribute to their success.

9. *Minimize obstacles.* Ask each member of your work group to identify the three most significant obstacles to his or her performance. Create a master list, and develop a strategy to eliminate the obstacles.

10. *Benchmark the best.* Study industries, organizations, and individuals that beat the competition by overcoming challenges and obstacles. Also, review case studies of those that did not—and lost.

11. *Address deficiencies.* Pay attention when someone has a performance problem. Unaddressed deficiencies can have a negative effect on every member of your team. By dealing with performance issues as early as possible, you can prevent them from growing more serious—and more distasteful for both you and the individual to face.

12. *Let your conscience be your guide.* Do the right thing no matter how inconvenient, unpopular, or painful it may seem. *That's* integrity!

13. *Enhance the work environment.* Ask fellow workers to submit three ideas for enhancing the quality of work life in your area. Create a master list of ideas, and start implementing the doable ones as quickly as possible.

14. *Spread the sparkle.* Get enthused about others who are enthusiastic—it's contagious and can snowball quickly. Recognize and reward those who help contribute to a culture of contagious enthusiasm.

15. *Display resilience.* It's not whether you get knocked down, it's whether you get up that counts. Take a hike—go on a 10-minute walk to calm down, reflect, and develop a bounce-back strategy.

16. *Show concern for others.* Remember special occasions. Send cards with personalized messages to your fellow workers on special days, such as birthdays and anniversaries with the organization.

17. *Spend one-on-one time with each member of your team.* Open these get-togethers with a general question, such as "How are things going with you?" Then really listen to what the person has to say. Listening is an important way to demonstrate that you care.

18. *Manage meetings effectively.* Supply participants with a written agenda two to three days before a meeting. Make sure the agenda includes meeting objective(s), issues to be discussed, start/end times and location, and information regarding who will be attending, how participants should prepare, and what they should bring. End all meetings with a short review of the results. Discuss what was accomplished and what, if anything, needs to be done after the meeting.

19. *Be sure everyone who reports to you has clarity of assignment and tools to succeed.* Do they know the grand plan and their place in it? Do they have equipment and supplies to do their best work?

20. *Communicate effectively.* Think before you speak, and plan before you write. Understand your message before expecting others to. Target your communication to the intended audience by using terminology they are likely to understand. Consider pretesting important communications on individuals who will give you candid feedback.

Improving Performance across Companies

Although bartering and trading can be acceptable when the work performed is simple and occurs at a discrete point in time, the best approach is to look beyond an isolated exchange and focus instead on building a long-term relationship. Partners who have mutual trust do not feel the need to check up on each other. Also, in many organizations, one's customers are often one's suppliers as well. Building a solid trust-based relationship pays dividends to both organizations, as the following example shows:

After years of relying on a weekly exchange of price incentives and shelf space, two consumer giants, Procter & Gamble and Wal-Mart, began to develop a trust-based relationship, sharing up-to-the-minute sales information, long-range buying plans, and current inventory figures. Eliminating a sea of promotional incentives allowed Procter & Gamble to provide the "everyday low prices" Wal-Mart required, while letting each company achieve a reasonable profit. At the same time, Wal-Mart agreed to pay invoices as presented and settle accounts at the end of the year.

Both companies have enjoyed substantial benefits with this new way of working: (1) Conflicts can be avoided and resolved more easily; (2) communication is more open, timely, and accurate; (3) Wal-Mart inventories have been cut from 30 days to 2 days, resulting in reduced cost; and (4) Procter & Gamble reports $500 million in annual savings as a result of the new level of partnership and trust.[37]

Leadership Challenge

Ren McPherson, past president of Dana Corporation, states: "Almost everybody agrees, 'people are our most important asset.' Yet almost no one really lives it. Great companies live their commitment to people." It is an old truth that applies today: The human side counts. And it is no secret that the number one factor is the character and actions of leaders.[38]

In his work on servant leadership, Robert Greenleaf proposes that the world can be saved as long as three truly great institutions exist—one in the private sector, one in the public sector, and one in the nonprofit sector. He believes that these organizations will achieve success through a spirit of community, and that their success will serve as a beacon for the world. The key in every case is **caring leadership** and the **empowerment of people.**[39]

The Quality Imperative

I f there is a single most important factor in efforts to empower employees, it is the quality challenge faced by companies struggling to compete in a global marketplace. Simply, quality products and service are demanded by consumers, and providing them requires a talented, committed, and empowered workforce.

Joseph Jablonski writes in *Implementing Total Quality Management,* "This is a cooperative form of doing business that relies on the talents and capabilities of both labor and management to continually improve quality and productivity using teams."[40] Implicit in this definition are three essential ingredients: (1) participative leadership, (2) continuous process improvement, and (3) the use of groups.

The philosophy behind the quality movement is that the people closest to the work usually have the experience and knowledge needed to come up with the best solutions to work-related problems. Ren McPherson, former president of Dana Corporation and dean of business at Stanford University, points out:

Until we believe that the expert in any particular job is most often the person performing it, we shall forever limit the potential of that person in terms of contribution to the organization and in terms of personal development. Consider a manufacturing setting: Within their 25-square-foot area, nobody knows more about how to operate a machine, maximize its output, improve its quality, optimize the material flow, and keep it operating efficiently than do the machine operators, material handlers, and maintenance people responsible for it. Nobody.[41]

W. Edwards Deming

The influence of one person, W. Edwards Deming, has been critical in the history of the quality movement. In 1947 he was recruited by American authorities in Japan to help prepare a census, and immediately he took an interest in the restructuring of the Japanese economy. In 1950, a 49-year-old Deming delivered a speech to the Japanese Union of Scientists and Engineers (JUSE) entitled "The Virtues of Quality Control as a Manufacturing Philosophy." This speech was to have a profound effect on Deming's audience. The Japanese believed in this teacher from the United States with his spartan dedication to work and Socratic teaching style, and they applied his ideas.[42]

Deming became a Japanese folk hero, and since 1951, the Deming Prize has been awarded annually in recognition of outstanding achievement in quality control. In an interview before his death in 1993, Deming said, "I think I was the only man in 1950 who believed the Japanese could invade the markets of the world, and would, within five years. They did this through a dedicated and sustained commitment to quality."[43]

The primary result of Deming's influence in Japan was that people at the production level were taught the statistical techniques of quality control, and then were delegated the task and the power to organize their work so that the quality of products could be improved. Also, Deming was able to convince top management of the necessity of personal involvement and commitment to building quality products.

In a lecture at the Hotel de Yama near Hakone, Japan, Deming produced a simple flow diagram to illustrate his concept of a quality system. That diagram, or a slight variation thereof, can be found in just about every Japanese corporation today. Essentially, Deming taught that the more quality you build into anything, the less it costs over a period of time.[44] He also taught the importance of designing a good system and process. To demonstrate this idea, Deming developed what he called the "Red Bead Experiment":

Ten people are picked and assigned jobs: six "willing workers," two "inspectors," one "chief inspector," and one "recorder." The objective is to show how a poorly managed system, not the workers, leads to defects and poor quality.

Deming explains that the "company" has received orders to make white beads. Unfortunately, the raw materials used in production contain a certain number of defects, or red beads.

With both the white and red beads in a plastic container, the six workers are given a paddle with fifty indentations in it and told to dip it into the container and pull it out with each indentation filled with a bead. They then take the paddle to the first inspector, who counts the red beads, or "defects." The second inspector does the same, and the chief inspector checks their tally, which the recorder then records.

Deming, playing the role of a misguided manager, acts upon the results. A worker drawing out a paddle with fifteen red beads is put on probation, while a worker with just six red beads gets a merit raise. In the next round, the worker who had six red beads now has eight, and the worker with fifteen has ten. In his "misguided manager" role, Deming thinks he understands what's happening: that the worker who got the merit raise has gotten sloppy—the raise went to his head—and the worker on probation has been frightened into performing better.

And so it continues—a cycle of reward and punishment in which management fails to understand that the defects are built into the system and that the workers have very little to do with it.

"We gave merit raises for what the system did; we put people on probation for what the system did," Deming says. "Management was chasing phantoms, rewarding and punishing good workers, creating mistrust and fear, trying to control people instead of transforming a flawed system and then managing it."[45]

Quality was Deming's message to the Japanese. They listened, they learned, and they practiced what Deming preached. Japanese manufacturers became profitable, well managed, and competitive. Deming describes a chain reaction for business success beginning with improving quality and resulting in jobs and more jobs. See Figure 13–1.

Increasingly, American organizations—public and private, large and small—have followed the example of the successful Japanese in their efforts to improve quality.

**Figure 13–1
The Deming Chain
Reaction**[46]

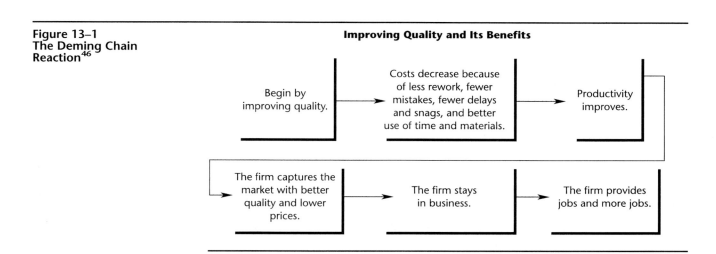

Improving Quality and Its Benefits

These organizations include General Electric, Motorola, Ford Motor Company, and the U.S. Army, Navy, and Air Force. Although quality improvement efforts were by no means universally successful, most organizations found their employees to be a valuable source of innovation and money-saving ideas. The following are typical examples:

Members of a team at Northrop Aviation were troubled because bits used to drill holes in titanium for F-5 fighter planes were breaking. The solution the group proposed: change the drilling angle, and make the bits from harder steel. This small change saved Northrop $70,000 in lost time.

In 1998, Boeing won the Malcolm Baldrige National Quality Award by achieving a 180-degree turnaround in quality with its C-17 military cargo jet. Using quality guidelines and improvement teams, Boeing cut the time it took to build a C-17 by 80% between 1994 and 1998. Productivity increased from $200,000 per employee to $327,000 per employee during this period of time.[47]

Experiences such as these are now commonplace as the quality movement and member empowerment have spread throughout American business, industry, and government.

No discussion about leadership, empowerment, and quality is complete without including Deming's 14 points for a successful workplace. These points or practices can be applied in both private and public organizations.

The Deming Way[48]

1. Create consistency and continuity of purpose. Plan products with an eye to the long-range needs of the company; don't succumb to the pressures of the quarterly report.

2. Set high standards. No company can compete in the world market until its management discards old notions about acceptable levels of mistakes, defects, and inadequate training and supervision.

3. Eliminate dependence on mass inspection for quality. Use statistical controls for incoming and outgoing goods.

4. Reduce the number of suppliers. Buy based on statistical evidence of quality, not price.

5. Recognize that there are two sources of quality problems: faulty systems (85 percent probability) and the production worker (15 percent probability). Strive to constantly improve the system.

6. Improve job training. Make continuous learning a way of life. Teach statistical techniques. The rudiments can be learned in a five-day intensive course.

7. Provide a higher level of supervision. Focus supervision on helping people to do a better job, and provide tools and techniques for people to have pride in their work.

8. Break down barriers between departments. Encourage problem solving through teamwork. Create a team consisting of design, research, sales, purchasing, and production personnel to eliminate errors and waste.

9. Stamp out fear by encouraging open, two-way communication.

10. Abolish numerical goals and slogans.

11. Use statistical methods for continuous improvement of quality and productivity.

12. Remove barriers to pride of work.

13. Institute a vigorous program of education and training to keep people abreast of new developments in methods, materials, and technologies.

14. Clearly define management's permanent commitment to quality and productivity.

Philosophical Roots of the Quality Movement

The following is a discussion of the philosophical roots of employee empowerment and the **quality movement.**

Beginning with Taylor

In 1911 Frederick W. Taylor wrote his famous book *Principles of Scientific Management,* which was eventually translated into dozens of languages. He developed one of the first monetary incentive systems to improve the productivity of workers who were loading pig iron onto railroad cars. His principles and incentive system were soon extended to many other industries, becoming the basis for a worldwide scientific management movement.

Taylor is recognized today as the father of modern management and of the industrial engineering discipline. His scientific management philosophy is summarized in four basic principles:

1. Develop a science for each element of an employee's work that replaces the old rule-of-thumb method.
2. Scientifically select, train, teach, and develop the worker. (In the past, the employee chose the job and was self-trained.)
3. Heartily cooperate with employees to ensure that all work is done in accordance with the principles of the science that has been developed.
4. Divide the work and responsibility between management and employee. Managers should take over all work for which they are better fitted than the worker. (In the past, the worker took almost all of the work and the greater part of the responsibility.)[49]

Taylor has been criticized for advocating an extreme division of labor, resulting in routine, repetitive, and boring jobs on assembly lines. Considering his scientific management philosophy in the frame of reference of the early 1900s, however, it is logical and even participative in nature. He advocated a systematic approach to problem solving, cooperation between labor and management, training of employees, a fair reward system, and proper assumption of responsibility by both labor and management. These were revolutionary concepts for that time. If only slightly modified, they apply to the enlightened leadership practices of today.[50]

The Human Relations School

In the 1920s, Elton Mayo, Fritz Roethlisberger, and a team of researchers from Harvard University conducted a series of studies at the Hawthorne Plant of the Western Electric Company in a suburb of Chicago. These studies were to profoundly affect management theory and practice. The Hawthorne studies marked the beginning of what would later be called the human relations school.

When the Harvard team began their work, their goal was to determine how environmental conditions, such as lighting and noise levels, affected employee productivity. They soon discovered that social factors and group norms influence productivity and motivation much more than do the combined effects of physical conditions, money, discipline, and even job security. In 1939 Roethlisberger summarized these findings in his famous book *Management and the Worker.*[51]

In the 1950s and 1960s, the writings of Abraham Maslow, of "hierarchy of needs" fame, and Douglas McGregor, known for "theory X, theory Y," reinforced the human relations school of thought. Other behavioral scientists, including Rensis Likert (four systems of management), Chris Argyris (integrating the individual and the organization), and Frederick Herzberg (motivation hygiene theory), joined these influential figures to set the stage for many participative management experiments in the United States and abroad.[52]

Experiments in Participative Management

Some of the early pioneers in participative management included large firms, such as Texas Instruments, AT&T, General Foods, and Procter & Gamble, as well as smaller firms, such as Harwood Manufacturing and Lincoln Electric Company. These companies became famous for their innovative approaches to employee relations. Many of the participative management experiments they conducted in the 1950s and 1960s bear a close resemblance to employee empowerment and quality improvement practices of today.

Texas Instruments used work simplification training for line workers to help solve manufacturing problems and improve productivity. AT&T used job enrichment programs to increase motivation and employee output. General Foods designed a plant from the ground up around a team concept, in which workers were classified into skill categories and could progress to the top category by learning how to do all the jobs needed to run the plant. Procter & Gamble independently developed a concept of group work in the 1940s and 1950s. Many of these experiments were so successful that they are still in place today. Factors common to all successful experiments included the following:

- Management attitudes toward workers were positive; employees were viewed as important assets to the success of the company.
- Workers were given increased scope and control over job activities.
- Workers felt that the projects they undertook were important and doable, and had real-life applicability.
- Training in human relations, problem-solving, and decision-making skills was conducted through formal and informal means.
- Opportunities for advancement based on acquiring new skills and knowledge were provided.
- Productivity and morale increased during the period in which experiments were conducted.[53]

Quality Synthesis

As business schools and colleges expanded during the 1970s, old-line professors steeped in classical principles of management distilled from Frederick Taylor had to defend their theories against the onslaught of young behavioral scientists oriented toward human relations. Some time passed before both groups came to understand that there is no single best way to manage in a complex environment. Both the classicist and the behaviorist had to find that there was good in both points of view. During the 1970s, 1980s, and 1990s, the quality movement became the catalyst for joining these two management views. Here was one management technique that combined participative leadership practices with a problem-solving orientation, and it was being fervently employed in a real-world lab by the industrious Japanese as they outstripped competitors and set new standards of quality.[54]

The leadership philosophy behind quality improvement efforts such as total quality management (TQM) and continuous quality improvement (CQI) is both *hard,* based on scientific management, and *soft,* concerned with the human side of work. It is this balance or blend that helps account for its general acceptance across the broad spectrum of managers today. By focusing on quality goals and using problem-solving tools and methods, quality improvement activities satisfy the needs of managers whose values lie with Frederick Taylor, the management classicists, and quantitative analysis. Such "hard-nosed" managers are drawn to the "end product" benefits of better products and services.

Likewise, by focusing on employee empowerment and personal growth, and by using group process techniques, quality improvement activities satisfy the needs of managers who trace their philosophical roots to Elton Mayo, Kurt Lewin, Abraham Maslow, Douglas McGregor, Rensis Likert, and other figures in the human relations and behavioral science school. These "soft-hearted" managers are especially pleased with the "in-process" benefits of improved morale, quality of work life, and the experience of community. See Figure 13–2.

Figure 13–2
The Leadership Philosophy behind Member Empowerment and the Quality Movement

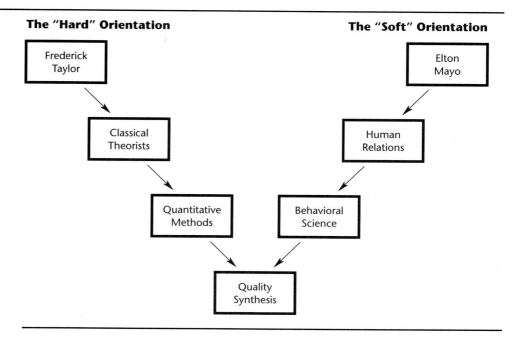

Improving Performance through Quality Initiatives

How effective is the quality movement? What results are experienced by participating organizations? A Government Accounting Office (GAO) report on American management practices shows U.S. companies are experiencing good results using quality improvement efforts to improve business performance.[55]

Background

Achieving high levels of quality has become an increasingly important element in competitive success. In recent years, a number of U.S. companies have found that they could not achieve world-class quality by using traditional approaches to managing product and service quality. To enhance their competitive position, American companies have reappraised the traditional view of quality and have adopted what is known as the total quality management model in running their businesses.

For many years the traditional way to achieve quality was through systematic final inspection. This approach is referred to as inspecting in quality. Intense foreign competition in general, and Japanese competition in particular, has led increasing numbers of U.S. companies to adopt total quality management practices that are prevention-based. This approach is often referred to as building in quality.

Results

■ Companies that adopted quality management practices experienced an overall improvement in business performance. In nearly all cases, companies that used total quality management practices achieved better employee relations, higher productivity, greater customer satisfaction, increased market share, and improved profitability.

■ Companies did not use a cookbook approach in implementing successful quality management systems, but common features that contributed to improved performance can be identified: Corporate attention was focused on meeting customer needs as a first priority; senior management led the way in building values into company operations; all employees were suitably trained, empowered, and involved in efforts to continuously improve quality and reduce costs; and systematic processes were integrated throughout the organization to foster continuous improvement.

■ The diversity of companies studied showed that quality management is useful for small companies (500 or fewer employees) as well as large companies, and for service companies as well as manufacturers.

■ Many different kinds of companies benefited from putting quality management practices into place. However, none of these companies reaped those benefits immediately. Companies improved their performance on average in about two and one-half years. Management allowed enough time for results to be achieved rather than emphasizing short-term gains.

Specific Findings

Specific findings revealed U.S. companies can improve performance through quality efforts.

■ Better employee relations were realized. Employees experienced increased job satisfaction and improved attendance; employee turnover also decreased.

■ Improved quality and lower cost were attained. Companies increased the reliability and on-time delivery of their product or service, and reduced errors, product lead time, and their cost of quality.

■ Greater customer satisfaction was accomplished, based on the companies' survey results of their consumers' overall perceptions about a product or service, the number of complaints received, and customer retention rates.

Financial Benefits of Improving Quality

A report in *Business Week* describes the financial impact of quality improvement efforts:

Total quality management (TQM) pays off handsomely. A study by the Georgia Institute of Technology and the College of William & Mary found that TQM award-winners posted 37% higher sales growth and 44% fatter stock prices, compared with a corporate control group. These results buttress similar findings for the stocks of 18 winners of the Malcolm Baldrige National Quality Award. They have outperformed the Standard & Poor's 500 stock index by over 100%.[56]

Implicit in the value system of the quality movement is the saying "If you always do what you have always done, you will always get what you have always gotten." This statement reflects the spirit of the childhood rhyme "Good, better, best. Never let it rest until the good gets better, and the better is the best."[57]

Part Four Summary

After reading Part Four, you should know the following key concepts, principles and terms. Fill in the blanks from memory, or copy the answers listed below.

Two kinds of leadership authority are top-down and bottom-up, both of which have merit. An approach to leadership that recognizes the value of both is (a)_____, emphasizing a commitment to people, as shown by (b)_____, _____, and _____. The essential character of leadership that involves people and gains their participation in decision making is (c)_____. The empowering leader raises the (d)_____ of others without lowering her or his own, primarily by (e)_____ to them, thus showing interest and respect. Three basic principles of an empowered workplace are to (f)_____, _____, and _____. The top six places employees prefer to get information are (g)_____, _____, _____, _____, _____, and _____. Management author Robert Greenleaf believed that the world would be saved by having three truly great institutions as role models—one in each sector of society—private, public, and nonprofit. In each case, the secrets of success would be (h)_____ and _____. The central figure in the history of the quality movement has been (i)_____, primarily because of his influence first in Japan, then in the United States. The (j)_____ synthesizes the benefits of scientific management, most associated with Frederick Taylor, and behavioral science, associated with individuals such as Abraham Maslow and Douglas McGregor.

Answer Key for Part Four Summary

a. **servant leadership,** page 121

b. **access, communication, support,** page 122

c. **democratic,** page 124

d. **psychological size,** page 129

e. **listening,** page 131

f. (any three) **trust in people, invest in people, recognize accomplishments, decentralize decision making, view work as a cooperative effort,** page 134

g. **immediate supervisor, small group meetings, top executives, policy handbook, orientation programs, member newsletter,** page 136

h. **caring leadership, the empowerment of people,** page 137

i. **W. Edwards Deming,** page 138

j. **quality movement,** page 141

Reflection Points—personal thoughts on leadership authority, empowerment in the workplace, and the quality imperative

Complete the following questions and activities to personalize the content of Part Four. Space is provided for writing your thoughts.

■ How do you rate as a servant leader? Discuss commitment to others as shown by access, communication, and support.

_____

_____

■ Describe a participative organization where leaders involve the people, gain understanding, and achieve good results. What do the leaders do? How do people react?

_____

_____

■ Discuss the use and abuse of leadership power. Is it necessarily true that power corrupts and absolute power corrupts absolutely? Cite examples of leaders who improved as a result of the responsibility of leadership.

_____

_____

■ Develop a five-point plan for organizational communication. What should be done to achieve the best communication possible—up, down, and sideways?

_____

_____

■ Implement one to five practical tips for a high-performance workplace. Discuss the results.

_____

_____

■ Critique "The Deming Way" as it applies to your workplace. Which points are present? Which are effective? Which points are missing? What are the results?

_____

_____

■ Use participative leadership to improve performance. Assemble a team, and discuss problems, bottlenecks, and opportunities. Select one and develop a recommendation. Follow up and evaluate.

_____

_____

Action Assignment

As a bridge between learning and doing, complete the following action assignment.

1. What is the most important idea you have learned in Part Four?

2. How can you apply what you have learned? What will you do, with whom, where, when, and, most important, why?

Part 5　Leadership Principles

14. Effective Leadership
15. Human Relations
16. The Team Concept

THE BOSS DRIVES; the leader coaches.

The boss wants power; the leader, good will.

The boss creates fear; the leader builds pride.

The boss says "I"; the leader says "We."

The boss places blame; the leader solves the problem.

The boss knows how; the leader shows how.

The boss uses people; the leader serves others.

The boss preaches; the leader teaches.

The boss takes credit; the leader gives credit.

The boss commands; the leader asks.

The boss says "Go"; the leader says "Let's go."

—William J. Stewart
Author and educator

Learning Points

In Part Five, you will discover the answers to these questions:
- How do you rate on the principles and practices of effective leadership?
- Why are human relations important, and what are the elements of an enlightened workplace?
- What are the characteristics of a high-performance group, and what can the leader do to develop communication, teamwork, and a one-team attitude?

Effective Leadership

How do you go about being an effective leader? Author and educator Warren Bennis provides a short-course answer distilled from years of study and experience: **"Be yourself. Figure out what you are good at. Hire only good people who care. Treat people the way you want to be treated. Focus on one or two critical objectives. Ask your co-workers how to get there. Listen well. Call the play. Get out of their way. Cheer them on. Count the gains. Start right now."**[1]

Certain principles of leadership have optimum positive influence on followers. Consider Amos Alonzo Stagg, Knute Rockne, Joe Paterno, Eddie Robinson, and Paul "Bear" Bryant in the field of sports. Although their styles were different, each followed universal principles of leadership that brought out the best in the pride and performance of people. These principles constitute leadership by competence. They apply at all levels of leadership and in all fields of work.[2]

For an evaluation of your competence as a leader (or an evaluation of your leader's competence), complete Exercise 14–1 and read the rationale that follows each question. Note that this questionnaire is an assessment of leadership behaviors, as opposed to personality traits. Followers are unable to read the minds of their leaders and can go only by what they see them do; therefore, it is important to consider how well you are *practicing* the principles of effective leadership.

**Exercise 14–1
Leadership Report
Card[3]**

Circle the appropriate number for each response, and read the accompanying rationale. If you are evaluating your leader, substitute *he* or *she* for *I,* and *his* or *her* for *my.*

A. I have a clear understanding of my responsibilities in order of priority.

   1. I haven't the foggiest.
   2. Things are vague.
   3. There is some confusion.
   4. Generally speaking, yes.
   5. Exactly.

Rationale:

■ If the leader is confused about personal goals and duties, how can the leader guide the behavior of others? The leader won't know in which direction to lead them.

B. All my people know what their job duties are in order of priority.

   1. None do.
   2. Some do.
   3. Most do.
   4. Almost all do.
   5. All do.

Rationale:

■ Job expectations must be understood and agreed upon for maximum job satisfaction and work performance.

■ Not knowing what is expected of you is a major cause of stress at work.

C. The jobs my people have are satisfying to them.

   1. Not really.
   2. Some are.
   3. So-so.
   4. More than most.
   5. Definitely yes.

Rationale:

■ A person's work is an important part of personal identity in Western society.

■ Work must be personally satisfying if high morale and productivity are to be achieved.

D. My people know whether they are doing a good job or if they need to improve.

   1. No, it's best they don't.
   2. Some do.
   3. I try to get to most of them.
   4. Practically all do.
   5. Yes, it's rare if they don't.

Rationale:

■ Not knowing how you are doing causes worry and anxiety and dissipates energy.

E. I recognize and reward good performance.

   1. The paycheck is enough.
   2. Sometimes.
   3. More often than not.
   4. Almost always.
   5. Always.

Rationale:

■ Appreciation for a job well done reinforces good work.

■ Ignoring a job well done reduces commitment. The employee begins to think, "If they don't care, why should I?" People need psychic, social, and economic reinforcement at work.

■ Recognition techniques that build morale include (1) personal thanks; (2) year-end celebrations; (3) courtesy time off; (4) traveling trophy; (5) money.

F. I have criticized an employee in the presence of others.

    1. I believe in making an example.

    2. Occasionally.

    3. Almost never.

    4. Once.

    5. Never, not once.

Rationale:

- Public criticism embarrasses, alienates, and ultimately outrages not only the employee being chastised, but all who are present as well.

- As Ralph Waldo Emerson said, "Criticism should not be querulous and wasting, all knife and rootpuller; but guiding, instructive and inspiring—a south wind, not an east wind."[4]

G. I care about the personal well-being of my people, and they know it.

    1. Honestly, no.

    2. Some of them, yes.

    3. Usually.

    4. Almost all of them, yes.

    5. Totally.

Rationale:

- If the leader does not show concern for people, they will either worry unnecessarily, or reduce allegiance to the leader. In either case, energy, time, and commitment are diverted from the work at hand.

- People resent being treated as unimportant; they want leaders to care about them and show respect for their interests, their problems, and their needs. Whether by personal hospital visits when they are ill, or by providing the best equipment and working tools available, or by sharing in the trials of battle and the rewards of victory, the effective leader shows consideration for others. Plutarch in *Lives* has this to say about the Roman leader, Julius Caesar:

  Caesar implanted and nurtured high spirits in his men: (1) first by gracious treatment and by bestowing awards without stint, demonstrating that the wealth he amassed from wars was a carefully guarded trust for rewarding gallantry, with no larger share for himself than accrued to the soldiers who merited it; and (2) secondly by willingly exposing himself to every danger and shrinking from no personal hardship of battle faced by his fellow soldiers.[5]

- A leader's ability to remember aspects of followers' personal lives (names of children, favorite hobbies, etc.) creates a bond that causes followers to admire and support the leader.

H. I have policies and procedures for employee development and cross-training.

    1. There is no need for this.

    2. I plan to someday.

    3. On occasion, for some employees.

    4. Yes, generally speaking.

    5. It is a major commitment I have.

Rationale:

- Employee training does six important things: builds skills, raises morale, cuts avoidable turnover and absenteeism, raises loyalty, reduces mistakes, and increases productivity.

I. I have given assignments to people without first considering the availability of their time and the competence they possess.

    1. Often.

    2. Occasionally.

    3. Rarely.

    4. I almost never do this.

    5. Never.

Rationale:

- Assigning work that is over a person's level of skill creates undue stress and is likely to result in a costly error.

- Assigning more work than is possible to accomplish in the time available creates frustration, low morale, resentment, and lower performance in the long run.

J. I have been accused of favoritism regarding some of my employees.

  1. Often.

  2. More than most.

  3. At times.

  4. Rarely.

  5. Never.

Rationale:

- The values of equality and fair treatment are widely shared in Western society; favoritism runs directly counter to these values.

K. I take personal responsibility for the orders I give and never quote a superior to gain compliance.

  1. Never.

  2. Rarely.

  3. Usually.

  4. Almost always.

  5. Always.

Rationale:

- Leaders who violate this principle lose the respect of their subordinates, upper management, and ultimately themselves as they become merely "paper leaders."

- The effective leader agrees with Harry Truman, who said, "The buck stops here" and "If you can't stand the heat, get out of the kitchen."

- When a leader refers to higher managers as "they," he or she drives a wedge between the employees and the organization, failing senior managers and employees as well.

- Karl Menninger's definition of loyalty can be helpful here:

  Loyalty doesn't mean that I agree with everything you say, or that I believe you are always right, or that I follow your will in blind obedience. Loyalty means that we share the same values and principles, and when minor differences arise, we work together, shoulder to shoulder, confident in each other's good faith, trust, constancy, and affection. Then together, we go forward, secure in the knowledge that few day-to-day matters are hills worth dying on.[6]

L. I do not promise what cannot be delivered, and I deliver on all promises made.

  1. I have dropped the ball often.

  2. I have failed occasionally.

  3. Usually.

  4. Almost without exception.

  5. Always.

Rationale:

- Broken promises lower employee confidence and respect for the leader.

- Disappointments deflate employee morale and performance, especially when they come from the leader.

M. My people understand the reasoning behind policies and procedures.

  1. Rarely.

  2. Occasionally.

  3. Sometimes.

  4. Usually.

  5. Always.

Rationale:

- Not knowing the purpose of a policy or procedure can result in mistakes.
- The following story shows the importance of understanding *why:* The members of a crew on a submarine were about to take battle stations, and the ship's Captain was worried about a young seaman whose job it was to close the watertight doors between certain compartments. The young man didn't seem to realize the purpose of his job, so the Captain undertook to impress him. He told him that if he failed his job, the ship would be lost. Not only that, some of the men aboard were specialists and it cost thousands to train each of them; they might be drowned. The Captain stated: "So you see how important it is that you do your job . . . this is a very expensive ship, and these men are very valuable." The young crewman replied: "Yes sir, and then there's me too." The Captain stopped worrying.[7]
- Uncertainty about policies can lead to paralysis.

N. The rules we live by are discussed and modified as needed.

    1. Rarely.

    2. Sometimes.

    3. Usually.

    4. Almost always.

    5. Always.

Rationale:

- People are more likely to follow a rule they help set.
- People need to know the appropriate limits of behavior and guidelines for conduct.
- Rules should be periodically reviewed for appropriateness; some rules may no longer be necessary or desirable.

O. I encourage my people to express disagreement with my views, especially if I'm dealing in a controversial area.

    1. Never.

    2. Rarely.

    3. Sometimes.

    4. Fairly often.

    5. Always.

Rationale:

- People have the need to express themselves on emotional issues without fear of reprisal.
- Good ideas can come from constructive disagreement.
- Remember Harry Truman's advice: "I want people around me who will tell me the truth as they see it. You cannot operate if you have people around you who put you on a pedestal and tell you everything you do is right. Because that can't be possible."[8]

P. My people know and feel free to use a right of appeal, formal and informal.

    1. There is no procedure for appeal.

    2. There is a procedure, but it is not widely known.

    3. Some do.

    4. Most do.

    5. All do.

Rationale:

- Not all decisions are good ones, and some should be reversed.
- Every rule must have an exception, and a review or appeal process can facilitate this.
- An appeal process is a defense against arbitrary and capricious treatment, and it meets the need for a sense of fairness.

Q. The last time I listened closely to a suggestion from my people was:

    1. I can't remember.

    2. Two months ago.

   3. A month ago.

   4. Last week.

   5. Within the past two days.

Rationale:

- Not listening shows disrespect, and people shut down when they do not feel respected.
- Important information and ideas may be lost unless two-way communication prevails.
- Ben Jonson's words make the point well: "Very few men are wise by their own counsel; or learned by their own teaching. For he that was only taught by himself had a fool to be his [teacher]."[9]
- One of the best ways to keep communication lines open is to be available. The simple act of placing your office in a position near the lobby, parking lot, or hall is a time-tested way to stay informed of employee needs and suggestions.

R. I encourage my people to participate in decisions affecting them unless compelling reasons prevent it.

   1. Rarely.

   2. Sometimes.

   3. Usually.

   4. Almost always.

   5. Always.

Rationale:

- Democracy is a political value taught in our society. It should come as no surprise when employees want to be involved in decisions that affect them.
- Participation leads to understanding; understanding leads to commitment; and commitment leads to loyalty.
- Peter Drucker states, "Good leaders know how to *tell*; great leaders know how to *ask*."

S. I have mastered both the job knowledge and technical skills of my work.

   1. I am totally out of my element.

   2. I need much improvement.

   3. I am OK.

   4. I am very good.

   5. I am excellent.

Rationale:

- Job knowledge helps the leader gain the respect and loyalty of people.
- Job expertise helps solve critical problems.
- Effective leaders are teachers and developers of people; this role requires keeping job knowledge current.

T. I have lost control of my emotions or faculties in the presence of my people.

   1. Often.

   2. Occasionally.

   3. Rarely.

   4. Almost never.

   5. Never.

Rationale:

- Emotional stability in the leader can be an anchor of strength for others.
- Past a certain point, as emotionality increases, objectivity and the ability to make good judgments decrease.

U. I set a good example for my people in the use of my time at work.

   1. If they did what I do, we'd be in trouble.

   2. I waste significant amounts of time.

3. Sometimes yes, sometimes no.

4. Usually.

5. I wish they would use me as a model.

Rationale:

- Because people are influenced primarily by the example the leader sets, leaders must follow effective time management practices.
- Effective time management results in efficiency and smooth operations in the work setting.

Scoring:

Add the numbers you circled for all 21 questions; record your total score here: _____

Interpretation:

Check the following list for an evaluation of your (or your leader's) competence as a leader.

Score	Evaluation
95–105	You should go to the head of the class. Your leadership practices can serve as a model for others. Your behavior concerning employee communication, rewards, decision making, assignment of work, and the example you set are ideal.
84–94	You are on solid footing as a leader. You understand and employ the basic principles of effective leadership, regardless of the level and field of work. People should be happy under your direction, and the quality of their work can be expected to be high.
63–83	You are doing some things right, and you are making mistakes in other areas. You are neither all good nor all bad in your leadership practices. Go back to the test, determine where your strengths are, and capitalize on those areas. Also, work diligently to raise your low scores. For example: Do you have good two-way communication with your people? Are you following the principles of effective motivation? Are you setting a good example by your own work habits and the use of your time?
62 and lower	Because of lack of training, lack of application, or lack of aptitude, you are not practicing the principles of good leadership. To diagnose the problem, answer these three questions: (1) Have you been reading the wrong book or following the wrong models of leadership? (2) Do you know the right answers but have been inattentive to practicing them? (3) Are you cut out for leadership, or do you feel more comfortable working alone—being responsible for your own work, as opposed to assigning, coordinating, teaching, coaching, and facilitating the work of others? Whatever the cause of your low scores, for the benefit of your employees and the quality of work of your group, you should address the problem and solve it. The best way to do this is to read the rationale for the correct answers and then make every effort to exhibit the correct behavior on the job.

Work Morale

The importance of morale has been recognized by all great leaders. Napoleon once wrote: "An army's success depends on its size, equipment, experience, and morale . . . and morale is worth more than all of the other elements combined." A person's morale can be diagnosed according to the percentage of time spent on the job in each of three states—work, play, and hell. Consider your own job. What percentage of your time is spent doing *work* (drudgery)? What percentage is spent at *play* (enjoyable, uplifting activities)? What percentage is *hell* (pain and torture)? Record your percentages below to assess your morale.

State	Percentage of time
Work	_____
Play	_____
Hell	_____
Total	100%

If less than 20 percent of your job is enjoyable, this problem will show up as your interest, commitment, and ultimately your performance go down. There is not enough satisfaction in your job. If more than 20 percent of your job life is hell, this problem will show up in your attitude, performance, relationships, and even your health. More than a day of your week is spent in a miserable state. An acceptable work (drudgery) quotient depends on the work ethic you have developed. Because of either Western world or Eastern world socialization, some people have a higher degree of self-discipline and tolerance for tedious labor.

Raising Employee Morale

Some policies and techniques for maximizing morale seem to work with the majority of employees in most cases. A review of 550 studies published since 1959 shows nine areas in which management can take action that will have positive effects on employee satisfaction and job performance. These are:

- *Pay and reward systems.* **Introduce a group bonus.**
- *Job autonomy and discretion.* **Allow workers to determine their own work methods.**
- *Support services.* **Provide service on demand from technical support groups.**
- *Training.* **Provide training and development for all employees.**
- *Organizational structure.* **Reduce the number of hierarchical levels.**
- *Technical and physical aspects.* **Break long production and assembly lines into smaller work units.**
- *Task assignments.* **Assign whole tasks,** including preparatory and finishing work.
- *Information and feedback.* **Solicit and utilize direct feedback from users—** clients, customers, other departments.
- *Interpersonal and group processes.* **Increase the amount and types of group interaction.**

Research shows that positive results can be obtained by using one or more of these techniques. Costs go down, and the quality of work and quality of work life improve.[10]

Work Morale and the Role of the Leader

Does morale make a difference, and does leadership count? Yes and yes, say Robert Levering and Milton Moskowitz in *The 100 Best Companies to Work for in America,* identifying Southwest Airlines as number 1 and quoting an enthusiastic employee: "Working here is an unbelievable experience. They treat you with respect, pay you well, and ask you to use your ideas to solve problems. They encourage you to be yourself. I love going to work!"[11]

Although he downplays his role in the success of the company, former CEO **Herb Kelleher** personifies the honest and caring leader who is committed to his people and who cares about their morale. As CEO, Kelleher spent his business day making sure employees believed in themselves and their company, and he did this in his own unique way. He smoked, arm-wrestled, drank Wild Turkey, rapped in music videos—and he loved it. His employees loved him, too. Kelleher states, "You can't just lead by the numbers. We've always believed that business should be enjoyable as well."[12]

Kelleher's attention to morale paid big dividends for Southwest Airlines. When he became CEO in 1982, the airline had just 27 planes; $270 million in revenues; 2,100 employees, and flew to 14 cities. By the time of his retirement in 2001, Southwest had become a $5.7 billion business with 30,000 employees and was flying to 57 cities. At $14 billion, Southwest's market capitalization was bigger than American's, United's, and Continental's combined. Most astounding of all was that, since the company first earned a profit in 1973, it never lost a penny. In an industry plagued by fare wars, oil crises, and other disasters, this is an amazing accomplishment—traced primarily to a caring leader who cared about his people.[13]

Practical Leadership Tips

The task of leadership is to manage morale, which means making sure people (1) feel they are given the opportunity to do what they do best every day; (2) believe their opinions count; (3) sense their fellow employees are committed to doing high-quality work; and (4) have made a direct connection between their work and the company's mission. By focusing on these key factors and by adhering to the following proven tips for being an effective leader, the leader can keep morale high and performance up in the work group or organization.[14]

1. **Be predictable.** One good rule for leading people is: Be consistent. If you give praise for an act today and criticism for the same act tomorrow, the result will be confusion.

2. **Be understanding.** Try to see things from the other person's view. How can you appreciate what another person is going through if you have never been there or at least listened?

3. **Be enthusiastic.** The atmosphere you create determines whether people will give their best efforts when you are not present. Why would *they* care if *you* do not?

4. **Set the example.** It is difficult to ask others to do something (for example, be at work on time—8:00 A.M.) if you, yourself, aren't willing to do it.

5. **Show support.** People want a leader they can trust in times of need and a person they can depend on to represent their interests. Care about your people and they will care about you. Mutual loyalty is an important force for getting things done, especially in emergencies and adverse conditions.

6. **Get out of the office.** Visit frontline people with your eyes and ears open. Ask questions, understand their concerns, and gain their support. This has to be done often enough to show that you care about their problems and their ideas.

7. **Keep promises.** When you make promises, keep them faithfully. One key to being an effective leader is credibility. Credibility is the formation of trust, and trust is an essential quality employees want in a leader.

8. **Praise generously.** Never let an opportunity pass to give a well-deserved compliment. Don't forget to show appreciation for effort as well as accomplishments, and do so in writing whenever possible.

9. **Hold your fire.** Say less than you think. Cultivate a pleasant tone of voice. How you say something is often more important than what you say. Most important, ask people, don't tell them. Discuss, don't argue.

10. **Always be fair.** Show respect, consideration, and support for all employees equally, but differentiate rewards based on performance. Reward good performers in a similar fashion, and nonperformers in a similar fashion, but don't reward good performers and nonperformers in the same fashion. Doing so is a sure way to demotivate good performers and lower the quality of work for all.

Morale of the Leader

An interesting question is what affects *leadership* morale? What reduces the enjoyment and increases the pain for leaders themselves? An *Industry Week* study of frontline supervisors and middle-level managers showed the following:[15]

Why Morale Is Low	Percentage Response	Solution
We're not a team (cohesion).	61%	Create a one-team attitude.
Bureaucracy stifles initiative.	39	Cut red tape and reduce paperwork.
My efforts aren't recognized.	39	Recognize jobs well done.
I'm locked into my job.	23	Provide career development.
No one tells me anything.	21	Keep people informed.
"They" want quantity, not quality.	21	Emphasize "doing jobs right."
Pay stinks.	12	Pay sufficient wages based on merit.
As a woman, I'm discriminated against.	6	Treat all people fairly.
All other reasons.	22	Case-by-case solution.

Psychological Health and the Concept of Flow

A satisfying work experience is important for emotional well-being. The Russian writer Fyodor Dostoyevsky expressed this when he wrote, "If it were considered desirable to destroy a human being, the only thing necessary would be to give his work a climate of uselessness."[16]

Thomas Jefferson, in a letter to Mrs. A. S. Marks, wrote, "It is neither wealth nor splendor, but tranquillity and occupation, which give happiness." Along these lines, University of Chicago psychologist Mihaly Csikszentmihalyi coined the term **flow** after studying artists who could spend hour after hour painting and sculpting with enormous concentration. The artists, immersed in a challenging project and exhibiting high levels of skill, worked as if nothing else mattered.

Flow is the confluence of challenge and skill, and it is what the poet Joseph Campbell meant when he said, "Follow your bliss." In all fields of work, from accounting to zookeeping, when we are challenged by something we are truly good at, we become so absorbed in the flow of the activity that we lose consciousness of self and time. We avoid states of anxiety, boredom, and apathy, and we experience flow. See Figure 14–1.

**Figure 14–1
The Experience of Flow
Combines High Challenge
and High Skill**[17]

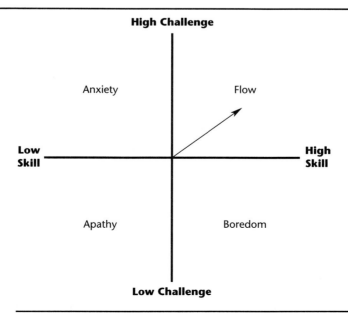

Note that low skill + low challenge = apathy and diminished work life; low skill + high challenge = anxiety and low self-esteem; high skill + low challenge = boredom and low creativity; high skill + high challenge = the experience of flow and work fulfillment.

What is it like to be in a state of flow? Csikszentmihalyi, in his book *The Evolving Self,* reports that over and over again, people describe the same dimensions of flow:

- A clear and present purpose distinctly known.
- Immediate feedback on how well one is doing.
- Supreme concentration on the task at hand as other concerns are temporarily suspended.
- A sense of growth and being part of some greater endeavor as ego boundaries are transcended.
- An altered sense of time that usually seems to go faster.[18]

Job Design and Work Satisfaction

What constitutes a good job? One of the best models of job design and work satisfaction shows intrinsic and extrinsic factors that are necessary for a rich job.[19] Intrinsic factors are:

1. **Variety and challenge.**
2. **Opportunity for decision making.**
3. **Feedback and learning.**
4. **Mutual support and respect.**
5. **Wholeness and meaning.**
6. **Room to grow.**

The first three must be optimal—not too much, which can add anxiety, nor too little, which produces boredom. The second three are open-ended. No one can have too much respect, growing room, or wholeness. Thus a rich job has optimal variety, responsibility, and feedback, and as much respect, growth, and wholeness as possible.

The rich job also includes extrinsic conditions of employment, including:

1. Fair and adequate pay.
2. Job security.
3. Benefits.
4. Safety.
5. Health.
6. Due process.

With this model as a basis, consider the employees in your jurisdiction. What steps can be taken to improve or maintain high job satisfaction?

Human Relations

Human relations are important to the individual and the society. As John Donne, the seventeenth-century English poet, wrote, in the language of his time:

No man is an Island, intire of its selfe;
Every man is a peece of the Continent,
A part of the maine;
If a Clod be washed away by the Sea, Europe is the lesse,
As well as if a Promontorie were,
As well as if a Mannor of thy friends, or of thine owne were;
Any man's death diminishes me,
Because I am involved in Mankinde;
And therefore;
Never send to know for whom the bell tolls;
It tolls for thee.[20]

In *The Different Drum,* psychiatrist Scott Peck writes: "We are all, in reality, interdependent. Throughout the ages, the greatest leaders of all of the religions have taught us that the journey of growth is the path away from self-love, and toward a state of being in which our identity merges with that of humanity."[21] Effective leaders understand this idea fully, and at a basic level feel connected with their fellow humans, care about the well-being of others, and relate effectively with people.

Human Relations in the Workplace

Psychologist William Menninger explains the importance of human relationships in the world of work:

The only hope for man to be fulfilled in a world of work is that he get along with his fellowmen—that he try to understand them. He may then be free to contribute to their mutual welfare—theirs and his. Insofar as he fails this, he fails himself and society.[22]

The first empirical evidence of the importance of human relations in the workplace was provided by studies conducted at Western Electric's Hawthorne plant, outside Chicago, Illinois, between 1927 and 1932. These studies were conducted by Elton Mayo, Fritz Roethlisberger, and other research personnel from Harvard University. The original purpose of the studies was to discover the effect of working conditions—noise, lighting, and the like—on employee performance. The final result was to demonstrate the critical role of human relations, particularly employee recognition and management support.[23]

The Hawthorne studies followed a period of American history marked by massive industrialization, exploitation of workers, and the use of scientific management to improve employee efficiency. As epitomized by Charlie Chaplin in the film *Modern Times,* the worker had been dehumanized in the pursuit of production and profit.

Among the findings commonly attributed to the Hawthorne studies are the following: (1) Productivity is affected by human relationships because the work environment is also a social environment; (2) a supportive leadership style and the amount of attention directed toward employees have positive influence on productivity; (3) there is a tendency for workers to set their own standards or norms for acceptable behavior and output.[24]

With the published results of the Hawthorne studies, the industrial community awakened to the fact that the worker must be treated as more than a machine, and that humanism in the workplace is good for both people and business. Participative work groups, enlightened leadership practices, and meaningful job assignments were recognized as important to prevent worker alienation, and a human relations movement began to take root.

Today it is a recognized fact that people have greater satisfaction and produce more when they are involved in their work, when they feel they are doing something important, and when their work is appreciated. Both quality of work and quality of work life are greatest when people are treated with dignity, trust, and respect.

Basic Beliefs about People

The quality of human relations in any workplace reflects its members', particularly its leaders', views of the essential nature and value of humanity itself.

- *Human nature.* It makes a great deal of difference whether one views people in general as good or evil. If we assume that people are basically good, we can believe that misbehavior is a reactive response rather than a manifestation of character. This positive view of people will lead to a search for causes in experience rather than in nature. If, on the other hand, we assume that people are inherently bad, then we are prone to assume that misbehavior is caused by something within the person that cannot be altered directly. Accordingly, our attention will focus on limiting freedom to choose and act through external restrictions and controls.

  The leader's view of human nature (inherently good or inherently bad) will color all his or her thoughts and actions in dealing with people.

- *Human value.* What is the basic value of human beings? This is a question as old as written history and probably as old as society itself. It stems from the debate as to whether people are ends in themselves or merely means to ends. In simple terms, we treat people as ends when we allow them to establish their own purposes and to choose for themselves. When we view people as ends, we reflect a humanistic view. In contrast, when we treat people as means, we limit their choices and use them primarily as instruments for our own purposes.

  The leader's opinion of the basic value of people will be revealed in his or her decisions and conduct, and these will influence both trust and goodwill engendered in others.

- *Where Do You Stand?* Personal history draws each of us toward some primary tendency that determines the general pattern of our relations with others. Small changes may occur to accommodate the various roles we play, but there seems to be a core pattern that represents our basic beliefs concerning human beings. We view people along the continuum of evil or good, depending on our personal experiences. Is your own view of people primarily positive or negative? Also, we tend to value people as objects to be used or subjects to be served. What experiences and factors have influenced your views and values? As a result, what principles and practices do you follow in your relations with others? How have your basic beliefs influenced your behavior toward others? How will this influence your experience as a leader?

Trust and Respect in Human Relations

Trust and **respect** are the key elements of all good relationships. Trust is expressed by an openness in sharing ideas and feelings. Respect is demonstrated by a willingness to listen to the ideas and feelings of others. Without trust and respect, human relations break down.

The rules for good relationships are to show respect by listening in a responsive manner and to show trust by expressing oneself honestly and openly. Exercise 15–1 provides an effective way to develop trust and respect, the foundation behaviors of good human relations.

**Exercise 15–1
The Dyadic
Encounter**[25]

Introduction:

A theme frequently thought and occasionally voiced when people meet or work together is, I'd like to get to know you, but I don't know how. This sentiment often is expressed in work groups and emerges in marriage and other dyadic (two-person) relationships. Getting to know another person involves a learnable set of skills and attitudes—self-disclosure, trust, listening, acceptance, and nonpossessive caring.

Through the dyadic encounter, a unique learning experience, people who need or want to communicate effectively can learn trust and respect by doing, as they build relationships and skills that can be applied both on the job and in the home.

The conversation that you are about to have is intended to result in more effective human relations. Tasks are accomplished more effectively if people have the capacity to exchange ideas, feelings, and opinions freely.

In an understanding, nonjudgmental manner, one person shares information with another, who reciprocates. This exchange results in a greater feeling of trust, understanding, and acceptance, and the relationship becomes closer.

Directions:

The following ground rules should govern this experience:

- Each partner responds to each statement before continuing to the next statement.
- Complete the statements in the order they appear, first one person responding and then the other.
- Do not write your responses.
- If your partner has finished reading, begin the exercise.

A. My name is . . . _____

_____

B. My hometown is . . . _____

_____

C. Basically, my job is . . . _____

_____

D. The reason I am here is . . . _____

_____

E. Usually, I am the kind of person who . . . _____

_____

F. The thing I like most is . . . _____

_____

G. The thing I dislike most is . . . _____

_____

H. My first impression of you was . . . _____

_____

I. On the job I am best at . . . _____

_____

J. My greatest weakness is . . . _____

_____

K. The best boss I ever had was . . . _____

_____

L. The worst boss I ever had was . . . _____
_____

M. I like people who . . . _____
_____

N. I joined this organization because . . . _____
_____

O. The next thing I am going to try to accomplish at work is . . . _____
_____

P. Away from the job, I am most interested in . . . _____
_____

Q. Society today is . . . _____
_____

R. What concerns me is . . . _____
_____

S. My most embarrassing moment was . . . _____
_____

T. I believe in . . . _____
_____

U. I would like to . . . _____
_____

V. What I like about you is . . . _____
_____

W. What I think you need to know is . . . _____
_____

X. You and I can . . . _____
_____

Y. During our conversation:
   a. your face has communicated . . . _____
_____

   b. your posture has conveyed . . . _____
_____

   c. your hands and arms have indicated . . . _____
_____

Z. Have a brief discussion of your reactions to this conversation. If time permits, you may discuss other topics. Several possibilities are projects at work, leadership practices, societal needs, and future goals. Or you may choose your own topics._____

_____
_____
_____

The Enlightened Workplace

Every so often, someone captures an important concept and expresses it in such a way that it penetrates and takes root in the society. Douglas McGregor and his book *The Human Side of Enterprise,* first published in 1960 and rereleased in 1985, stand like a lighthouse and beacon over the sea of literature on leadership. McGregor's book and his famous "Theory Y" speech, delivered at MIT's Alfred P. Sloan School of Management in 1957, changed the entire concept of organizational life for the second half of the twentieth century.[26] See Table 15–1 for the three propositions and five beliefs of Theory X in contrast to the four dimensions of Theory Y.

Table 15–1 **Two Theories of** **Management—X and Y[27]**	**Theory X: Three Propositions and Five Beliefs** The conventional conception of management's task in harnessing human energy to meet organizational requirements can be stated broadly in terms of three propositions: **1.** Management is responsible for organizing the elements of productive enterprise—money, materials, equipment, people—in the interest of economic ends. **2.** With respect to people, this is a process of directing their efforts, motivating them, controlling their actions, and modifying their behavior to fit the needs of the organization. **3.** Without this active intervention by management, people would be passive—even resistant—to organizational needs. They must therefore be persuaded, rewarded, punished, and controlled—their activities must be directed. This is management's task. We often sum it up by saying that management consists of getting things done through other people. Behind this conventional theory there are five beliefs—less explicit, but widespread: **1.** The average person is by nature indolent—working as little as possible. **2.** The average person lacks ambition, dislikes responsibility, and prefers to be led. **3.** The average person is inherently self-centered and indifferent to organizational needs. **4.** The average person is by nature resistant to change. **5.** The average person is gullible, not very bright, and the ready dupe of the charlatan and the demagogue. Conventional organization structures and managerial policies, practices, and programs reflect these assumptions. **Theory Y: Four Dimensions** We require a different theory of the task of managing people based on more adequate assumptions about human nature and human motivation. The broad dimensions of such a theory are as follows: **1.** Management is responsible for organizing the elements of productive enterprise—money, materials, equipment, people—in the interest of economic ends. **2.** People are not by nature passive or resistant to organizational needs. They have become so as a result of experience in organizations. **3.** The motivation, potential for development, capacity for assuming responsibility, and the readiness to direct behavior toward organizational goals are all present in people. Management does not put them there. It is a responsibility of management to make it possible for people to recognize and develop these human characteristics for themselves. **4.** The essential task of management is to arrange organizational conditions and methods of operation so that people can achieve their own goals best by directing their own efforts toward organizational objectives. This is a process primarily of creating opportunities, releasing potential, removing obstacles, encouraging growth, and providing guidance. It is a liberating and empowering process in contrast to a system of beliefs, policies, and practices that can best be described as "management by control."

McGregor married the ideas of social psychologist Kurt Lewin to the theories of Abraham Maslow. To these, he added his own perspective drawn from his experiences as a professor and practicing leader. The essence of McGregor's message is that people react not to an objective world, but to a world fashioned from their own perceptions and assumptions about what the world is like. Not content to merely describe alternative theories, McGregor went on to identify leadership strategies that could be used to create enlightened workplaces.[28]

McGregor emphasized the human potential for growth, elevated the importance of the individual in the enterprise, and articulated an approach to leadership that undergirds all types and forms of organization. McGregor's prescriptions for an enlightened workplace are as follows:[29]

- The practice of inclusion versus exclusion, based on democratic ideals; the active involvement of all concerned.
- Mutual satisfaction of individual needs and group goals through effective interpersonal relationships between leaders and followers.
- Leadership influence that relies not on techniques of coercion, compromise, and bargaining, but on openness, honesty, and working through differences.
- A conception of humanity that is optimistic versus pessimistic, and that argues for humanistic treatment of people as valuable and valuing, as opposed to objects for manipulation and control.
- A transcending concern for human dignity, worth, and growth, captured best by the phrase "respect for the individual."
- A belief that human goodness is innate, but that it can be thwarted by a dysfunctional environment, and that one's full potential can best be achieved in a healthy climate characterized by trust, respect, and authentic relationships.
- The importance of free individuals to have courage to act and accept responsibility for consequences.

To show the difference enlightened leadership can make, contrast conditions in two investment firms:[30]

Firm 1. This firm refers to one-half of its staff as the professionals and the rest of the employees as office staff. While the office staff members, primarily secretaries, do not expect to earn the wages of college graduates with multiple degrees, they resent the inference that if one group is professional, it follows that everyone else is unprofessional. In this firm, morale is low, turnover is high, and work performance is reduced.

Firm 2. This firm considers its investment counselors and support staff to be directly associated. One or more counselors and a secretary form a team, and the company ties the secretary's bonus and other forms of recognition to the performance of the people he or she supports. Here, esprit de corps runs at stratospheric levels, performance is high, and the firm is prosperous.

Firm 2 puts into practice McGregor's prescriptions for inclusion, shared goals, respect for all people, and personal responsibility.

The Team Concept

The Russian writer Leo Tolstoy once said, "All happy families resemble one another, and every unhappy family is unhappy in its own way." The same can be said for groups. Rather than a single thread, there is a tapestry of qualities that characterize all effective groups. Fully functioning groups and excellent teams possess 12 key characteristics:

1. *Clear mission.* The task or objective of the group is well understood and accepted by all.

2. *Informal atmosphere.* The atmosphere is informal, comfortable, and relaxed. It is a working atmosphere in which everyone is involved and interested. There are no signs of boredom.

3. *Lots of discussion.* Time is allowed for discussion in which everyone is encouraged to participate, and discussion remains pertinent to the task of the group.

4. *Active listening.* Members listen to each other. People show respect for one another by listening when others are talking. Every idea is given a hearing.

5. *Trust and openness.* Members feel free to express ideas and feelings, both on the issues and on the group's operation. People are not afraid to suggest new and different ideas, even if they are fairly extreme.

6. *Disagreement is OK.* Disagreement is not suppressed or overridden by premature group action. Differences are carefully examined as the group seeks to understand all points of view. Conflict and differences of opinion are accepted as the price of creativity.

7. *Criticism is issue-oriented, never personal.* Constructive criticism is given and accepted. Criticism is oriented toward solving problems and accomplishing the mission. Personal criticism is neither expressed nor felt.

8. *Consensus is the norm.* Decisions are reached by consensus, in which it is clear that everyone is in general agreement and willing to go along. Formal voting is kept to a minimum.

9. *Effective leadership.* Informal leadership shifts from time to time, depending on circumstances. There is little evidence of a struggle for power as the group operates. The issue is not who controls, but how to get the job done.

10. *Clarity of assignments.* The group is informed of the action plan. When action is taken, clear assignments are made and accepted. People know what they are expected to do.

11. *Shared values and norms of behavior.* There is agreement on core values and norms of behavior that determine the rightness and wrongness of conduct in the group.

12. *Commitment.* People are committed to achieving the goals of the group.

In Exercise 16–1 on the next page, a group can evaluate itself and improve both team spirit and team effectiveness based on the results. By reinforcing strengths and addressing deficiencies, people can take steps to build and sustain a high-performance group. When this is done, together everyone can accomplish more.

**Exercise 16–1
Characteristics of an
Effective Group**[31]

Consider each of the following characteristics. Evaluate your group as it is operating now
(1 is the lowest rating; 10 is the highest).

1. Clear mission

    1   2   3   4   5   6   7   8   9   10

2. Informal atmosphere

    1   2   3   4   5   6   7   8   9   10

3. Lots of discussion

    1   2   3   4   5   6   7   8   9   10

4. Active listening

    1   2   3   4   5   6   7   8   9   10

5. Trust and openness

    1   2   3   4   5   6   7   8   9   10

6. Disagreement is OK

    1   2   3   4   5   6   7   8   9   10

7. Criticism is issue-oriented, never personal

    1   2   3   4   5   6   7   8   9   10

8. Consensus is the norm

    1   2   3   4   5   6   7   8   9   10

9. Effective leadership

    1   2   3   4   5   6   7   8   9   10

10. Clarity of assignments

    1   2   3   4   5   6   7   8   9   10

11. Shared values and norms of behavior

    1   2   3   4   5   6   7   8   9   10

12. Commitment

    1   2   3   4   5   6   7   8   9   10

Scoring:

Add all the circled numbers to find your overall score. Then see the following chart to find
your group's effectiveness rating.

Score	Rating
108–120	Excellent
84–107	Good
49–83	Average
25–48	Poor
12–24	Failing

Interpretation:

Refer to the following discussion to interpret your group's rating. Note that each characteristic is important, so strive to improve low ratings, regardless of the overall total.

Excellent   *This is a top-notch group regarding communication and teamwork.* The atmosphere is warm and supportive. The focus of attention and effort is on the mission. Creativity is encouraged and success can be expected. Ask yourself if you have ever been a member of an excellent group—in the home, workplace, or community at large. If you have, you know firsthand how satisfying and productive such a group can be.

Good   *This is a strong group for morale and teamwork.* There is enthusiasm and an overall spirit of cooperation and dedication to accomplishing the mission. Conditions are good. In a society where people are free to live and work where they choose, these are the groups that attract and keep good people; then these people work as a team to achieve shared goals.

Average   *Conditions are neither all good nor all bad regarding group effectiveness.* Genuine effort is required to build on strengths and improve weaknesses. As is, the group is average. If you are a member or leader of such a group, you are probably suffering from cognitive dissonance and won't be satisfied until conditions are in line with your ideals. You will want to begin today to achieve agreement on purpose, create an atmosphere of trust and respect, and employ democratic leadership practices.

Poor   *This is a poor group environment.* Major work is needed to improve attitudes and performance. Without attention to team building, failure can be expected. Does this mean that a group that is presently poor can take steps to improve? Definitely. It happens all the time. Case after case can be seen in which a poor-performing team improves group dynamics and becomes a championship team. Simply, they develop the 12 characteristics of an effective group.

Failing   *Major change in group composition is in order.* Leaders and members may be reassigned. It is true that not everyone is meant to be in a group together. Personal and social factors may exist that make staying together unacceptable. What is the answer? Separation and reorganization so that talented and dedicated individuals are neither lost nor harmed.

Positive versus Negative Group Member Roles

How do you develop a high-performance group? As with everything else in life, success depends on the individual and what he or she chooses to do. And like most other things in life, it depends also on the example and direction of leaders. A high level of group performance can be achieved when formal leaders and influential members of the group model and reinforce positive versus negative group member roles. Roles that help build and sustain a high-performance group are as follows:[32]

- **Encourager.** This person is friendly, diplomatic, and responsive to others in the group. The encourager makes others in the group feel good and helps them make contributions to fulfill their potential. The encourager is a cheerleader, coach, and group advocate.

- **Clarifier.** The clarifier restates problems and solutions, summarizes points after discussion, and introduces new or late members to the group by bringing them up to date on what has happened. The gift of the clarifier is to create order out of chaos and replace confusion with clarity.

- **Harmonizer.** The harmonizer agrees with the rest of the group, brings together opposite points of view, and is not aggressive toward others. The harmonizer brings peace versus war, love versus hate, cooperation versus competition, and unity versus discord.

- **Idea generator.** The idea generator is spontaneous and creative. This person is unafraid of change and suggests ideas that others do not. Often these ideas are just what is needed to solve a problem. The idea generator is almost always a creative and unconventional thinker. Pose a problem, and ideas will flow. Idea generators are rich in ideas—half-baked or fully baked.

- **Ignition key.** This person provides the spark for group action, causing the group to meet, work, and follow through with ideas. The ignition key is often a practical organizer who orchestrates and facilitates the work of the group. In this sense, the ignition key plays a leadership role in group action.

- **Standard setter.** This person's high ideals and personal conduct serve as a model for group members. The standard setter is uncompromising in upholding the group's values and goals, and thus inspires group pride. The standard setter is often an expert, possessing knowledge and skills deemed important by the group.

- **Detail specialist.** This person considers the facts and implications of a problem. The detail specialist deals with small points that often have significant consequences in determining the overall success of a group project. A vigilant finisher, the detail specialist searches for errors and omissions and keeps the group on red alert. To understand the importance of the detail specialist, consider Benjamin Franklin's words:

> A little neglect may breed mischief: for want of a nail, the shoe was lost; for want of a shoe, the horse was lost; for want of a horse, the rider was lost; for want of a rider, the battle was lost; for want of a battle, the war was lost; for want of a war, the cause was lost. The cause could be something of great importance—life, liberty, the pursuit of happiness—lost for *want of a nail.*

Group member roles that reduce group success are:[33]

- *Ego tripper.* This individual interrupts others, launches into long monologues, and is overly dogmatic. The ego tripper constantly demands attention and tries to manipulate the group to satisfy a need to feel important.

- *Negative artist.* This person rejects all ideas suggested by others, takes a negative attitude on issues, argues unnecessarily, and refuses to cooperate. The negative artist is pessimistic about everything and dampens group enthusiasm.

- *Above-it-all person.* This member withdraws from the group and its activities by being aloof, indifferent, and excessively formal, and by daydreaming, doodling, whispering to others, wandering from the subject, or talking about personal experiences when they are unrelated to the group discussion. The above-it-all person has a "don't care" attitude that detracts from group progress.

■ *Aggressor.* This person attacks and blames others, shows anger or irritation against the group or individuals, and deflates the importance or position of the group and the members in it.

■ *Jokester.* This person is present for fun, not work. The jokester fools around most of the time and will distract the group from its business just to get a laugh.

■ *Avoider.* This person does anything to avoid controversy or confrontation. The avoider is dedicated to personal security and self-preservation, and is unwilling to take a stand or make a decision.

As a practical measure, consider your own work group or organization, and ask, Who is playing positive versus negative group member roles? Who is providing encouragement, harmony, new ideas? Take the time to let members know how important they are to the group's success, and how appreciated they are for their efforts. Be specific and be personal if you want to reinforce these helpful behaviors. Above all, be sure that your own actions are positive and constructive. For example, where a negative artist may complain about the wind, the effective leader adjusts the sails. This positive example is instructive and helpful for all.

Designing Teams for Success

When a group approach is appropriate, the questionnaire in Exercise 16–2 can be used to construct teams for balance and diagnose existing teams for potential strengths and weaknesses. Note that the questionnaire evaluates **problem-solving style,** not ability.

Exercise 16–2
Problem-Solving Styles—Darwin, Einstein, Socrates, and Henry Ford[34]

There are 10 sets of phrases below. Rank each set by assigning a 4 to the phrase that is *most* like your problem-solving style, a 3 to the one *next most* like your style, a 2 to the one *next most* like your style, and a 1 to the phrase that is *least* like your problem-solving style. Be sure to assign a different number to each phrase in the set. There can be no ties.

Example: __2__ Experiential   __1__ Reflective   __3__ Theoretical   __4__ Active

E	R	T	A
_____ Following instincts	_____ Weighing evidence	_____ Developing thoughts	_____ Accomplishing goals
_____ Relying on feelings	_____ Considering facts	_____ Considering potentialities	_____ Trying things out
_____ Being perceptive	_____ Measuring effects	_____ Thinking things through	_____ Taking action
_____ Emotional involvement	_____ Impartial investigation	_____ Rational analysis	_____ Practical use
_____ Being aware	_____ Questioning details	_____ Using reason	_____ Performing deeds
_____ Letting intuition guide	_____ Recording information	_____ Summarizing truths	_____ Applying solutions
_____ Present-oriented	_____ Evaluation-oriented	_____ Future-oriented	_____ Achievement-oriented
_____ Open to experience	_____ Thorough observation	_____ Conceiving ideas	_____ Applying knowledge
_____ Conscious of events	_____ Studying data	_____ Forming theories	_____ Taking risks
_____ Concrete experience	_____ Unbiased inquiry	_____ Abstract thinking	_____ Producing results

Scoring:

When you have completed the questionnaire, find the total score for each column. Record that number in the appropriate space below:

_____	_____	_____	_____
Total for E column	Total for R column	Total for T column	Total for A column

Record your totals for E, R, T, and A on the appropriate axes in Figure 16–1, and connect the scores with straight lines to make a picture of your problem-solving style. The longest line of your four-sided figure indicates your preferred style—Charles Darwin, Albert Einstein, Socrates, or Henry Ford.

Interpretation and Discussion:

All problem solving involves having experiences (E), reflecting on results (R), building theories (T), and taking action (A). These processes or activities constitute four steps of the problem-solving cycle (see Figure 16–2). The following is a description of this cycle, including the strengths and potential weaknesses of each style—Charles Darwin, Albert Einstein, Socrates, and Henry Ford.

**Figure 16–1
A Picture of Your Problem-
Solving Style**

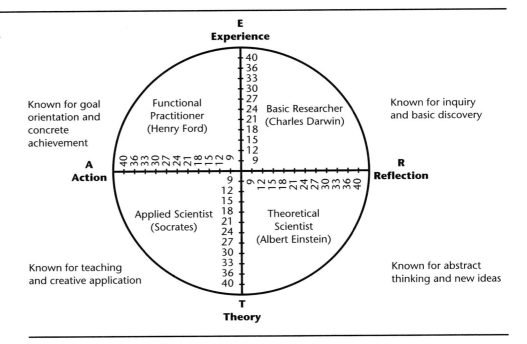

**Figure 16–2
The Problem-Solving Cycle**

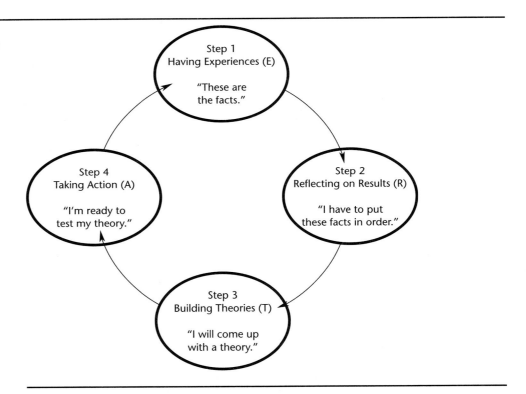

Having experiences (step 1) is followed by reflecting on results (step 2). If the longest line of your four-sided figure is between E and R (see Figure 16–3), your preferred style of problem solving is like that of Charles Darwin (1809–1882), author of *On the Origin of Species by Means of Natural Selection* and *The Descent of Man and Selection in Relation to Sex.* About himself, Darwin wrote, "My mind seems to have become a kind of machine for grinding general laws out of large collections of facts."[35]

As a Darwin, your strengths are observing, recording facts, and identifying alternatives. Gathering data is enjoyable to you. By style, you are a basic researcher and you love the discovery process. Darwins are known in every field—social science, natural science, the

**Figure 16–3
The Charles Darwin
Problem-Solving Style**

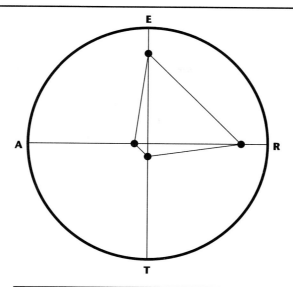

arts, business, and the professions—for their thorough data collection and objective analysis. Carried to an extreme, however, the Darwin style of problem solving can lead to paralysis as each new fact becomes even more interesting than the last, resulting in indecision. It is important to look before leaping, but it is possible to look so long that one never leaps. Consider the case of Darwin himself, who had developed his theories of human evolution years before another scientist, Alfred Russell Wallace, came to similar conclusions and would have received credit for these theories had not Darwin at last published.

After the data are gathered, theory building takes place (step 3). At this stage, assumptions are developed and ideas are formulated. One moves from the world of experience into the world of theory, while remaining in the mode of reflecting rather than acting. If the longest line of your figure is between R and T (see Figure 16–4), your preferred style of problem solving is that of the theoretical scientist—the Albert Einstein style. Abstract conceptualization and blue-sky thinking are your forte. In his description of the world, Einstein wrote, "Physical concepts are free creations of the human mind, and are not, however it may seem, uniquely determined by the external world." The Einstein style of problem solving is like that of the typical philosopher. Carried to an extreme, however, it can result in castles in the air with little practical value. This is the style of the husband whose wife says, "That's good, Albert, but when are you going to *do* something?"

**Figure 16–4
The Albert Einstein
Problem-Solving Style**

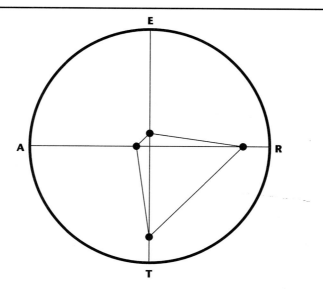

After theories have been developed, they must be tested (step 4). If your longest line is between T and A (see Figure 16–5), your preferred style is that of the applied scientist. Your strength is not in collecting and analyzing data, but in translating ideas so that they can be put into action. As such, yours is the style of the teacher Socrates (470–399 B.C.):

We know Socrates as one of the greatest teachers in history, perhaps the greatest of the great men produced by Athens. His name commands admiration, honor, and reverence. Men and women were his objective; to them he had a mission. He wandered through the streets and down to the marketplace, or often he would go to the public gymnasium. Then he started business—the business of teaching. Socrates was the founder of moral philosophy. He was scoffed at for taking his examples from common life, but he did so to lead plain people to goodness, truth, and beauty.[36]

Figure 16–5
The Socrates Problem-Solving Style

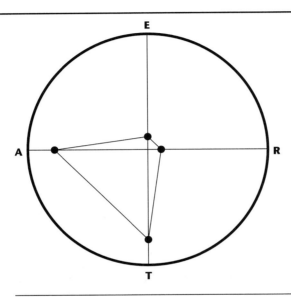

A more modern example of the Socrates problem-solving style is Thomas Alva Edison: "The only invention I can really claim as absolutely original is the phonograph," explained Edison. "I'm an awfully good sponge. I absorb ideas from every source I can and then I put them to practical use. Then I improve them until they become of some value. The ideas that I use are mostly the ideas of other people who don't develop them themselves."

Comfortable with ideas, but wanting to apply them, the applied scientist moves from a reflective to an active orientation. This person enjoys coordinating and problem-solving activities. When taken to the extreme, the Socrates style of problem solving may result in impressive, but incomplete, performance because these individuals dislike details. The Socrates-type person may give a beautiful speech, but fail to do thorough research.

Taking action automatically results in new experiences (step 1), so the problem-solving cycle never completely ends. In work, and in life, when one problem is solved, another arises. If your longest line is between A and E (see Figure 16–6), your style of problem solving is like that of Henry Ford (1863–1947), whose strength was achieving results. Upton Sinclair described Henry Ford, the functional practitioner, as follows:

Henry Ford was now fifty-five; slender, gray-haired, with sensitive features and a quick, nervous manner. His long, thin hands were never still, but were always playing with something. He was a kind man, unassuming, not changed by his great success, the world's first billionaire. Having had less than a grammar-school education, his speech was full of the peculiarities of the plain folk of the Middle West. He had never learned to deal with theories, and when confronted with one, he would scuttle back to the facts like a rabbit to its hole. What Ford knew he had learned by experience, and if he learned more, it would be in the same manner.[37]

Figure 16–6
The Henry Ford Problem-Solving Style

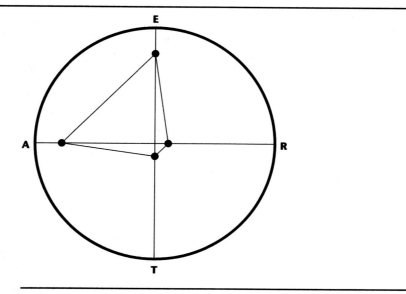

If the functional practitioner knows what needs to be done, the goal will usually be accomplished. This is a person of deeds and action, more than ideas and contemplation. But here, as with the other problem-solving styles, a strength may become a liability when carried to the extreme. If the functional practitioner does not have sufficient facts, or fails to work from a well-conceived plan, there may be tremendous accomplishment—of the wrong thing.

The versatile style of problem solving is represented by Figure 16–7. This individual is equally comfortable with each step of the problem-solving cycle—having experiences, reflecting on results, building theories, and taking action. As such, this person does not have structural strengths or weaknesses resulting from style preference.

Figure 16–7
A Versatile Style of Problem Solving

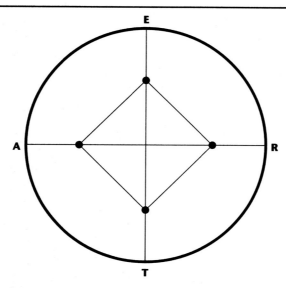

There are several important points to remember concerning styles of problem solving:

1. All problem solving involves four steps—having experiences, reflecting on results, building theories, taking action—and each step must be performed well for overall effectiveness. For example, an independent businessperson with a Socrates style must take extra care to consider details as well as concepts, and should remember to get the facts before making decisions, even if this does not come naturally.

2. It is possible to have preference for more than one style of problem solving. For example, a person may be equally comfortable as a Henry Ford and a Socrates. Such a person relates to the world in both an experiential and a theoretical sense. In either case, this person shows a bias for action.

3. When people with different styles of problem solving live or work together, **tolerance of differences** is required. A Henry Ford manager must be patient with the seeming lack of effort put forth by an Einstein employee, and a Socrates wife must try to understand her Darwin husband's preference for having experiences and reflecting on results over forming ideas and applying knowledge. Appreciation of the characteristics and needs of each type of person can go a long way toward improving relationships and increasing performance.

4. Most people have difficulty changing their styles of problem solving. This can be seen in school when a Henry Ford student fails or drops out. Often the cause is the nature of the curriculum and the style of instruction versus the ability of the student. The functional practitioner, who wants to apply knowledge and accomplish tangible results, may have difficulty relating to book reading and theoretical discussion.

An organization or group needs all four styles of problem solving. A balance of basic research, theoretical science, applied science, and functional practice helps maximize individual as well as group performance. Consider the following story:

Fred was a successful research chemist when he suffered a heart attack. During his stay in the hospital, his work was performed by younger employees. Like many large organizations, Fred's company was rich in talent, and others were qualified to do his job.

When Fred recovered and returned to work, he retained his title, his office was the same, and his income was unchanged. However, he had lost a significant part of his job—his duties were now make-work assignments, while important responsibilities and decision making were handled by others. Whereas Fred had been physically ill before, he now became depressed, and his overall health began to deteriorate. Fred had been placed on the shelf, and he knew it.

At that time, Fred's company began research and development on a new product, and the "Problem-Solving Styles" questionnaire was used to create a balanced team. On the team was a theoretical scientist, who could write formulas from wall to wall, but whom few could understand. This was the Einstein. Also on the team was an applied scientist, who could understand the Einstein's ideas and who knew how to bridge the gap between thinking and doing. The team had a Socrates. The team also had a Henry Ford, who was known for his practical nature. He was a goal-oriented person with the ability to produce results. What was missing on the new product team was a Charles Darwin, a basic scientist, who would be sure that all the facts were gathered and all the data were considered. Fred was chosen to be the team's Darwin.

Within a year, the team developed one of the company's most successful products. A year after that, Fred's wife phoned him at work. By accident, she reached his boss. She said: "Oh, Mr. Johnson, I have been wanting to talk to you for so long. I have wanted to thank you . . . for giving my Fred back to me."[38]

Fred's story shows how the needs of the individual and the needs of the organization are interwoven and how both can be met by creating a balanced team incorporating all four styles of problem solving.

Leader as Team Builder

What do the U.S. Supreme Court, the University of Kentucky basketball team, a first-rate business project group, and the Twelve Apostles have in common? Each is a team, has work to do, must work together, has a variety of members, faces ambiguous situations, must choose a path, must overcome obstacles, needs high performance, and needs leadership.[39]

Teamwork is essential for group success. The testimony of Michael Jordan, a superb individual contributor, is instructive for people in all fields of work: "One thing I believe to the fullest is that if you think and behave as a team, the individual accolades will take care of themselves. Talent wins games, but teamwork and intelligence win championships."[40]

Leaders in every endeavor know the power of the team concept for achieving results. Effective leaders value teamwork as a virtue, and they demonstrate this by their own efforts as team builders and champions of the group.

The Importance of Hiring and Developing Winners

The task of the leader is to recruit and develop team members who can perform successfully in the type of sport and level of league they are in. Winning performance is A and B levels, not C, D, or F, for every team member, as well as for the leader her- or himself.

This simple principle is employed by every successful athletic coach, yet it is too often overlooked by the leader in the workplace. The result is inadequate performance—loss of product, people, and profit—and, inevitably, replacement of the leader.

What can the leader do? The answer is to commit to excellence and model this ideal personally. The leader must follow this dictum: Hire the best and develop the rest. The successful leader hires the best talent available (A and B players), then trains and develops all other personnel to perform at A and B levels.

What happens to individuals who cannot or will not perform at A and B levels? For the sake of customers and co-workers and ultimately themselves, they are reassigned. The caring leader considers the interests of all, knowing effective performance is required and the individual may be better suited for another sport or league. As difficult or unpleasant as the task may be, action must be taken.[41]

How to Create a High-Performance Team

Effective leaders understand that all the individual competence in the world will not result in a high-performance team. An essential component of success is the leader's ability to take a group of people and develop them into a team, including creating a spirit of cooperation and a one-team attitude. The best leaders develop successful teams by following 11 time-tested practices:

- Show enthusiasm for the work of the group. The leader's emotion ignites and energizes the team.
- Make timely decisions based on agreed upon goals. In this way, leaders show decisiveness and consistency.
- Promote open-mindedness, innovation, and creativity by personal example and a conducive work climate.
- Admit mistakes and uncertainties, modeling honesty as a virtue.
- Be flexible in using a variety of tactics and strategies to achieve success.
- Have persistence and lasting power, never giving up on hope or effort.
- Give credit to others for the team's accomplishments, meeting people's needs for appreciation and recognition.

■ Keep people informed about progress and problems, celebrating victories and fine-tuning efforts.

■ Keep promises and follow through on commitments, earning the trust and confidence of others.

■ Train for success; master fundamentals and practice for perfection.

■ Put others first and self last, embodying the spirit of the caring leader.[42]

Research shows why some teams are successful and others are not. One study evaluated a number of high-performance teams, including national champion sports teams, heart transplant surgical teams, the crew of the USS *Kitty Hawk,* and others, to determine the characteristics that make them successful. Eight characteristics were always present:

1. A clear, elevating goal.
2. A results-driven structure.
3. Competent team members.
4. Unified commitment.
5. A collaborative climate.
6. Standards of excellence.
7. External support and recognition.
8. Principled leadership.

When any one feature is lost, team performance declines. The most frequent cause of team failure is letting personal or political agendas take precedence over clear and elevating team goals.[43]

Stages in the Life of a Group

Regardless of size or type, a group typically goes through predictable stages over the course of time. Figure 16–8 is an illustration of four stages in the life of a group, as described by Glenn Parker and Roy Lacoursiere.[44] By understanding these stages, including major issues, typical member behavior, and effective leadership actions at each stage, the leader can help a group move quickly to the high-morale–high-performance status of an effective team.

Stage I—**Forming.** In the start-up stage, the group is formed, but its purpose and members' expectations are unclear. This stage incorporates all the discomfort and apprehension found in any new social situation. It is characterized by caution and tentative steps to test the water. Individuals try to determine acceptable behavior and the nature of the group's task, as well as how to deal with each other to get work done. Interactions are superficial and tend to be directed toward the formal leader. Skills and knowledge as a team are undeveloped. See Table 16–1.

Stage II—**Storming.** The initial stage of forming is followed by a period of storming. In this stage, individuals react to what has to be done, question authority, and feel increasingly comfortable being themselves. This stage can be characterized by conflict and resistance to the group's task and structure, even as productivity begins to increase as skills and knowledge develop. Group members express concerns and frustrations, and feel fairly free to exchange ideas. Members learn to deal with differences to work together to meet the group's goals. A group that doesn't get through this stage successfully is marked by divisiveness and low creativity. See Table 16–2.

Figure 16–8
Stages in the Life of a
Group

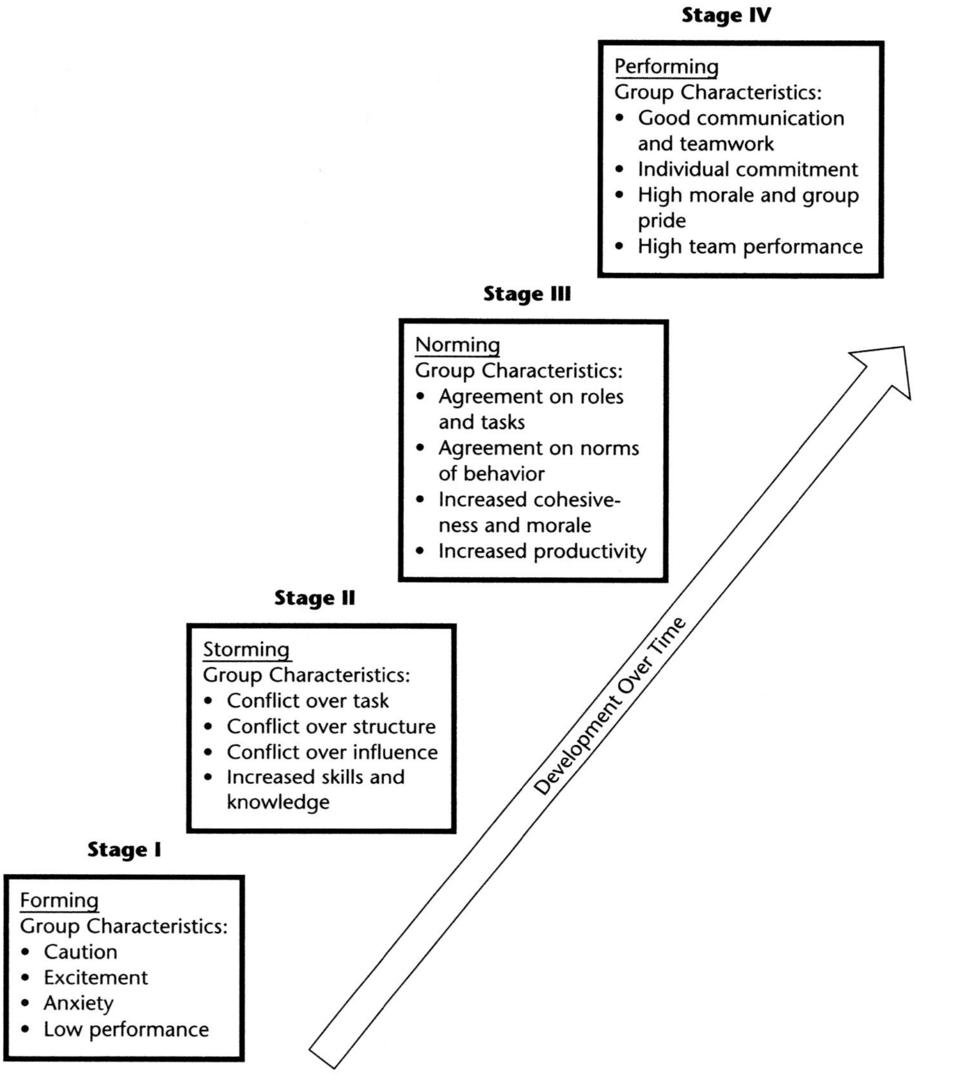

Stage IV

Performing
Group Characteristics:
• Good communication
  and teamwork
• Individual commitment
• High morale and group
  pride
• High team performance

Stage III

Norming
Group Characteristics:
• Agreement on roles
  and tasks
• Agreement on norms
  of behavior
• Increased cohesive-
  ness and morale
• Increased productivity

Stage II

Storming
Group Characteristics:
• Conflict over task
• Conflict over structure
• Conflict over influence
• Increased skills and
  knowledge

Stage I

Forming
Group Characteristics:
• Caution
• Excitement
• Anxiety
• Low performance

Development Over Time

Table 16–1
Forming

Major Issue Is Development of Trust, Including Answers to These Questions:
1. What is going to happen?
2. Who is who in the group?
3. Where do I fit in the group?
4. How will I be treated?

Member Behavior Is Characterized by
1. Anxiety.
2. Search for structure.
3. Silence.
4. Caution with leader and other group members.

Leaders Can Reduce Uncertainty by
1. Explaining purpose and goals.
2. Providing time for questions.
3. Allowing time for members to get to know each other.
4. Modeling expected behaviors.

Table 16–2 Storming	**Major Issue Is Increased Conflict from**
	1. Openly dealing with problems.
	2. Increasing group interaction.
	3. Power struggles for influence.
	4. Increasing independence from leader.
	Member Behavior Is Characterized by
	1. Confrontation with the leader.
	2. Polarization of team members.
	3. Testing of group tolerance.
	4. Fight-or-flight behavior.
	Leaders Can Reduce Conflict by
	1. Hearing all points of view.
	2. Acknowledging conflict as opportunity for improvement.
	3. Adhering to core values, such as truth, trust, and respect.
	4. Staying focused on the goal.

Stage III—**Norming.** The stage of storming is usually followed by a third stage in the life of a group, a period of norming. In this stage, norms of behavior are developed that are considered necessary for the group to accomplish its task. These norms can be explicit or implicit. In any case, a greater degree of order begins to prevail and a sense of group cohesion develops. Members now identify with the group and develop customary ways for resolving conflict, making decisions, and completing assignments. In this stage, members typically enjoy meetings and freely exchange information. Productivity continues to increase as group skills and knowledge further develop. See Table 16–3.

Table 16–3 Norming	**Major Issue Is Development of Norms for**
	1. Team member behavior.
	2. Decision-making processes.
	3. Resolving differences.
	4. Leadership behavior.
	Member Behavior Is Characterized by Shift from
	1. Power struggle to affiliation.
	2. Confusion to clarity.
	3. Personal advantage to group success.
	4. Detachment to involvement.
	Leaders Can Encourage Norm Development by
	1. Modeling listening skills.
	2. Fostering an atmosphere of trust.
	3. Teaching and facilitating consensus.
	4. Providing team-centered learning.

Stage IV—**Performing.** Stage three is usually followed by a fourth stage, performing. This is the payoff stage in the life of a group. People are able to focus their energies on the task, having worked through issues of membership, purpose, structure, and roles. The group is now focused on solving problems and completing tasks. Members take initiative, and their efforts emphasize results. As the group achieves significant milestones, morale goes up and people have positive feelings about each other and the accomplishments of the group. The group is no longer dependent solely on the leader for direction and support; instead, each member takes on leadership roles as necessary. At this stage, the group shows the characteristics of an effective team. See Table 16–4.

Table 16–4
Performing

Major Issue Is Group Performance, Including
1. Using a wide range of task and process behaviors.
2. Monitoring and taking pride in group accomplishments.
3. Focusing on goals as well as interpersonal needs.
4. Maintaining the values and norms of the group.

Member Behavior Is Characterized by
1. Interpersonal trust and mutual respect.
2. Active resolution of conflict.
3. Active participation.
4. Personal commitment to the success of the group.

Leaders Can Help the Group Succeed by
1. Being prepared for temporary setbacks.
2. Focusing on task accomplishments *and* interpersonal support.
3. Providing feedback on the work of the group.
4. Promoting and representing the group.

It is helpful to view each of the stages in the life of a group from two points of view. The first is *interpersonal relationships.* The group moves through predictable stages of testing and dependency (forming), tension and conflict (storming), building cohesion (norming), and finally, establishing functional role relationships (performing). Each stage focuses on problems inherent in developing relationships among group members.

At the same time, the group is struggling with *accomplishing tasks.* The initial stage focuses on task definition and the exchange of information (forming). This is followed by discussion and conflict over the task (storming). Next comes a period of sharing interpretations and perspectives (norming). Finally, a stage of effective group performance is reached (performing).[45]

Avoiding Groupthink

As a group settles on norms of behavior in stage III and into a mode of performance in stage IV, there is a risk of falling into a pattern of groupthink. This is a well-documented pitfall in group dynamics identified by psychologist Irving Janis in *Victims of Groupthink.* Janis defined groupthink as "a mode of thinking that people engage in when they are deeply involved in a cohesive group, and when the members' striving for unanimity overrides their motivation to realistically appraise alternative courses of action." Groupthink is an important concept for a leader to understand.[46]

When people meet in groups, they are often under strong pressure to conform to the majority view. When they don't conform, they risk being isolated or cast aside. In such situations, people may make errors in judgment and conduct based on a desire to preserve group harmony and to continue to be accepted by the group and its leader.

Janis describes additional factors that, when combined with cohesiveness, can foster groupthink. These factors are a highly insulated group with restricted access to external information, and a stressful decision-making context, such as that brought on by budgetary crises, external pressure, or a history of recent setbacks. As a result of the trilogy of group cohesiveness, isolation, and stress, a group can arrive at decisions that are unsuccessful and possibly even catastrophic.[47]

Janis describes eight symptoms that can give a group early warning that groupthink may be present. The following is a description of these symptoms with cases in history to illustrate their effects:[48]

1. Illusion of invulnerability. A feeling of power and authority is important to any decision-making group. It gives members confidence that they will be able to carry through on any decisions reached. However, if they come to believe that every decision they reach will automatically be successful, then they become prey to an illusion of invulnerability. Janis showed that American military leaders had this illusion in choosing not to fortify Pearl Harbor more heavily prior to the disastrous attack by the Japanese that led to U.S. entry into World War II.

2. Belief in the inherent morality of the group. People want to believe in the rightness of their actions. In the extreme, this can lead to exhortations that "God is on our side." Such claims fulfill an important function—they relieve responsibility for justifying decisions according to rational procedures. People do this as a way to protect self-esteem.

3. Rationalization. When a final decision is reached, it is normal to downplay the drawbacks of the chosen course. The problem in a group arises when legitimate objections exist, but they are overshadowed by the perceived negative reaction to anyone who voices those objections. Key engineers in the NASA *Challenger* decision ultimately withdrew their objections to the ill-fated launch, not because of any correction in the admittedly problematic O-rings, but rather, because they rationalized the risk of catastrophic launch failure as only "possible," while the risk of censure and ostracism for continuing to speak out against the launch became a virtual certainty.

4. Stereotypes of out-groups. President Truman and his advisors fell victim to the temptation to falsely characterize enemy groups in 1950 with the decision to cross the 38th parallel, a line drawn by the Chinese Communists as a "line in the sand" between North and South Korea. The decision was made despite repeated warnings from Communist China that to do so would be viewed as a declaration of war by the United States on China. How could Truman and his advisors have so seriously misinterpreted the Chinese warnings? The decision was based largely on a false stereotype of the Chinese Communists as being weak and dominated by Russia, who, it was believed, did not want war. The stereotype proved false, and the Korean "police action" became a resounding failure as the Chinese attacked with massive force.

5. Self-censorship. As one of the principles on which our country was founded, the ability to express oneself without censorship has always been highly valued. It has also been considered a healthy safeguard against group coercion in our work lives. But the fact is, the most common form of censorship is the one we commit on ourselves under the guise of group loyalty, team spirit, or adherence to company policy.

The decision by President Kennedy and his advisors to send a band of Cuban exiles into the Bay of Pigs has been ranked as the greatest foreign policy mistake of the Kennedy administration. The day after the Bay of Pigs fiasco, JFK said, "How could I have been so stupid?" The answer is that Kennedy and his advisors suppressed their doubts, censoring themselves to make the operative belief seem like the truth.

6. Direct pressure. Pressure on group members can surface in many forms. The net effect is the same: Group members are encouraged to keep dissident views to themselves. As one example, Janis reported that during Watergate, "Nixon time and again let everyone in the group know which policy he favored, and he did not encourage open inquiry." Another example involves the *Challenger* disaster. Several engineers made the recommendation to postpone the *Challenger* launch. According to the Rogers Commission report, certain group members responded with direct pressure on those engineers to alter their views, with statements such as "I'm appalled that they could arrive at the recommendation" and "At that rate, it could be spring before the shuttle would fly."

7. Mindguards. A bodyguard is someone charged with the protection of another person's physical well-being. In groupthink, a corollary entity may surface to protect the group from disturbing thoughts and ideas—a mindguard. Interestingly, such mindguards typically perform their function not within the group itself, but far from the confines of group discussion. Data, facts, and opinions that might bear directly on the group are deliberately kept out of the group's purview. Generally, this is done with a variety of justifiable intentions—time is running short, a regular member will summarize for the group, and not pertinent and perhaps saddest of all, the group has already made up its mind.

8. Illusion of unanimity. Finally, the rationalizations, psychological pressures, and mindguards have their effect—the group coalesces around a decision. Drawbacks are downplayed, and the invulnerability and morality of the final course are reinforced. Doubting group members may even feel that they have adequately put their own fears to rest. More likely, it is simply the sense of relief that the struggle has come to an end. An illusion of unanimity sets in.

In contrast to the destructive forces of groupthink are a number of techniques that a leader can employ to help ensure a rational consideration of all available courses of action:

1. The leader should assign the role of critical evaluator to each member, encouraging the group to give open airing of ideas, including objections and doubts. This practice should be reinforced by the leader's acceptance of criticism of his or her own judgments.

2. When charging a group with a task, the leader should adopt an impartial stance instead of stating personal opinions and preferences. This approach will encourage open discussion and impartial probing of a wide range of policy and problem-solving alternatives.

3. The leader should set up outside evaluators to work on the same policy question. This tactic can prevent the group from being insulated from important information and suggestions.

4. When the agenda calls for evaluation of decision or policy alternatives, at least one member should play devil's advocate, functioning as a lawyer in challenging the testimony of those who advocate for a position.

5. After reaching a preliminary consensus about what seems to be the best policy or decision, the group should hold a "second chance" meeting, at which every member expresses as clearly as possible all residual doubts and rethinks the entire issue, before making a final decision.[49]

Team Building Interventions and Techniques

There are many approaches to team building. The most common is for members of a group to develop and grow together over the normal course of time as the team responds to challenges and successfully performs its natural functions. Consider this example:

From time to time, the tribe gathered in a circle. They just talked and talked and talked, apparently to no purpose. They made no decisions. And everybody could participate. There may have been wise men or wise women who were listened to a bit more—the older ones—but everybody could talk. The meeting went on, until it finally seemed to stop for no reason at all and the group dispersed. Yet after that, everybody seemed to know what to do because they understood each other so well. Then they could get together in smaller groups and do something or decide things.[50]

Team building can be enhanced by experiential strategies and activities. Educational workshops in retreat settings are increasingly popular. This off-site format focuses on topics such as communication, teamwork, characteristics of effective groups, positive versus negative group member roles, and workshop/labs to improve team performance—goal setting, values clarification, problem solving, decision making, and the like.

Some organizations use adventure and challenge experiences that can be quite effective at building relationships, developing group identity, and increasing team pride. These interventions are usually conducted in field settings and involve a range of activities that include "ground" experiences, or low-course initiatives, to build team spirit and skills, and "ropes," or high-course challenges, that build individual confidence and pride. There are many varieties of challenges including rafting, rowing and riding.

One of the best ways to develop and sustain team effectiveness is to periodically meet in a conducive atmosphere, free of interruptions, and discuss important issues. Meaningful questions include:

- *Where have we been?* What forces and events have brought us to this point?

- *Where are we now?* What are our current "prouds" and "sorries"? What are our strengths, weaknesses, opportunities, and threats?

- *What is our purpose or mission?* What is our reason for existence?

- *What should be our goals?* What should we accomplish to fulfill our mission?

- *What are our values?* What principles should guide us in moral dilemmas?

- *Who are our stakeholders?* Who cares about our work and what will it mean to them when we are successful?

- *What should be our strategy?* What initiatives should we have to accomplish our goals and achieve our mission? What strategic, measurable, action-oriented, and timely projects and activities should we undertake?

- *What are the critical factors that define success?* How do we know what great performance looks like?

- *How should we work together to fulfill our potential?* What should we continue doing, start doing, or stop doing? How should we monitor progress? Who should do what by when?

Exercise 16–3 is an easy-to-use and highly effective exercise for team building. It is a variation of Kurt Lewin's famous force field theory for improving team performance. A good approach would be to have individuals complete the exercise alone and then work as a group to develop and improve team effectiveness.

**Exercise 16–3
Team Excellence**[51]

Answer the following questions, first individually, then as a group.

To operate as a team, what do we need?

_____

_____

_____

_____

What should we continue doing?

_____

_____

_____

_____

What should we start doing?

_____

_____

_____

_____

What should we stop doing?

_____

_____

_____

_____

How should we monitor our progress?

_____

_____

_____

_____

Actions to be taken, including *who* should do *what* by *when,* are as follows:

_____

_____

_____

_____

_____

_____

_____

_____

_____

_____

_____

The Role of the Leader in the Team Concept

It is true that good teams can boost productivity and accomplish the seemingly impossible. It is also true that poor teams reduce effectiveness and generally create problems. Is there something that can be done to ensure team success? Research shows that success is enhanced if an organization understands and effectively manages five team processes:[52]

1. Buy-in—how the work of the team is legitimized and goals are set.
2. Accountability—how individual and team performance is managed and rewarded.
3. Learning—how performance is improved and skills developed.
4. Infrastructure—how the work of the team is systemized and resources accessed.
5. Partnering—how people interact and work together to achieve success on the team and across organizational units.

A key factor in all five team processes is **leadership.** Teams perform most successfully when they have a leader who facilitates the work of the group to accomplish buy-in—agreement on direction; accountability—clarity of assignments; learning—the development of members; infrastructure—allocation of resources; and partnering—a supportive work climate. The most effective team leaders are caring individuals who have a passion for the work and a concern for people.[53]

Organizations can empower their people and improve performance through the use of teams, but successful teams require effective leadership. For optimum results, a designated leader should coordinate the group, advocate for the team across the organization, access needed resources and processes, and ensure that results are supported by, and meaningful to, the organization.[54]

Part Five Summary

After reading Part Five, you should know the following key concepts, principles, and terms. Fill in the blanks from memory, or copy the answers listed below.

Leadership author Warren Bennis details advice to leaders based on years of study, including (a) _____, _____, _____, _____, _____, _____, and _____. Research shows nine ways an organization can raise morale, including (b) _____, _____, _____, _____, _____, and _____. A master at building morale and achieving business success was (c) _____, who believed that you can't lead just by the numbers; business must also be enjoyable. Specific leadership actions that build morale include (d) _____, _____, _____, and _____. High morale and high performance result when a person is in a state of (e) _____, versus apathy, anxiety, or boredom. This state comes from the confluence of high challenge and high skill. The best (most rich) jobs are characterized by (f) _____, _____, _____, _____, _____, and _____. The key elements of good relationships are (g) _____, shown by listening in a responsive manner, and (h) _____, shown by expressing oneself honestly and openly. Douglas McGregor's book (i) _____changed the entire concept of organizational life for the second half of the twentieth century. The characteristics of a high-performance work group and the need for positive versus negative group member roles are practical applications of McGregor's ideas. Positive roles include (j) _____, _____, _____, _____, _____, _____, and _____. In the design of teams for success, (k) _____ is important, as is (l) _____. Stages in the life of a group are (m) _____, _____, _____, and _____. There are potential pitfalls to effective group decision making, including (n) _____, _____, _____, _____, and _____.

Organizations can empower their people through the use of teams, but successful teams require effective (o) _____ to coordinate the group, advocate for the team, access needed resources or processes, and ensure that meaningful results are achieved.

Answer Key for Part Five Summary

a. (any seven) **be yourself, figure out what you are good at, hire good people, treat people fairly, focus on key objectives, ask your co-workers how to achieve the objectives, listen well, call the play, get out of the way, cheer them on, count the gains, start right now,** page 148

b. (any six) **introduce a group bonus, allow workers to determine their own work methods, provide technical support services, provide training, reduce the number of hierarchical levels, break production into small work units, assign whole tasks, gain direct feedback from users, increase group interaction,** page 155

c. **Herb Kelleher,** page 155

d. (any four) **be predictable, be understanding, be enthusiastic, set the example, show support, get out of the office, keep promises, praise generously, hold your fire, always be fair,** page 156

e. **flow,** page 157

f. **variety and challenge, opportunity for decision making, feedback and learning, mutual support and respect, wholeness and meaning, room to grow,** page 158

g. **respect,** page 160

h. **trust,** page 160

i. *The Human Side of Enterprise,* page 163

j. **encourager, clarifier, harmonizer, idea generator, ignition key, standard setter, detail specialist,** page 169

k. **problem-solving style,** page 170

l. **tolerance of differences,** page 176

m. **forming, storming, norming, performing,** pages 178–80

n. (any five) **illusion of invulnerability, belief in the inherent morality of the group, rationalization, stereotypes of out-groups, self-censorship, direct pressure, mindguards, illusion of unanimity,** pages 181–83

o. **leadership,** page 187

Reflection Points—personal thoughts on effective leadership, human relations, and the team concept

Complete the following questions and activities to personalize the content of Part Five. Space is provided for writing your thoughts.

■ How do you rate on principles of effective leadership? What are your strengths? What areas do you need to improve?

_____

_____

■ What is your level of morale? What practical steps can the leader take to keep morale high and performance up in a work group or an organization?

_____

_____

■ Have you ever been a member of a high-performance work group? Describe conditions.

_____

_____

■ Discuss positive and negative group member roles. Which positive roles do you usually play when you perform at your best? Which negative roles do you need to eliminate?

_____

_____

■ What is your style of problem solving—Charles Darwin, Albert Einstein, Socrates, or Henry Ford? Does your career or current job allow you to capitalize on the strengths of your style—inquiry and discovery, abstract thinking, teaching and advising, execution of results?

_____

_____

■ What should a leader do to build a top-performing team? What policies and practices have worked for you? What have you seen work for others?

_____

_____

■ Use the "Team Excellence" exercise to develop and sustain team effectiveness. Discuss results.

_____

_____

Action Assignment

As a bridge between learning and doing, complete the following action assignment.

1. What is the most important idea you have learned in Part Five?

2. How can you apply what you have learned? What will you do, with whom, where, when, and, most important, why?

Part 6 Understanding People

17. **Human Behavior**
18. **The Art of Persuasion**
19. **The Diversity Challenge**

A FRIEND ASKED MICHELANGELO: "How's the work going at the Sistine Chapel?"

Michelangelo answered:

"About the same. You know, I really never should have started this thing. Four years, on and off, I've been at it. What I really wanted to do was a tomb for Julius II. But they made a decision and I'm stuck with it. The worst thing is that I had to start at the entrance of the chapel first, which I thought was a stupid idea. But they wanted to keep the chapel open as long as possible while I was working."

His friend inquired: "What's the difference?"

Michelangelo replied:

"What's the difference? Here I am trying to do a ceiling mural on the creation of man, right? But I have to start with the end of the whole scheme, and then finish with the beginning. Besides, I've never painted a ceiling before, and I'm not very experienced at murals either."

The friend sympathized: "Boy, that's tough."

Michelangelo went on:

"And on top of that, the scaffolding material I have to use is dangerous. The whole thing shakes and wiggles every time I climb up there. One day it's boiling hot, and the next day it's freezing. It's dark most of the time. Working on my back, I swallow as much paint as I put on the ceiling. I can't get any decent help. The long climb up and down the ladders will kill me yet. And to top everything, they are going to let the public in and show the thing off before it's even finished. It won't be finished for another year at least. And that's another thing, they are always nagging me to finish. And when I'm finished, what then? I've got no security. And if they don't like it, I may be out of work permanently."

The friend responded: "Gee, Michelangelo, that's tough. With no job security, such poor working conditions, irritating company policies, and inadequate subordinates, you must really be dissatisfied with your job. Are you ready to quit?"

Michelangelo replied:

"What? Quit? Are you crazy? It's a fascinating challenge. And I'm learning more and more every day about murals and ceilings. I've been experimenting and changing my style for these last few years, and I'm starting to get a lot of recognition from some very important people. You can see for yourself that it's going to be one of the finest achievements of all time. I'm the only one responsible for the design, and I'm making all of the basic decisions. It may bring me other opportunities to do even more difficult work.

"Quit? Never. This is a terrific job."[1]

Learning Points

In Part Five, you will discover the answers to these questions:
- Why do people do what they do? What does it take to motivate you?
- Do you have emotional intelligence? What are your strengths and weaknesses in the art of persuasion?
- Why is diversity an important subject for leadership effectiveness? What can the leader do to tap the benefits of diversity and avoid the pitfalls of prejudice?

Human Behavior

"I wonder why she acts that way." "People! I'll never understand them." "We've met the enemy, and they are us." If you have ever had such thoughts as these, this chapter will be of interest to you. Understanding why people do what they do is important for employee morale and job performance. When the work is done, this understanding is important in dealing with family and friends.

Business leader Lee Iacocca prescribes a formula for success: "Effective leaders focus on three "p"s—**people, products,** and **profit**—in that order." Mark McCormack, author of *What They Don't Teach You at Harvard Business School,* explains the importance of understanding people:

Whether it is a matter of closing a deal or asking for a raise, of motivating a sales force or negotiating one to one, of buying a new company or turning around an old one, business situations almost always come down to people situations. Those individuals with a finely tuned people sense, and an awareness of how to apply it, invariably take the edge.[2]

Psychological Forces

Physical and emotional needs are important determinants of human behavior, helping explain why people work, why they have certain personal goals, and what they want in their relationships with others. Psychologist Abraham Maslow divides human needs into five categories progressing from basic needs for **survival** and **security,** to social needs for **belonging** and **respect,** to the complex need for **fulfillment.**[3]

1. *Survival.* The needs that are taken as the starting point for motivation theory are the physiological, or basic body tissue, needs. Taking a breath of air and acting in self-defense are normal expressions of such needs. Survival needs that motivate behavior include:

Health. Anyone who has ever been sick or felt pain knows the overwhelming desire to get well and feel better.

Nutrition. When you are hungry, you seek food, and it is natural for this need to influence your actions.

Exercise. Who has not felt the normal urge to stretch limbs, tense muscles, and breathe deeply?

Rest. Can you recall a time when the primary thing you wanted to do was to sleep? You needed rest, and your behavior was influenced by this need.

Shelter. Without protection from climate and weather, people become uncomfortable and may even die; the need for shelter can be a powerful motivator.

Survival needs are basic, strong, and natural forces within the person. Psychologist Viktor Frankl tells of his experiences in a Nazi concentration camp during World War II:

What did the prisoner dream about most frequently? Of bread, cake, cigarettes, and nice warm baths. During waking hours prisoners were concerned, above all else, with what they would get for their evening meal and how much would be available. When they received food, they were torn between whether they should consume all of it immediately, or save a part of it for that later time when their stomachs would hurt from hunger. In short, whether awake or asleep, their greatest concern was for the most basic physical needs—food and physical comfort.[4]

2. *Security.* Once survival needs are satisfied, security needs become important. Freedom from threat and protection from loss are major security goals, helping explain our interest in savings accounts, medical insurance, seniority rights, and burglar alarms. All ages and types of people experience the need for security. Both the child who is afraid of the dark and the worker who fears unemployment feel the need for security, and the drive to satisfy this need influences their actions.

Security needs can motivate the behavior of societies as well as individuals. In the United States during the 1950s, fallout shelters were common, and an elaborate civil defense program was in place because of fear of nuclear attack. Justifiably or not, people believed that the danger of nuclear war decreased during the 1970s, 80s, and 90s. Consequently, fallout shelters lapsed into ill repair and often went unstocked, and civil defense readiness was reduced during that period.

Typically, when people feel they have fair and reasonable protection, such as when they have an early warning system in the case of national security or a financial nest egg in the case of material security, they can tolerate quite a bit of uncertainty. However, if conditions are dangerous or events appear out of control, the need for security can become a powerful motivator.

3. *Belonging.* When survival and security needs are satisfied, the need for belonging emerges. Each person strives to secure a place as an accepted member in a social milieu. This is true for people in all cultures, whether aggressive or peaceful, primitive or advanced. Every individual makes a distinct effort to belong to some aspired social group. If you have ever felt a need for love or a need to express love, you have experienced a natural need for belonging, and this has influenced your behavior.[5]

The need for belonging is a normal human need. People are psychologically built so that they require this interaction. Studies of children in institutions in which they do not receive affection show that they do not develop normally, in spite of the fact that all their physical needs are met.[6] The following shows the life-and-death importance of the need for love:

The evidence is now compelling that emotionally deprived animals, including humans, are less resistant to stress effects and to disease than emotionally satisfied animals, that they have higher morbidity and mortality rates, and that they tend to be less developed physically and behaviorally.

Death is but an extreme consequence of the general physical and psychological decline that affects children completely starved of emotional interchange. They die from deprivation of love, just as if they had been deprived of food and died from hunger—for what they indeed die from is an unsatisfied hunger for love.

In the late 1920's, several hospital pediatricians began to introduce a regular regimen of "mothering" in their wards. Dr. J. Brennemann, who for a time had attended an old-fashioned foundling home where the mortality rate was nearer 100 percent than 50 percent, established the rule in his hospital that every baby should be picked up, carried around, and "mothered" several times a day. At Bellevue Hospital in New York, following the institution of "mothering" on the pediatric wards, the mortality rate for infants fell from 55 percent to less than 10 percent.

In short, it was discovered that infants need something more than the satisfaction of basic, physical needs if they are to make any progress—that is, to survive and grow and develop in physical and mental health. That something came to be recognized as what was later called "Tender Loving Care."[7]

4. *Respect.* Once survival, security, and belonging needs are satisfied, people are motivated by the need for respect—the need to be considered favorably by self and others. The pursuit of fame, regardless of the field—business, government, the arts—can be explained only by the powerful need for respect. It is natural to want the recognition and honor of others. When this need is not satisfied, an individual feels inferior, weak, and discouraged. William James, American philosopher and founder of psychology as a discipline, writes:

We are not only gregarious animals, liking to be in sight of our fellows, but we have an innate propensity to get ourselves noticed, and noticed favorably, by our kind. No more fiendish punishment could be devised, were such a thing physically possible, than that one should be turned loose in society and remain absolutely unnoticed by all the members thereof.[8]

The need for recognition is a major determinant of behavior from youth through adulthood:

A youngster may excel in school to win the praise of parents.

A teenager may diet or exercise to be considered attractive.

A young adult may choose a certain career or mate to achieve the respect of others.

An older adult may build a business or become a community leader to be considered successful.

5. *Fulfillment.* After physical and social needs are satisfied, people are motivated by the need for fulfillment. These people may or may not please others by what they do, and their efforts may or may not result in the attainment of intended goals. Regardless of the consequences, if a person does something because it is valued personally, then the act itself is fulfilling.

In studying the characteristics of the fulfilled person, Maslow identified people he believed lived rich and fulfilling lives. Included were Albert Einstein, Eleanor Roosevelt, Ludwig van Beethoven, and Albert Schweitzer. Maslow found that these people shared 15 characteristics of self-actualization.[9] To evaluate your own development as a self-actualized person, complete Exercise 17–1.

Exercise 17–1
Characteristics of the Self-Actualized Person

Rate yourself on the following characteristics. Circle the number that best represents your current status (1 is low; 10 is high).

1. Acceptance of self and others

   1   2   3   4   5   6   7   8   9   10

2. Accurate perception of reality

   1   2   3   4   5   6   7   8   9   10

3. Close relationships

   1   2   3   4   5   6   7   8   9   10

4. Personal autonomy (independence)

   1   2   3   4   5   6   7   8   9   10

5. Goal-directedness; achievement orientation

   1   2   3   4   5   6   7   8   9   10

6. Naturalness (spontaneity)

   1   2   3   4   5   6   7   8   9   10

7. Need for privacy

   1   2   3   4   5   6   7   8   9   10

8. Orientation toward growth and new experience

   1   2   3   4   5   6   7   8   9   10

9. Sense of unity with nature

   1   2   3   4   5   6   7   8   9   10

10. Sense of brotherhood with all people

   1   2   3   4   5   6   7   8   9   10

11. Democratic character

   1   2   3   4   5   6   7   8   9   10

12. Sense of justice

   1   2   3   4   5   6   7   8   9   10

13. Sense of humor

   1   2   3   4   5   6   7   8   9   10

14. Creativity

   1   2   3   4   5   6   7   8   9   10

15. Personal integrity (high principles)

   1   2   3   4   5   6   7   8   9   10

Scoring and Interpretation:

Add the numbers you circled to find your total score; then compare it with the corresponding description.

Score	Progress
15–45	Not great—should definitely improve
46–120	Just OK—needs work
121–150	Very good—keep going!

The characteristics I want to improve are:

_____

_____

_____

_____

_____

Action steps I will take are:

_____

_____

_____

_____

_____

_____

The English author–philosopher Julian Huxley summarizes the need for fulfillment with the following observation:

Human life is a struggle—against frustration, ignorance, suffering, evil, the maddening inertia of things in general; but it is also a struggle for something. Fulfillment seems to describe better than any other single word the positive side of human development and human evolution—the realization of inherent capacities by the individual and of new possibilities by the race; the satisfaction of needs, spiritual as well as material; the emergence of new qualities of experience to be enjoyed; the building of personalities.[10]

Motivation in the Workplace

The word *motivation* comes from the Latin term meaning "to move." Ancient scholars were fascinated by the fact that some objects in the world seem to be self-movers, while other objects remain stationary unless acted upon by some outside force. They assumed that motion was caused by a spirit inside the object—a "little man" of some kind—that pushed or impelled the object into action. Whenever the "spirit was moved," so was the object or body that the spirit inhabited.[11]

The effective leader must motivate people to accomplish tasks. This involves understanding the needs of others and arranging conditions so that individual needs can be met while advancing the organization. In this way, the little man, or *spirit* of the individual, is awakened and liberated. The performance that results can be tremendous.

The importance of motivation is suggested in findings that most people believe they could give as much as 15 to 20 percent more effort at work than they now do with no one, including their own supervisors, recognizing any difference. Perhaps even more startling, these workers also believe they could give 15 to 20 percent less effort with no one noticing any difference.[12]

Exercise 17–2 evaluates motivation in the work setting. By completing this exercise, you will better understand the role of needs in the world of work.

Exercise 17–2
Motivation at Work[13]

Rank your responses for each of the following questions. The response that is most important or most true for you should receive a 5; the next, a 4; and on down to the least important or least true which should receive a 1.

Example: The work I like best involves

    A   __4__   Working alone.

    B   __3__   A mixture of time spent with people and time spent alone.

    C   __1__   Giving speeches.

    D   __2__   Discussion with others.

    E   __5__   Working outdoors.

1. Overall, the most important thing to me about a job is whether or not

    A   _____   The pay is sufficient to meet my needs.

    B   _____   It provides the opportunity for fellowship and good human relations.

    C   _____   It is a secure job with good employee benefits.

    D   _____   It allows me freedom and the chance to express myself.

    E   _____   There is opportunity for advancement, based on my achievements.

2. If I were to quit a job, it would probably be because

    A   _____   It was a dangerous job, such as working with inadequate equipment or poor safety procedures.

    B   _____   Continued employment was questionable because of uncertainties in business conditions or funding sources.

    C   _____   It was a job people looked down on.

    D   _____   It was a one-person job, allowing little opportunity for discussion and interaction with others.

    E   _____   The work lacked personal meaning to me.

3. For me, the most important rewards in working are those that

    A   _____   Come from the work itself—important and challenging assignments.

    B   _____   Satisfy the basic reasons people work—good pay, a good home, and other economic needs.

    C   _____   Are provided by fringe benefits—such as hospitalization insurance, time off for vacations, and security for retirement.

    D   _____   Reflect my ability—such as being recognized for the work I do and knowing I am one of the best in my company or profession.

    E   _____   Come from the human aspects of working—that is, the opportunity to make friends and to be a valued member of a team.

4. My morale would suffer most in a job in which

    A   _____   The future was unpredictable.

    B   _____   Other employees received recognition, when I didn't, for doing the same quality of work.

    C   _____   My co-workers were unfriendly or held grudges.

    D   _____   I felt stifled and unable to grow.

    E   _____   The job environment was poor—no air conditioning; inconvenient parking; insufficient space and lighting; primitive toilet facilities.

5. In deciding whether or not to accept a promotion, I would be most concerned with whether

    A   _____   The job was a source of pride and would be viewed with respect by others.

    B   _____   Taking the job would constitute a gamble on my part, and I could lose more than I gained.

    C   _____   The economic rewards would be favorable.

    D   _____   I would like the new people I would be working with, and whether or not we would get along.

    E   _____   I would be able to explore new areas and do more creative work.

6. The kind of job that brings out my best is one in which

A _____ There is a family spirit among employees and we all share good times.

B _____ The working conditions—equipment, materials, and basic surroundings—are physically safe.

C _____ Management is understanding, and there is little chance of losing my job.

D _____ I can see the returns on my work from the standpoint of personal values.

E _____ There is recognition for achievement.

7. I would consider changing jobs if my present position

A _____ Did not offer security and fringe benefits.

B _____ Did not provide a chance to learn and grow.

C _____ Did not provide recognition for my performance.

D _____ Did not allow close personal contacts.

E _____ Did not provide economic rewards.

8. The job situation that would cause the most stress for me is

A _____ Having a serious disagreement with my co-workers.

B _____ Working in an unsafe environment.

C _____ Having an unpredictable supervisor.

D _____ Not being able to express myself.

E _____ Not being appreciated for the quality of my work.

9. I would accept a new position if

A _____ The position would be a test of my potential.

B _____ The new job would offer better pay and physical surroundings.

C _____ The new job would be secure and offer long-term fringe benefits.

D _____ The position would be respected by others in my organization.

E _____ Good relationships with co-workers and business associates were probable.

10. I would work overtime if

A _____ The work is challenging.

B _____ I need the extra income.

C _____ My co-workers are also working overtime.

D _____ I must do it to keep my job.

E _____ The company recognizes my contribution.

Scoring:

Place the values you assigned to A, B, C, D, and E for each question in the spaces provided in the scoring key on page 203. Notice that the letters are not always in the same place for each question. Then add each column to obtain a total score for each motivation level.

The five motivation levels are as follows (each will be discussed in the "Interpretation" section—see page 204):

Level I   Survival needs

Level II   Security needs

Level III   Belonging needs

Level IV   Respect needs

Level V   Fulfillment needs

Scoring Key

Motivation Level

	I	II	III	IV	V
1.	A _____	C _____	B _____	E _____	D _____
2.	A _____	B _____	D _____	C _____	E _____
3.	B _____	C _____	E _____	D _____	A _____
4.	E _____	A _____	C _____	B _____	D _____
5.	C _____	B _____	D _____	A _____	E _____
6.	B _____	C _____	A _____	E _____	D _____
7.	E _____	A _____	D _____	C _____	B _____
8.	B _____	C _____	A _____	E _____	D _____
9.	B _____	C _____	E _____	D _____	A _____
10.	B _____	D _____	C _____	E _____	A _____
Totals	_____	_____	_____	_____	_____

Next, make a graphic representation of your motivation at work on the motivation graph in Figure 17–1. Find the number on the scale that corresponds to each motivation level, and draw a line across that point in the column. Then fill in the area, creating a bar chart of your needs at work. See the sample motivation graph on page 204 (Figure 17–2).

The highest points of your motivation graph indicate the most important needs identified by you in your work. The lowest points show those needs that have been relatively well satisfied or de-emphasized by you at this time.

Figure 17–1
Motivation Graph

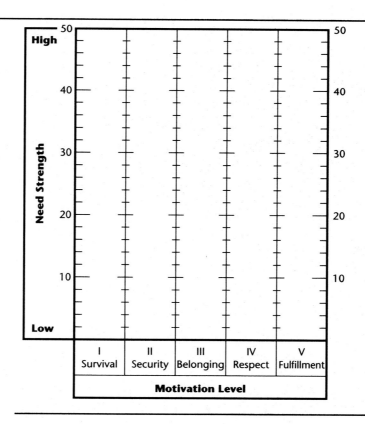

Figure 17–2
Sample Motivation Graph

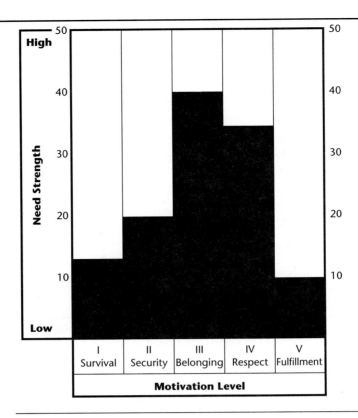

Interpretation:

The following is a description of the five motivation levels. Also included are policies and practices an organization should consider to help satisfy employee needs at each motivation level. In a real sense, the five best gifts to give employees are survival, security, belonging, respect, and fulfillment.

Level I: Survival Needs:

People motivated at the first level are concerned with physical and economic survival. If they do not presently have a job, they feel the need to find one. If they do have a job, their goal is to keep it and to have a safe work environment. There is also concern for comfort and the avoidance of physical irritations such as inadequate space, inefficient equipment, and inconvenient parking, rest room, and eating facilities.

A worker motivated at the first motivation level is concerned primarily with issues that are secondary to the actual job being done. Any job that meets physical and economic needs is acceptable; the nature of the work itself is relatively unimportant.

Physical needs may dominate the behavior of a person who has no job or who is in economic difficulty. Consider the plight of millions of people during the Great Depression, or that of an individual today who has lost a job, whose children need clothing, and whose dependent parents are ill. Consider Ma's words in John Steinbeck's *The Grapes of Wrath:*

But I like to think how nice it's gonna be, maybe, in California. Never cold. An' fruit ever'place, an' people just bein' in the nicest places, little white houses in among the orange trees. I wonder—that is, if we all get jobs an' all work—maybe we can get one of them little white houses. An' the little fellas go out an' pick oranges right off the tree. They ain't gonna be able to stand it, they'll get to yellin' so.[14]

An organization can meet the survival needs of its employees by providing:

- Sufficient pay.
- Safe working conditions.
- Safe equipment, tools, and materials.
- A supportive physical environment, with good lighting, heating, air conditioning, and rest rooms.

Does your organization meet the survival needs of its employees? Evaluate on a scale of 1 to 10 (1 is low; 10 is high): _____

Level II: Security Needs:

People motivated at the second level feel the need for security and predictability in their lives. They want assurance that their jobs are not subject to loss or change. As a result, there is a concern for benefits of a protective nature, such as health insurance, retirement income, and seniority rights. There is also a need for signs of stability from upper management.

The second motivation level, like the first, involves issues that are peripheral to the work itself; therefore, any job that provides economic protection and a dependable work environment will be valued by the person motivated at this level.

Security needs may erupt at all levels of responsibility and in all lines of work if business conditions are poor or if managers act in a threatening way. Think of how you would feel if you sensed that your job was in jeopardy; or imagine the concern you would feel if the equipment, supplies, and other resources required to perform your job were taken away.

An organization can meet the security needs of its employees by providing:

- Proper tools, equipment, and materials to do the job.
- Job aids, such as training manuals and technical assistance.
- Economic protection through insurance and retirement programs.
- Job security through career counseling, in-service training, and seniority systems.
- Confidence in management through stable and dependable actions of managers.

How well does your organization meet its employees' security needs? Evaluate on a scale of 1 to 10 (1 is low; 10 is high): _____

Level III: Belonging Needs:

People motivated at the third level are concerned with being accepted members of the work group or organizational family. A sense of belonging and the giving and receiving of support are important incentives at this level.

When belonging needs are the primary source of motivation, employees value work as an opportunity for establishing warm and satisfying human relationships. Jobs that allow them the opportunity to interact with people and to create friendships are likely to be valued, regardless of the nature of the work itself. A person motivated at this level may be more interested in human relations than job duties when considering which career to pursue or which company to join.

Employee needs for belonging are normal. How these needs are met (whether by counterproductive cliques and gripe sessions or by constructive work groups and employee meetings) can influence the success of an organization.

An organization can meet the belonging needs of its employees by providing the following:

- Communication sessions between employees and management (these are most effective when conducted in small groups).
- Celebration of holidays, birthdays, and special events.
- Expressions of consideration, such as notes of appreciation, hospital visits, and sympathetic understanding when employees have personal problems.
- Job participation vehicles, such as regular staff meetings, annual employee meetings, employee task forces, committees, and performance improvement teams.
- Communication outlets, such as employee newsletters, notices from management, bulletin boards, and annual reports.
- Most important, an open-door policy in which every employee feels free to share concerns and suggestions with every other employee, regardless of level of responsibility.

How well does your organization support the belonging needs of its employees? Rate conditions on a scale of 1 to 10 (1 is low; 10 is high): _____

Level IV: Respect Needs:

The fourth motivation level reflects a person's need for recognition. The respect of others for one's special traits or competencies is important. Based on social esteem, the individual develops a sense of self-worth.

This is the first motivation level that is closely related to the nature of the work and depends on aspects of the job itself for satisfaction. Work that provides the opportunity to display skills that one feels others respect will be valued and will have motivation strength. The person who is primarily interested in self-image or reputation is motivated at the fourth motivation level.

An organization can meet its employees' needs for recognition by providing:

■ Individual incentives for high performance, such as achievement awards, worker-of-the-month honors, attendance awards, and recognition for suggestions.

■ Public acclaim for outstanding contributions at award banquets, retirement dinners, and annual meetings.

■ Opportunities to improve job status through training programs, job titles, and promotions.

■ Tangible rewards, such as increased pay, bonuses, commemorative plaques, letters of recognition, gifts, and privileges.

■ Most important, day-to-day recognition and praise for a job well done.

Does your organization provide recognition for employees' achievements? Evaluate on a scale of 1 to 10 (1 is low; 10 is high): _____

Level V: Fulfillment Needs:

When a person is motivated at the fifth level, his or her primary concern is to fulfill personal values and to experience growth. There is an interest in mental and emotional challenges and a desire to demonstrate life values on the job. Writer Studs Terkel explains the motivation of employees at the fifth level:

It's about a search, too, for daily meaning as well as for daily bread, for recognition as well as cash, for astonishment rather than torpor; in short, for a sort of life rather than a Monday through Friday sort of dying.

There are, of course, the happy few who find a savor in their daily job: The Indiana stonemason who looks upon his work and sees it is good; the Chicago piano tuner who seeks and finds a sound that delights; the bookbinder who saves a piece of history; the Brooklyn fireman who saves a piece of life.

But don't these satisfactions, like Jude's hunger for knowledge, tell us more about the person than about the task? Perhaps. Nonetheless, there is a common attribute here: a meaning to their task well over and beyond the reward of the paycheck.[15]

Once people reach a certain level of material comfort and social needs are met, they care more about fulfillment; in plain English, they are more interested in what they actually do all day. Add a strong economy and a small labor pool, and the fifth motivation level is all the more important.

The nature of one's work is particularly critical for satisfying fulfillment needs, because the job itself must allow a good deal of freedom of expression and opportunity for experimentation. When the fifth motivation level is dominant, the individual channels more creative and constructive energy into the work activity than she or he would if motivated solely by the need for respect, belonging, security, or survival.

An organization can meet the fulfillment needs of its employees by:

■ Discussing organization values and goals in light of individual values and goals, and tailoring job duties to accomplish both.

■ Providing the opportunity for personal growth, through both on-the-job assignments and outside activities. For example, an organization may support an employee's involvement in community service activities or may support his or her continuing education efforts.

How well does your organization meet its employees' needs for fulfillment? Evaluate on a scale of 1 to 10 (1 is low; 10 is high): _____

Why People Do What They Do

There are nine points to remember about human motivation. With these in mind, you will better understand why people do what they do, both on the job and in their lives away from work. These points can also explain the complicated relationship between personal goals and work behavior.[16]

1. **A satisfied need is not a motivator.** It is not what people have that motivates behavior; it is what they do not have, or what they have done without. One person may be motivated by a need to never be hungry again; another, by a need to never be dependent again; another, by a need for love; another, by a need to be "somebody" someday; and yet another, by a need for self-expression. Each is motivated by a need that is not fully satisfied.

2. **Employee motivation and company success are related.** In his book *The Human Equation,* Jeffrey Pfeffer shows that profit is directly related to a company's effectiveness in motivating its workforce. He identifies seven practices that successful companies share: (1) employment security; (2) selective hiring of new personnel; (3) empowered teams and decentralization of decision making as the basic principles of organizational design; (4) comparatively high compensation, contingent on organizational performance; (5) extensive training; (6) reduced status distinctions and barriers, including dress, language, office arrangements, and wage differences across levels; and (7) extensive sharing of financial and performance information throughout the organization.[17]

This list shows that three of the practices—job security, above-average wages, and reduced wage differentials—address lower-level needs; and three practices— empowered teams, extensive training, and information sharing—address higher-level needs. The remaining practice, selective hiring, is made possible because these companies are desirable places to work. Pfeffer concludes that high performance requires both good pay and an enriched work environment.

3. **Psychological needs and social values are not the same.** Both Adolf Hitler and Mohandas Gandhi may have been motivated by the need for respect (the fourth motivation level), but their actions reflected different social values. One believed in totalitarianism and war, and the other struggled for democratic ideals through nonviolent demonstration. Similarly, two employees may be motivated by fulfillment needs—both behaving for self-discovered, self-defined reasons. Yet the actions of one may be harmful to other people, while the actions of the other may help other people. The psychological forces are the same, but the values are not. Psychological needs explain human motivation; social values are the concern of ethics.

4. **The same act can satisfy any of the five motivation levels.** Consider that a person may work for any of the following reasons: (1) because there is no food to eat, thus meeting survival needs; (2) because job stability is in danger, thus meeting security needs; (3) to be an accepted member of a work group, trade, or profession, thereby meeting belonging needs; (4) to be recognized as important, skillful, or otherwise worthy of admiration, thus meeting respect needs; (5) for the personal satisfaction experienced doing the job, thereby meeting fulfillment needs.

5. **All people have the same needs, but to different degrees and accompanied by different wants.** *What* it takes to satisfy these needs and *how much* is required are unique to each person. To illustrate: (1) Sue's affection satisfies Bill's need for belonging, while Jim's belonging needs are satisfied by acceptance into his work group. (2) Jill's need for respect will be satisfied when she is recognized as a skilled actress, while Karen's need for respect is reflected in her goal to win an Oscar. Jill and Karen feel their needs to different degrees, showing that some people have a greater need for ego satisfaction.

6. **A person can be deficiency-motivated, bringing harm to self or others.** It is possible to have an extreme fixation on a natural need, so strong that it can lead to neurotic and even destructive behavior. For example, a person can be so hungry for

love that the need becomes destructive. In the following passage, Gustave Flaubert describes Madame Bovary's relationship with her husband:

> She had to have her chocolate every morning, attentions without end. She constantly complained of her nerves, her chest, her liver. The noise of footsteps made her ill. When people went away, solitude became odious to her; if they came back, it was doubtless to see her die.
>
> When Charles returned in the evening, she stretched forth two long thin arms from beneath the sheets, put them around his neck, and having him sit down on the edge of the bed, began to talk to him of her troubles: he was neglecting her; he loved another; she had been warned she would be unhappy; and she ended by asking him for a dose of medicine and a little more love.[18]

No matter how much Charles showed his wife that he loved her, she was never satisfied, and in the end, her need for proof that she was loved ended in a diminished life and early death.

In contrast, the healthy individual is growth-motivated and reasons, I have satisfied this need; now I am ready to satisfy other needs. This point is important in interpersonal relations, especially leader–follower relationships. For example, when someone is deficiency-motivated and psychologically stuck at one of the need levels (except the fifth), direction from others is needed. In this case, help and advice from the wise would be appropriate. On the other hand, when someone is growth-motivated, the primary need is for understanding and nonpossessive caring. Those who want to help should listen in a nonjudgmental way as the person talks and discovers his or her own answers.[19] Good books that can be used to understand and deal with deficiency-motivated and growth-motivated people are *The Road Less Traveled* by Scott Peck and *If You Meet the Buddha on the Road, Kill Him!* by Sheldon Kopp.

7. **Unsatisfied needs can harm your health, as surely as if you were physically stricken.** If you feel the need for recognition, but no one respects you; if you feel the need for love, but no one cares; if you feel the need for self-expression, but have no outlets, you can develop a motivation condition as harmful as physical illness. Consider the following case:

> Tim wanted to be an artist. He felt the need to express himself, and art was to be the means. The fact that no one else liked his work, and that he could not sell his paintings, mattered little to Tim; he was happy. Then Tim met Sarah. They fell in love and were married.
>
> A year later, twins were born to Tim and Sarah. With this change in his life, Tim's mind turned to food, clothing, and other needs for the children. Soon he went to work in an automobile factory as a production worker. Tim loved his family, and he was proud of himself for sacrificing his need for self-expression—his desire to paint—in the interest of his family.
>
> By the time four years had passed, Tim was experiencing poor physical health and recurrent depression. His inner need to paint, sidetracked because of the need to earn a living, would not be quieted. He felt incomplete and unhappy. Tim developed problems at work and became increasingly irritable.[20]

8. **Leadership is important in meeting employee needs and preventing motivation problems.** What a leader does will vary with the circumstances. Sample actions include improving job safety (survival needs), clarifying job assignments (security needs), offering a word of encouragement (belonging needs), providing praise for a job well done (respect needs), and offering new skills development (fulfillment needs). In any case, such leadership motivates employees and brings out their best in job performance. It is an example of enlightened and servant leadership.[21]

9. **The ideal is to integrate the needs of the individual with the goals of the organization.** If the needs of the individual can be satisfied while advancing the work of the organization, the ultimate in employee morale and organization effectiveness will be achieved. Too many people are dissatisfied and perform below their potential because their jobs are not motivating. Many employees care more about off-the-job projects than on-the-job duties because these outside activities satisfy their psychological needs. The failure to integrate individual needs and organizational goals can represent a significant loss or brain drain for the organization.[22]

The Art of Persuasion

Management author Fred Fiedler writes, "Leadership is the use of influence to accomplish a task."[23] This point is supported in *Working with Emotional Intelligence,* a book that explains the importance of understanding and dealing with people.[24] Author Daniel Goleman explains that although technical skills are important, **emotional intelligence (EI)** is the essential and indispensable requirement for effective leadership. One person may call this practical wisdom, and another may call it commonsense leadership. No matter what label is put on the skill, leadership success requires the ability to understand and deal effectively with people.[25] The following story is a practical example of emotional intelligence:

The owner of a fast-food franchise was having trouble with employee turnover. The majority of his employees were teenage students, and few would remain for an entire semester.

In an attempt to solve the problem, he sat down one day and wrote down everything he could think of about them. He noted the fact that they went to school; that most of them sought teacher approval and parental approval; that they liked money; that they were working to buy things, but were thinking about college. Most had pride in their school grades, were competitive, and were working to develop a work ethic. All sought recognition and some were worried about the future.

As he studied this list, the owner focused his attention on certain words: money, work ethic, pride in grades, teacher approval, parental approval, competitive, recognition, and college.

Then an idea hit him: a bonus plan based on grade-point averages. Any student who works for a whole semester and earns a 2.5 to 3.0 GPA would be awarded a 15-cent-per-hour bonus for all hours worked that semester. The ante would be upped to 25 cents per hour for students earning better than 3.0.

The cost was small—less than 5 percent of his payroll costs for the time period. The advantages were many:

Students were encouraged to work for the entire semester.

The bonus attracted better students, who tended to be better workers.

Guidance counselors and teachers did his recruiting for him, recommending his restaurant to students looking for work.

Parents encouraged their children to work at his place.

Great public relations for the restaurant—he received free newspaper and television coverage.[26]

A high-profile example of the importance of understanding and dealing effectively with people is the case of Louis V. Gerstner, Jr., former chairman and chief executive of IBM. By 1996, Gerstner was leading his company back to success, rebounding from nearly a decade of problems.[27] Business analysts and management authors would say that IBM had recommitted to its core values of service to the customer and performance excellence, as it took the efforts of literally thousands of talented and dedicated employees to create a resurgence of IBM. However, a particularly visible success factor was the *leader* Gerstner's personal ability to deal with people. In particular, Gerstner was effective in his personal appeals to major customers. A case in point was a visit to Toronto, where Gerstner held a conference with 20 top executives:

Seated at a horseshoe-shaped table, and dressed in shirtsleeves, the IBM top executive held forth for 90 minutes in a casual, but powerful presentation. There were no slides, no computerized overheads, and no prepared speech. Gerstner chatted about a wide range of subjects, including the changes that technology is bringing to business and society. Most of the CEOs in the room were impressed by the relevance of his discourse to their companies. In the words of the chairman and CEO of Rubbermaid, "He was able to connect." Lou Gerstner was filling a leader's quintessential responsibility—influencing key people to think and act in ways to benefit his organization.[28]

Goleman summarizes the character and ability of successful leaders with the phrase "nice guys finish first." The research on leadership success shows that the best commands, forces, and companies are run not by Captain Ahab types who terrorize their people, but by caring leaders with emotional intelligence to balance a people-oriented personal style with a decisive command role and willingness to make difficult decisions. These leaders do not duck the tough problems—technical or personnel. They are purposeful, decisive, and businesslike; but equally characteristic, they are positive, warm, and understanding with people. They are democratic in their character and show respect for all people regardless of position or status. They are appreciative, trustful, and even gentle in their dealings with people, although sometimes this trait is below the surface of a dignified and formal appearance. Goleman emphasizes that the successful leader is a caring leader who can understand people and deal with them effectively.[29]

The elements of emotional intelligence include self-awareness, impulse control, persistence, confidence, self-motivation, empathy, and social deftness. It is difficult to single out one trait as most important because different aspects of emotional intelligence come into play in different situations. One overall characteristic, however, is persuasiveness. Can you get buy-in for your ideas from the people around you? The most effective leaders have a finely honed ability to influence others. To evaluate your emotional intelligence in the workplace, complete Exercise 18–1.

Exercise 18–1
What Is Your EI
at Work?[30]

The following 25 statements represent aspects of emotional intelligence. Using a scale from 1 to 4 (1 is low; 4 is high), estimate how you rate on each trait.

_____ I usually stay composed, positive, and unflappable, even in trying times.

_____ I can think clearly and stay focused on the task at hand under pressure.

_____ I am able to admit my own mistakes.

_____ I usually or always meet commitments and keep promises.

_____ I hold myself accountable for meeting my goals.

_____ I am organized and careful in my work.

_____ I regularly seek out fresh ideas from a wide variety of sources.

_____ I am good at generating new ideas.

_____ I can smoothly handle multiple demands and changing priorities.

_____ I am results-oriented, with a strong drive to meet my objectives.

_____ I like to set challenging goals and take calculated risks to reach them.

_____ I am always trying to learn how to improve my performance, including asking advice from people younger than I am.

_____ I readily make sacrifices to meet an important organizational goal.

_____ The company's mission is something I understand and can identify with.

_____ The values of my team—or of our division or department, or the company— influence my decisions and clarify the choices I make.

_____ I actively seek out opportunities to further the overall goals of the organization and enlist others to help me.

_____ I pursue goals beyond what is required or expected of me in my current job.

_____ Obstacles and setbacks may delay me a little, but they don't stop me.

_____ Cutting through red tape and bending outdated rules are sometimes necessary.

_____ I seek fresh perspectives, even if that means trying something totally new.

_____ My impulses or distressing emotions don't often get the best of me at work.

_____ I can change tactics quickly when circumstances change.

_____ Pursuing new information is my best bet for cutting down on uncertainty and finding ways to do things better.

_____ I usually don't attribute setbacks to a personal flaw (mine or someone else's).

_____ I operate from an expectation of success rather than a fear of failure.

Scoring and Interpretation:

Add your ratings for all 25 items: _____. A score below 75 indicates a need for improvement. Remember, however, that EI is not a permanent state. As Goleman notes in *Emotional Intelligence* and *Working with Emotional Intelligence,* "Emotional intelligence can be learned, and we can each develop it, in varying degrees, throughout our lives. It is sometimes called maturity."

Elements of the Art of Persuasion

The successful leader must master the elements of the art of persuasion, including (1) **an understanding of people,** (2) **the effective use of words,** and (3) **the ability to manage conflict.**

An Understanding of People

Napoleon Bonaparte was a master of persuasion because he understood people. Few leaders in history have been able to stimulate others to action as Napoleon could. The secret of his leadership was simple: He first determined what people wanted most; then he did everything in his power to help them get it. Most of us take just the opposite tack: We first decide what we want; then we try to persuade others to want the same thing as badly as we do. Napoleon knew better. He always keyed his plea to what his army wanted most at the moment:

When his army was half starved, Napoleon promised them food in exchange for victory. When they were homesick and thinking of deserting, he appealed to their pride by asking them how they wanted to return home: as conquering heroes or with their tails tucked between their legs? When they were fighting in Egypt under the pyramids, he appealed to their sense of history: "Forty centuries are looking down upon you," he told them. Helping others to achieve *their* goals—that is the essence of leadership.[31]

Understanding others requires the ability to listen effectively. By wanting to listen and listening well, the leader shows that he or she cares about people, wants to know the truth, and wants to make a positive difference in the lives of others. The act of listening demonstrates respect and builds a bond of trust like no other. It is this bond that is the primary source of the leader's persuasive ability.[32]

Understanding others also requires sensitivity to their needs. The ability to see things from the other person's view, to walk a mile in the other person's shoes, is called empathy, and it is important in all human relations, especially leadership. Vince Lombardi was famous for saying, "Coaches who can outline plays on a chalk board are a dime a dozen. Give me a leader who can get inside his players, find their talents, read their minds, and motivate them."

The Effective Use of Words

Vocabulary, clarity, and eloquence can be used to persuade others to take action, especially in difficult times. Leaders can inspire with a phrase:

"Of the people, by the people, for the people"—Abraham Lincoln

"The only thing we have to fear is fear itself"—Franklin Roosevelt

"Ask not what your country can do for you—ask what you can do for your country"—John F. Kennedy

These motivational words are etched in the memories of most Americans.

In times of crisis, the conviction of a leader conveyed by his or her words can be a determining factor in the course of events. Consider the tenacity of the English people during World War II, inspired by a determined Winston Churchill who braced Britons to their task. Churchill told his people that even though all of Europe may fall to the German onslaught:

We shall not flag or fail. We shall go on to the end. We shall fight in the seas and oceans, we shall fight on the beaches, we shall fight on the landing grounds, we shall fight in the fields and in the streets, we shall fight in the hills; we shall never surrender.[33]

Churchill expressed his nation's gratitude to its airmen who, although outnumbered, fought bravely and defeated the German Luftwaffe, by saying, "Never in the field of human conflict was so much owed by so many to so few." Then Churchill declared:

Let us therefore brace ourselves to our duties, and so bear ourselves that, if the British Empire and its Commonwealth last for a thousand years, men will say, "This was their finest hour."[34]

About the importance of words and the power of persuasion, Churchill said, "If you have an important point to make, don't try to be subtle or clever. Use a pile driver. Hit the point once. Then come back and hit it again. Then hit it a third time a tremendous whack!"[35]

One of the best examples of the power of words to inspire people and persuade them to action is that of Patrick Henry, revolutionary and patriot, who proclaimed in 1775:

Is life so dear, or peace so sweet, as to be purchased at the price of chains and slavery? Forbid it, Almighty God! I know not what course others may take; but as for me, give me liberty, or give me death![36]

Day-to-day leaders are unlikely to face the magnitude of challenges that Winston Churchill did; nonetheless, they are still required to communicate their ideas and inspire their subordinates. They may not have the skill with words to the degree that Patrick Henry did, but they still must be convincing in conveying information and effective in generating emotion. Some ability to communicate can be learned in a good course on public speaking and developed further with practice. However, more important than technique is to *speak the truth* and *speak from the* **heart**. These two principles are required for credibility and trust, the fundamental elements of successful leadership. The best advice to the leader is to forget personal ego. Instead, concentrate on the audience. Consider what is important to them, and address their interests honestly, directly, and to the point.

The Ability to Manage Conflict

Conflicting purposes and personalities are inevitable in dealing with people, and they are part of the normal functioning of a healthy group. Without knowledge and skill in managing conflict, the leader will fail to achieve her or his full potential.[37] There are many strategies for dealing with conflict. The following points should be remembered:[38]

- Recognize that conflict is natural; indeed, nature uses conflict as an agent for change, creating beautiful beaches, canyons, and pearls.
- The issue is not *whether* we will have conflict in life—we will. Everyone has his or her share. How we handle conflict makes the difference.
- We can view conflict as either a problem or an opportunity. We can dwell on the negative or accentuate the positive. By choosing optimism over pessimism, we can be energized by events and focused in our efforts. With energy and focus, we are better equipped to resolve conflicts and achieve our goals.
- Dealing with conflict effectively is rarely about who is right and who is wrong; it is more about what different people need and want. If everyone's needs are satisfied reasonably and everyone's wants are considered fairly, conflict can be a gift of energy that can result in a new and better condition for all.
- An important issue to address is, Do all parties want to resolve the conflict, and will all sides try with goodwill to settle their differences? If the answer is no, the best course is to agree to disagree, invite third-party resolution, and walk separate paths. Every student of history knows that war is the unacceptable alternative.
- If people want to resolve the conflict, it helps to reframe the problem. Reframing can be done by having each person see things from the other person's point of view. See things from the customer's standpoint, the employee's eyes, or the owner's perspective. In so doing, each party restates the problem from the other person's standpoint. This process often provides the breakthrough needed for constructive dialogue and the resolution of the problem.

The effective leader knows that conflict is an inevitable fact of human life, that no two people will see eye to eye on every issue all the time, and that what is needed is creative conflict, not destructive conflict.[39]

In dealing with conflict, people fall into habits and patterns by placing different emphasis on cooperativeness and assertiveness. *Cooperativeness* is the desire to satisfy another person's needs and concerns; *assertiveness* is the desire to satisfy one's own needs and concerns. Figure 18–1 shows five styles of conflict that result from various combinations of cooperativeness and assertiveness.[40]

Figure 18–1
Styles of Conflict[41]

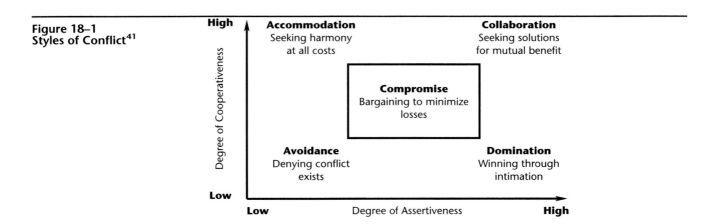

Avoidance:—Being both uncooperative and unassertive, downplaying disagreement, withdrawing from the situation, and staying neutral at all costs. Avoidance pretends that a conflict doesn't really exist.

Accommodation—Being cooperative but unassertive, letting the wishes of others rule; smoothing over or overlooking differences to maintain harmony. Accomodation plays down differences and highlights similarities to reduce conflict.

Domination—Being uncooperative but assertive, working against the wishes of others, engaging in win–lose strategies, and forcing others through the exercise of authority. Domination uses force, skill, or authority to "win" a conflict.

Compromise—Being moderately cooperative and assertive, bargaining for acceptable solutions in which each party wins some and loses some. Compromise occurs when each party to the conflict gives up something of value to the other.

Collaboration—Being both cooperative and assertive, trying to satisfy everyone's concerns as fully as possible by working through differences, finding and solving problems so that everyone gains. Collaboration involves working through conflict differences and solving problems so that everyone wins.

The various styles of conflict can have very different outcomes. Conflict by avoidance and conflict by accommodation often create lose–lose situations. No one achieves one's true desires, and the underlying reasons for conflict often remain.

Conflict by domination and conflict by compromise tend to create win–lose situations. In extreme cases, one party achieves its desires to the complete exclusion of the other party's desires. Trust and goodwill are two common casualties.

Collaboration seeks to reconcile underlying differences. It results in win–win situations where issues are resolved to the mutual benefit of all parties. Collaboration is the most preferred of the styles of conflict.[42]

To personalize the concept of styles of conflict, complete Exercise 18–2.

**Exercise 18–2
Styles of Conflict**[43]

Consider how you behave in conflict situations. In the space to the left of each statement, write the number that indicates how likely you are to respond in the manner indicated: 1 = very unlikely; 2 = unlikely; 3 = likely; 4 = very likely.

_____ **1.** I am firm in pursuing my goals.

_____ **2.** I try to win my position.

_____ **3.** I give up some points in exchange for others.

_____ **4.** I feel that differences are not always worth arguing about.

_____ **5.** I try to find a position that is intermediate between the other person's and mine.

_____ **6.** I am considerate of the other person's wishes.

_____ **7.** I show the logic and benefits of my positions.

_____ **8.** I consider the merits of all points of view.

_____ **9.** I try to find a fair combination of gains and losses for both parties.

_____ **10.** I try to achieve maximum benefit for all parties.

_____ **11.** I try to avoid unpleasantness for myself or others.

_____ **12.** I try to soothe the other person's feelings and preserve our relationship.

_____ **13.** I attempt to get all concerns and issues out in the open.

_____ **14.** I avoid taking positions that would create controversy.

_____ **15.** I try not to hurt others' feelings.

Scoring:

Total the numbers assigned to items 1, 2, and 7 to find your *domination* score: _____
Total the numbers assigned to items 8, 10, and 13 to find your *collaboration* score: _____
Total the numbers assigned to items 3, 5, and 9 to find your *compromise* score: _____
Total the numbers assigned to items 4, 11, and 14 to find your *avoidance* score: _____
Total the numbers assigned to items 6, 12, and 15 for your *accommodation* score: _____

A high score for each style of conflict is 9–12; a low score for each style is 3–6.

Interpretation:

Research indicates that each style has a role to play in work situations but that the best overall approach is collaboration. Only collaboration can lead to problem solving that is most beneficial to all parties, resulting in true conflict resolution. You should consider any patterns that may be evident in your scores and think about how to best handle the conflict situations in which you become involved.[44] Remember, collaboration involves working through differences and solving problems so that everyone wins.

To exercise the art of persuasion, a leader must consider each person as an individual, learn what motivates that person, and then act to satisfy personal needs while at the same time accomplishing the goal. This process requires an understanding of people, the effective use of words, and the ability to manage conflict.

UNIT
19

The Diversity Challenge

If there is one word that characterizes America's workplace, that word is *diversity*. The U.S. workforce is composed of more minorities, recent immigrants, and women than ever before, and this pattern is expected to continue in the years to come. In addition, business has become increasingly global, so leaders are challenged to deal effectively with a wide variety of people and customs. The cross-cultural leader must be patient, understanding, willing to learn, and flexible. All these characteristics are part of **cultural sensitivity,** an awareness of and a willingness to investigate the reasons people of another culture act as they do.[45]

A leader with cultural sensitivity will achieve a bond of trust and respect with people. This relationship is essential for employee satisfaction and effective performance. Table 19–1 presents a sampling of appropriate and inappropriate behaviors in a variety of countries. It is important to emphasize the word *sensitivity* because cultural stereotypes do not always apply with every individual. The caring leader knows that each person must be considered as a unique individual, case by case.

Table 19–1	Protocol Do's and Don'ts[46]	
	Do's	Don'ts
	Europe	
Great Britain	DO hold your fork (tines pointed down) in the left hand and your knife in the right hand throughout the meal. DO say please and thank you—often.	DON'T ask personal questions. The British protect their privacy. DON'T gossip about royalty.
France	DO be punctual for appointments. DO shake hands (a short, quick pump) when greeting, being introduced, and leaving. Only close friends kiss cheeks.	DON'T expect to complete any work during the French two-hour lunch. DON'T try to do business during August—*les vacances* (vacation time).
Italy	DO write business correspondence in Italian for priority attention. DO make appointments between 10 A.M. and 11 A.M., or after 3 P.M.	DON'T eat too much pasta, as it is not the main course. DON'T hand out business cards freely. Italians use them infrequently.
Spain	DO write business correspondence in English, unless your Spanish is impeccable. DO take business lunches at 2:30 P.M. and dinner at 9 P.M. or 10 P.M. Be prepared to dine until midnight or later.	DON'T expect punctuality. Your appointments will arrive 20 to 30 minutes late. DON'T make the American sign for "OK" with your thumb and forefinger. In Spain, this sign is vulgar.
	Asia	
Japan	DO find a highly respected third party to act as your introducer to the lower-ranking person with whom you need to work.	DON'T attempt to get a deal going by directly approaching a target who is below the top level in the organization.
China	DO print your business cards and stationery without black borders.	DON'T use black borders because in China, black is associated with death.
Korea	DO say "yes," "perhaps," or "I will carefully consider your suggestion."	DON'T say "no." Koreans feel it is important to have visitors leave with good feelings.
	Mexico and Latin America	
Mexico	DO meet two or three times before expecting to consummate a deal.	DON'T fly into a Mexican city in the morning and expect to close a deal by lunchtime.
Brazil	DO create a good impression by expressing an interest in the Portuguese language.	DON'T attempt to impress Brazilians by speaking a few words of Spanish; Portuguese is the official language of Brazil.

Table 19–2 shows how diversity policies and practices are being used in American business and industry. Education sessions on valuing differences usually include one or more of the following:

- Fostering awareness and acceptance of individual differences.
- Helping participants understand their own feelings and attitudes about people who are "different."
- Exploring how differences might be tapped as assets in the workplace.
- Enhancing work relations between people who are different from one another.[47]

**Table 19–2
Managing Diversity within Private and Public Employers[48]**

Program or Policy	Percentage of Employers with an Existing Policy or Program	Percentage of Employers Needing a Policy or Program or Greater Effort
Building a Valuing-Diversity Culture		
Discussion groups to promote tolerance and understanding	49.9	75.1
Diversity training for supervisors	38.0	74.5
Efforts to change corporate culture to value differences	37.0	61.4
Team building for diverse groups that must work together	35.3	68.8
Diversity task force to recommend policy changes where needed	34.6	44.9
Holding managers accountable for increasing diversity in managerial ranks	32.7	65.5
Awareness training to reduce prejudice	11.6	26.2
Educational Initiatives		
Incentives for younger workers to complete their education	65.5	72.7
Basic education classes (reading, math)	29.8	57.1
Classes in English for non-English-speaking employees	21.4	64.8
Career Support		
Minority internships	58.1	62.2
Networking among minority groups	41.7	70.3
Programs to steer women and minorities into pivotal jobs—key positions critical to rapid advancement	25.7	61.8
Specific goals to diversify middle and upper management	27.7	57.1
Accommodating Special Needs		
Scheduled days off to accommodate religious preferences	58.2	40.5
Policies to hire retirees for temporary assignments	45.1	51.6
Day care arrangements or benefits	24.5	48.8
Work-at-home arrangements	19.5	32.7
Job redesign to accommodate disabled employees	17.3	49.4
Translation of written materials (manuals, newsletters) into several languages	12.6	21.0

Managing Diversity

Although diversity is the new reality, many leaders are unprepared to handle it. Often their previous experiences have not covered the kinds of situations that arise in today's multicultural settings.[49] One short example gives diversity a human perspective, showing how difficult it can be for employer and employee as well:

An American nursing supervisor gave a directive to one of her Filipino nurses, and the supervisor wanted it to be done stat! For the supervisor, that meant now, immediately, before anything else. The Filipino nurse, meaning no disrespect but with a different time orientation, completed what she had been doing and then complied with the supervisor's request—five to ten minutes later than expected. To the nurse, stat meant soon. A few minute's delay was acceptable. She could complete her work in a short time, then take care of the supervisor's request. She certainly did not see her behavior as insubordinate. The supervisor saw this situation differently. The nurse was either casual about her duties or disrespectful of authorities.[50]

In addition to different perceptions about time, people can have different ideas about work habits, communication patterns, social roles, and a myriad of other workplace issues. For example, employee motivation practices continue to reflect white male experiences and attitudes. Some of these methods can be highly dysfunctional when applied to women or to African Americans, Asians, Hispanics, or Native Americans. Consider a few examples:[51]

■ A manager was pleased with a new breakthrough achieved by one of his Native American employees. Therefore, he recognized her with great fanfare and personal praise in front of all the other employees. Humiliated, she didn't return to work for days.

■ After learning that a friendly pat on the back would make employees feel appreciated, a manager took every chance to pat his subordinates. His Asian employees, who hated being touched, avoided him like the plague.

■ Concerned about ethics, a manager declined a gift offered him by a new employee, an immigrant who wanted to show gratitude for her job. He explained the company's policy about gifts. She was so insulted that she quit.

■ A new employee's wife, an Eastern European, stopped by the office with a bottle of champagne, fully expecting everyone present to stop and celebrate her husband's new job. When people merely said "hello" and then returned to work, she was mortified. Her husband quit within a few days.

Dealing with diversity effectively means behaving in a way that creates trust and respect among people, and gains benefits from their differences. An analogy makes the point well: If you were planting a garden and wanted to have a variety of flowers, you would never think of giving every flower the same amount of sun, the same amount of water, and the same type of soil. Instead, you would cultivate each flower according to its needs. Neither the rose nor the orchid is more or less valuable because it requires unique or special treatment.[52]

Leaders of diverse work groups may wonder, How can I possibly learn about all these people? The answer is that although you can't learn all there is to know about every culture, the more you know, the more successful you will be. In addition, people will appreciate your efforts.

Diversity Prescription

In the enlightened workplace, there is a philosophy of pluralism and a relentless effort to eliminate racism, sexism, ageism, and other discriminations. Where this occurs, all people have reason to believe that they are accepted and respected and that their voices will be heard. The prescription is to turn walls in our minds and hearts into bridges that join and make a structure that is stronger than its individual cells. The prescription is to value diversity as a strength. To that end, remember:

■ All people should be treated with respect and dignity—we must have an *eyes-level* approach rather than an *eyes-up* or *eyes-down* approach in our dealings with people, regardless of social status.

■ Every person should model and reinforce an essentially democratic character and humanistic approach to life.

■ Valuing diversity provides strength and a positive advantage for organizations operating in multicultural environments.

In *The New Leaders: Guidelines on Leadership Diversity in America,* Ann Morrison reports the results of her study on diversity practices in U.S.-based private and public organizations. The practices considered most important are:

1. **Top management's personal involvement.**
2. **Targeted recruitment.**
3. **Internal advocacy groups.**
4. **Emphasis on Equal Employment Opportunity statistics.**
5. **Inclusion of diversity in performance evaluations.**
6. **Inclusion of diversity in promotion decisions.**
7. **Inclusion of diversity in management succession.**
8. **Diversity training groups.**
9. **Networks and support groups.**
10. **Work and family policies that support diversity.**[53]

Benefits of Diversity

The following are the benefits organizations receive by valuing and managing diversity as an asset:

- Increase in workforce creativity.
- Broader range of knowledge and skill.
- Better decisions based on different perspectives.
- Better services provided to diverse populations.
- Ability to recruit excellent talent from the entire labor pool.[54]

Far from being a stumbling block, diversity in the workplace can be a springboard for opportunity and excellence.

Diversity Strategies and Techniques

Dealing with diversity is no easy task, and it never ends. But it is the right thing to do, and it is worth the effort for all involved. The following are strategies and techniques that can help individuals and organizations manage diversity effectively.[55]

What Individuals Can Do

- Connect with and value your own culture. Assess how your background translates into your own lifestyle, values, and views.
- Think about how it feels to be different by remembering times when you felt that you were in the minority. Examine how you felt and the impact on your behavior.
- Try to understand each person as an individual, rather than seeing the person as a representative of a group.
- Participate in educational programs that focus on learning about and valuing different cultures, races, religions, ethnic backgrounds, and political ideologies.
- Make a list of heroes in music, sports, theater, politics, business, science, and so forth. Examine your list for its diversity.
- Learn about the contributions of older people and people with visual, hearing, or other impairments. Consider how their contributions have helped us all.

- Learn more about other cultures and their values through travel, books, and films, and by attending local cultural events and celebrations.
- Continually examine your thoughts and language for unexamined assumptions and stereotypical responses.
- Include people who are different from you in social conversations, and invite them to be part of informal work-related activities, such as going to lunch or attending company social events.
- When dealing with people, try to keep in mind how you would feel if your positions were reversed.

What Organizations Can Do

- Include employees from a variety of backgrounds in decision-making and problem-solving processes. Use differences as a way of gaining a broader range of ideas and perspectives.
- Develop mentoring and partnering programs that cross traditional social and cultural boundaries.
- Develop strategies to increase the flow of applicants from a variety of backgrounds. For example, if you commonly recruit students from college campuses, ensure that the student populations represent a diversity of backgrounds.
- Look for opportunities to develop employees from diverse backgrounds and prepare them for positions of responsibility. Tell them about the options in their present careers, as well as other career opportunities within the organization.
- Show sensitivity in the physical work environment. Display artwork and literature representing a variety of cultures, and make structural changes to ensure accessibility.
- Form a group to address issues of diversity. Invite members who represent a variety of backgrounds.
- Implement training programs that focus on diversity in the workplace—programs designed to develop a greater awareness and respect for differences.
- Pay attention to company publications such as employee newsletters. Do they reflect the diversity of ideas, cultures, and perspectives present in the organization?
- Evaluate official rules, policies, and procedures of the organization to be sure all employees are treated fairly.
- Talk openly about diversity issues, respect all points of view, and work cooperatively to solve problems.

Why Tolerance Is Important

Tolerance is important because intolerance can lead to discrimination, and discrimination can have harmful effects. Put yourself in the shoes of writer–psychiatrist Alvin Poussaint:

A white policeman yelled, "Hey, Boy, come here." Somewhat bothered, I retorted: "I'm no boy." He then rushed at me, inflamed, and stood towering over me, snorting, "What d'ja say, Boy?" Quickly he frisked me and demanded, "What's your name, Boy?" Frightened, I replied, "Dr. Poussaint. I'm a physician." He angrily chuckled and hissed, "What's your first name, Boy?" When I hesitated, he assumed a threatening stance and clenched his fists. As my heart palpitated, I muttered in profound humiliation, "Alvin." He continued his psychological brutality, bellowing, "Alvin, the next time I call you, you come right away, you hear? You hear?" I hesitated. "You hear me, Boy?"[56]

Poussaint was humiliated and, in his words, "psychologically castrated." Frustration and powerlessness are burdens prejudiced people may intentionally or unknowingly place on others. Poussaint was the victim of discrimination born of intolerance.

Table 19–3   **Patterns of Intergroup Relations**[57]

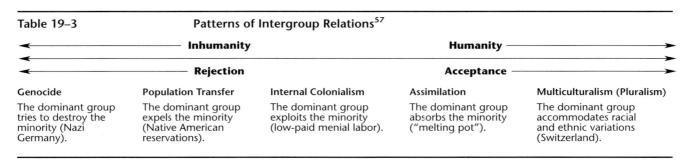

←—————————— Inhumanity		Humanity ——————————→		
←—————————— Rejection		Acceptance ——————————→		
Genocide	**Population Transfer**	**Internal Colonialism**	**Assimilation**	**Multiculturalism (Pluralism)**
The dominant group tries to destroy the minority (Nazi Germany).	The dominant group expels the minority (Native American reservations).	The dominant group exploits the minority (low-paid menial labor).	The dominant group absorbs the minority ("melting pot").	The dominant group accommodates racial and ethnic variations (Switzerland).

Patterns of intergroup relations can exist along a continuum from inhumanity and rejection to humanity and acceptance. See Table 19–3.

Most people would agree that the direction of progress is toward assimilation and multiculturalism (pluralism). For progress to occur, there truly must be social tolerance. The need for social tolerance is captured best in the following story:

The Cold Within

Alexander Pope

Six human beings were trapped one day
In black and bitter cold.
Each one possessed a stick of wood,
Or so the story's told.

With dying fire in need of logs,
The first one held hers back;
For of the faces around the fire,
She noticed one was black.

The next one looking across the way
Saw one not of his church,
And couldn't bring himself to give
The fire his stick of birch.

The third one sat in tattered clothes;
He gave his coat a hitch.
Why should he give wood to use
To warm the idle rich?

The richest man sat back and thought
Of the gold he had in store,
And how to keep what he had earned
From the lazy, shiftless poor.

The black man's face bespoke revenge
As the fire passed from his sight;
For all he saw in his stick of wood
Was a chance to spite the white.

And the last man of this forlorn group
Did naught except for gain.
Giving only to those who gave
Was how he played the game.

The logs held tight in death's still hands
Was proof of human sin.
They didn't die from the cold without;
They died from the cold within.

Gender Diversity in the Workplace

Diversity takes many forms and one of the most obvious is gender. The participation of women in the workplace continues to increase. Today's leaders must address the changing composition of the workforce and the special needs of women. Deloitte & Touche LLP is an organization taking practical measures with flexible work arrangements—flextime, work-at-home, flexplace, job sharing, and other initiatives. In 1991, the CEO of the company identifed the retention and advancement of women as a business imperative for the 1990s, providing the business rationale for developing a program that includes flexible work arrangements. Part of the firm's mission and one of its guiding principles is its commitment to flexibility. Recognizing that success depends on the understanding and support of key constituents within the firm, Deloitte & Touche used newsletters from top management, partner meetings, press conferences, and interviews with the media to communicate the reasons behind this undertaking, its progress, the firm's goals, and plans for implementation.

Communication across Genders

With the changing role of women in American society from wife and mother, to wife and mother and career person as well, there has been a merging of the sexes in the workplace. This has brought the need for better understanding between men and women as work associates. Communication plays an important part in this equation.

In *You Just Don't Understand: Women and Men in Conversation,* linguist Deborah Tannen builds a strong case for her hypothesis that boys and girls grow up in different worlds of words. Tannen notes that boys and girls play differently, usually in same-sex groups, and that their ways of using language in their games are separated by a world of difference:

Boys tend to play outside, in large groups that are hierarchically structured. Their groups have a leader who tells others what to do and how to do it, and resists doing what other boys propose. It is by giving orders and making them stick that high status is attained. Another way boys achieve status is to take center stage by telling stories and jokes, and by sidetracking or challenging the stories and jokes of others. Boys' games have winners and losers and elaborate systems of rules that are frequently the subjects of arguments. Finally, boys are frequently heard to boast of their skill and argue about who is best at what.

Girls, on the other hand, play in small groups or in pairs; the center of a girl's social life is her best friend. Within the group, intimacy is the key, and differentiation is measured by relative closeness. In their most frequent games, such as jump rope and hopscotch, everyone gets a turn. Most of girls' activities, such as playing house, do not have winners or losers. Although some girls are certainly more skilled than others, they are expected not to boast about it, or show that they think they are better than the others. Girls don't give orders; they express their preferences as suggestions, and suggestions are likely to be accepted. Whereas boys say, "Gimme that!" and "Get outta here!" girls say, "Let's do this," and "How about doing that?" Anything else is put down as "bossy." They don't grab center stage—usually, they don't want it—so they don't challenge each other directly. Much of the time, they simply sit together and talk. Girls are not accustomed to jockeying for status in an obvious way; they are more concerned with being accepted and liked.[58]

Tannen believes differences developed in childhood cast a long shadow into adulthood. When men and women talk to each other about troubles, for example, there is a potential problem because each expects a different response. Men may ignore or avoid dealing with feelings and emotions, preferring instead to attack underlying causes. Women, expecting to have their feelings supported, may misconstrue men's aggressive approach and feel that they themselves are being attacked. In general, where men seek status, women seek connection.[59]

Tannen explains that from childhood, there is a tendency for men to use conversation to negotiate status; women talk to create rapport. The clash of the two styles can lead to frustration—in personal relations, of course, but in the office as well, from the female manager who feels she isn't heard in meetings, to the male executive who is baffled when his gruff orders spark resentment or anger.[60]

To the question, Who talks more, women or men? seemingly contradictory evidence is reconciled by differences between public speaking and private speaking. Men generally are more comfortable doing public speaking, whereas women usually feel more comfortable doing private speaking. Another way of capturing these differences is by using the terms *report talk* and *rapport talk*. For most men, report talk is primarily a means of preserving independence or negotiating and maintaining status in a hierarchical social order. To the man, talk is for information that can equate to power. For most women, the language of conversation is primarily a language of rapport. To the woman, talk is for interaction that can equate to love. Telling things is a way to show involvement, and listening is a way to show she is interested and cares.[61]

What should we do about differences in the way men and women communicate? Should women try to change to be more like men, or vice versa? Neither change is the answer. It is important to simply recognize that natural differences exist. When people don't know there are differences in communication styles, and that they are formed in the normal course of growing up, they end up attributing communication problems to someone's bad intentions or lack of ability. [62]

Women in Leadership Positions

Historically, women in high leadership positions have come from nonprofit organizations, educational institutions, and public office; increasingly, they come from the business world. The "2000 Catalyst Census of Women Corporate Officers and Top Earners" reveals that women constituted 12.5 percent of the corporate officer ranks of Fortune 500 Companies, more than one-third of small businesses in the United States were owned or operated by women (women-owned businesses generated over $3 trillion annual sales), and women constituted nearly half of the managerial workforce. (As of 1997, they held 49 percent of managerial and professional specialty positions, up from 36 percent in 1976).[63]

The Center for Creative Leadership has identified six success factors for women in high leadership positions:

- *Help from above.* Women in high levels of leadership have typically received the support of influential mentors.

- *A superior track record.* Held to high standards, executive-level women have usually managed effectively and have developed an excellent record of performance.

- *A passion for success.* Senior-level women have been determined to succeed. They worked hard, seized responsibility, and achieved their objectives.

- *Outstanding people skills.* Successful women executives typically utilize participative leadership, employee empowerment, and open communication to foster trust and high levels of morale among subordinates.

- *Career courage.* Successful women leaders have demonstrated courage to take risks, such as taking on huge responsibilities.

- *Mental toughness.* Senior-level women are seen as tenacious, demanding, and willing to make difficult decisions.[64]

**Figure 19–1
Long-Term Perspective on
Change: Few New Cracks in
the Glass Ceiling**[65]

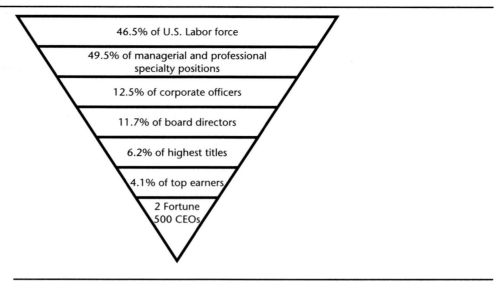

Although the trend is positive for women in leadership positions, Figure 19–1 shows that each rung on the responsibility ladder is progressively more difficult to climb. At each level, a higher percentage of women are sidetracked.

Several factors can sidetrack women in the workplace. The "glass ceiling" is a catchphrase for the impediments women face as they seek top leadership positions. Sidetracking mechanisms include:

- *Lack of encouragement.* Women are often ignored in the grooming of executives for senior-level jobs. Men are more often moved around and cross-trained within the company to learn about different aspects of the business.[66]

- *Lack of opportunity followed by disillusionment.* In a national poll of middle-management women, 71 percent reported not having the same chances for promotion to top executive jobs as their male counterparts. Once there, unequal rewards can be a demotivator. At the managerial level, on average, for every dollar earned by white men, white women earn 74 cents, African-American women earn 58 cents, Hispanic women earn 48 cents, and Asian and other women earn 67 cents.[67]

- *Closed corporate culture.* Many women who enter the executive suite do so by modeling established behavior patterns and management customs. Those who do not conform find that the alternative is to leave the organization.[68]

- *Women's ghettos and the feminization of jobs on the corporate staff.* Some women accept or are shunted into staff jobs that are difficult to exchange for line jobs, where salaries and responsibilities are usually greater. Many of these staff jobs are devoid of responsibility for finance and operations, two important disciplines for senior leaders to master.[69]

- *Double standards.* Women may have to be more competent than men to be accepted by the dominant group. This double standard can be seen when mistakes made by males are tolerated, but mistakes made by females are not tolerated, and when, to be promoted, a woman must be clearly superior to every male candidate. Table 19–4 shows how double standards can be used to judge the behavior of men and women in business.

Table 19–4 Judging Behavior Based on Double Standards[70]	Man	Woman
	A businessman is aggressive.	A businesswoman is pushy.
	He is careful about details.	She's picky.
	He loses his temper because he's so involved in his job.	She's a complainer.
	He follows through.	She doesn't know when to quit.
	He's firm.	She's stubborn.
	He makes wise judgments.	She reveals her prejudices.
	He is a man of the world.	She's been around.
	He isn't afraid to say what he thinks.	She's opinionated.
	He exercises authority.	She's tyrannical.
	He's discreet.	She's secretive.
	He's a stern taskmaster.	She's difficult to work for.

Leadership, Diversity, and Personal Example

Leadership plays a pivotal role in dealing with diversity. To be most effective, leaders should:

- *Empower others.* Share power and information, solicit input, and reward people based on performance without regard to race, gender, age, personality, job classification, and so on; encourage participation and share accountability.

- *Develop people.* Provide opportunities for growth, and then model and coach desired behaviors; delegate responsibility to those who have the ability to do the work; individualize training and development efforts.

- *Value diversity.* View diversity as an asset; understand diverse cultural practices; facilitate integration among people; help others identify their needs and options to be productive contributors.

- *Communicate.* Clearly communicate expectations, ask questions to increase understanding, and show respect through listening; develop communication across cultural and language differences; provide ongoing feedback with sensitivity to individual differences.[71]

The effective leader is **integrative.** This approach involves bringing together people of different cultures, races, genders, personalities, and stages of development, and integrating them into a whole that is greater than the sum of its parts. This integration is not simply a melting-down process; rather, it is a building up in which the identity of the individual is preserved, yet simultaneously transcended. The effective team that results does not eliminate diversity. Instead, it welcomes other points of view, embraces opposites, and seeks to understand all sides of every issue.

As important as leadership is, in the final analysis, it falls on each person to do the right thing. In *The Measure of Our Success,* Marian Wright Edelman writes:

Remember that the fellowship of human beings is more important than the fellowship of race and class and gender. Be decent and fair and insist that others be so in your presence. Don't tell, laugh at, or in any way acquiesce to racial, ethnic, religious, or gender jokes, or to any practices intended to demean rather than enhance another human being. Walk away from them; stare them down; make them unacceptable. Through daily moral consciousness, face up to rather than ignore voices of division. Remember that we are not all equally guilty, but we are all equally responsible for building a decent and just society.[72]

Part Six Summary

After reading Part Six, you should know the following key concepts, principles, and terms. Fill in the blanks from memory, or copy the answers listed below.

Business leader Lee Iacocca's prescription for success focuses on
(a) _____, _____, and _____, with the emphasis on
(b) _____ as the most important aspect of the formula. Psychological determinants of behavior include five human needs identified by Abraham Maslow—needs for (c) _____, _____, _____, _____, and _____. There are many principles of human motivation, including (d) _____, _____, _____, and _____. Leadership success requires the ability to understand people and deal with them effectively, and this requires (e) _____, a term developed by Daniel Goleman. Elements of the art of persuasion include (f) _____, _____, and _____. Effective speaking requires speaking from the (g) _____. Managing conflict most effectively requires
(h) _____, versus avoidance, accommodation, domination, and even compromise. The American workplace is increasingly diverse and increasingly global; thus leaders are challenged to deal with a wide variety of people and customs. Managing diversity requires (i) _____, elements of which are patience, understanding, willingness to learn, and flexibility. There are 10 practices that are most important in tapping the constructive potential of diversity, including (j) _____, _____, _____, _____, and _____. The effective leader in a multicultural environment is (k) _____, embracing other points of view and seeking to understand all perspectives of every issue, while developing a whole that is greater than the sum of its parts.

Answer Key for Part Six Summary

a. **people, products, profit,** page 193

b. **people,** page 193

c. **survival, security, belonging, respect, fulfillment,** page 193

d. (any four) **a satisfied need is not a motivator; employee motivation and company success are related; psychological needs and social values are not the same; the same act can satisfy any of the five motivation levels; all people have the same needs; a person can be deficiency-motivated; unsatisfied needs can harm your health; leadership is important in meeting employee needs; the ideal is to integrate individual needs with organizational goals,** pages 207–8

e. **emotional intelligence,** page 209

f. **an understanding of people, the effective use of words, the ability to manage conflict,** page 213

g. **heart,** page 214

h. **collaboration,** page 215

i. **cultural sensitivity,** page 219

j. (any five) **top management's personal involvement, targeted recruitment, internal advocacy groups, emphasis on Equal Employment Opportunity statistics, inclusion of diversity in performance evaluations, inclusion of diversity in** promotion decisions, inclusion of diversity in management succession, diversity training groups, network and support groups, work and family policies that support diversity, page 222

k. **integrative**, page 228

Reflection Points—personal thoughts on human behavior, the art of persuasion, and the diversity challenge

Complete the following questions and activities to personalize the content of Part Six. Space is provided for writing your thoughts.

■ What motivational needs do you feel in the workplace? What needs are satisfied or unimportant at this time? Does your job allow the satisfaction of your motivational needs?

_____

_____

■ Discuss what a company should do to meet employee needs for (a) survival, (b) security, (c) belonging, (d) respect, and (e) fulfillment. What policies and practices would you recommend?

_____

_____

■ How important is emotional intelligence for leadership success? Do you know a leader who is a master at understanding and dealing with people?

_____

_____

■ Consider the elements of the art of persuasion in the leadership process. Evaluate yourself in the areas of understanding others, using words effectively, and dealing with conflict. Which areas are your strengths? Which do you need to improve?

_____

_____

■ What experiences have you had in dealing with diversity? Have you ever witnessed firsthand the harmful effects of intolerance and discrimination?

_____

_____

■ Discuss gender diversity in the workplace, including the increasing numbers of women in the workforce and in leadership positions. If you have ever had an opposite-sex leader, discuss the pros and cons of your experience.

_____

_____

Action Assignment

As a bridge between learning and doing, complete the following action assignment.

1. What is the single most important idea you have learned in Part Six?

2. How can you apply what you have learned? What will you do, with whom, where, when, and, most important, why?

Part 7   Multiplying Effectiveness

20. **Effective Delegation**
21. **How to Assign Work**
22. **The Role of Personality**

WHEN I WAS BUILDING MICROSOFT, I set out to create an environment where software developers could thrive. I wanted a company where engineers liked to work. I wanted to create a culture that encouraged them to work together, share ideas, and remain highly motivated.

—Bill Gates
Co-founder, Microsoft

Learning Points

In Part Seven, you will discover the answers to these questions:

- How can a leader multiply personal effectiveness by delegating authority? What are the rules for effective delegation?
- How should a leader give orders? What principles should be followed?
- What are the leadership needs of different types of people? What is your own personality—traditional, participative, or individualistic?

Effective Delegation

UNIT 20

The effective leader is an arithmetic artist, subtracting and dividing when less can be more, adding and compounding to achieve a greater good. In this way, the leader enlists the energies and improves the effectiveness of the group. Consider the case of Microsoft's **Bill Gates** and the ability he has shown to multiply his effectiveness through the efforts of others.

Gates writes: "Develop your people to do their jobs better than you can. Transfer your skills to them. This is exciting but it can be threatening to a manager who worries that he is training his replacement. Smart managers like to see their employees increase their responsibilities because it frees the managers to tackle new or undone tasks."[1]

Successful leadership means picking the right people for the right assignments and developing them. These followers are not clones of the leader, but are people who have talents that may be dormant or underdeveloped.

In her wonderful book *Jesus CEO,* management author Laurie Beth Jones writes regarding targeted selection: "Who would pick someone who smells like fish and mud? Who would pick an unpopular tax collector? Who would pick leaders from filthy wharves and toil-filled fields? But He did, and together they changed the world."[2]

Effective leadership involves seeing qualities in others unknown to themselves and treating others in a way that brings out their best. The effective leader uses the multiplication key—the ability to **delegate**—to develop others and achieve more success than would otherwise be possible.

If you have doubts as to the importance of delegation, consider that the life span of most businesses is one and a half generations. The pattern is this: A person starts a business, and it lasts through his or her working lifetime. It takes successors only half a working generation to put the company out of business.[3]

The question is *why*? Surely the founder does not intend this result. The answer is failure to develop people because of failure to delegate power. By withholding authority, leaders guarantee that their companies will have short life spans. When the leader is unable or unwilling to develop others through effective delegation, no provision is made for continuation of the business and its lasting success.[4]

In today's downsized, fast-paced, and high-tech workplace, delegation is not only advisable but also necessary for success. All employees need to be involved if the full value of their skills is to be realized.

There are two ways of exerting leadership strength: One is pushing down through intimidation; the other is pulling up through delegation. Pulling up through delegation is infinitely more effective, and it is the chosen approach of the successful leader.

Delegation Success Story

Think again of the famous success story of Herb Kelleher and Southwest Airlines—this time as an instance of truly effective delegation.

Herb Kelleher may have built Southwest Airlines from a doodle scratched on a cocktail napkin to the most successful airline in history, but he is the first to say he did not do it alone. Caring, competent and committed leadership may be required, but literally thousands of *turned on* employees were also necessary. The triggering switch: effective delegation. Two notable examples are Jim Parker, general counsel for 15 years and now CEO, and Colleen Barrett, originally a secretary and now president of the company.[5]

There are many reasons leaders fail to delegate. Some do not know how. Others do not think their employees will do the job as well as they themselves will. Others do not trust their employees to follow through. Still others fail to delegate because they fear their employees will show them up by doing a better job.

Regardless of the cause, failure to delegate should be corrected for two important reasons:

1. Delegation gives the leader time to carry out important responsibilities in the areas of establishing direction, aligning resources, and energizing people.

2. Delegation gives employees a sense of accomplishment and job satisfaction, and helps prepare them for more difficult tasks and additional responsibility. Employees who are bored and underused come alive when important jobs are delegated to them.[6]

Delegation is the key to multiplying the effectiveness of the leader and the group as a whole. Exercise 20–1 can be used to diagnose delegation strengths and areas for improvement. Complete the exercise based on yourself as a leader or based on a leader you know.

Exercise 20–1
Delegation Diagnosis[7]

Answer each of the following 25 questions. Do not debate too long over any one; go with your first reaction.

	Yes	No
1. Do you spend more time than you should doing work your employees could do?	___	___
2. Do you often find yourself working while your employees are idle?	___	___
3. Do you feel you should be able to answer personally any question about any project in your area?	___	___
4. Is your in-box usually full?	___	___
5. Do your employees take initiative to solve problems without your direction?	___	___
6. Does your operation function smoothly when you are absent?	___	___
7. Do you spend more time working on details than you do on planning and supervising?	___	___
8. Do your employees feel they have sufficient authority over personnel, finances, facilities, and other resources for which they are responsible?	___	___
9. Have you bypassed your employees by making decisions that were part of their jobs?	___	___
10. If you were incapacitated for an extended period of time, is there someone trained who could take your place?	___	___
11. Is there usually a big pile of work requiring your action when you return from an absence?	___	___
12. Have you ever assigned a job to an employee primarily because it was distasteful to you?	___	___
13. Do you know the interests and goals of every person reporting to you?	___	___
14. Do you make it a habit to follow up on jobs you delegate?	___	___
15. Do you delegate complete projects as opposed to individual tasks whenever possible?	___	___
16. Are your employees trained to their maximum potential?	___	___
17. Do you find it difficult to ask others to do things?	___	___
18. Do you trust your employees to do their best in your absence?	___	___
19. Are your employees performing below their capabilities?	___	___
20. Do you always give credit for a job well done?	___	___
21. Do employees refer more work to you than you delegate to them?	___	___
22. Do you support your employees when their authority is questioned?	___	___
23. Do you personally do those assignments that only you could or should do?	___	___

24. Does work pile up at any one point in your operation?   _____   _____

25. Do all your employees know what is expected of them in order
of priority?   _____   _____

Scoring:

Give yourself 1 point for each *Yes* answer for numbers 5, 6, 8, 10, 13, 14, 15, 16, 18, 20,
22, 23, and 25: _____.

Give yourself 1 point for each *No* answer for items 1, 2, 3, 4, 7, 9, 11, 12, 17, 19, 21,
and 24: _____.

Record your total score here: _____.

Interpretation:

Score	Evaluation
20–25	You follow effective delegation practices that help the efficiency and morale of your work group. These skills maximize your effectiveness as a leader and help develop the full potential of your employees.
14–19	Your score is OK, but nothing special if you are striving for excellence in leadership. To improve your delegation skills, review the questions you missed and take appropriate steps so that you will not repeat those delegation mistakes.
13 and below	Delegation weakness is reducing your effectiveness as a leader. The overall performance of your work group is lower than it should be because you are either unable or unwilling to relinquish power to others. In addition, delegation mistakes may cause dissatisfaction among employees. At the minimum, they will not develop job interest and important skills unless you improve in this area. Remember Andrew Carnegie's admonition: "It marks a big step in a supervisor's development to realize that other people can be called upon to help do a better job than one can do alone."

Rules for Effective Delegation

The following rules for effective delegation apply to leading individuals as well as groups. Leaders who incorporate these rules will maximize the job performance and work morale of employees, and will increase the overall productivity of their work groups.[8]

- **Share power with employees.** Fight the natural fear, common to all leaders, of losing control. Remember, to hoard your power is to lose it. Only by delegating authority to others will you accomplish more and greater work.

- **Don't delegate the bad jobs, saving the good ones for yourself.** Don't be like the supervisor who always calls on her or his assistant for the dirty work, late-night work, and disciplining, reserving for her- or himself all the easy assignments and the ones that bring reward.

- **Know your employees.** Effective delegation requires knowing the aptitudes and interests of all your employees. If all else is equal, assign social tasks to employees who enjoy dealing with people, fact finding and report preparation to those who enjoy investigation and writing, and hands-on work to employees who like personal involvement. Include idea-oriented employees in brainstorming or in formulating policies. Capitalize on the special strengths of all your employees.

- **Use delegation as a development tool.** Improve the knowledge, skills, and attitudes of employees by delegating tasks that are meaningful and challenging and that raise their abilities to new levels.

- **Delegate work fairly among all employees.** Recognize the fact that some employees have higher capacity levels, but don't overburden those employees while underworking others. Delegation that is perceived as unfair lowers the morale and performance of both the overused and underused workers.

- **When you delegate authority, be sure to back your employees if that authority is questioned.** When all else is equal, support your employees. If someone has made a mistake, discuss the mistake privately; then let that person correct the problem him- or herself.

- **Let employees know what decisions they have authority to make and delegate decision making to the lowest possible level.** This approach improves effectiveness and efficiency by avoiding referrals through many departments and levels of an organization to solve a problem or receive an answer.

- **Delegate with consistency.** Don't go on delegation campaigns, overwhelming employees sometimes and underusing them other times.

- **Delegate whole tasks so that employees can see projects through to completion; allow sufficient time to get jobs done.** Avoid the "Zeigarnik effect," a term attributed to the Russian researcher Bluma Zeigarnik, in which employee morale, commitment, and performance deteriorate because employees are not able to finish tasks. Work that has not been started may or may not be a motivator, but unfinished tasks almost always demotivate.[9]

- **Insist on clear communication.** Obtain agreement to provide regular feedback on progress and problems. An effective technique is to post a visible calendar with assignment due dates marked. Clear communication and conscientious follow-up will ensure the success of delegated tasks.

- **Make good use of questions when delegating work.** Encourage employees to ask questions to clarify assignments. Also, ask what you can do to help them succeed.

- **Explain the importance of assignments.** Show employees how assigned tasks can satisfy important individual needs, as well as advance the goals of the organization.

- **Learn to live with work styles that are not like your own.** Establish high standards of performance and do not tolerate low-quality work; however, balance this requirement with the fact that no two people are exactly alike, and another person's approach to a task may not be the same as your own.

- **Avoid delegating tasks that are pets, personal, or petty.** Some tasks should not be delegated: (1) If an assignment is a *pet,* that is, one unique to your own interest or skill, you should do it; perhaps no one else will be able to do it as well; (2) if a task is private or *personal,* do it yourself; otherwise, it puts an unfair burden on your employees; (3) if a task is *petty,* never delegate it; to do so lowers self-respect and the respect of your employees.

- **Follow the three D's for all work—do it, delegate it, or ditch it.** *Do* assignments yourself; *delegate* work to competent employees as soon as possible; *ditch* unimportant tasks. In any case, don't let assignments pile up, as they will ultimately reduce the efficiency of your work group.

By applying proven rules for effective delegation, leaders can multiply personal effectiveness, develop employee talents, have good leader–follower relations, and obtain the highest possible level of job performance.

How to Assign Work

Meg Whitman, CEO of eBay, walked into an online flea market and became inspired. She joined the company and was successful because she recognized opportunity, made a decision, and gave the orders to make it work. Whitman knew people she could depend on to get the job done, and she assigned work effectively.

Assigning work effectively is one of the most important skills of the successful leader. The following is a list of proven principles for performing this leadership task:[10]

- **Consider the availability of the employee's time and whether this is the ideal person to do the job.** If the employee's schedule is heavily loaded, explain the priority level of the work. A common mistake is for the leader to assign a job to the one who can get it done, even if this is the same person over and over again. This practice creates three problems: (a) The overworked employee becomes resentful; (b) the overworked employee does not know the priority of many assignments; and (c) the abilities of underworked employees are wasted or never developed.

- **Use work assignments as a means of developing people.** If a task does not have to be done perfectly or within a certain time period, try giving it to an employee who has never done it before. Besides showing you have faith in the employee, you will be developing another person who will be familiar with the job if the regular performer is not available.

- **Know exactly what you want to communicate before giving an order.** Confusion on the leader's part creates doubt and lack of confidence in employees. If you are giving a speech to your employees, prepare and practice it so that what you say will be clear and understandable. If you are going to have a conference with your employees, make notes of the important points you want to cover and refer to them, if needed, during the meeting. If you are assigning a task, rehearse for clarity, and write it down if it is complex or has more than one part or step.

- **If many duties or steps are involved in an order, follow oral communication with a note, and keep a copy.** Keeping records of important conferences, orders, and rules can be helpful. As a reference, a note (short and to the point) can be an excellent memory aid. However, don't become memo crazy; this practice encourages defensive behavior and wastes time, paper, and goodwill.

- **Ask rather than tell, but leave no doubt that you expect compliance.** This approach shows both courtesy and respect. The adage "You can catch more bears with honey than you can with vinegar" applies here. You can usually obtain more cooperation by asking for assistance than by commanding others to do a job.

- **Use the correct language for the employee's training level.** Recognize the fact that many people will not understand your words and terms as readily as you do. Most occupations and jobs have abbreviations, slang words, and technical language that the new or untrained person will not understand. What does "one BLT without, rush!" mean to a new employee, particularly if the person is from a foreign country? For such a person, understanding the English language may be difficult, even without acronyms and jargon.

- **Make assignments in a logical sequence, using clear and concise language.** People remember things best that are clearly stated. If you skip around and are vague, employees will miss the point of your message or will easily forget it.

- **Be considerate but never apologetic when asking someone to do a job.** Imagine that a water main breaks on a cold, snowy night and Bill, the foreman, says to Joe, the laborer: "Joe, I feel so sorry for your having to go down in that hole in this freezing weather. It's going to be like ice! Boy, am I glad I don't have to go . . . brrrr!"

  If Joe wasn't feeling sorry for himself before Bill started talking, he would be now. A better way for Bill to make the request would be: "Joe, I have some dry clothes for you in the truck, and a thermos of coffee will be ready when you come up. Good luck." The rule is: No apologies, just consideration.

- **Talk deliberately and authoritatively, but avoid shouting across a room or making an unnecessary show of power.** Save your power until it is needed. You reduce effectiveness and put people on the defensive if you are constantly forceful. The familiar statement, "She doesn't raise her voice very often, but when she does, everyone listens," exemplifies this principle.

- **Take responsibility for the orders you give.** Avoid quoting others to gain compliance or to relieve yourself of personal responsibility, as when a leader says, "Don't blame me. The boss says we have to do it." If you do not take personal responsibility for the orders you give, the results will be (a) loss of respect from your employees, (b) loss of confidence from your supervisor, and (c) reduced commitment to follow your orders.

- **Give people the opportunity to ask questions and express opinions.** This is a vital point because (a) employees may be confused by an assignment, and questions can help clarify instructions; (b) employees may have information or know something you do not; (c) when you encourage questions and self-expression, you demonstrate respect for employees; and (d) when you allow the opportunity to ask questions and express opinions, you will be rewarded with increased creativity and commitment from your employees.

- **Follow up to make sure assignments are being carried out properly, and modify them if the situation warrants.** Some leaders say, "I don't have time to follow up; I am too busy giving orders." The folly here is that unless there is follow-up, an inappropriate order or assignment may be repeated. Without follow-up, one never learns from experience.

If follow-up reveals that an order is a mistake, admit the error. A leader who has the attitude "right or wrong, that is my decision" does three things if the decision is wrong: (a) loses the opportunity to correct the mistake; (b) loses the respect of people who are concerned about the quality of work; and (c) sets an example of egotism and closed-mindedness.

Career Stages, Nature of Work, and Focus of Work

Three interrelated concepts—career stages, nature of work, and focus of work—influence job performance. These concepts and the typical progression of careers are shown in Figure 21–1.

Figure 21–1
Progression of Careers[11]

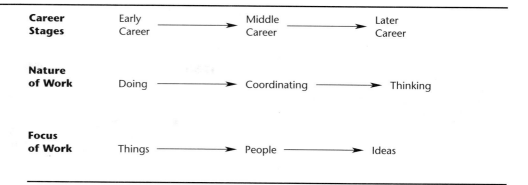

Career Stages	Early Career	→	Middle Career	→	Later Career
Nature of Work	Doing	→	Coordinating	→	Thinking
Focus of Work	Things	→	People	→	Ideas

In the early career, the individual is usually performing tasks. These tasks may include physical effort and working with tools, machines, and materials. Or the job may involve working with people, providing direct service. During this career stage, time is spent learning and applying the skills of the trade or profession. In the beginning, the individual's role may be that of apprentice or trainee. After training, the role may be that of colleague and independent contributor. The type of work performed represents frontline responsibility in the occupation or organization. Police officer, carpenter, programmer, salesperson, and technician are job titles typical of this stage.

In middle career, the individual may spend more time coordinating people. This stage may involve leadership and training responsibilities. If so, the nature of the job becomes less that of doing the work and more that of directing the work of others—coaching them and developing their potential. Work in the middle career includes mid-level responsibility in the occupation or organization. Coordinator, supervisor, and manager are typical job titles.

At the highest levels of an occupation or organization, thinking is the primary activity, and the primary focus of attention is on ideas, such as plans and policies. Duties include determining the long-range direction of the organization, making strategic decisions regarding products and finances, and establishing the ethical tone of the organization. In most cases, the individual is not faced with these responsibilities until the later career stage. Owner, president, chairman, and executive director are common titles of office.

Not everyone experiences the career progression outlined here, because of personal choice or the unique nature of the work. A farmer may choose to maintain a one-person operation for his or her entire working life; similarly, the nature and focus of the artist's work will probably remain the same regardless of career stage.

It is important to match the personal interests of the individual with the demands of the job. Imagine a president of a department store spending most of her time displaying merchandise and running the cash register instead of making long-range plans and developing a management team; or imagine a salesperson spending an inordinate amount of his time thinking about price, profit, and public policy rather than focusing on customer service and the care of merchandise. When personal interests and job requirements are mismatched, morale and performance are sure to deteriorate, for both the president and the salesperson.

Management Roles and Skills

Top managers establish the organization's goals, overall strategy, and operating policy. These individuals officially represent the organization to the external environment.

Middle managers are responsible for implementing the policies and plans developed by top management and for supervising and coordinating the activities of lower level managers. They can be significant sources of innovation and productivity when given the autonomy to make decisions affecting their operating units.

Front-Line managers supervise and coordinate the activities of operating employees. They typically spend a large proportion of their time coordinating, facilitating and supporting the work of subordinates.

Figure 21–2 shows the types of skills needed for effective performance at each level of management. The varying amounts of skills needed are represented by the different-sized blocks. Note that **relational skill,** the ability to understand and work effectively with people, is equally important at all levels of responsibility.

**Figure 21–2
Types of Skills Needed at
Each Level of Management
Responsibility**[12]

Management Level	Skills	Responsibilities
Top-level Management	Conceptual Skills	Strategic Planning and Decision Making
Middle-level Management	Relational Skills	Coordination & Planning for Implementation
First-level Management	Technical Skills	Implementation

A description of each type of skill follows:

Technical skill refers to detailed job knowledge, hands-on expertise, and the specialized use of equipment, techniques, and procedures. Both the technical expert and the work group supervisor should have a high degree of technical skill. Examples include a computer specialist designing a program, a lawyer preparing a legal document, and a maintenance supervisor overseeing a repair job.

Relational skill includes the ability to motivate, coordinate, and advise other people, either as individuals or as a work group. Sensitivity in human relations and a willingness to help others are essential elements of relational expertise. Success at all levels of management—first, middle, and top—requires good human relation skills. Examples include an office supervisor handling an employee performance problem, a sales manager coordinating a sales force, and a plant superintendent solving a problem between the manufacturing and scheduling departments.

Conceptual skill refers to the ability to think abstractly. Long-range planning, strategic decision making, and the weighing of ethical considerations in employee, customer, and government relations all require conceptual skills. Examples include a labor relations vice president evaluating a proposed labor agreement and a company president deciding whether to support a community service project.

Figure 21–3 shows the amount of time each level of management normally spends on the four processes or functions of management—planning, organizing, directing, and controlling. Note that the conceptual skills needed increase at each higher level of responsibility.

Figure 21–3   Normal Distribution of a Manager's Time[13]

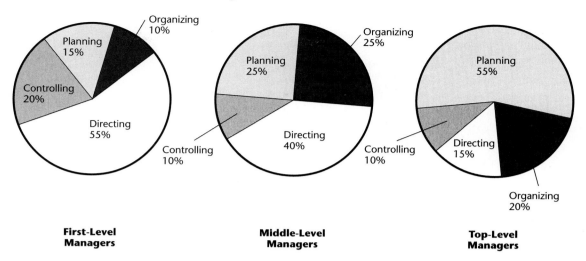

First-Level Managers   **Middle-Level Managers**   **Top-Level Managers**

Management Processes/Functions

Planning includes charting a direction, determining strategies to succeed, and making policy decisions.

Organizing involves aligning structure, people, and resources to achieve goals.

Directing entails supervising, facilitating, coaching, and developing people.

Controlling focuses on tracking progress against plans and making corrections.

To increase understanding of the different functions of management at each level of responsibility, complete Exercise 21–1.

**Exercise 21–1
Functions and Levels
of Management—
In-Box Practice[14]**

Each of the individuals described below occupies one of three levels of management: first, middle, and top. Each is also involved in one of the four management functions: planning (P), organizing (O), directing (D), and controlling (C). Read the descriptions; then fill in the chart that follows.

Manager A of Wolverine World Wide has hired a market research company to investigate Asian markets for Wolverine shoes. If the market studies are promising, Manager A will set up a distribution network in Asia.

Manager B is responsible for cleaning the buildings and taking care of repairs for the county schools. He has spent the past weeks making a schedule, ordering equipment, and assigning work teams.

Manager C has trained her employees in the proper way to present the meal when the restaurant's customers order this evening's special.

Manager D is reviewing the company's three main sales goals for the current year. By next week, she will have a detailed progress report ready to present at the monthly meeting of the company's sales managers.

Manager E wants to use the company's surplus funds to buy a wholesale food distributor. However, the asking price for the distribution company is more than the amount of money on hand. So Manager E has contacted the bank about a 10-year loan to finance the purchase.

Manager F has decided that the human resources department needs an additional employee to interview job applicants. Manager F writes a help-wanted advertisement to place in the local newspaper.

Manager G has spent the morning resolving an argument between three of the company's clerical workers. The workers all want to take their lunch breaks at the same time, but one of the workers needs to remain in the office to answer the telephone.

Manager H is conducting a performance review of senior officers, focusing on quality of production, customer satisfaction, market share, employee morale, and financial performance.

Manager	Management Level First, Middle, Top	Management Function P, O, D, C
A		
B		
C		
D		
E		
F		
G		
H		

Answer Key:

A	Middle	P
B	First	O
C	First	D
D	Middle	C
E	Top	P
F	First	O
G	First	D
H	Top	C

The Vital Shift—Moving from Doer to Coordinator to Thinker

In the U.S. workplace, the reward for being an outstanding producer is often promotion into management. Success is measured by status in the organization, as blue-collar workers aspire to white-color jobs and first-line leaders strive to rise to executive levels. In much of the rest of the world, mobility is less the norm as people are hired into either blue- or white-collar jobs and are expected to remain there, and as management positions are typically filled on the basis of education or social standing. The opportunity to become a manager and rise in the organization is not as common elsewhere as it is in the United States.[15]

A promotion to supervisor can be more than a job change; for many people, it can be a culture shock. The progression through career stages and management levels is not always a smooth one. As seen in Figure 21–4, some of the most difficult times are the periods of vital shift, when a person leaves one type of work and moves to another.

Moving from a period of doing things, through a period of coordinating people, to a period of thinking about ideas can be difficult because different interests and skills are involved at each stage. When the transition is not made successfully, the result is the overpromotion syndrome popularized by author Laurence J. Peter. According to the **Peter Principle,** the individual may be dissatisfied because the new work is not interesting or may feel inadequate because needed skills are missing. At the same time, the organization and those it serves are harmed because the individual lacks competence in performing the tasks of the position.[16]

Figure 21–4
Vital Shifts–Moving from Doer to Coordinator to Thinker[17]

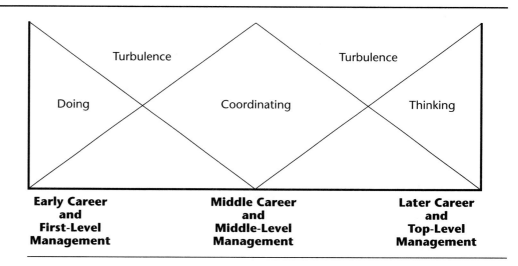

The New-Job Tryout

One of the best ways to successfully make a vital shift is to use the new-job tryout. This approach allows an individual to work at a different type of job or level of responsibility for an interim period of time to see if the work is agreeable and can be performed effectively. If either the person or the organization decides the employee should not continue in the new job, employee pride is easily preserved because the job was considered a two-way tryout. Without such a trial period, fear of embarrassment or an unwillingness to hurt people's feelings may result in a person's being retained in an unsuitable position, even when this harms the individual or the organization. The new-job tryout helps solve this problem. For example, before a permanent job assignment is made, the secretary may try out office management, the tradesperson may try out supervision, or the captain may try out the chief's position.

The Role of Personality

When problems occur at work, they are rarely caused by lack of technical skill or lack of desire to do the job; they are often caused by **personality differences.** When people approach a common task from different points of view, barriers can occur that lower performance and reduce opportunities for all. Whenever you are dealing with other people, personality plays a vital part.

Many interesting models and well-developed instruments can be used to understand personality differences. Self-report questionnaires can help people learn more about themselves, understand other people, and improve human relations.

The questionnaire in Exercise 22–1 measures **style of interpersonal relations,** an important element in dealing with people. It will allow you to better understand yourself and the people in your world. This understanding can help in the leadership process and in the development of communication, teamwork, and a one-team attitude.

As you complete the questionnaire and interpret the results, keep in mind that no questionnaire can capture the full flavor and uniqueness of a single human being. There is no one just like anyone else anywhere in the world. Each individual is biologically different because we are products of millions of ancestors, no two of whom were exactly alike. Additionally, each person is unique in his or her experiences, resulting in perceptions and judgments that are different from every other person's.

Also note that the following problems may exist with self-report questionnaires: (1) Answers may be inaccurate (e.g., an unemployed parent may feel justified in lying on an employment test); (2) the relationship between test scores and other behaviors may be unknown or lack dependability (e.g., there may be no correlation between test scores and job performance); and (3) the same test taken on different occasions may produce different results (e.g., a person's mood and recent experience may influence scores). Thus, no questionnaire should be used as a basis for decision making unless it has been proved valid and reliable.

**Exercise 22–1
Interpersonal Style
Questionnaire**[18]

This questionnaire consists of 26 statements. There are no right or wrong answers. The best answers are your true opinions.

For each statement, indicate which of the three alternatives—*a, b,* or *c*—is *most true* or *most important* to you by circling *a, b,* or *c* in the "Most" column. Then choose the *least true* or *least important* of the two remaining alternatives, and circle its letter in the "Least" column. For example, if *a* is circled under "Most," then either *b* or *c* should be circled under "Least." For every statement, be sure you circle one alternative in each column.

Do not skip any questions, and do not debate too long over any one statement. Your first reaction is desired.

	Most			Least		
	T	P	I	T	P	I
1. When I enter new situations, I let my actions be guided by						
a. my own sense of what I want to do.						
b. the direction of those who are responsible.						
c. discussion with others.	b	c	a	b	c	a
2. When faced with a decision, I consider						
a. precedent and traditions.						
b. the opinions of the people affected.						
c. my own judgment.	a	b	c	a	b	c
3. People see me as						
a. a team player.						
b. a free spirit.						
c. a dependable person.	c	a	b	c	a	b
4. I feel most satisfied when						
a. I am working on personal goals.						
b. I do things according to standards.						
c. I contribute to a project.	b	c	a	b	c	a
5. I try to avoid						
a. not being myself.						
b. disappointing those in authority.						
c. arguments with my friends.	b	c	a	b	c	a
6. In my opinion, people need						
a. guidelines and rules for conduct.						
b. warm and supportive human relationships.						
c. freedom to grow.	a	b	c	a	b	c
7. Over time, I have learned						
a. no person is an island.						
b. old paths are true paths.						
c. you pass this way only once.	b	a	c	b	a	c
8. I want to be treated						
a. as a unique person.						
b. as an equal.						
c. with respect.	c	b	a	c	b	a
9. I avoid						
a. not meeting my responsibilities.						
b. compromising my personality.						
c. the loss of good friends.	a	c	b	a	c	b

	Most	Least
	T P I	**T P I**

10. What the world needs is

    a. more people who think independently.

    b. more understanding among diverse people.

    c. more people who respect and abide by the law.

	Most	Least
10.	c b a	c b a

11. I am most happy when

    a. I am free to choose what I want to do.

    b. there are clear guidelines and rewards for performance.

    c. I share good times with others.

	Most	Least
11.	b c a	b c a

12. I am most responsible to _____ for my actions:

    a. family and friends

    b. higher authorities

    c. myself

	Most	Least
12.	b a c	b a c

13. To be a financial success, one should

    a. relax; money is not important.

    b. work in cooperation with others.

    c. work harder than others.

	Most	Least
13.	c b a	c b a

14. I believe

    a. there is a time and place for everything.

    b. promises to friends are debts to keep.

    c. the one who travels fastest travels alone.

	Most	Least
14.	a b c	a b c

15. I want the value of my work to be known

    a. soon after completion.

    b. with the passage of time.

    c. while I am doing it.

	Most	Least
15.	b a c	b a c

16. A group member should support

    a. the decisions of the majority.

    b. only those policies with which he or she personally agrees.

    c. those who are in charge.

	Most	Least
16.	c a b	c a b

17. I believe feelings and emotions

    a. should be shared with discretion.

    b. should be shared openly.

    c. should be kept to oneself.

	Most	Least
17.	c b a	c b a

18. The people I enjoy working with are

    a. free-thinking.

    b. well organized.

    c. friendly.

	Most	Least
18.	b c a	b c a

19. I value

    a. teamwork.

    b. independent thinking.

    c. order and organization.

	Most	Least
19.	c a b	c a b

20. I believe in the saying

    a. all work and no play makes Jack a dull boy.

    b. united we stand, divided we fall.

    c. there are no gains without pains.

	Most	Least
20.	c b a	c b a

	Most			Least		
	T	**P**	**I**	**T**	**P**	**I**

21. My work day goes best when I

    a. have freedom of operation.

    b. know what is expected of me.

    c. experience fellowship with good companions.   b c a   b c a

22. If I suddenly received a large sum of money, I would

    a. use most of it now for the things I want.

    b. invest most of it for the future.

    c. spend half of it now and save the rest.   b c a   b c a

23. I grow best by

    a. following established truths.

    b. interacting with others.

    c. learning from personal experience.   a b c   a b c

24. It is important that I

    a. plan a year or two ahead.

    b. live my life to the fullest now.

    c. think about life in a long-term way.   c a b   c a b

25. I am known for

    a. making my own decisions.

    b. sharing with others.

    c. upholding traditional values.   c b a   c b a

26. I work best

    a. with structure and organization.

    b. as a member of a team.

    c. as an independent agent.   a b c   a b c

Scoring:

Step 1:

Add the total number of circled letters for each of the six columns. Put these totals in the boxes below marked T, P, and I. Each "Most" and "Least" section total should be 26.

Most				**Least**		
T	P	I		T	P	I

     (Total = 26)   (Total = 26)

Step 2:

Determine your scores for T, P, and I by using the following formula:

Score = 26 + Most − Least. For example, if your T Most was 20 and your T Least was 12, your T score would be 26 + 20 − 12 = 34. Complete the following equations:

T Score = 26 + _____ − _____ = _____
                    T Most   T Least

P Score = 26 + _____ − _____ = _____
                    P Most   P Least

I Score = 26 + _____ − _____ = _____
                   I Most   I Least

        (Your total should be 78.)   Total = _____

Interpretation:

The letters T, P, and I represent three styles of interpersonal relations:

T = Traditional

P = Participative

I = Individualistic

If your highest score is T, you are **traditional.** You are known for your high standards and sense of tradition. If your highest score is P, you are **participative.** Caring about people and serving others are high values for you. If your highest score is I, you are **individualistic,** loving freedom and personal independence. If you are within 1 point of the same score for all three, you have built-in versatility for dealing with different types of people. If your two high scores are T and I, there are two opposite forces in your world asking you to act two different ways. One force is saying "be traditional," and the other is saying "be individualistic." Although this dichotomy can present problems, it can also be good if it allows you to accomplish your values and goals in life. Values and goals are more important than style of interpersonal relations. Note that occasionally it may be difficult for others to understand you because of the different signals you send.

Types of People and Types of Culture

One way to show that all styles of interpersonal relations have equal value is to identify people in history who represent distinctly different styles and who are each held in high esteem.

Traditional When historians identify people who have had the most impact on humankind, the name of Moses always makes the top 10. His leadership style exemplified traditional behavior. A woman in history who was traditional was the longest-reigning monarch of all the European monarchs. Indeed, a whole era or period of history was named after Queen Victoria, known for her moral strength and high standards of conduct.[19]

Participative A woman in history who was participative was Eleanor Roosevelt. She was people-caring and people-serving. Always concerned with the welfare of others, she focused her life on the betterment of society.[20] Some of the best products of the United States have been the ideas and accomplishments of participative Benjamin Franklin. Indeed, without Franklin, the United States would not exist as we know it today.

There were few activities in which Benjamin Franklin did not excel. Philosopher, inventor, diplomat, printer, scientist—he was all of these and more. By his many achievements, including discovering electricity and helping to write the Constitution, Franklin left his mark upon the face of America and the world.[21]

Individualistic One of America's most influential thinkers was the individualist Henry David Thoreau, who wrote:

> If a man does not keep pace with his friends,
> perhaps it is because he hears a different drummer.
> Let him step to the music he hears,
> however measured or far away.[22]

An example of a woman who was individualistic is Joan of Arc, who led the French people by her conviction and brave example.[23]

If you were an employer, you would probably have trouble deciding which of these individuals to hire. Each has special qualities and would make valuable contributions. However, each is different in style of interpersonal relations, and each would require different treatment to be both happy and productive.

Personality and Culture People are products of their culture—family, town, and country. Thus, style of interpersonal relations is influenced by how we are raised. Societies teach and reinforce behavior traits; just as individuals are traditional, participative, and individualistic, so are whole groups of people.[24]

Because personality is a social construct, it involves cross-cultural variations. Studies across cultures show that style of interpersonal relations is a basic dimension or characteristic.[25] Traditional social orientations put the needs and interests of the group above the individual. Individualistic social orientations involve separating the self from others. Participative social orientations seek a middle ground between individualistic and traditional styles with an emphasis on warm and supportive human relations.[26]

Traditional cultures tend to be formal and structured, such as those of England, Germany, and Spain. Many non-Western cultures, including those of Japan, China, and India, are traditional in nature.[27] Participative cultures develop in melting pot societies: The United States is about 20 percent traditional, 60 percent participative, and 20 percent individualistic. Individualistic cultures include the French, Italian, and Greek.

It is important to note that there are exceptions to these generalizations. For example, it is possible for an individual Frenchman to be more traditional than the most traditional German; and there may be a German who is more individualistic than the most individualistic Frenchman. It is also important to note that human traits vary in degrees, so that a person typically is a mixture of all three styles. While you may be primarily participative, you probably have a few traditional and individualistic characteristics as well.

Describing whole groups of people according to interpersonal style should not obscure the extensive diversity and variation that characterize each individual person. Also, it should be noted that certain qualities belong potentially to all people, such as basic honesty, concern for others, and open-mindedness.[28]

Understanding Others

The leader in the work setting typically interacts with a variety of people, each with his or her individual style. Certain characteristics distinguish each style of interpersonal relations. As you read the following descriptions, think about the people with whom you live and work. The descriptions will help explain why some people are easy for you to understand, although you may not always agree with them (they are like you), and why other people are difficult for you to understand (they are different from you). Think also about the ways these different types of people should be treated to bring out their best.

Form of control. Traditionals are comfortable with rules, policies, and procedures. They believe that without such guidelines, social breakdown occurs. Participatives prefer interpersonal commitment as a form of control. The participative says, "I will do this. Will you do that?" Social ties are their preferred form of control. For individualists, *control* is a negative word. They dislike the idea of restricted freedom. In this spirit, Thoreau wrote, "The only obligation I have is to do at any time what I think is right."[29]

Basis of action. The basis of action for traditionals is direction from authorities in which they believe. These authorities may be parental, supervisory, governmental, or religious. In any case, traditionals believe those in charge should determine the course of action to be taken. Discussion and agreement with others are the basis of action for participatives. Democracy is their preferred form of government, and participative management is their favorite style of leadership. The basis of action for individualists is direction from within. The individualist has an internal compass to establish direction and a personal yardstick to measure the rightness and wrongness of behavior. A concept in psychology called locus of control asks, "Who is in charge, the world or me?" The individualist says "me."

To be avoided. Traditionals avoid deviation from authoritative direction. Therefore, systems and procedures to guide behavior should be available. They appreciate job descriptions with responsibilities clearly defined. Business plans, life plans, and road maps for travel are important to them. Participatives avoid confrontation and strive to reach agreement if at all possible. Interpersonal conflict and misunderstanding are particularly painful. Abraham Lincoln, who had both traditional and individualistic moments, was mostly participative. In this fashion he wrote, "Am I not destroying my enemies when I make friends of them?"[30] Individualists avoid not being themselves. Congruency is important to them. They strive to be true to their essential nature. Individualists realize that life is a progression of social roles, but they insist on choosing their own parts.

Perception of responsibility. Traditionals believe highest allegiance should go to superordinate powers. These powers may be in the church, community, workplace, or home. Participatives feel responsibility to help others. They try not to disappoint family, friends, and colleagues. Participatives relate to the little boy who told Father Flanagan of Boys Town, "He ain't heavy, he's my brother." They are the practicing humanitarians. They see themselves as their brothers' keeper. "To thine own self be true and thou cannot be false to any man," advises Polonius, in *Hamlet.* This is an individualistic principle. Individualists assign first responsibility for their own actions to their own conscience.

Goals desired. Traditionals value organization and order. They believe the mission, goals, and objectives of an organization should be identified, and that each person's role should be made clear. Work plans and organization charts are helpful job aids for traditionals. Participatives value group consensus and smooth human relations. By interpersonal style, they make good personnel officers, counselors, and work group supervisors. Participatives are harmonizing agents. Individualists value independence and freedom. "Give me wings and let me fly" and "no rules for me" are interpersonal needs felt by individualists. They are especially uncomfortable with close supervision. Assignments that allow as much freedom as possible are ideal for individualists (assuming they have the ability and desire to accomplish the work). Consider Patrick Henry, the individualist, who said, "Give me liberty, or give me death." You may also recall that some people sought to kill him.

Basis for growth. Traditionals believe there is a time and place for everything, and the best way to grow is by following the established order. They value traditions in all areas of life—family, work, and religion. Philosophically, traditionals relate to Ecclesiastes 3:1–2: "To every thing there is a season, and a time to every purpose under the heaven: A time to be born, and a time to die; a time to plant, and a time to pluck up that which is planted." Participatives enjoy human interaction and prefer to grow in this manner. A participative would make a poor Robinson Crusoe—stranded on a deserted island. Participatives like to teach others and learn from them as well. Sharing is a basic interpersonal value. In the work setting, they especially appreciate group involvement activities. Staff meetings and collaborative work teams are seen as growth opportunities by participatives. Individualists prefer growth through introspection and self-analysis. It is important for them to get away occasionally and think, "How do I feel about this; what is my philosophy on that, and what are my beliefs on this?" Individualists grow best through personal experience and self-discovery. A sentiment that reflects their nature is expressed by the poet Robert Frost, who wrote:

> I shall be telling this with a sigh
> Somewhere ages and ages hence:
> Two roads diverged in a wood,
> And I—
> I took the one less traveled by,
> And that has made all the difference.[31]

Position in relation to others. Traditionals are comfortable as members of the hierarchy. Whether at the top, in the middle, or on the first rung of the ladder, they value structure and organizational clarity. Many people who are in top positions in organizations are traditionals. Note that George Washington was traditional in his style of interpersonal relations. Participatives are comfortable as members of the team. In fact, the *team* acronym, *t*ogether *e*veryone *a*ccomplishes *m*ore, is a participative concept. Participatives make good work group and committee members, because they enjoy working with and through others. Indeed, committees are creatures of the participative personality. They are tools not only to get the job done, but also to meet social needs. Individualists are most comfortable as separate people. For all their lives, they have seen the group go one way, and, almost instinctively, they have gone the other. By personality type, individualists are the pioneers of society—the first to do this and the first to go there. If Daniel Boone were to complete the "Interpersonal Style Questionnaire," he would be an individualist—as would Christopher Columbus, the explorer and navigator. For their needs to be met, individualists must express themselves as the unique individuals they see themselves to be, not as members of a group or bureaucracy.

Material goods. The traditionals are excellent competitors. Witness the success of the Germans and Japanese in the international marketplace. And witness the New England Yankee, who came from Puritan stock and formed the basis of the American free market system. Participatives collaborate to get material goods. Teamwork comes naturally, as the participative says, "If we help each other, together we will accomplish more." Being involved in barn building, potluck suppers, and volunteer fire departments are participative activities. Individualists tend to take material goods for granted, thinking that everyone should have them. Compared to material wealth, personal independence is far more important.

Identification and loyalty. The traditional's first loyalty is to the organization—the U.S. Marine Corps, the FBI, the Roman Catholic Church. Pride in the organization is especially important to traditionals. This is the reason organizations need legends, logos, and other means to build "Yankee spirit" and achieve "Celtic pride." The participative's first loyalty is to the group—the shoulder-to-shoulder work group, team, or department. Inclusion and a sense of belonging are important values for participatives. Edwin Markham's short verse captures the essence of the participative personality:

> He drew a circle that shut me out,
> Heretic, rebel, a thing to flout;
> But Love and I had the wit to win—
> We drew a circle that took him in.[32]

Loyalty is not a major value for individualists, but when they have it, they have it intensely for the person or ideal they deem worthy.

To show how different personalities value loyalty in different ways, imagine three Marine Corps privates—traditional, participative, and individualistic. The traditional's highest loyalty will be to the corps and all it represents; the participative's first loyalty will be to his comrades in arms, the platoon; and the individualist's primary allegiance will be to those individuals and ideals who have earned his respect and support. Indeed, when thinking of patriotism, the traditional imagines an old Uncle Sam, finger pointing, saying, "I want you"; service for the participative is based on such ideas as "united we stand, divided we fall"; and the individualist's ideal is to preserve "the land of the free."

One can see these orientations surface when personalities clash. If you ever have an argument with a traditional, realize the importance placed on responsibility and duty. If you ever have an argument with a participative, know that what is valued is brotherhood and love. If you ever have conflict with an individualist, know that what is important is freedom and liberty. These differences explain why people can fail to communicate and still respect each other at a basic level. Participatives and individualists realize that traditionals uphold an important quality with commitment to responsibility, while traditionals and individualists recognize the universal value in the participative's commitment to love. Finally, traditionals and participatives see the importance of the individualist's dedication to freedom.

Time perspective. The time perspective for traditionals is the future. Because of this, they often have supplies, tools, and money when others do not. For participatives, the time perspective is the near future—tomorrow or next week; they can wait that long. The time perspective for individualists is the present—today. Don't talk to them about the past; they will say, "The past is gone." And don't talk to them about the future; they will say, "The future may never come." Individualists are primarily interested in here-and-now experience and living life fully in the moment.

It is interesting to see the influence of all three styles in American culture—traditional, participative, and individualistic. It can be argued that this diversity gives strength to the society. Consider the tenets that reflect each style. America is a nation of laws (traditional), conceived by and for people (participative), and dedicated to freedom and the rights of individuals (individualistic).

A summary of the styles of interpersonal relations is presented in Table 22–1.

Table 22–1
Interpersonal Styles

Behavior/Value	Traditional	Participative	Individualist
Form of control	Rules, laws, and policies	Interpersonal commitments	What I think is right or needed
Basis of action	Direction from authorities	Discussion and agreement with others	Direction from within
To be avoided	Deviation from authoritative direction	Failure to reach agreement	Not being oneself
Perception of responsibility	Superordinate powers	Colleagues and self	Self
Goals desired	Compliance	Consensus and smooth human relations	Individual freedom
Basis for growth	Following the established order	Human interaction	Introspection and personal experience
Position in relation to others	Member of hierarchy	Peer group member	Separate person
Material goods	Competition	Collaboration	Taken for granted
Identification and loyalty	Organization	Group	Individual
Time perspective	Future	Near future	Present

Dealing with Different Types of People

Differences in personality can result in perceptions and judgments that are poles apart. You have undoubtedly seen individuals and groups who should be working together smoothly but are not. An awareness of the nature and needs of different types of people is the first step in building relationships. This awareness can lead to new levels of cooperation and success.

Although each person is unique and should be treated according to individual makeup, the following guidelines are useful for meeting the needs of and bringing out the best in people with each style of interpersonal relations. Remember that most people have characteristics of all three styles but tend to develop a preference for one or two over the other(s). The most ardent individualist will have traditional moments, and vice versa.

- *Meeting the needs of traditionals.* Provide work rules and job descriptions with duties spelled out in priority order. Provide an organization chart showing reporting relationships; respect the chain of command. Respect traditions and established ways; appeal to historical precedent. Avoid changes when possible; if impossible, introduce changes slowly. Accentuate reason over emotion when handling problems. Mind your manners and language; be courteous. Establish a career plan with benchmarks for progress, rewards expected, and time frames. Provide tangible rewards for good performance, preferably money. Recognize good work with signs of status, such as diplomas, uniforms, medals, and titles. Reinforce company loyalty through service pins, award banquets, and personal appreciation. Communicate the mission, goals, and objectives of the organization, and provide an action plan. Keep work areas organized, clean, and safe. Finally, be clear and logical when giving orders.

- *Meeting the needs of participatives.* Include them in the decision-making process; use participative management. Provide opportunity for off-the-job social interaction—company picnics, recreation programs, and annual meetings. Emphasize teamwork on the job through task forces, committee projects, quality improvement teams, and other group involvement activities. Have regular, well-run staff meetings; provide ample opportunity for sharing ideas. Ask for opinions, listen to what is said, and then demonstrate responsiveness. Get to know the person—family makeup, off-the-job interests, and personal goals. Appeal to both logic and feelings when dealing with problems; emphasize a joint approach and talk with, not at, the person. Use communication vehicles such as bulletin boards, newsletters, focus groups, telephone hot lines, and the open-door policy to exchange information. Allow people skills to shine in public relations, teaching, and mediation projects. Provide growth opportunities through in-service training and staff development programs. Finally, keep human relations smooth; consider personal feelings.

- *Meeting the needs of individualists.* Recognize independence and personal freedom; don't supervise too closely. Provide immediate reward for good performance; don't delay gratification. Talk in terms of present; de-emphasize past and future. Provide opportunities for growth through exploration and self-discovery. Keep things stimulating; keep things fun. Focus on meaningful personal experiences, satisfying interpersonal relationships, and important social causes. Provide individual job assignments, and assign work by projects when possible. Accentuate feelings as well as logic when handling problems. Reward good performance with personal time off and personal fulfillment activities. Keep things casual; minimize formality. Avoid rigid controls; allow for questions and creativity. Finally, treat the individualist as a separate person, not as a member of a group or organization.

The concept of interpersonal style is like being right-handed or left-handed. Although people are able to use either hand, they usually prefer one over the other. The preferred hand is generally better developed, making it more efficient and effective to use. You can demonstrate this for yourself by first writing your name as you normally would. Then change hands and sign your name. You can do it, even though it is difficult and feels unnatural.

Solving Personality Differences

Differences in personality can result in communication problems unless there is appreciation for the needs and contributions of different kinds of people. Unless the idea is accepted that it is OK to be different, misunderstanding can develop over any dimension of interpersonal style. When differences occur, there are four steps you can take to improve communication.

Step 1: Talk it out. Silence results in emotional wear and tear on everyone. At the same time, it prevents any possibility of solving problems. The silent treatment is a negative treatment; anyone can be negative. Use the positive approach and talk it out:

- *Where:* Talk it out in private so that all parties can communicate in an uncensored and honest way. Unless the truth is known, a problem will never be fully resolved.

- *When:* Talk it out when people are fresh. Otherwise, they won't be able to think clearly, much less express themselves clearly.

- *How:* Be sure every word spoken passes three important tests—is it true, is it necessary, is it kind?

Step 2: Be understanding. Look at things from the other person's view. As an old saying goes, "You can't understand another person until you have walked a mile in his shoes." So see things from the woman's point of view; see the man's side. See things from the boss's perspective; see them through the customer's eyes. See things from the different perspectives of traditionals, participatives, and individualists. Empathy can go a long way toward promoting understanding.

Also, try to understand the forces—past and present—in another person's life that may have influenced and helped shape her or his personality. You may understand Mary better if you know what it was like to be raised as an only child in the 1970s. You may understand John better if you know what it was like to be raised in a large family in the 1950s. Consider the differences between being brought up a Roman Catholic in Cleveland, Ohio; growing up Jewish in New York City; and being raised a Baptist in Birmingham, Alabama. If you do not know what it was like being a child in Mexico City in 1980, you may want to ask.

Step 3: Be flexible. Be willing to compromise. If people are frozen in different styles or points of view, no amount of talking will result in good relations. Remember, everyone must be flexible. If one party is always the one to compromise, a sense of fairness is violated and the relationship will ultimately deteriorate. People may stay in a relationship physically but leave it emotionally.

Step 4: Be tolerant. Recognize that differences in personality are unavoidable, that few people live or work with their identical twin, and that tolerance of different styles—traditional, participative, and individualistic—is necessary if communication, teamwork, and a one-team attitude are to be achieved.

Leadership Needs and Organizational Contributions of Different Styles

An important point to remember is that different types of people need different treatment to be satisfied and to achieve their full potential. The absence of planning and clear guidelines is particularly upsetting to traditionals. Conflict and impersonal relationships take an especially heavy toll on participatives. Strict rules and close supervision represent a hostile environment for individualists. The most effective leaders honor the needs of all three types of people. They establish structure and high standards for traditionals, provide warmth and social interaction for participatives, and encourage creativity and personal growth for individualists.

Although different organizations may attract different types of people—the structure and order of the military may appeal to traditionals, human interaction and service to others may meet participative needs, and freedom of action and creative expression may appeal to individualists—remember that each interpersonal style has positive qualities and that an organization with variety can benefit by a balance of styles.

- *Traditionals* bring roots, stability, and discipline that every organization needs if it is going to grow and prosper. They provide systems and procedures that allow a lot of people to work together in an organized way.

- *Participatives* are interactive and friendly. They provide the glue that holds people together. As leaders, they are participative; as followers, they are good team players. Participatives are the harmonizing agents needed by every family, work group, and organization. Participatives provide warmth and support by their very nature.

- *Individualists* provide new ideas and creativity. They are independent and resist close supervision, but when personally motivated, they are dynamic and creative. An organization needs creativity within to remain vibrant and develop new markets, new products, and new initiatives, especially if it exists in a competitive environment.

Mixing Personalities to Strengthen the Group

In building a team, some leaders select members in their own image. They choose associates with personalities similar to their own. This approach can limit the potential of the group in meeting its goals. Leaders should instead consider what members with different styles can gain from each other. The following table shows how each style of interpersonal relations can add balance, flexibility, and overall effectiveness to a group or organization.

Strengths of Traditionals	Strengths of Participatives	Strengths of Individualists
■ Provide clarity of assignment.	■ Care about people.	■ Challenge the system.
■ Organize efforts.	■ Bring harmony and peace.	■ Find flaws in procedures.
■ Give attention to detail.	■ Teach and give counsel.	■ Tackle problems with zest.
■ Adhere to standards.	■ Give encouragement to others.	■ Provide reform where needed.
■ Appreciate traditions.	■ Instill team spirit.	■ Generate new ideas.
■ Remember facts and figures.	■ Persuade and motivate.	■ Focus energies on the present.
■ Give structure and order.	■ Are sensitive to others and aware of their needs.	■ Accentuate possibilities.
■ Provide consistency.	■ Provide warmth and support.	■ Celebrate the individual.

As an organization experiences greater diversity, there is a need for greater tolerance. With sufficient tolerance, the different positive qualities of traditional, participative, and individualistic types of people can help the organization achieve its full potential. By nature, traditionals provide needed structure and organization, participatives add warmth and supportive human relations, and individualists bring creativity and the capacity for change from within.

Interpersonal Styles and Leadership Effectiveness

For a practical application showing that all three styles of interpersonal relations are important for organizational success, consider the case of five organization presidents:

- The first president was individualistic. He was a creative visionary whose genius was to found and physically create the organization. He was innovative and entrepreneurial.

- The second president was traditional, combining courtly ways with a basic goodness of character. His concern for people became a model and standard for others who would continue to serve the organization.

- The third president was participative, a master of diplomacy and persuasion. Gifted at finding the middle ground in disputes and the high ground in direction, he brought stability to the organization.

- The fourth president was versatile, with roughly equal amounts of all three styles. His administrative approach was traditional, or chain-of-command; his manner in dealing with people was participative; and his international initiatives were individualistic.

- The fifth president was a mixture of individualistic and participative. His creativity and ability to work with people were extraordinary, and he met the organization's traditional needs through excellent subordinates who provided needed structure and organization.

How can five people be so different, yet so effective? The answer is that as important as interpersonal style is, there are other factors that are even more important. These are character, leadership, and tolerance of diversity.

- *Character.* Each of the five presidents told the truth as he believed it to be, and in any moral dilemma, consideration of others came first. Think about it: We will forgive a person anything—odd dress, strange habits, even personality differences—when character is good.

- *Leadership.* All five presidents employed universal principles of effective leadership. Each had a vision and a plan. Each kept job knowledge current to solve problems and develop others. Each demonstrated a humanistic approach in dealing with people.

- *Diversity.* All five presidents showed understanding, responsiveness, and flexibility in relating to all types of people—young and old, black and white, male and female, and traditional, participative, and individualistic. Each was tolerant of differences and valued diversity as a strength.

In dealings with other people, the leader's challenge is to understand and value different types of people, and to be wise, caring, and flexible in meeting their needs. To the degree this challenge is met, individuals will be served and organizations will prosper by the gifts they bring.

What does it take to meet this challenge? First is a sincere belief that the greatest good for all individuals can best be achieved by working together. Second is the knowledge that diversity enriches individuals and groups. Third is the day-to-day practice of considering the interests and meeting the needs of others. Ask yourself how you are doing in these three key areas, and what you can do to improve.

Part Seven Summary

After reading Part Seven, you should know the following key concepts, principles, and terms. Fill in the blanks from memory, or copy the answers listed below.

Business leader (a) _____ recommends developing others and delegating authority as a means of freeing up the leader to tackle new or undone tasks, thus multiplying the leader's effectiveness. In today's workplace, the ability to (b) _____ is not only desirable but also essential for organizational success, because all the talents of all employees need to be fully utilized. Established rules for effective delegation include (c) _____, _____, _____, _____, and _____. (d) _____ is one of the most important and useful leadership skills. Proven principles for assigning work effectively include (e) _____, _____, _____, _____, _____, and _____. (f) _____, the ability to work well in cooperation with people, is equally important at all levels of management responsibility. The (g) _____, popularized by author Laurence Peter, refers to being overpromoted to one's level of incompetency. When communication, teamwork, and attitude problems occur at work, often the cause is (h) _____. Just as individuals are different, so are whole groups of people different in (i) _____. (j) _____ bring roots, stability, and discipline to the workplace. They respect the chain of command, and respond positively to high standards of work and conduct, as well as clear and logical orders. (k) _____ are warm and friendly, providing the harmony, peace, and teamwork that every work group needs. They respond positively to participative leadership and consideration in human interactions.

(l) _____ are dynamic and creative when personally motivated. They avoid close supervision and respond positively to individual assignments requiring unconventional ideas and methods. When conflicts occur between different personalities, constructive steps are (m) _____, _____, _____, and _____.

Answer Key for Part Seven Summary

a. **Bill Gates,** page 232

b. **delegate,** page 232

c. (any five) **share power with employees; don't delegate the bad jobs, saving the good ones for yourself; know your employees; use delegation as a development tool; delegate work fairly among all employees; be sure to back your employees if delegated authority is questioned; let employees know what decisions they have authority to make and delegate decision making to the lowest possible level; delegate with consistency; delegate whole tasks and allow sufficient time to get jobs done; insist on clear communication; make good use of questions when delegating work; explain the importance of assignments; learn to live with work styles that are not like your own; avoid delegating tasks that are pets, personal, or petty; follow the three D's for all work—do it, delegate it, or ditch it,** pages 237–38

d. **Assigning work effectively,** page 239

e. (any six) **consider the availability of the employee's time and whether this is the ideal person to do the job; use work assignments as a means of developing people; know exactly what you want to communicate before giving an order; if many** duties or steps are involved in an order, follow oral communication with a note, and keep a copy; ask rather than tell, but leave no doubt that you expect compliance; use the correct language for the employee's training level; make assignments in a logical sequence, using clear and concise language; be considerate but never apologetic when asking someone to do a job; talk deliberately and authoritatively, but avoid shouting or making an unnecessary show of power; take responsibility for the orders you give; give people the opportunity to ask questions and express opinions; follow up to make sure assignments are being carried out properly, and modify them if the situation warrants, pages 239–40

f. **relational skill,** page 242

g. **Peter Principle,** page 247

h. **personality differences,** page 248

i. **style of interpersonal relations,** page 248

j. **Traditionals,** page 253

k. **Participatives,** page 253

l. **Individualists,** page 253

m. **talk it out, be understanding, be flexible, be tolerant,** pages 258–59

Reflection Points—personal thoughts on effective delegation, how to assign work, and the role of personality

Complete the following questions and activities to personalize the content of Part Seven. Space is provided for writing your thoughts.

■ Discuss the role of delegation in the leadership process. Do you know a leader with delegation weakness? Do you know a leader with delegation strengths? Compare and contrast their leadership styles and effectiveness.

_____

_____

■ Do you know a leader who is effective at assigning work and giving orders? What principles and techniques are used?

_____

_____

■ Discuss career stages, nature of work, and focus of work as these factors apply in your occupational life. Where are you now? Do your personal interests match the demands of your job?

_____

_____

■ Have you developed the technical, relational, and conceptual skills appropriate for the work you do? Discuss.

_____

_____

■ Discuss the concept of the vital shift and the pros and cons of the new-job tryout. Give real-life examples.

_____

_____

■ Discuss the role of personality in your work experience. Are you primarily traditional, participative, or individualistic? Does your organization value your style of interpersonal relations? Is your supervisor wise, caring, and flexible in meeting your needs?

_____

_____

Action Assignment

As a bridge between learning and doing, complete the following action assignment.

1. What is the most important idea you have learned in Part Seven?

2. How can you apply what you have learned? What will you do, with whom, where, when, and, most important, why?

Part 8   Developing Others

23. **The Leader as Teacher**
24. **Helping People Through Change**
25. **Burnout Prevention**

THE BEST WAY OF EDUCATING PRINCES is to teach them to become intimate with all sorts and conditions of men. Their commonest handicap is that they do not know their people. People are always masked in their company because they are the masters. They meet many subjects, but no real people. Hence, bad choice of favorites and ministers that dims the fame of kings and ruins their subjects. Teach a prince to be sober, chaste, pious, generous, and you will teach him how to love his people and his kingly dignity; and you will implant in him every virtue at the same time.

—Marquis of Vauvenargues, 1715–1747
Maxims and Reflections of Luc de Clapiers

Learning Points

In Part Eight, you will discover the answers to these questions:
- What is the role of the leader as teacher and developer of people?
- What can a leader do to help people through change? What are the roles of attitude and personal example?
- Where are you in the burnout process? What steps can be taken for emergency, short-term, and long-term aid?

23

The Leader as Teacher

The Native American totum for *teacher* is Wolf. As the moon rises every night, Wolf always finds something new to learn from it. Leaders, too, in exploring life may discover new truths to share with the rest of the clan, the human race. How does a leader show concern for others? An important way is by taking interest in people and by helping them grow to their full potential. The signs of caring leadership appear primarily among the followers. Are the followers engaged in their work and striving to do their best? Are they learning and growing in knowledge, skill, and attitude?[1]

Many leaders view **developing others** as the most relevant and rewarding of all their tasks. Effective leaders at all levels of responsibility—chief executive, middle manager, and frontline supervisor—are aware that the failure experienced by Roger in the following story can occur in the adult world of work as well.

Why Can't Roger Learn?[2]

When Roger was first observed in the classroom, he was beginning to fail and to feel defeated, but he was trying. When the observers walked in, he was listening with obvious interest to a story his teacher was reading. He sat quietly for at least 15 minutes. After the story, the teacher wrote some letters of the alphabet on the blackboard and requested that the children copy them on a sheet of paper she passed out. Roger picked up the crayon and looked at his neighbor's paper to see what he was supposed to do; he then started to write. The teacher moved over to him, took the crayon out of his hand and said firmly and with minor irritation, "Not a crayon, Roger; use a pencil."

Roger glanced at the little girl on his right, in obvious embarrassment. He wanted her to like him. He turned back to the teacher and said in a small voice, "I don't have a pencil." The teacher turned to the class and announced, "Some of us are not prepared. Who has a pencil to lend Roger?" Another child, eager to please the teacher, moved over to Roger and handed him a pencil. Roger was looking at the floor in embarrassment, but managed to thank him. In a few moments he again tried to find out how to do the assigned task. He watched his neighbor, but the child turned to him and said angrily, "Stop looking. Do your own stuff."

Finding no answer to his dilemma, Roger decided to escape by going up to sharpen his pencil. Another child was ahead of him, so Roger waited patiently for his turn. His smallness in comparison to the other children was very evident. Two other children came to sharpen their pencils and pushed Roger aside. He allowed the intrusion, because what can be done when others are so much bigger and aggressive? Another child came up and also attempted to push Roger aside. Anger flooded over his face. He had to show them that he had importance too. He attempted to push the intruder away saying, "It's my turn." The teacher noticed Roger pushing and said angrily, "Roger, take your seat, immediately." The teacher then glanced over at the observers, grimaced with distaste, and shook her head. She was sure that they shared insight into Roger's problems.

Roger walked dejectedly back to his seat. After a few moments of depressed staring at his paper, he leaned toward the girl on his left and whispered desperately, "How do you do it?" The girl frowned and said, "Shh-h," and hit him on the head with her pencil.

The teacher noticed difficulty again and assuming that Roger was responsible (after all, he is such a problem), said in exasperation, "Roger, will you please pay attention to your paper!"

Roger glanced around the room to see if everyone else was looking at him. He stared down at his shoe, his face red. He could have been saying, "What's wrong with me? Why can't I do anything right? Why does everyone hate me?" He still wanted to try; he had not reached the place where complete failure and hostility had taken over. Therefore, he attempted to do something about the hated paper before him. He made some marks; then, as though talking to himself, he said, "Is this good?" He glanced over at the paper of the boy on his right. As if in answer to his own question, he said, "Oh, ugh. Look at his." He wanted to think somebody was doing worse than he was. The boy stuck out his tongue at him, and Roger turned listlessly back to his paper.

The teacher was coming up the aisle again and paused at Roger's seat. "Roger, we are not writing our names, we are just practicing M's." She hurried over to the blackboard without showing him what to do and started moving through the next lesson. Several more letters were presented. Roger became restless. He didn't understand. He wiggled in his seat and then stood up. The children began to practice the letters again. Roger became very frustrated as he found he was unable to form them. He let his paper fall to the floor.

"Pass your papers to the end of the table," the teacher said. "Roger, get your paper," said the little girl next to him, "Roger, I'm telling. We have to pass them down." The angry voice of the teacher was once again heard. "Roger, get your paper off the floor." Roger complied, but he hit the paper with his pencil. He didn't like it. It was no good. He felt bad. He didn't want anyone else to see it.

The teacher gave all the children another piece of paper to continue the letter-making practice. Roger somehow found new determination and tried again. He followed the teacher's movements in the air, whispering to himself in concentration. The angry little girl leaned over to him and said, "Shh-h," and hit him on the head with her pencil again. Roger wanted her to like him, so he did nothing. But his frustration had to be expressed. He zoomed his pencil in the air, making a quiet airplane noise. He forgot the task. The teacher scolded him again and wearily exhorted him to pay attention.

The observation lasted only one hour. What happens over time to such a person, who experiences hour after hour of failure? Two months after the initial observation, Roger refused to try any learning task. He often crawled on the floor like an animal, making odd noises. He could not sit still for more than five minutes, and he hit his peers and yelled at them. His teacher became frantic. His mother was so worried that she came to school often and peered through the window of the schoolroom door. "He cries every day about school. He says everyone hates him," she explained.

Failure and a particular kind of punishment had distorted Roger. In many schools where administrators and teachers are unaware of the seriousness of allowing a child to fail or of using aversive techniques to change behavior, they still ask about such a child, "Why did it happen?" "Probably the parents," the accusing answer echoes down the school halls.

Effective leaders know that Roger's failure wasn't necessary, that preventing such failure is important, and that their own ability to teach is often the key. It is a proven fact that expectation of failure can help bring about failure. Conversely, expectation of success can help bring about success. Children have been found to score from two to three points higher when an IQ test is administered by a teacher who conveys expectation for success, than when the same test is given by a teacher who does not convey high expectations. This phenomenon is called the Pygmalion effect.[3]

Leadership author and educator John Gardner explains the importance of the leader as teacher and developer of people:

> If one is leading, teaching, dealing with young people or engaged in any other activity that involves influencing, directing, guiding, helping or nurturing, the whole tone of the relationship is conditioned by one's faith in human possibilities. That is the generative element, the source of the current that gives life to the relationship.[4]

Are leaders who are interested in employee development on the wrong track? Are they overly concerned with a relatively unimportant subject? Are they too employee-centered to the detriment of organizational goals? Take the test in Exercise 23–1 to see for yourself the importance of developing others. You will find that training helps both employee morale and job performance.

Exercise 23–1
Numbers Never Lie

Directions:

Your task is to circle the numbers in Figure 23–1, beginning with 1 and proceeding sequentially through 2, 3, 4, and so forth, to 60. Do not skip any numbers. You are to circle as many as possible within a 60-second time limit.

Figure 23–1
Numbers Worksheet

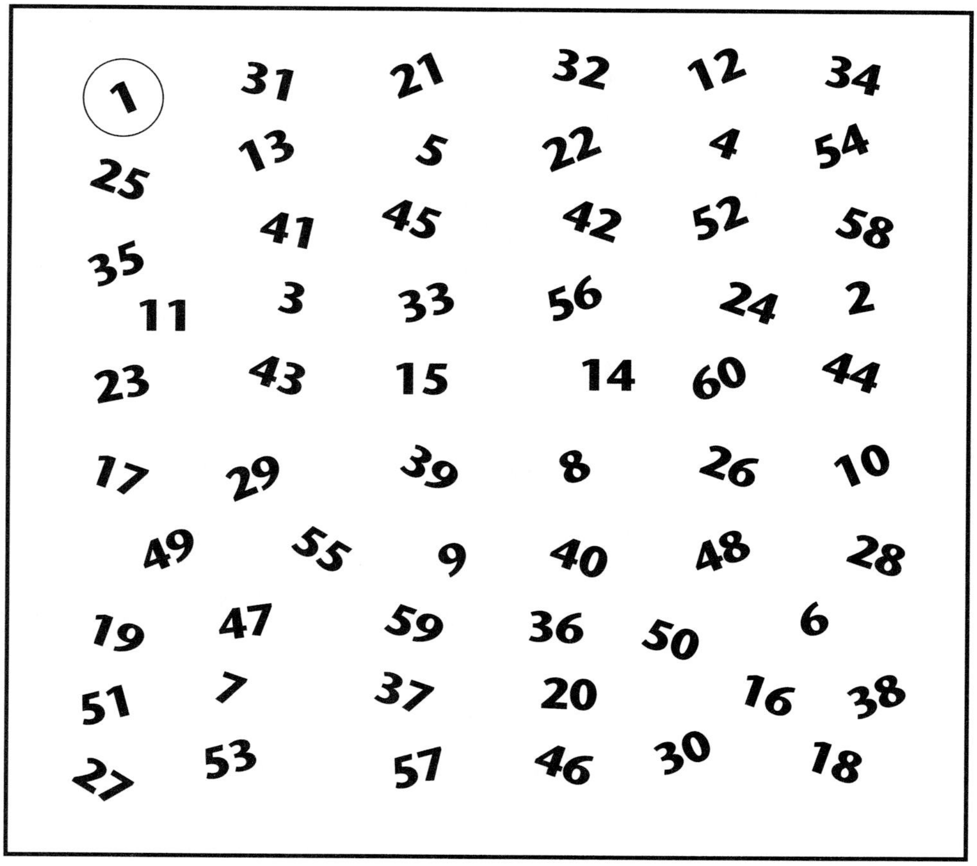

Discussion:

Now that you have completed the task, how did you do? How do you feel? Perhaps you did not do as well as you would have liked, and probably you feel frustrated, much like Roger did in the foregoing story.

Further Directions:

At this point, you are asked to repeat the task, but this time you will be given the benefit of training.

Step 1:

Draw a straight line between the dots at the top and bottom of Figure 23–2.

Step 2:

Draw a straight line from the dot at the left side of the figure to the dot on the right side of the figure.

Figure 23–2
Numbers Worksheet

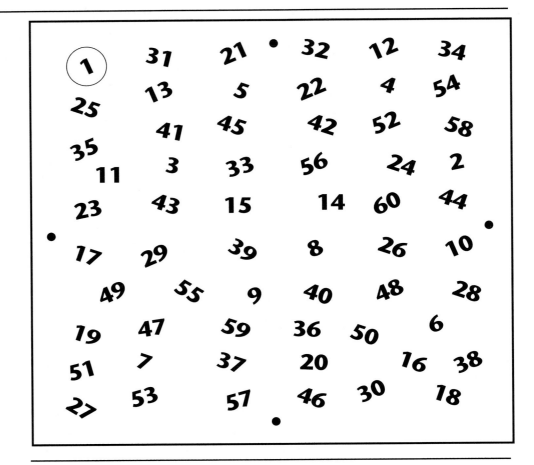

Step 3:

You now have four quadrants. Notice that all the odd numbers are on the left side of the vertical line; the even numbers are on the right side. Notice also that the first five numbers are in the top half of the figure, the next five numbers are in the bottom half of the figure, and so on for every sequence of five numbers up to 50. Finally, notice that numbers 51 to 60 alternate back and forth from the lower left quadrant to the top right quadrant.

Step 4:

Your task is to circle the numbers in Figure 23–2, beginning with 1 and proceeding sequentially through 2, 3, 4, and so forth, to 60. Do not skip any numbers. You are to circle as many as possible within a 60-second time limit.

Further Discussion:

How did you do this time? How do you feel? Typically, people will do at least 25 percent better—and even as much as 100 percent better. Usually, they feel much less frustrated. Both performance and attitude improve because training has been provided. Again, think of Roger and how his life might have changed for the better if his teacher had taken the time to give him proper instructions.

The number counting that you did in the exercise was a simple task. In the work setting, however, many complex and important jobs are performed—everything from repairing cars to repairing bodies. Consider the potential for improving the quality of work and the quality of work life through proper training. Imagine the benefit we would gain with even a 25 percent improvement in job performance and satisfaction.

The Development of Others

Motivation expert Zig Ziglar once observed that he had read a lot of birth announcements, all of them indicating that the newborn was a boy or a girl. None of them announced the arrival of a farmer, a doctor, an engineer, or a member of any other profession. Performers in every field are developed, not born. Effective leaders recognize the importance of developing people. Like the productive farmer who plants good seeds and cares for them properly, effective leaders view developing others as an essential key to success.

Leading is like coaching in many ways. In basketball, for example, the coach cannot cross the line and move onto the playing court. She works in advance of playing time and on the side of the action. Before the game, she prepares her players by anticipating the problems they will face and by readying them to meet those problems. She trains, advises, and encourages, but she never touches the ball. The coach cannot do the players' work for them. Instead, she is a mentor and teacher.[5]

The leader as teacher is a concept that has been with us for centuries. The term *mentor* is derived from *The Odyssey,* in which Homer describes Ulysses as choosing his trusted friend, Mentor, to look after his son, Telemachus, as Ulysses begins his 10-year journey. Mentor gave Telemachus good counsel, and he cared for and protected him as his teacher. These attributes have been central to our modern concept of mentoring in the workplace.[6]

Types of Teacher/Leaders

Just as there is no single best way to lead, there is no one best way to develop others. Each leader brings unique personal experiences and talent to the task. The following list describes five types of teacher/leaders.[7] Keep in mind that not all types are appropriate for all learners in all circumstances.

- *Shamans* heal through the use of personal power. They focus the attention of their followers on themselves. When this approach is combined with unusual gifts and skills, shamans are charismatic. They have power, energy, and commitment that they use to energize others.

- *Priests* claim power through office. They are agents of omnipotent authority, and the people who follow them are taught to see themselves as set apart from others. Priests establish structure, order, and continuity—a past program and a plan for the immediate and distant future. Priests operate in a hierarchy with roles and duties in a hierarchical ladder.

- *Elected leaders* undergo trials, self-transformation, training, or some other rite to achieve their positions. Elected leaders derive power not only from their own experience, but also from the mandate of their followers. Consent of followers constitutes much of the power of these teacher/leaders.

- *Missionaries* are goal-directed. Usually, missions involve a utopian view of the future and a program for achieving reforms. Missionaries teach out of personal conviction, believing in certain ideals and seeing it as a duty to pass on these ideals to others.

- *Mystic healers* seek the source of illness and health in the follower's personality. Mystic healers try to discover the statue in the marble and seek, like Michelangelo, to find what can be created from the raw material. To be successful, these teacher/leaders require unselfish motivation and considerable sensitivity, as well as flexibility to vary treatment according to the nature and needs of each individual.

Much of contemporary leading and teaching incorporates the priestly, elected, and missionary types. The priest brings continuity and hierarchy to the task, as power is delegated by the most powerful, and people at each level, division, or unit are differentiated from others. The elected leader gains authority by election, and followership is by consent of the governed. Missionaries can be found in many organizations that have some kind of central mission—economic, religious, political, social service, or other. Shamans and mystic healers may or may not operate within the bounds or the dictates of an organization. Their approach to developing others tends to be individualistic and personalized.

Principles of Developing Others

Like pine trees that are stunted if they grow near the timberline, more fully developed if they grow farther down the mountainside, and tall and green if they grow in the valley, people also experience maximum development under certain conditions. **Personal conditions conducive to growth are the following:**[8]

1. People grow when there is a felt need.
2. People grow when they are encouraged by someone they respect.
3. People grow when their plans move from general goals to specific actions.
4. People grow as they move from a condition of lower to higher self-esteem.
5. People grow as they move from external to internal commitment.

Organizational conditions conducive to growth are the following:[9]

1. Basic respect for the worth and dignity of all people is a cardinal value.
2. Individual differences are recognized, and a variety of learning experiences are provided.
3. Each person is addressed at his or her level of development and is helped to grow to fuller potential.
4. Good communications prevail—people express themselves honestly and listen with respect to the views of others.
5. Growth is rewarded through recognition and tangible signs of approval—commendation, promotion, income, and the like.

Principles to follow in developing others include the following:

1. *Have a respectful attitude.* Deep inside each person is the desire to achieve something, to be somebody. If you tap into that desire and demonstrate that you believe in the person, self-respect can be ignited. Ultimately, it is self-respect or self-esteem that fuels success. Consider the story of the banker and the beggar:

> There was a banker who would regularly drop a coin in a beggar's cup. Unlike most people, the banker would insist on receiving one of the pencils the beggar had with him. The banker would say, "You are a merchant, and I always expect to receive good value from the merchants with whom I do business."
>
> One day the beggar was gone. Some years later, the banker walked by a concession stand, and there was the former beggar, now a shopkeeper. The shopkeeper said, "I always hoped you might come by some day. You are largely responsible for me being here. You kept telling me that I was a merchant. I started thinking of myself that way. Instead of a beggar receiving gifts, I started selling pencils, lots of them. You gave me self-respect and caused me to look at myself differently."[10]

2. *Build self-esteem.* The importance of developing self-esteem can be seen in the following story:

Thomas J. Watson, Jr. (1914–1993), son of the founder of IBM, initially had trouble living up to his father's charisma and achievements. Watson Sr. was one of the great entrepreneurs of the 20th Century. He put IBM on the map and gave the world the motto THINK. In contrast, Watson Jr. even needed a tutor to get through the IBM sales school. "I had no distinctions, no successes," he writes in *Father, Son & Company.*

When Watson started taking flying lessons, however, something important happened. "What a feeling," he says. "I was good at flying, instantly good. I poured everything I had into this activity and gained a lot of personal self-confidence." This small success led to greater successes. Watson became an officer in the U.S. Air Force during WWII. It was in the Air Force that he discovered he had "an orderly mind, the ability to focus on what was important, and to put it across to others."

Watson eventually became the CEO of IBM and launched the company into the Computer Age. In fifteen years, he multiplied IBM's earnings almost tenfold. By the time he retired, the IBM he shaped was the greatest success story of America's postwar boom, routing computer-industry rivals like General Electric, RCA, and Sperry-UNIVAC. During his tenure, IBM created more wealth for its shareholders than any company in business history, an achievement that led *Fortune* magazine in 1987 to declare Watson, "The greatest capitalist who ever lived."[11]

3. *Use the correct medium or combination of techniques.* Consider whether one-on-one coaching, formal education, professional conferences, or on-the-job learning is the best method, or whether a combination of approaches would be most appropriate.

Sabbaticals in various forms are ideal ways to keep fresh and motivated. They have long been a tradition in universities and can be equally effective in the business world. One example is the company with five leaders for every four turns or departments. By rotation, one person is available at any time to study and work on projects that otherwise would never be addressed. New products, markets, and enthusiasm are the by-products of such a system of working sabbaticals. This is a good way to combat the typical syndrome where people get promoted, learn the job, then get bored, and pass the feeling on to others.

4. *Use coaching versus judging in developing people, considering purpose, timing, focus, and process.*[12]

Purpose. Judging serves to label performance. Coaching serves to improve performance.

Timing. Judging is time-specific, such as a quarterly review. Coaching is ongoing and provided as needed.

Focus. Judging is standardized for all subjects. Coaching is tailored to each individual.

Process. Judging is unilateral, one-way. Coaching is interactive, two-way.

5. *Practice.* Practice builds proficiency. Most things people learn involve more than abstract thinking; they must be learned with the senses and muscles as well. By actually repairing a car, a person will learn more about automobile maintenance than by merely reading about it. As the Greek dramatist Sophocles said, "Knowledge must come through action." And as Confucius said, "I listen and I hear; I see and I remember; I do and I understand."[13]

Practice is especially important in the development of leaders. As leadership expert Henry Mintzberg explains: "The idea that you can take intelligent but inexperienced young people who have never managed anybody and turn them into highly effective leaders via two years of classroom training is unrealistic. This is the reason cooperative education, internships, and other learn-by-doing assignments are so important."[14]

Training in the Workplace

Both the organization and the individual are helped if people have multiple skills, if they can move easily across functional boundaries, if they are comfortable switching between regular duties and special projects, if growth is valued, and if continuous learning is a way of life. In such organizations, there is an understanding that the employer and employee share responsibility for maintaining proficiency and achieving success. Employers give employees the chance to develop enhanced employability in exchange for better productivity and commitment to the company's purpose for as long as the employee works there.[15]

The American Society of Training and Development (ASTD) states that the overall U.S. commitment to training is approximately 1.4 percent of payroll, with better employers providing substantially more—from 2 to 5 percent of payroll. New employee orientation and leadership development are the two most cited types of training. See Table 23–1 for examples of corporate training expenditures.[16]

Table 23–1
Examples of Corporate Annual Training Expenditures[17]

Company	Total Annual Training Expenditure*	Percentage of Payroll
IBM	$750 million	5 percent
General Electric	$260 million	4 percent
Xerox	$257 million	3.5 percent
Texas Instruments	$45 million	3.5 percent
Motorola	$42 million	2.6 percent
Honeywell	$30 million	2.5 percent

*These expenditures do not include training participants' salaries. If salaries were included, annual expenditures would roughly double.

Through research on best practices, ASTD has developed a model of training that supports organizational effectiveness and contributes to individual productivity. Table 23–2 shows a model of highly effective training, including targeted training needs and types of training provided.

Table 23–2
Model of Highly Effective Training[18]

Targeted Training Needs	Types of Training Provided
Ensuring organizational performance	Executive development
	Management training and development
	Supervisory training and development
	Staff/employee training
Meeting strategic goals	Strategic planning, team building, employee orientation, quality improvement
Implementing new technology	Technical training
	Scientific and engineering training
	Technician training
	Craft and apprentice training
	Employee skill training
	Data processing and computer training
	Information systems training
Engaging customers	Sales and marketing training
	Customer service training
Protecting employees and communities	Health and safety training
	Regulatory compliance (e.g., meeting environmental standards)
Ensuring job readiness	Basic skills training

Developing Leaders

Organizations typically identify a leadership gap and then seek to fill the gap through training efforts. Competency and performance goals are usually set for achieving business results and developing people-building skills. Interventions include classroom instruction, seminars, performance coaching, mentoring, and action learning, or field activities. Are the results worth the effort? An example from sports shows the big dividends leadership development can pay:

In the book *Sacred Hoops,* coach Phil Jackson talks about his work with Michael Jordan. With such a gifted athlete, no coach could do much to improve his basketball play. So Jackson focused his efforts with Jordan on making the superstar a true leader of the team. And it worked. In 1989, five years after joining the league and the same year that Jackson became head coach of the Bulls, Jordan began to see his role not just as stealing balls and scoring points, but as a leader whose job also was to help raise the level of play of every other player on the team. It is this contribution, Jordan's ability to help his teammates better players, more than his superb athletic talent, that made the Chicago Bulls the world's winningest basketball team.[19]

Robert Katz, in his book *Skills of an Effective Administrator,* explains that leadership is a learned skill. Although people possess varying amounts of aptitude to lead, their skills can be improved through training and practice. Furthermore, even those lacking strong innate ability can improve their performance through coaching and learning. This is the rationale for the establishment of leadership schools—Plato's Academy, 387 B.C.; Aristotle's Lyceum, 355 B.C.; Oxford University, A.D. 1117; Harvard University, A.D. 1636; and the U.S. military academies, as well as over 1,000 corporate universities found in American business, industry, and government by A.D. 2000.[20]

One good way to learn is by **studying the masters,** those who have gone before. If you observe carefully, you will note a trace of Jonathan Winters in Robin Williams. The Beatles learned from Chuck Berry. Matisse learned from Gauguin. The most effective performers are honest in appraising their current skills and humble enough to learn from others. They copy, adapt, and sometimes surpass the heroes who were the source of their inspiration. They take to heart Yogi Berra's famous slogan, "You can observe a lot by watching."[21]

Individuals who want to develop leadership effectiveness should identify superb leaders and learn from their example. They should observe their behavior and ask questions. Understanding the values and goals of successful leaders, the rationale for their decisions and actions, the principles underlying their skills and techniques, and the resources they use to solve problems and make decisions can serve as an excellent foundation for developing one's own leadership ability.

Although much of what is labeled as leadership development is classroom-based and is provided in courses, seminars, and lectures, important growth can come from on-the-job experiences. These experiences usually force people to rise to a challenge or endure a trial they have never faced before. Out of adversity can come meaningful development that cannot be easily achieved in the classroom setting. Experiences having developmental possibilities include early work experience, first-time supervision, responsibility for starting something from scratch or for fixing something (turnaround), expansion of job scope, special projects and task force assignments, and line to staff switch. As an example, an international assignment may help develop a leader to be more open-minded, tolerate ambiguity, appreciate different perspectives, improve communication effectiveness, and raise self-confidence.[22]

Noel Tichy, author of *The Leadership Engine,* states that great organizations—such as IBM, Intel, GE, and Wal-Mart (when they are great)—don't have just one strong leader or a few here and there; they have many good leaders at all levels of the organization. They make leadership development and leadership excellence a strategic commitment and basis of success.[23]

The Employer–Employee Relationship

The employer–employee relationship is an important subject for both the individual and the organization, and it is especially important for people in leadership positions. The following is a discussion of what employers want in an employee and how to attract and keep good people.

What Employers Want in an Employee

The number one quality employers want in an employee is honesty. The need for trust is paramount because the employer relies on the employee to serve its customers, protect its property, and uphold its reputation. Employee honesty is essential.

Next, the employer wants someone who will take initiative and be a self-starter. The employee who is eager to serve is viewed as an asset. Specific skills are less important than the underlying qualities of self-motivation, desire to learn, and personal commitment.

Next, employers want employees with (1) work effectiveness; (2) communication skills; (3) the ability to get along well with others; (4) creative responses to setbacks and obstacles; (5) a high attitude–low maintenance approach to work; and (6) leadership potential.[24]

The shift from career dependence to career self-leadership is a reality in today's work environment. The following are basic rules for succeeding in one's work:

Rule 1: **Put your best foot forward.** Ask what is expected of you and with whom you will be working; then exceed expectations. Build good working relationships from the beginning.

Rule 2: **Deliver results.** Be known for reliability and performance. Stay on task, and persevere in the face of challenge. Let your deeds speak louder than the words you use.

Rule 3: **Be considerate.** Work cooperatively to accomplish tasks. Lend a helping hand to others in need, and have a one-team attitude in dealing with people.

Rule 4: **Be creative.** Keep an open mind, and look for ways to improve your organization and the work you do. Be original and open to new ideas.

Rule 5: **Have integrity.** Remember, success comes from doing the right things for the right reasons in the right way. Keep your thinking cap on to *know* what is right. Keep your character strong to *do* what is right.

How to Attract and Keep Good People

Attracting and keeping good employees is an ever-increasing concern for today's employers. The investment in time, money, and energy to hire a good employee is high, and the cost in lost time, lost money, and psychic letdown if the company loses a good employee is even higher. Consider that the financial cost alone (in 1999) averaged $2,250 for turning over one semiskilled employee after a 90-day probation period.[25]

It is important to know what attracts the best employees to a company and what makes them stay. These are two of the oldest issues in the business world, and maybe the most important.[26]

Now the Gallup Organization, of Princeton, New Jersey, claims to have answered how to keep good people once and for all. Marcus Buckingham, a senior consultant at the Gallup School of Management, explains that the opinion-polling company has identified 12 questions that appear to measure the core elements needed to attract and keep the most loyal, productive, and talented employees.

Gallup culled these dozen from the multitude of questions it has asked in interviews with more than 1 million employees during the past 25 years. Using factor analysis, regression analysis, concurrent validity studies, focus groups, and follow-up interviews, Gallup statisticians isolated the questions that most accurately measure the likelihood that a given workplace will attract and keep the best people. The exact wording of the questions is important.

1. Do I know what is expected of me at work?
2. Do I have the materials and equipment I need to do my best work right?
3. At work, do I have the opportunity to do what I do best every day?
4. In the last seven days, have I received recognition or praise for good work?
5. Does my supervisor, or someone at work, seem to care about me as a person?
6. Is there someone at work who encourages my development?
7. At work, do my opinions seem to count?
8. Does the mission of my company make me feel like my work is important?
9. Are my co-workers committed to doing quality work?
10. Do I have a good friend at work?
11. In the last six months, have I talked with someone about my progress?
12. At work, have I had opportunities to learn and grow?

It isn't just that employees who answer yes to these questions are more likely to stay with the company; the beauty of these 12 questions, according to Gallup, is that they address factors that are particularly important to the most talented and most productive employees.[27]

Of the 12, the most powerful questions are those with a combination of the strongest links to the most business outcomes. On the basis of this perspective, the first six are the most powerful questions. As a leader, if you want to know what you should do to maintain a strong and productive work group, addressing these six questions would be an excellent place to start.

Helping People Through Change

Nearly 2,500 years ago, the Greek philosopher Heraclitus noted that one can never cross the same river twice. In other words, change is a constant in life. In *Managing at the Speed of Change,* Daryl Conner writes that the volume, speed, and complexity of change are increasing in modern times. In our personal lives, we are constantly having to adjust to family changes, job changes, and health changes. In society at large, we face escalating changes in government, educational, religious, and other institutions.[28]

Change in the Workplace

Change is the label under which we put all of the things that we have to do differently in the future. In general, people dislike change. It makes a blank space of uncertainty between what is and what might be. The four major types of change in the workplace are:[29]

1. *Structure.* Change in structure is often severely resisted by people. Mergers, acquisitions, right-sizing, and reengineering activities typically involve tremendous change.

2. *Tasks.* Changes in the environment, including products and processes, require changes in tasks. Driving forces include customer needs, productivity improvement, and quality initiatives.

3. *Technology.* Innovations in this area have dramatically increased the rate of change. No industry, trade, or profession is immune to change caused by technological advancements.

4. *People.* Change in any of the above variables can result in changing relationships—change in managers, employees, co-workers, and customers, and change within a given person, such as change in knowledge, attitude, and skills.

A particularly stressful change in the American workplace is the downsizing and reorganization activities resulting from reengineering business, reinventing government, and other management initiatives. Employees who are victims of job loss, particularly those in their middle years, face enormous economic, social, and personal stress. Employees who remain with an organization often experience the "survivor syndrome." They are afraid they will be part of the next round of cuts, and they feel sadness and guilt over their co-workers' fate. In addition, they often have more work to do personally if production demands do not reflect the reduced number of people to do the job.

Many lessons have been learned from studying the downsizing of organizations, but four stand out: (1) People need to be flexible and willing to change to preserve important values and goals; (2) people need a positive attitude toward lifelong learning to remain viable in the workplace; (3) career education is a survival skill, since people must learn to manage their own careers; and (4) change can be expensive—consider that if 100 employees with an average annual salary of $24,000 go through a six-month change or transition resulting in two hours of distraction per day, the cost is $276,000.[30]

How prevalent is change in the workplace? During the 1990s, 85 percent of U.S. companies experienced at least one major transformation—merger, acquisition, restructure, or the like. A recent study found that 42 percent of the North American companies surveyed engaged in 11 or more change initiatives in a five-year period. In essence, the report describes a "change frenzy" that is creating cynical, demoralized employees and failing to produce meaningful improvements. The result is frontline workers who are overstressed by all of the changes created by managers frantically searching for the next formula for success. Consider the following letter from an apologetic and enlightened management:[31]

Dear Employees:

For the last decade, we have been trying to change our organization. Because we are frightened for our economic future, we kept looking for—and finding—another program du jour. We've dragged you through quality circles, excellence, total-quality management, self-directed work teams, re-engineering, and God knows what else. Desperate to find some way to improve our profitability, we switched from change to change almost as fast as we could read about them in business magazines.

All of this bouncing from one panacea to the next gave birth to rampant bandwagonism. We forgot to consider each change carefully, implement it thoughtfully, and wait patiently for results. Instead, we just kept on changing while you progressed from skepticism to cynicism to downright intransigence because you realized that all of these changes were just creating the illusion of movement toward some ill-defined goal.

Now we've got a lot of burned-out workers and managers, tired of the change-of-the-month club and unlikely to listen to our next idea, no matter how good it might be. For our complicity in this dismal state of affairs, we are sincerely sorry.

The Management

Managing People Through Change

Figure 24–1 depicts the all-too-common responses to change at various organizational levels.

Figure 24–1
Organizational Response to Change[32]

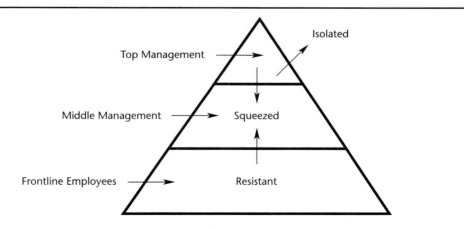

Top management. Top leaders may underestimate the impact of change on lower levels of the organization. They expect employees to go along when a change is announced and blame middle managers if people resist or complain. They may be so insulated that they truly don't know the results of their decisions and programs.

Middle management. Managers in the middle feel pressure to implement organizational change, but often lack information and top leadership direction to be successful. They may feel squeezed between resistant or withdrawn subordinates and demanding but out-of-touch superiors.

Frontline employees. Frontline people may feel threatened by changes announced by management and may respond with denial and resistance, leading often to worry and protective behavior. At this point, employees may shut down and be morale casualties. In this state, lack of willingness to take initiative and to be accountable is not uncommon.

Rules to Guide Leaders in Implementing Change

When organizations have the right goals in mind—they want to be customer-focused, quality-conscious, empowered, and profitable—and the reason for change is accounted for by market competition, customer demands, and other forces, the question of how to implement or manage change should be addressed. Seven rules should guide leaders in all change efforts:

1. *Have a good reason for making a change.* Consider each change carefully against the following criteria: Will it support the organization's purpose and goals; does it reflect the organization's basic principles and core values?

2. *Personalize change.* Let people know where you stand. Why is the change important to you? How will you be affected if the change is successful or if it fails? Why is this change important to them? What do they stand to gain or lose?

3. *Implement change thoughtfully.* Follow four proven principles: Involve the people who are affected by the change; go slow, giving people time to adjust; keep people informed through constant personal communication; be available.

4. *Put a respected person in charge of coordinating change.* Select someone who is trusted by all. Then tap the constructive power of the group through transition teams to plan, coordinate, and communicate change efforts. Provide training in new knowledge, attitudes, and skills to support change.

5. *Tell the truth.* When change is necessary, give the facts and rationale, not sugar-coated pep talks. Trust goes up when the truth is shared. Only after people know the truth and come to terms with negative feelings can they focus effectively on the future.

6. *Wait patiently for results.* It takes time for a seed to grow, and it takes time to realize benefits from change. Change that is too rapid can be destructive. Rush the process and reduce the results.

7. *Acknowledge and reward people.* As change is made, take time to recognize people and show appreciation. Acknowledge the struggles, sacrifices, and contributions people have made. A word of thanks goes a long way.

Social psychologist Kurt Lewin identified a three-step process for helping people through change: First, unfreeze the status quo; second, move to the desired state; third, live by conditions that become the new, but not rigid, status quo.[33]

- *Unfreezing* involves reducing or eliminating resistance to change. As long as people drag their heels about a change, it will never be implemented effectively. To accept change, people must first deal with and resolve feelings about letting go of the old. Only after people have dealt successfully with endings are they ready to make transitions.

- *Moving to the desired state* usually involves considerable two-way communication, including group discussion. Lewin advised that the person leading change should make suggestions and encourage discussion. Brainstorming, benchmarking, field study, and library research are good techniques for channeling the energies of the group. The best way to overcome resistance to change is to involve people in the changes that will affect them.

- *Living by new conditions* involves such factors as pointing out the successes of the change and finding ways to reward the people involved in implementing the change. Recognizing the contributions of others shows appreciation for their efforts and increases their willingness to participate in future change efforts.

Understanding Complex Organizational Change

There are many models for understanding organizational change. One of the best is an eight-stage process provided by John Kotter of Harvard University. Kotter's model summarizes the steps necessary to produce successful change. The first four steps unfreeze the status quo and energize the organization around a new vision. The remaining four steps help move the organization to the desired state, including implementing new practices and reinforcing changes in the organizational culture.[34] See Figure 24–2.

Figure 24–2
The Eight-Stage Process of Creating Major Change

1. Establishing a Sense of Urgency
- Examining the market and competitive realities
- Identifying and discussing crises, potential crises, or major opportunities

2. Creating the Guiding Coalition
- Putting together a group with enough power to lead the change
- Getting the group to work together like a team

3. Developing a Vision and Strategy
- Creating a vision to help direct the change effort
- Developing strategies for achieving that vision

4. Communicating the Change Vision
- Using every vehicle possible to constantly communicate the new vision and strategies
- Having the guiding coalition role-model the behavior expected of employees

5. Empowering Broad-Based Action
- Getting rid of obstacles
- Changing systems or structures that undermine the change vision
- Encouraging risk taking and nontraditional ideas, activities, and actions

6. Generating Short-Term Wins
- Planning for visible improvements in performance, or "wins"
- Creating those wins
- Visibly recognizing and rewarding people who made the wins possible

7. Consolidating Gains and Producing More Change
- Using increased credibility to change all systems, structures, and policies that don't fit together and don't fit the transformation vision
- Hiring, promoting, and developing people who can implement the change vision
- Reinvigorating the process with new projects, themes, and change agents

8. Anchoring New Approaches in the Culture
- Creating better performance through customer—and productivity—oriented behavior, more and better leadership and more effective management
- Articulating the connections between new behaviors and organizational success
- Developing means to ensure leadership development and succession management

Kotter has identified common errors and their consequences in creating organizational change. These are presented in Figure 24–3.[35]

Figure 24–3
Eight Errors Common to Organizational Change Efforts and Their Consequences

Common Errors
- Allowing too much complacency
- Failing to create a sufficiently powerful guiding coalition
- Underestimating the power of vision
- Undercommunicating the vision by a factor of 10 (or 100 or even 1,000)
- Permitting obstacles to block the new vision
- Failing to create short-term wins
- Declaring victory too soon
- Neglecting to anchor changes firmly in the corporate culture

Consequences
- New strategies aren't implemented well.
- Acquisitions don't achieve expected synergies.
- Reengineering takes too long and costs too much.
- Downsizing doesn't get costs under control.
- Quality programs don't deliver hoped-for results.

The empowerment of people is a key element for successful organizational change. Table 24–1 presents five principles leaders should follow for tapping the constructive power of all employees.

Table 24–1
Empowering People to Effect Change[36]

- **Communicate a clear, compelling vision to employees.** If employees have a shared sense of purpose, it will be easier to initiate actions to achieve that purpose.
- **Make structures compatible with the vision.** Unaligned structures block needed action.
- **Provide the training employees need.** Without the right skills and attitudes, people feel unempowered.
- **Align information and personnel systems to the vision.** Unaligned systems block needed action.
- **Confront supervisors who undercut needed change.** Nothing disempowers people the way a bad boss can.

Myths and Realities in Dealing with Change

There are a number of myths and realities in dealing with change.[37] One myth is that change will go away, when the reality is that change is here to stay. If you have lived long enough, you have witnessed firsthand the truth of this statement as you have seen your own body change, your family change, your work change, and even your mind change.

Another common myth is that you can just keep on doing things the way you have been, when the reality is that if your world is changing—home, work, and society—then you may have to change as well. For example, if the marketplace or technology or other external forces require doing business differently, you may not succeed if you are unwilling to make adjustments. Sometimes, to protect family, health, and other high-priority values, people have to make changes. As Charles Darwin wrote, "It is not the strongest of the species that survive, nor the most intelligent, but the one most responsive to change."[38]

The Importance of Attitude

What a person does when change occurs depends on his or her attitude. At one extreme, the individual may shut down and declare, "I will never change." A more effective approach is to keep an open mind and say, "Let's consider the possibilities."

In all areas of life, attitude affects our happiness, effectiveness, and general well-being. Attitude can make or break your career, your relationships, and even your health. We have all known someone with an attitude problem.

Some people take the attitude of the victim when change occurs. This robs them of personal energy and makes them less appealing to others. In contrast, other people view change as a challenge and focus on the opportunities and benefits that change can bring.

The power of attitude to change people's lives is reflected in this statement: Life is 10 percent what happens to you and 90 percent how you react to it. If you change your attitude, your attitude will change you. Figure 24–4 shows an attitude curve in response to change.

Figure 24–4   Attitude Curve in Response to Change[39]

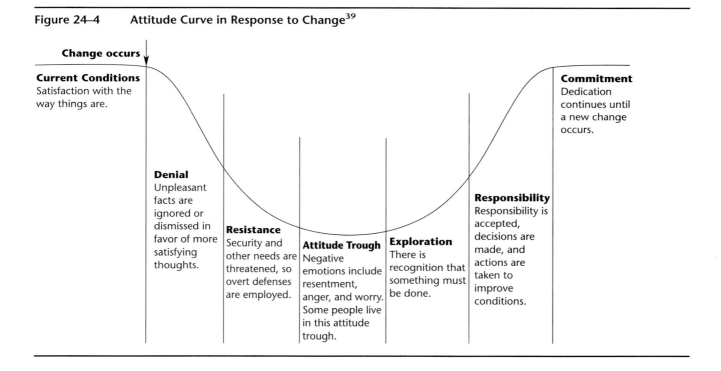

Figure 24–5 shows effective responses in dealing with change. Denial, resistance, and negative attitudes are avoided in favor of proceeding directly to states of **exploration, personal responsibility,** and **commitment.** This positive reaction is most likely to happen when people:

■ Believe the change is the right thing to do.

■ Have influence on the nature and process of the change.

■ Respect the person who is championing the change.

■ Expect the change will result in personal gain.

■ Believe this is the right time for change.[40]

Figure 24–5   Effective Responses in Dealing with Change

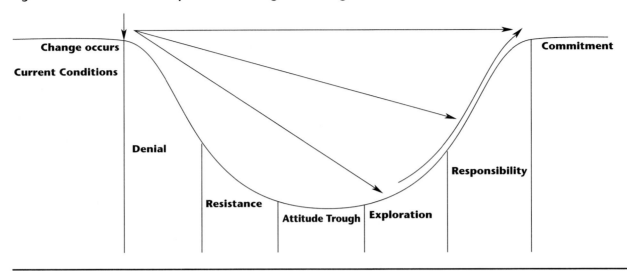

Strategies for Dealing with Change

Change often means loss, and loss can be difficult to deal with. Change may mean loss of security, confidence, relationships, direction, or possessions. Healthy coping means dealing with loss realistically and letting go of what must be given up in order to move on. You must adopt the belief that it is never too late to change your attitude and set your life on a new and positive course.

At each phase of the attitude curve, there are strategies that can be taken to help deal successfully with change.

	What the Individual Can Do	What Others Can Do
Denial	Don't put your head in the sand like an ostrich. Remember the adage "He who drinks from the cup of denial will sleep in the inn of defeat." Live by the principle, Know the truth and it will set you free.	Provide information. Answer questions. Communicate, communicate, communicate, ideally in person.
Resistance	State how you feel. Get it off your chest.	Listen and acknowledge feelings. Show understanding. Listening shows respect for others and may yield important and otherwise unknown information.
Attitude Trough	Say this is intolerable—enough is enough. Resolve to improve. Say good-bye to the past. Be willing to alter techniques.	Model and reinforce positive actions. Be patient.
Exploration	Have an open mind. Consider all possibilities. Coping includes fact finding and visioning an ideal future.	Focus on priorities. Channel energy in a helpful way. Brainstorm ideas and alternatives. Provide helpful training. Set short-term goals.
Responsibility	Have courage. Take action. Accept the consequences.	Encourage and expect the best. Help with planning and goal setting. Show support when decisions are made.
Commitment	Learn from the past. Enjoy the present. Plan for the future.	Acknowledge and celebrate accomplishments. Help prepare for future challenges.

Initiating Change

Thus far, our discussion about change has dealt with reacting healthfully and effectively to a changing world. What about initiating change? What if one's goal is to change others or improve conditions? These are admirable ambitions; but a word of advice from a Church bishop (name unknown) of Westminster Abbey (A.D. 1100) is worth remembering:[41]

When I was young and free and my imagination had no limits, I dreamed of changing the world. As I grew older and wiser, I discovered the world would not change, so I shortened my sights somewhat and decided to change only my country.

But it, too, seemed immovable.

As I grew into my twilight years, in one last desperate attempt, I settled for changing only my family, those closest to me, but alas, they would have none of it.

And now as I lie on my deathbed, I suddenly realize: *If I had only changed myself first,* then by example I would have changed my family.

From their inspiration and encouragement, I would then have been able to better my country and, who knows, I may have even changed the world.

More modern, but similar, advice on this issue is provided by the Indian political and spiritual leader Mohandas Gandhi, who said, "If you would change the world, then you must be the way you want the world to be."

UNIT 25

Burnout Prevention

D anger lurks in modern society, and the victim is often the dedicated and talented person. This danger is called burnout, and it can occur both on the job and in the home. The dictionary definition of *burn out* is "to fail, wear out, or become exhausted due to excessive demands on one's strength, resources, and energy."

In the human sphere, **burnout** is what happens when a person experiences physical, psychological, and spiritual fatigue and is unable to cope. Lack of energy and low vitality are characteristics of physical fatigue. Symptoms of psychological fatigue include depression and loss of sharpness in thinking and feeling. Spiritual fatigue is characterized by lack of interest and meaning in life, resulting in unhappiness and pessimism.[42]

Burnout can strike the businessperson with too many pressures and too little time, the homemaker with too much work and not enough appreciation, and the friend who is tired of being his or her "brother's keeper." The following are common types of burnout victims. Do any sound familiar to you?

- **Superpeople,** who want to do everything themselves because no one else can or will, and they have never let anyone down.
- **Workaholics,** who are driven to meet unreasonable demands placed on them (either self-incurred or assigned by others).
- **Burned-out Samaritans,** who are always giving to others while receiving little help or appreciation in return.
- **Mismatched people,** who do their jobs well but who do not like what they are doing.
- **Midcareer coasters,** who may once have been high performers but whose enthusiasm is gone.
- **Overstressed students,** who are holding down full-time jobs and full course loads.[43]

Burnout was introduced to the scientific literature in the early 1970s by psychologists Herbert Freudenberger and Christina Maslach. The evocative image of their term has made it a popular topic in the print and electronic media since that time. Extensive research has also been carried out. One literature search of the *Psychological Abstracts* revealed more than 1,000 research articles and nearly 100 books on burnout.[44]

Burnout is a great equalizer. It is blind to age, sex, color, and creed. It is a condition that can affect both white- and blue-collar workers as well as those who work at home. Job burnout is widespread in modern society. It is hazardous, and it can be contagious. If left unchecked, it can harm individual health, human relationships, and organization effectiveness.

A study by the American Academy of Family Physicians reported the extent of job stress for five occupations. Researchers surveyed 4,473 people working as business executives, teachers, secretaries, garment workers, and farmers, and found the number who usually or always work under stress to be high—80 percent of the business executives, 66 percent of the teachers and secretaries, 44 percent of the garment workers, and 35 percent of the farmers.

Participants in this study identified the major sources of stress to be work overload, pressure from superiors, deadlines, and low salaries. Probably the most important finding was the relationship discovered between job stress and health. Individuals reporting high work stress had two to four times as many health problems, including allergies, migraines, backaches, depression, insomnia, and other classic signs of burnout.[45]

The result of burnout is that a company loses its best people at a critical point, or it leaves them so stressed that their attitude sabotages projects. The result for the individual can be even more tragic, as the following story shows.

We Buried Joe Today

People were surprised when Joe suffered a sudden fatal heart attack since he didn't seem ill or particularly out of condition. Joe was a salesman in his late fifties, who went into sales thirty years ago because he could sell anything. He was a great talker, people liked him, and he was known for his tremendous energy. One day, Joe accepted a position with a large corporation. He liked the idea of having a big product to push and wanted the security that working for a big company offered him.

Gradually, though, Joe found that what he had accomplished was under siege by younger people who had the kind of energy and enthusiasm that, after two decades on the job, Joe found hard to muster routinely. The facts before Joe were scary—his mortgage payments and living expenses were high, his children were in college, and the prospect of retirement loomed darkly before him. The benefits of his work—a larger home and more expensive toys—suddenly caused more worry than joy.

Joe became troubled over whether he could maintain the pace that he set for himself and his company expected him to meet. He began pushing himself harder and harder to perform, complaining almost daily that he was losing his touch, that his memory wasn't as sharp, that he couldn't make the number of sales calls he used to, and that he couldn't put in the hours he did twenty-five or thirty years ago.

Joe's fears led to increased irritability. He had trouble sleeping and found himself in a constant state of worry. He even began drinking to relax and to help him fall asleep. Trying to overcome his alcohol-induced sleep, he began drinking more and more coffee in the morning to lift the veil of drowsiness. Joe also kept his fears and concerns shielded from what was potentially his greatest support system—his wife and family.

Finally, Joe's boss called him into his office one day. Joe had been anticipating this particular call with extreme dread for weeks. He had seen the trend—his good accounts gradually were being siphoned to younger people, he no longer was invited to management meetings, and he sensed that people were talking behind his back. Even as Joe became more frantic and desperate, working harder and longer, his territory was dwindling around him. Joe was at the wrong end of a dangerous game of burnout. When the call came, Joe knew exactly what it meant. He never made it to his boss's office.[46]

The following is a formula for the burnout process:

Too many demands on strength and resources over a prolonged period of time

+

High expectations and deep personal involvement in the work one does

+

Too few actions taken to replenish the energy consumed in meeting these demands

= Burnout

Job burnout can be prevented and overcome. This effort requires self-understanding and the support of others. For a better understanding of the job burnout phenomenon, take the test in Exercise 25–1 to evaluate your own status (homemakers should evaluate conditions at home).

**Exercise 25–1
Up in Smoke—Are You
Burned Out?[47]**

For each question, indicate your most accurate response by circling the number in the appropriate column.

Do you	Never	Rarely	Sometimes	Often	Always
Feel less competent or effective than you used to feel in your work?	1	2	3	4	5
Consider yourself unappreciated or "used"?	1	2	3	4	5
Dread going to work?	1	2	3	4	5
Feel overwhelmed in your work?	1	2	3	4	5
Feel your job is pointless or unimportant?	1	2	3	4	5
Watch the clock?	1	2	3	4	5
Avoid conversations with others (co-workers, customers, and supervisors in the work setting; family members in the home)?	1	2	3	4	5
Rigidly apply rules without considering creative solutions?	1	2	3	4	5
Become frustrated by your work?	1	2	3	4	5
Miss work often?	1	2	3	4	5
Feel unchallenged by your job?	1	2	3	4	5
Does your work					
Overload you?	1	2	3	4	5
Deny you rest periods—breaks, lunch time, sick leave, or vacation?	1	2	3	4	5
Pay too little?	1	2	3	4	5
Depend on uncertain funding sources?	1	2	3	4	5
Provide inadequate support to accomplish the job (budget, equipment, tools, people, etc.)?	1	2	3	4	5
Lack clear guidelines?	1	2	3	4	5
Entail so many different tasks that you feel fragmented?	1	2	3	4	5
Require you to deal with major or rapid changes?	1	2	3	4	5
Lack access to a social or professional support group?	1	2	3	4	5
Involve coping with a negative job image or angry people?	1	2	3	4	5
Depress you?	1	2	3	4	5

Scoring and Interpretation:

Add all the circled numbers, and record your total: _____

Score	Category
94–110	Burnout
76–93	Flame
58–75	Smoke
40–57	Sparks
22–39	No fire

- *Burnout.* If your score is 94 to 110, you are experiencing a very high level of stress in your work. Without some changes in yourself or your situation, your potential for stress-related illness is high. Consider seeking professional help for stress reduction and burnout prevention. Coping with stress at this level may also require help from others—supervisors, co-workers, and other associates at work, and spouse and other family members at home.

- *Flame.* If you scored from 76 to 93, you have a high amount of work-related stress and may have begun to burn out. Mark the questions on which you scored 4 or above, and rank them in order of their effect on you, beginning with the ones that bother you the most. For at least your top three, evaluate what you can do to reduce the stresses involved, and act to improve your attitude or situation. If your body is reflecting the stress, get a medical checkup.

- *Smoke.* Scores from 58 to 75 represent a certain amount of stress in your work and are a sign that you have a fair chance of burning out unless you take corrective measures. For each question on which you scored 4 or above, consider ways you can reduce the stresses involved. As soon as possible, take action to improve your attitude or the situation surrounding those things that trouble you most.

- *Sparks.* If your score is from 40 to 57, you have a low amount of work-related stress and are unlikely to burn out. Look over those questions on which you scored 3 or above, and think about what you can do to reduce the stresses involved.

- *No fire.* If your score is 22 through 39, you are mellow in your work, with almost no job-related stress. As long as you continue at this level, you are practically burnout-proof.

Dealing with Burnout

Although you may be in a state of burnout, the "phoenix phenomenon" can occur. You can rise from the ashes to a new level of energy and commitment, depending on your use of corrective strategies. Strategies for dealing with burnout include **emergency aid, short-term actions,** and **long-term solutions.**[48]

Examples of emergency aid:

1. Doing deep breathing.
2. Engaging in positive self-talk.
3. Taking a physical retreat.
4. Talking with a friend.

Sample short-term actions:

1. Reducing workload.
2. Setting priorities.
3. Taking care of your body.
4. Accentuating the positive.

Important long-term solutions:

1. Clarifying values.
2. Renewing commitments.
3. Making lifestyle changes.
4. Developing personal competencies.

For many people, both the job and the home represent potential sources for high stress and burnout. For this reason, having at least one safe haven is important. Ideally, if things are going badly on the job, rest and comfort can be found in the home. Similarly, if home conditions involve pressure, conflict, and frustration, having a satisfying work life helps. The person who faces stress on the job and stress in the home at the same time is waging a war on two fronts and is a prime candidate for burnout.

The Leader's Role in Burnout Prevention

Executives can institute the following 10 practices to prevent burnout in the workplace:

1. Clarify the mission, goals, and values of the organization, and *live* these personally.
2. Clearly communicate role expectations. People need to know their place in the plan.
3. Maintain a healthy work environment—meet physical, safety, and emotional health needs.
4. Manage work processes so that individuals and groups are neither overloaded nor underloaded.
5. Maintain an effective balance between continuity and change. While self-renewing change is vital for keeping up with shifting conditions, change should not occur at a pace so fast that it produces widespread stress.
6. Foster a spirit of belonging and teamwork throughout the organization through personal involvement, effective communication, and morale-building activities.

7. To the degree possible, allow people flexibility to work at the pace and manner that will ensure personal satisfaction while maintaining needed productivity.

8. Provide people opportunity for ongoing involvement in decisions affecting them.

9. Have career development policies and activities that help people achieve their full potential.

10. Provide assistance in times of stress. Services ranging from fitness programs to counseling centers can be provided within the organization, or referral networks can be established.[49]

In *Managing Stress for Mental Fitness,* Merrill Raber and George Dyck list 10 strategies for supervisors to follow in helping employees manage job stress:

1. Maintain a safe and organized work environment.

2. Clarify work unit goals and objectives.

3. Be sure individual job expectations and instructions are clear.

4. Evaluate workloads and deadlines. Are they reasonable?

5. Have regular reviews to provide accurate and timely feedback; give assurance that good work is appreciated.

6. Show patience, understanding, and support in dealing with employee problems.

7. Deal with personality differences directly and constructively.

8. Coach and develop employees to their full potential.

9. Involve people, as much as possible, in decisions that affect them.

10. Keep communication lines open with an open-door policy.[50]

Job Stress

Michael Losey, president of the Society for Human Resource Management, describes the impact of stress on the individual in the modern-day workplace:

The feverish pace most corporations have set for themselves is perhaps the largest contributor to workers' high stress levels. Facsimile machines, beepers, computers, cellular telephones, and other products of the modern workplace have fueled the problem. Automation has left many workers virtually on call twenty-four hours a day. They feel a sense of "never punching out" and "no down time for rest." Clients and bosses can and do contact employees at home, in the car, at restaurants, during family outings—basically anywhere, at any time. As Henry David Thoreau once said, men have become the tools of their tools.[51]

Juliet Schor, Harvard economist and author of *The Overworked American: The Unexpected Decline of Leisure,* sheds light on historical forces and events that have helped create the overstressed American worker:

It all began with the Pilgrims who reduced leisure by dropping from the calendar more than 50 holidays enjoyed by the English since medieval times. Sunday was declared to be the only toil-free day. By the time the Industrial Revolution arrived in America, the Pilgrims' work ethic was woven thoroughly into management's expectations; so much so that labor unions had to work for a century to secure eight-hour workdays with at least one day of rest.

With the end of World War II and the increased prosperity and leisure of the next thirty years, most unions reduced their vigilance. When the era of layoffs and vast cutbacks came to first one and then another industry and company during the '70s, '80s, and '90s, employees were unprepared to resist the side effects of "downsizing." Today companies routinely ask employees, including managers, to do the work of 1.3 people—for the same pay and with less time off. Overtime is at a modern-day high (an average of 4.7 hours a week) while in the last decade, the average yearly vacation and other paid absences decreased by 3.5 days. These are patterns that are expected to continue.[52]

More than 100 million Americans spend approximately one-third of their day on the job. Currently, five major forces or trends are sources of stress for increasing numbers of these people:

- **New technology.** Job skills and tasks are changing rapidly. No one can ignore the revolution in work caused by computer technology. Nearly every employee, from the frontline worker to the corporate executive, has been affected by the introduction of the computer in the workplace.[53] No longer can a person just walk in the door and be a decent citizen. Now it's walk in the door, be a decent citizen, and know how to run several computer programs. More than 50 million workers use computers every day, along with other products of modern technology—faxes, cellular phones, and e-mail. This situation creates virtual offices for workers on the go, accelerating information transfer and changing the way products are developed and services provided.[54] Check here if new technology affects you. _____

- **Workforce diversity.** New members of the workforce are increasingly diverse and possess skill sets and value systems that are different from those of earlier generations. These differences, along with differences in race, gender, nationality, and creed, can result in a social mix that is highly stressful.[55] Check here if workforce diversity affects you. _____

- **Global competition.** The intensification of international competition brings pressure to perform and fear of failure. This phenomenon has been studied extensively in the case of Japan and the manufacture of automobiles, but it involves many other countries and a multitude of industries.[56] In the relatively sheltered era of the 1960s, 7 percent of the U.S. economy was exposed to international competition. That number grew to 70 percent during the 1980s, and it is expected to climb higher with every passing year.[57] Check here if global competition affects you. _____

- **Organizational restructure.** The phenomenon of organizational restructuring—mergers, takeovers, reengineering, and rightsizing—is a continuing drumbeat reported in newspapers, magazines, and television. For an enormous number of people, these developments are sources of uncertainty, worry, and stress.[58] Displaced workers typically experience pay cuts, as downward mobility is the norm more than the exception. The reality for most people caught in organizational restructure is that spending power and standards of living decline.[59] Check here if organizational restructure affects you. _____

- **Changing work systems.** There is an emerging redefinition of work itself, with a growing disappearance of the job as a fixed bundle of tasks. In its place is an emphasis on fluid and constantly changing work assignments required to fulfill ever-increasing demands of customers. Change in how work is accomplished has become a way of life in the workplace, as many new concepts are tried, adapted, and discarded, only to be replaced by newer approaches. Quality teams, process improvement, and semiautonomous work groups are examples of trends in which traditional methods of hierarchical supervision are replaced by work teams and self-direction in a general shift from tier to peer.[60] Check here if you are affected by changing work systems. _____

Stress at Work and Public Policy

The good news is that the majority of U.S. workers are psychologically sound and are coping relatively well with work and with life in general. The bad news is that substantial numbers of people do not enjoy this condition, but are afflicted by the job stress syndrome. Some of these people are struggling with personal or family problems that often have repercussions on the job. Further good news, however, is that in recent years the mental health community and some governmental agencies have focused attention and resources on the subject of work and well-being.[61]

One product of collaboration between the National Institute of Occupational Safety and Health, the Association of Schools for Public Health, and experts from the American Psychological Association, labor, and industry is agreement on a blueprint for protecting the health and well-being of American workers. The four cornerstones of this blueprint are:

- Well-designed jobs.
- Evaluation systems to detect psychological disorders and underlying risk factors.
- Education of workers and managers on the signs, causes, effects, and control of work-related psychological disorders.
- Improved mental health service delivery for workers.[62]

Women, Work, and Stress

Many women do not work for wages, yet the stress in their lives can be fully as great as for those who do. The tasks required for maintaining a home and raising children may result in overload or underload, depending on the person and the situation. For those who choose or are required to hold down a job and raise a family at the same time, significant levels of stress can result. The amount of pressure these women face, the conflict they experience, and the frustration they feel can be enormous.

Sociologist Arlie Hochschild describes the working mother's plight in her book *The Second Shift*. After working a full day on the job, she then puts in a full shift at home. In fact, women work an average of 15 hours a week more than their husbands do.[63] The typical problem unfolds like this: Wanting to be a model mother and a wonderful wife, as well as a perfect professional, the modern woman is increasingly overcommitted and overstressed.

Perhaps you have heard the saying "Man must work from sun to sun, but a woman's work is never done." Consider that this expression was coined before the current era when more and more women have the responsibility of a job outside the home in addition to the traditional roles of mother and homemaker. If you are this woman, or if you live with her, you know the syndrome firsthand—day after day of constant work morning until night. If you do not know such a person yourself, you can learn from reading the description of a working mother's day.

A Day in the Life of a Working Mother

She is up at 6:00 A.M., has a shower and her makeup on by 6:30, at which time she wakens her husband and kids. She makes breakfast and everyone eats by 7:15. Everyone needs something—lunch money, a doctor's note, or a newspaper tucked under the arm—on the way to the door.

As she drives to work, she makes three stops: drops off Jessie at day care, picks up dry cleaning, and buys donuts for the monthly office meeting. It is 7:55 when she swings into the parking lot. She grabs her high-heel shoes (because she's supposed to dress great, too), and dashes across the drive and into the door at 8:00 sharp.

She no longer feels fresh as a daisy as she confronts her desk and the to-do list ahead. By 8:15 and with a kickoff coffee, she is focused and in the work groove. Her pace is steady as she moves efficiently through the day, from meeting to memo to meeting again. Her energy holds up as she maintains a high level of production, pausing just once for a personal break. She loves her work and is proud of her company, so her job is not a negative.

Lunch time is used for errands, the normal pattern for most workdays. She buys a card for her friend who has just had surgery and has lunch while she drives, including a soda from the cooler that she keeps in the car.

From 1:00 P.M. on, the day goes crazy. A supplier slips up, a customer complains, a coworker has problems, and then she gets the message she most hates to hear—"Your son's school called." She handles them all and still finishes the key account report by the end of the day.

As she straightens her office and prepares to go home, she thinks of the day and what it has meant. She is relieved that her son's school problem was easily handled, but she is also thankful that she could have called on her husband if the problem had required a trip to school. It was work as normal, but what does that mean? It was money for the family, but was it enough? It was time, which is life, and was it well spent?

These are good questions for the future, but more important is the flurry of activity that lies ahead. First is day-care pickup of little Jessie, then a swing by school for Billy. Both of these are must-hits and they are always eventful, with progress reports, funny stories, laughter, and sometimes tears.

She arrives home at 5:45 but can't sit down or even start dinner because Susie is standing in the driveway and needs to be at her dance lesson by 6:00.

While she waits for Susie, she uses the time productively to outline the talk she has to give the next day. The company believes in employee involvement and her team presentation has to go well.

She's off again by 7:30, but now it's so late she decides to zip by the fast-food drive-through rather than cooking the meal she had planned. At 8:00 she is ready to set the food out, talk with the kids, and meet her husband.

Dinner goes well, but as with most things, it seems a little late and a little rushed, plus dishes, homework, and laundry are yet to be done.

At 10:00 she has a choice: do the family bills, check the news, return her mom's call, sew Billy's pants, write her friend's card, or talk with her husband. She wants to talk with Fred, but he is concentrating on Billy's Cub Scout project. She does 1 through 5, and then it's time for bed.

She is too tired to fall asleep, plus she is waiting on Fred. She thinks about the family, each one in turn—their health, their happiness, and what they need. She then thinks about herself. She is tired but happy. She knows she is spending her chips, but she wouldn't change if she could. Her only question is, can I keep it up? And, how do others do it who don't have a husband?

The Executive Monkey Studies

Whether yours is a high-stress field, such as law enforcement, or a low-stress profession, such as library science, and regardless of whether you are satisfied or bored with your job, if you feel the responsibility of office, yet feel out of control, then the case of the "executive monkey" and related research will be of interest to you.

"Executive monkeys develop ulcers" was the conclusion of a study Joseph Brady did in 1958.[64] In this study, Brady placed pairs of monkeys in an environment where both received electric shocks. A red light signaled the shock period. However, the monkeys were not shocked if one of them operated a lever that prevented the flow of electric current. See Figure 25–1.

**Figure 25–1
The Executive Monkey
Studies**

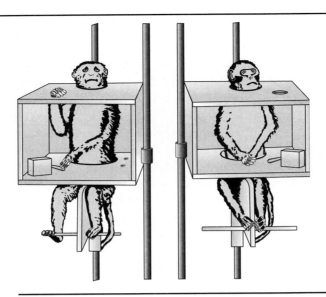

In each pair of monkeys, the executive monkey (so named because of the analogy to human executive situations) was the one having access to an operational lever and was able to learn the relationship between the light, the lever, and the shocks. The other, nonexecutive, monkey had a nonoperational lever and therefore was unable to learn any way to prevent the flow of electric current. The only thing this monkey knew was that every once in a while there was a shock, but the monkey didn't know why.

In this study, the executive monkeys, who were responsible for saving their partners and themselves, developed ulcers and died, while the uninformed, nonexecutive monkeys remained healthy. The results of the study suggested that the burden of responsibility, including the need to maintain a high degree of vigilance and the pressure to make decisions, was the cause of the high level of stress resulting in death.

A follow-up study on rats conducted by Jay Weiss of Emory University provided additional information as to the demise of the executive monkeys.[65] One primary difference between the Weiss study and the Brady study was that Weiss used a warning tone to signal the imminent onset of electric current. Weiss showed that the executive animals were much more able to cope with responsibility and avoid ulcers if they were given feedback on their behavior. He did this by arranging conditions so that the lever, when operated, would prevent shock and would also turn off the warning tone that preceded the shock. This provided clear evidence to the executive animal, in the form of tone cessation, that shock could be avoided, whereas Brady's executive monkeys received no such assurances.

Weiss's animals learned through feedback that they could control their situation, whereas Brady's monkeys felt less control. The conclusion was that pressure to perform without feeling in control can result in health problems and even death. Weiss found that the responsibility of office was not the cause of debilitating stress, but the feeling of frustration and being out of control was.

Based on results of executive animal studies, you may decide against assuming significant responsibilities in life (such as becoming a parent or supervisor, or having a business of your own). On the other hand, you may recognize the penalties in wear and tear that may accompany responsible positions but decide that the price is justified by the personal, social, and economic rewards. In any case, the executive animal studies demonstrate the importance of having a sense of control when one assumes responsibility.

Robert Karasek of Columbia University has found that people with little control over their jobs, such as assembly-line workers and cooks, have higher rates of heart disease than people who can choose the pace and method of their work. People who deal with the public but have little opportunity for independent decision making are those most negatively affected. The combination of high psychological demands and low personal control appears to raise the risk of heart disease by "about the same order of magnitude as smoking or having a high cholesterol level."[66]

If you are in a position to accept responsibility, be sure you have adequate power to influence the events for which you will be held responsible. In addition, as a leader, be sure to delegate to subordinates sufficient authority as well as responsibility to accomplish tasks. The following is a classic experiment demonstrating the importance of feeling in control—not only to manage stress, but to maximize job performance:

Adult subjects were given complex puzzles to solve and a proofreading chore. In the background was a loud, randomly occurring distracting noise; to be specific, it was a combination of two people speaking Spanish, one person speaking Armenian, a mimeograph machine running, a desk calculator, a typewriter, and street noise—producing a composite, nondistinguishable roar. The subjects were split into two groups. Individuals in one set were just told to work at the task. Individuals in the other were provided with a button to turn off the noise, a modern analog of control—the off switch. The group with the off switch solved five times the number of puzzles as their cohorts and made but a tiny fraction of the number of proofreading errors. Now for the kicker: . . . none of the subjects in the off switch group ever used the switch. The mere knowledge that one can exert control made the difference.[67]

Part Eight Summary

After reading Part Eight, you should know the following key concepts, principles and terms. Fill in the blanks from memory, or copy the answers listed below.

Many leaders view (a) _____ as the most rewarding of all their tasks. Types of leaders as teachers include shamans, priests, elected leaders, missionaries, and mystic healers. People grow best when there is a felt need, when they are encouraged by someone they respect, when their plans move from general goals to specific actions, when they move from a condition of lower to higher self-esteem, and when they move from external to internal commitment. These are (b) _____. One good way to learn leadership is by (c) _____, and learning from their examples. Good rules for succeeding in one's career include (d) _____, _____, _____, _____, and _____. What do employees want from their employers, and how do you keep good people? The six most powerful answers are (e) _____, _____, _____, _____, _____, and _____. Types of change going on in the American workplace involve (f) _____, _____, _____, and _____. There are seven rules for guiding people through change: (g) _____, _____, _____, _____, _____, _____, and_____. Effective responses in dealing with change include (h) _____, _____, and _____, versus denial, resistance, and the attitude trough. Types of burnout victims include (i) _____, _____, _____, and _____. The formula for the burnout process is this: Too many demands on strength and resources + high expectations and deep personal involvement + too few actions to replenish the energy consumed = (j) _____. Strategies for dealing with burnout include (k) _____, such as deep breathing, positive self-talk, physical retreat; (l) _____, such as reducing workload, setting priorities, taking care of one's body; and (m) _____, such as clarifying values, making lifestyle changes, developing personal competencies. Five major forces or trends are sources of stress for increasing numbers of people: (n) _____, _____, _____, _____, and _____. The most stressful jobs have high-demand tasks with little relief, power, or pay. The combination of high demand with low personal control and small psychic or financial compensation is a formula for stress that the good leader can help prevent or solve.

Answer Key for Part Eight Summary

a. **developing others,** page 266

b. **personal conditions conducive to growth,** page 272

c. **studying the masters,** page 275

d. **put your best foot forward, deliver results, be considerate, be creative, have integrity,** page 276

e. **let people know what is expected of them, give them materials and equipment to do the job right, give them the chance to do what they do best every day, provide recognition and praise for good work, show that you care about them as people, encourage their development,** page 276

f. **structure, tasks, technology, people,** page 278

g. **have a good reason for making a change, personalize change, implement change thoughtfully, put a respected person in charge, tell the truth, wait patiently for results, acknowledge and reward people,** page 280

h. **exploration, responsibility, commitment,** page 283

i. (any four) **superpeople, workaholics, burned-out Samaritans, mismatched people, midcareer coasters, overstressed students,** page 286

j. **burnout,** page 286

k. **emergency aid,** page 291

l. **short-term actions,** page 291

m. **long-term solutions,** page 291

n. **new technology, workforce diversity, global competition, organizational restructure, changing work systems,** page 293

Reflection Points—personal thoughts on the leader as teacher, helping people through change, and burnout prevention

Complete the following questions and activities to personalize the content of Part Eight. Space is provided for writing your thoughts.

■ Discuss the vignette "Why Can't Roger Learn?" What could the teacher have done to keep Roger from failing?

_____

_____

■ What is your style of developing others? Are you a shaman, a priest, an elected leader, a missionary, or a mystic healer in your approach to teaching? How did you develop your style?

_____

_____

■ Apply conditions conducive to growth to your own development. What factors are present that will help you fulfill your potential?

_____

_____

■ Apply the findings of the Gallup organization to attract and keep good people. Answer all 12 questions personally; then indicate the answers your employees would give. Use this exercise to capitalize on strong points and to shore up weaknesses.

_____

_____

■ Apply the attitude curve in dealing with change in your own work and career. Where are you now—denial, resistance, attitude trough, exploration, responsibility, or commitment?

_____

_____

■ Identify a change initiative in which you are either the owner or a principle player. Apply the seven rules for helping people through change to critique your efforts. Discuss success points and areas for improvement.

_____

_____

■ Discuss job stress and burnout prevention based on your own experiences. Discuss the role of the leader, as well as effective coping techniques.

_____

_____

Action Assignment

As a bridge between learning and doing, complete the following action assignment.

1. What is the most important idea you have learned in Part Eight?

2. How can you apply what you have learned? What will you do, with whom, where, when, and, most important, why?

Part 9 Performance Management

26. **Managing Performance**
27. **Professional Performance**
28. **Sustaining Discipline**

YOU CANNOT BE DISCIPLINED in great things and undisciplined in small things. There is only one sort of discipline—*perfect* discipline. Discipline is based on pride as a soldier, on meticulous attention to detail, and on mutual respect and confidence. It can only be obtained when all officers are so imbued with the sense of their moral obligation to their men and their country that they cannot tolerate negligence.

—General George Patton
U.S. Army

Learning Points

In Part Nine, you will discover the answers to these questions:
- Have you mastered performance management as a leadership skill? Do you know how to set goals, provide feedback on progress, and correct performance problems?
- What is your level of performance in the areas of statesmanship, working with and through others; entrepreneurship, achieving results; and innovation, generating new and usable ideas?
- Do you model and reinforce high standards of professional conduct? Do you uphold core values, using a caring confrontation when corrective action is necessary?

Managing Performance

UNIT 26

Performance management is at the heart of leadership success. It is important to have a vision; it is important to have values; it is important to have leadership qualities, such as vitality, persistence, and concern for others; it is important to have the power of leadership position. But all of these will result in little actual accomplishment without performance management skills. Effective leadership requires the art of clearly communicating goals, coaching others to succeed, and correcting poor performance.[1]

- **Performance planning** establishes direction and clarity of assignment. It provides the foundation on which individual and group performance can be developed and evaluated.

- **Performance coaching** involves the development and encouragement of people. The leader's challenge is to help individuals grow and fulfill their personal potential while advancing the organization's success.

- **Correcting poor performance** includes modifying and improving performance when mistakes are made.

In their best-selling book on leadership, *The One Minute Manager,* Ken Blanchard and Spencer Johnson teach three secrets to leadership success that correspond with performance planning, coaching, and correcting. These are leadership techniques that work at all levels of leadership and in all work environments. The three secrets are:

- One-minute goal setting for performance planning.
- One-minute praising for performance coaching.
- One-minute reprimand for correcting poor performance.[2]

These three secrets are drawn from the basic principles of behavioral psychology—the power of goals to focus and energize behavior; the need for feedback to reinforce or modify behavior; and the importance of praise as a recognition technique.[3]

One-minute goal setting. One-minute goal setting involves identifying three to five goals that are critical to success, and writing these on a single sheet of paper—in 250 or fewer words. It is important to include the individual in the goal-setting process, because there is a strong relationship between personal involvement and future success. The individual needs psychological investment, and participation in goal setting helps accomplish this purpose.

One-minute praising. One-minute praising involves showing appreciation for effort and accomplishments. It is based on two ideas: (1) People need feedback as a way of tracking and sustaining progress; and (2) what gets rewarded gets repeated. One-minute praising has four characteristics:

1. Praise is immediate.
2. Praise is specific.

3. Praise is sincere.

4. The individual is encouraged.

One-minute reprimand. The one-minute reprimand is saved for individuals who are trained and who know what to do, but make mistakes. The one-minute reprimand has four characteristics:

1. Correction is immediate.

2. Correction focuses on behavior, not on the character of the person.

3. Correction is sincere.

4. The individual is encouraged.

By mastering the three secrets of the one-minute manager, the effective leader can raise the productivity of individuals and groups. Use Exercise 26–1 to practice these secrets.

Exercise 26–1
The Performance
Management Lab

One-Minute Goal Setting:

Use 250 or fewer words to identify the three to five most important goals of your job (or the job of another person). Include *what* the goals are, *why* they are important, and the *time frame* for action.

Goal 1: _____

_____

_____

_____

Goal 2: _____

_____

_____

_____

Goal 3: _____

_____

_____

_____

Goal 4: _____

_____

_____

_____

Goal 5: _____

_____

_____

_____

One-Minute Praising:

Look for the opportunity to recognize and reinforce good performance. When you deliver praise, be *timely* (if you wait too long, you may lose goodwill); be *specific* (explain why the performance is good and what it means to others); be *sincere* (show that you care about the person and what has been done); and *encourage* the person (set the stage for future success).

One-Minute Reprimand:

If attitudes or actions result in mistakes, correct performance in an effective way. Be *immediate* (don't store or save up punishment); be *specific* (let people know the impact of their behavior); be *sincere* (show how important good performance is to you; show your interest and show that you care); *encourage* the person (emphasize positive qualities and your confidence in him or her).

Taking Aim and Taking Stock

Effective job performance requires setting objectives and measuring results. The following experiment shows the importance of having clear goals and obtaining accurate feedback on performance:

A group of professional golfers participated in an interesting experiment. Each was given a basket of balls and was asked to drive them as far and as straight as possible, with the fairway lights off. The golfers hooked and sliced their drives, and balls were popping up and dribbling off the tee . . . not at all the performance you would expect from professionals. After they had finished, each was given another basket of balls and asked to drive these as far and as straight as possible—this time, with the lights on. The golfers hit ball after ball, straight as an arrow, 275 to 325 yards down the fairway. What was the difference between the two experiments? The answer is clear goals and accurate feedback on performance. There were no lights in the first experiment; thus, the golfers could not see the target, nor could they learn the results of their efforts. In the second experiment, lights provided a clear goal and accurate feedback, so that eyes, hands, and muscles could make adjustments to achieve the desired objective.[4]

The following story shows the importance of setting performance objectives and measuring results for the work group:

The famous industrialist Charles Schwab was visiting a steel mill that was producing far below its potential. The superintendent of the plant couldn't understand why—he had coaxed the employees, threatened them, sworn and cursed, but nothing seemed to work. Schwab asked the superintendent for a piece of chalk, and turning to the nearest worker, he asked, "How many heats did your shift make today?" "Six," was the answer. Without saying a word, Schwab drew a large "6" on the floor and walked away. When the night shift came in, they asked what the "6" meant. A day-shift worker said, "We made six heats today, and Schwab wrote it on the floor. " The next morning, when Schwab walked through the mill, he saw "7" on the floor—the night shift had made seven heats. That evening, he returned to the plant and saw that the "7" had been erased, and in its place was an enormous "10." Within a short period of time, one of the lowest producing plants was turning out more work than any other mill in the company. The employees had set performance goals, and they enjoyed recording the results.[5]

Setting Performance Objectives

Management author Peter Drucker explains the importance of setting performance objectives:

Each person, from the highest level to the lowest level, should have clear objectives that support the success of the organization. As much as possible, lower level employees should participate in the development of higher level objectives as well as their own, thus enabling them to know and understand their supervisor's goals as well as their own place in the plan.[6]

Setting performance objectives is important in four major areas—quantity, quality, timeliness, and cost. One or more of these areas will fit every person's job:[7]

Quantity. The most common method of measuring performance depends to some degree on quantity. In one way or another we tally number of sales made, dollar volume generated, number of hours billed, number of fenders painted, or any amount that may be processed or produced.

Quality. This is one of the most important areas for which standards apply. Measurements of quality include at least two factors: errors and appearance. *Errors* can include monitoring rejects, misfiles, safety records, customer complaints, miswelds, wrong diagnoses, and countless other areas. *Appearance* deals with items other than rejects or specific errors and is more subjective in judgment. It covers such areas as neatness, a person's manner in answering the telephone, a receptionist's greeting of visitors, or a service representative's explanation to a dissatisfied customer.

Timeliness. This area includes such time factors as meeting deadlines for on-time shipments, on-time departures and arrivals, and absenteeism. Timeliness can also involve the development of new and workable approaches. The most creative idea needs the right moment for its introduction.

Cost. Cost includes the four *M's* of management: manpower, material, machines, and methods. For example, is the person able to perform while controlling expenditures for labor, inventory, equipment, and corporate services? Can the person live within a reasonable budget?

Performance objectives should be measurable. A generalized objective, such as "improve customer service," provides no guidelines for achieving success. When performance objectives are specific and measurable, however, the individual can know when, and to what extent, those objectives have been achieved. The following list consists of examples of measurable objectives for improving customer service:

1. Develop and implement a system that allows tracking, following up, and resolving customer complaints.
   The system should identify the number and types of complaints, actions taken by whom, and date of resolution.
   Maintain progress charts and graphs, and post them in places where employees can see them. This system is to be completed by January 1, 2003.
2. Achieve 98 percent on-time delivery by January 1, 2004.
3. Develop a blue-ribbon service system for our top 20 national accounts by January 1, 2005, by assigning one person to service each account.

Conducting Performance Reviews

After performance objectives have been established, progress should be reviewed to capitalize on strengths and improve weaknesses. Performance reviews keep communication lines open, help motivate employees, and give peace of mind to both employer and employee.[8]

Performance reviews should include three steps: preparation, implementation, and follow-up. Both the supervisor and the employee should be trained in carrying out each of these steps. Table 26–1 contains a performance review checklist for supervisors and employees.

Performance reviews should be used to solve job problems and develop employee competence. Table 26–2 lists characteristics of three types of performance reviews: the tell-and-sell method, the tell-and-listen method, and the problem-solving method. If the supervisor uses the problem-solving method and plays the role of coach, employees usually experience less fear, and productivity improves.

Multisource evaluations can be useful for improving performance. Approximately 90 percent of Fortune 1000 companies use some form of multisource assessment, including evaluations from supervisors, employees, peers, and customers. These assessments are called 360-degree feedback because the individual is rated by a whole circle of people.[9]

Research shows that the evaluation of leaders by employees can be a valuable tool for improving leadership effectiveness. The questionnaire in Exercise 26–2 can be used to evaluate the performance of supervisors and managers.

**Table 26–1
Performance Review
Checklist**[10]

What to Do before the Performance Review

As an employee, you should:

- Consider your strong points and formulate a plan to utilize them fully.
- Determine the areas in which you need to improve. Devise a plan to strengthen your performance in these areas.
- Think about what your supervisor can do to help you improve.

As a supervisor, you should:

- Consider your employee's strong points and think about how you can reinforce or capitalize on these.
- Think about your employee's weak areas and consider actions for improvement.
- Think about what you can do to help your employee improve.
- Provide advance notice of the performance review; solicit employee input.

What to Do during the Performance Review

As an employee, you should:

- Explain your strengths and weaknesses. Be thorough in expressing each one.
- Discuss issues that may not be apparent to the supervisor that hinder your performance.
- Present ideas to improve future performance; don't dwell on past mistakes, either to save face or to fix blame.
- Present what you think your supervisor can do to help you improve.
- Listen carefully to your supervisor's reactions; these are important indications of attitudes, priorities, and perceptions that will be useful in future dealings.
- Obtain final agreement on what each of you will do. Don't settle for "Let's discuss this again at a later date." Try to get as much commitment and agreement as possible.

As a supervisor, you should:

- Create a positive climate—quiet, private, and free from interruptions.
- Tailor the conversation to suit the needs of your employee. Stop talking and listen. Have your employee begin by explaining each strength and weakness in his or her own words. Provide ample time for the full development of each point; avoid interrupting.
- Ask questions based on your prior preparation as well as on new information developed during the conversation. Encourage your employee to do the same.
- Be open and flexible to issues that may come up that you may not know about. Take a problem-solving versus problem-blaming approach.
- Ask how you can help your employee do a better job; listen carefully and take notes.
- Establish new performance objectives, standards, and completion dates. Make your expectations clear. Be direct and honest.
- Write down points of discussion and agreement. Review them so that both you and your employee have the same understanding.
- Remember that a performance review should involve two-way communication. Be prepared to compromise and be flexible. Remember also that you are the supervisor and, as such, are responsible for resolving differences.
- End the meeting on an upbeat, positive, and future-focused note.

What to Do after the Performance Review

As an employee, you should:

- Keep your supervisor informed of progress toward meeting objectives.
- Discuss with your supervisor as soon as possible any changes that occur that affect your objectives.

As a supervisor, you should:

- Develop a system of checks and reminders to be sure that performance objectives are being met.
- Show your employee that you want him or her to succeed. Provide positive reinforcement for progress made toward accomplishing objectives.

Table 26–2   **Three Types of Performance Reviews**[11]

	Tell-and-Sell Method (Supervisor acts as judge)	Tell-and-Listen Method (Supervisor acts as advisor)	Problem-Solving Method (Supervisor acts as coach)
Objective	To evaluate and get employee to change.	To communicate evaluation and encourage discussion.	To stimulate employee growth and development.
Assumptions	Employees want to correct weaknesses if they know them. Any person can improve if he or she chooses. The supervisor is qualified to evaluate the employee.	People will change if defensive feelings are removed.	Growth can occur without focusing on faults. Discussion of job problems leads to improved performance.
Reactions of employee	Defensive behavior is suppressed. Attempts are made to cover up hostility.	Defensive behavior is expressed. Employee feels accepted.	Behavior is oriented toward problem solving.
Skills required	Persuasiveness; patience.	Listening and reflecting feelings; summarizing.	Listening and reflecting feelings; using exploratory questions; summarizing.
Attitude	People profit from criticism and appreciate help.	One can respect the feelings of others if one understands them.	Discussion develops new ideas and mutual interests.
Motivation	Use of positive or negative extrinsic incentives (motivation is not related to task content).	Reduced resistance to change.	Increased freedom; increased responsibility (use of intrinsic motivation in that interest is inherent in the task).
Gains	Success is most probable when the employee respects the supervisor.	Employee develops a favorable attitude toward the supervisor, which increases the probability of success.	Some improvement is almost assured.
Risks	Loss of loyalty; inhibition of independent judgment.	Need for change; improvement may not be recognized.	Employee may lack ideas. Change may be different from what the supervisor had in mind.
Values	Perpetuates existing values and practices.	Permits supervisor to change views as a result of employee responses; some upward communication.	Both employee and supervisor learn, since experience and views are pooled. Change is facilitated.

**Exercise 26–2
How Does Your
Supervisor Rate?**[12]

Rate your supervisor on each criterion by circling the appropriate response.

Criteria	Responses		
Does the supervisor provide clarity of assignment?	Very well	Fairly well	Not very well
Are high standards of performance required?	Usually	Sometimes	Seldom
Is concern shown for employee needs and welfare?	Frequently	Sometimes	Rarely
Does the supervisor ensure that proper materials and equipment are available?	Very well	Fairly well	Not very well
Is favoritism shown in dealing with employees?	Never	Sometimes	Frequently
Do employees feel free to discuss job-related problems?	Whenever necessary	Sometimes	Seldom
Are employees given incomplete or confusing information?	Seldom	Sometimes	Almost always
Are employees told why they are being asked to do a particular job?	Almost always	Sometimes	Rarely
Are employees recognized for good job performance?	Almost always	Sometimes	Seldom
Is the supervisor honest in all dealings with people?	Always	Sometimes	Almost never
Does the supervisor keep job knowledge current?	Very well	Fairly well	Not very well
Is the advice of employees sought in dealing with job-related problems?	Frequently	Sometimes	Seldom
Does the supervisor assign the right jobs to the right people?	Almost always	Sometimes	Rarely
Are employees criticized or otherwise belittled in the presence of others?	Never	Sometimes	Frequently
Are employees told in advance about changes that will affect them?	Almost always	Sometimes	Rarely
Does the supervisor encourage and support employee development?	Yes	Sometimes	No
Are employees kept waiting for decisions or information?	A short time	Varies	A long time
Are employee confidences kept?	Always	Sometimes	Seldom
Does the supervisor provide constructive feedback on employee performance?	Frequently	Sometimes	Rarely
Is blame shifted to employees for supervisory errors?	Never	Sometimes	Almost always

Scoring and Interpretation:

Count the number of items circled in the first column; then multiply that number by 3 and record the total: _____

Count the number of items circled in the second column; then multiply that number by 2 and record the total: _____

Count the number of items circled in the third column; record that number as the total: _____

Add the totals for the three columns to find the overall score: _____

Score	Evaluation
56–60	Excellent/outstanding
46–55	Very good/effective
35–45	Average/improvement encouraged
25–34	Poor/needs improvement
20–24	Failing/must change

Professional Performance

Performance, as the following story shows, is important in all fields of work:

A mother was having a hard time getting her son to go to school one morning. "Nobody likes me at school," said the son. "The teachers don't and the kids don't. The superintendent wants to transfer me, the bus drivers hate me, the school board wants me to drop out, and the custodians have it in for me." "You've got to go," insisted the mother. "You're healthy. You have a lot to learn. You've got something to offer others. You're a leader. Besides, you're forty-nine years old, you're the principal, and you've got to go to school."[13]

The questionnaire in Exercise 27–1 evaluates job performance in three important areas—**statesmanship, entrepreneurship,** and **innovation.** Complete the questionnaire alone or with another person, such as a co-worker, subordinate, or supervisor. Points to remember are the following:

- Factors measured by the questionnaire are important for success in every field of work, from steel fabrication to public service. Every industry and profession requires statesmanship, the ability to work with and through other people; entrepreneurship, the ability to achieve results; and innovation, the ability to generate new and usable ideas.

- The questionnaire measures job behavior, not personal qualities. To increase objectivity, evaluation is based on actual rather than potential performance.

- Results on the questionnaire are based on a normative group. Scores show how you compare with individuals considered top producers and those considered poor producers in U.S. business and industry.

- How high or low you score is less important than what you do about your results. It is important to know where you stand to capitalize on strengths and improve weaknesses.

**Exercise 27–1
The Performance
Pyramid**[14]

Read the following sets of statements. For each set, place a check mark next to the statement that is most like your behavior on the job at this time. Although it may be difficult to select one statement over the others, you must choose one statement in each set.

1. _____ a. You are interested in what will work, not what might work.

_____ b. You are willing to listen to anyone's ideas.

_____ c. You seek out the ideas and opinions of others.

_____ d. You are tolerant of those whose ideas differ from yours.

2. _____ a. You rarely get worked up about things.

_____ b. You measure up to what is expected of you in output.

_____ c. You are one of the top producers of results.

_____ d. You are busy with so many things that your output is affected.

3. _____ a. You avoid changing existing methods and procedures.

_____ b. You continually search for better ways to do things.

_____ c. Sometimes you think of things that could be improved.

_____ d. You often make suggestions to improve things.

4. _____ a. You go out of your way to help others.

_____ b. You rarely spend time on other people's problems.

_____ c. Other people often come to you for help.

_____ d. You lend a hand if others request your assistance.

5. _____ a. You have selected assignments that have had a good future.

_____ b. Most jobs you have worked on have resulted in significant contributions.

_____ c. You would be much further ahead if you had not been assigned so many things that turned out to be unimportant.

_____ d. Some of your time has been wasted on things that you never should have undertaken.

6. _____ a. You have changed the whole approach to your work.

_____ b. You have initiated many changes in the work you are doing.

_____ c. From time to time, you have made a change in the way you do your work.

_____ d. You go along with established ways of working, without upsetting things.

7. _____ a. You seek consensus in settling disagreements.

_____ b. You do not concern yourself with the affairs of others.

_____ c. You will yield a point rather than displease someone.

_____ d. Once your mind is made up, you prefer not to change it.

8. _____ a. You follow the motto "better safe than sorry."

_____ b. You avoid taking risks except under rare circumstances.

_____ c. You will gamble on good odds any time.

_____ d. You sometimes take risks when the odds are favorable.

9. _____ a. You are well known for your creativity.

_____ b. You often think of new ways of doing things.

_____ c. You are conservative and rarely experiment with new ideas.

_____ d. From time to time, you introduce new ideas.

10. _____ a. You sometimes trust the wrong people.

_____ b. Your judgment about people is usually correct.

_____ c. You have as little to do with others as possible.

_____ d. Your ability to work with people is outstanding.

11. _____ a. You prefer doing work yourself rather than planning work for others.

_____ b. You plan work and hold performance to schedule.

_____ c. You make plans, but adjust to day-to-day changes.

_____ d. You rarely make plans.

12. _____ a. Your ideas are almost always used.

_____ b. You frequently say to yourself, I wish I had thought of that.

_____ c. Your ideas are sometimes put into practice.

_____ d. Your ideas are often adopted.

13. _____ a. You consider alternatives before making decisions.

_____ b. You wait as long as possible before making decisions.

_____ c. You make decisions before weighing the consequences.

_____ d. You involve others in decisions that affect them.

14. _____ a. You rarely push to have your plans adopted.

_____ b. Inevitable roadblocks prevent you from accomplishing your goals.

_____ c. You are known for getting difficult jobs done.

_____ d. If you want something done, you find a way to get it done.

15. _____ a. You believe change should be gradual, if it should occur at all.

_____ b. You are open to change and new methods.

_____ c. You prefer traditional and established ways.

_____ d. You are innovative in your ideas and approach to work.

Scoring:

Follow the steps below to complete the scoring matrix and the Performance Pyramid.

Step 1:

In the Self-Evaluation columns of the scoring matrix, circle the number that corresponds to the lettered statement you checked in each set of statements in the questionnaire. For example, if you checked statement c. for item 1, you would circle 7 in the Self-Evaluation column.

Step 2:

If another person evaluated you, circle the appropriate numbers in the Partner's Evaluation columns. For example, if your partner checked statement b. for item 1, you would circle 5 in the Partner's Evaluation column.

Step 3:

Add the circled numbers in each column of the scoring matrix to find your total scores on statesmanship (A), entrepreneurship (B), and innovation (C). Record the totals in the appropriate spaces at the bottom of the columns.

Step 4:

Plot your results on the Performance Pyramid in Figure 27–1. (See the sample in Figure 27–2.) If there is a difference between your self-evaluation and your partner's evaluation, use either an average of the two scores or your self-evaluation scores. In general, you know your own performance best. Nevertheless, you should discuss points of agreement and disagreement with your partner; you may be doing an exceptional job and not communicating this to your partner.

Scoring Matrix

	Statesmanship			Entrepreneurship			Innovation	
	Self-Evaluation	Partner's Evaluation		Self-Evaluation	Partner's Evaluation		Self-Evaluation	Partner's Evaluation
1. a.	1	1	**2.** a.	1	1	**3.** a.	1	1
b.	5	5	b.	5	5	b.	7	7
c.	7	7	c.	7	7	c.	3	3
d.	3	3	d.	3	3	d.	5	5
4. a.	7	7	**5.** a.	5	5	**6.** a.	7	7
b.	1	1	b.	7	7	b.	5	5
c.	5	5	c.	1	1	c.	3	3
d.	3	3	d.	3	3	d.	1	1
7. a.	7	7	**8.** a.	1	1	**9.** a.	7	7
b.	1	1	b.	3	3	b.	5	5
c.	3	3	c.	7	7	c.	1	1
d.	5	5	d.	5	5	d.	3	3
10. a.	3	3	**11.** a.	3	3	**12.** a.	7	7
b.	5	5	b.	7	7	b.	1	1
c.	1	1	c.	5	5	c.	3	3
d.	7	7	d.	1	1	d.	5	5
13. a.	5	5	**14.** a.	3	3	**15.** a.	3	3
b.	1	1	b.	1	1	b.	5	5
c.	3	3	c.	5	5	c.	1	1
d.	7	7	d.	7	7	d.	7	7
A _____	A _____		B _____	B _____		C _____	C _____	

Figure 27–1
Your Performance Pyramid

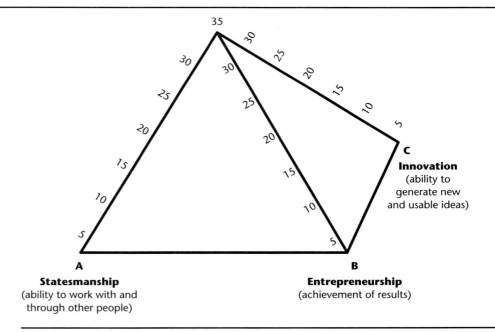

A
Statesmanship
(ability to work with and
through other people)

B
Entrepreneurship
(achievement of results)

C
Innovation
(ability to
generate new
and usable ideas)

**Figure 27–2
Sample Performance
Pyramid**

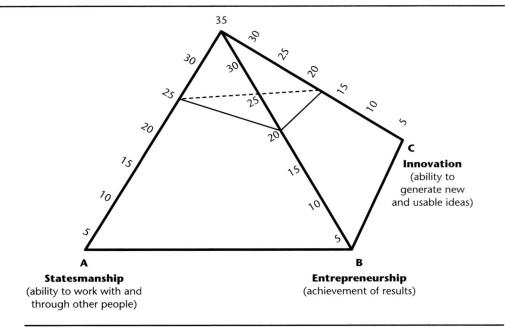

Interpretation:

High scores represent strengths in job performance; low scores represent areas you should strive to improve. Use the following information to evaluate your scores:

Score	Evaluation
30–35	Extremely high performers receive these scores. As a result of ability, experience, motivation, and attitude, these individuals produce top results. If such a person were to leave, it is likely that the organization would suffer significantly.
20–29	Good performers receive these scores. They are pivotal people in their organizations and are solid producers. In college, these scores represent very good work.
15–19	People who receive these scores are doing their jobs. They are doing what is expected of individuals in their positions—no more and no less. Although these scores are acceptable, they are not extraordinary.
14 and below	People whose performance needs improvement receive these scores. Such scores reflect problems in ability, experience, motivation, or attitude. Counseling and training should be considered.

Improving Performance

What can you do to maintain high performance or to improve in the areas of statesmanship, entrepreneurship, and innovation?

- First, you have to want to perform at your best; you must not be complacent.
- Second, you have to know the essential behaviors that represent statesmanship, entrepreneurship, and innovation.
- Third, you have to apply principles and practices to perform these behaviors.

The following discussion of each performance area includes behaviors that reflect high performance and principles as well as techniques that can be used to improve performance.

Statesmanship

Statesmanship is the ability to work with and through other people. A statesman is skillful in human relations and is able to multiply personal accomplishments through the efforts of others. Statesmanship is based on the attitude and practice of servant leadership and the empowerment of people. The following describes the role of the statesman:

A statesman is not a dictator, but rather a developer of effective relationships. The statesman is one who guides rather than leads, helping others to make decisions rather than making decisions alone. The statesman believes that if everyone works together, more can be accomplished.[15]

Consider Abraham Lincoln. Throughout his life, Lincoln was always willing to teach others what he had learned himself. From childhood onward, he was the statesman—storyteller, speech maker, and always the ringleader. As one boyhood comrade relates:

When he [Lincoln] appeared, the boys would gather and cluster around him to hear him talk . . . He argued much from analogy and explained things hard for us to understand by stories, maxims, tales, and figures. He would almost always paint his lesson or idea by some story that was plain and near to us, so that we might instantly see the force and bearing of what he said.[16]

Examine the following behaviors that represent a high level of statesmanship:

- You seek out the ideas and opinions of others.
- You go out of your way to help others.
- You seek consensus in settling disagreements.
- Your ability to work with people is outstanding.
- You involve others in decisions that affect them.

If you would like to increase your ability to work with and through others, develop good human relations skills and use the four-step method listed below to solve problems.

Develop Good Human Relations Skills

The following principles will help you accomplish this goal:

1. *Let people know where they stand.* You should communicate expectations and then keep people informed on how they are doing. If criticism is necessary, do it in private; if praise is in order, give it in public.

2. *Give credit where due.* Look for extra or unusual performance, and show appreciation as soon as possible. You should not wait until December to say thank you for something done in July. If you do, for six months the person probably will be thinking, "If she doesn't care, why should I?" In addition, you will have missed the opportunity to reinforce good performance. As psychologist Gordon Allport writes: "Not only does human learning proceed best when the incentive of praise and recognition is used, but the individual's capacity for learning actually expands under this condition."[17]

3. *Tell people as soon as possible about changes that will affect them.* Keep people informed, and tell them why change is necessary. Many people dislike change, and they especially dislike sudden changes. Therefore, new ideas and methods are more easily accepted when introduced gradually.

4. *Make the best use of each person's ability.* No two people are exactly alike, so let each person shine as only that person can. Take the time to look for potential not now being used. Also, never stand in a person's way. To do so creates resentment, reduces morale, and ultimately results in reduced performance.

Use the Four-Step Method to Solve Problems

Statesmanship requires problem-solving ability. The following four-step method can be used for solving any problem:

1. *Get the facts.* As Mark Twain said, "Get the facts first; then you can distort them as much as you please." You simply cannot solve a problem without first knowing the facts, so (a) review all records; (b) talk with the people concerned; (c) consider opinions and feelings; and (d) look at all sides. Seeing things from more than one point of view can help in the problem-solving process. Abraham Lincoln tried to understand the views of both the North and the South when he said:

> I have no prejudice against the Southern people. They are just what we would be in their situation. If slavery did not now exist among them, they would not introduce it. If it did now exist among us, we would not instantly give it up. This I believe of the masses of North and South.

2. *Weigh and decide.* After getting all the facts, you must weigh each fact against the others, fit the pieces together, and consider alternatives. Consider the effects that different courses of action will have on individuals and groups. Sometimes it is a good idea to sleep on a problem so that you do not jump to conclusions or overreact. It is easy to rush the thinking step of the problem-solving process and forget critical details.

3. *Take action.* After you have gathered the facts and determined a course of action, carry out your plan. Harry Truman realized the importance of this step in the problem-solving process. He believed that statesmanship required taking action, which was why he said, "The buck stops here" and "If you can't stand the heat, get out of the kitchen."

Many people occupy positions requiring statesmanship but are indecisive and fail to act. Have you ever been affected by someone in authority—supervisor, parent, or public official—who could not, or would not, take action? Consider what William James wrote: "There is no more miserable human being than one in whom nothing is habitual but indecision."[18]

4. *Follow up.* Follow-up is an essential, but often neglected, step in the problem-solving process. Some people say, "I'm so busy taking action that I don't have time to follow up." With this attitude, they may make the same mistakes over and over. Such people are not learning from experience.

Statesmanship requires asking, Did my action(s) help the quality of work or the quality of work life? If not, admit this fact and try to find a better solution. Contrast the willingness to admit mistakes with the approach taken by many people that "right or wrong, that is my decision." By taking time to follow up on actions and being willing to admit mistakes, the statesman achieves three important goals: (a) the respect of all who are watching; (b) another chance to solve the problem; and (c) the opportunity to set an example of honesty and thoroughness in problem solving.

Herb Kelleher, former CEO of Southwest Airlines, states:

> One thing I knew was to admit mistakes. If I discovered a decision I made was a mistake, I would just stop it. You have to look at things the way a scientist would: this experiment didn't work out; it's over. You can't get emotional about it. That's the key so far as I'm concerned: there's no ego involved. You can't keep something on life support for years and years because you've let your self-esteem get tied up in things.[19]

Entrepreneurship

Entrepreneurship is the ability to achieve results, regardless of obstacles. It takes entrepreneurship to build a plant on time, to produce a quality product, and to close a sale. An entrepreneur is action-oriented, but knows that it is not just action, but achievement, that counts. Effective performance in any field requires entrepreneurship. Consider the story of entrepreneur Henry Ford, who founded and built the Ford Motor Company. Ford believed in honesty and hard work and often asked, "Did you ever see dishonest calluses on a man's hands?"

Profile of an Entrepreneur

How It Began

. . . There was a crank in front, and you had to turn it over to start the engine. It made a mighty sputtering, then a roaring, and shook the vehicle most alarmingly; but it held together, and Mr. Ford got in and started. He had a kerosene lamp in front, and by this dim light went down the street paved with cobblestones. Mrs. Ford stood in the rain for a long time, wondering if she would ever see her husband again.

The young inventor was gone a long time, and came back pushing the contraption. A nut had come loose, with all the shaking. But he was exultant; in spite of bumpy cobblestones and muddy ruts, he had gone where he wished to go. "You're wet clear through," said his wife, as he let her lead him into the kitchen, take off his wet things, hang them up, and give him hot coffee. He was talking excitedly all the time. "I've got a horseless carriage that runs," said Henry Ford.

The Early Years

. . . He observed when they [the cars] bumped into each other, and devised plans to keep them from doing so. He examined materials, read contracts, discussed selling campaigns, and prepared advertisements shrewdly addressed to the mind of the average American, which he knew perfectly, because he had been one for forty years. It was his doctrine that any man who wanted to succeed in business should never let it out of his mind; and he had practiced this half a lifetime before he began to preach it.

In the first year the sales of the Ford Motor Company brought Ford a million and a half dollars, nearly one-fourth of which was profit. From then on, all his life, Henry Ford had all the money he needed to carry out his ideas. He took care of his money, and used it for that purpose.

Tough Times for the Men

. . . Under this new deal, the chassis came to him [the worker] with spindlenuts already screwed on; it was Abner's job to put in a cotter-pin and spread it. The next man wielded a scoop, pasting a gob of brown grease into the cavity; by the time he had smoothed it level, the chassis had moved on to another, who screwed on the hubcap. Abner's job rested his tired legs, but his back began to ache abominably, and his arms were ready to give out from being held up in front of him continually. But he hung on like death and taxes, for he was over forty, the dangerous age for workers in any factory.

Mission Accomplished

. . . Henry had a seemingly inexhaustible market for his cars. He was employing more than two hundred thousand men, paying wages of a quarter of a billion dollars a year. He had developed fifty-three different industries, beginning alphabetically with aeroplanes and ending with wood-distillation. He bought a broken-down railroad, and made it pay; he bought coal mines, and trebled their production. He perfected new processes—the very smoke that had once poured from his chimneys was now made into automobile parts.[20]

The following behaviors represent a high level of entrepreneurship:

- You are one of the top producers of results.
- Most jobs you have worked on have resulted in significant contributions.
- You will gamble on good odds anytime.
- You plan work and hold performance to schedule.
- If you want something done, you find a way to get it done.

Entrepreneurship in any field requires **good work habits, a belief in oneself,** and **the willingness to take risks.** All three of these qualities depend primarily on the individual. The following action plan will help you maximize entrepreneurship.

Exercise Good Work Habits

The achievement of results requires a positive attitude and the ability to stick with a job until it is done, even when others may give up. As a Polish proverb says, "If there is not enough wind, row." The following poem by Edgar Guest shows the kind of attitude that is necessary to accomplish difficult tasks:

> Some said it couldn't be done.
> But he, with a chuckle, replied
> That maybe it couldn't, but he would be one
> Who wouldn't say so until he tried.
>
> So he buckled right in with a bit of a grin,
> If he worried, he hid it.
> He started to sing, as he tackled the thing
> That couldn't be done—and he did it.[21]

The high performer goes the extra mile, living by the maxim that triumph is the "umph" added to "try." If you exercise good work habits, you will be rewarded both financially and personally as word gets out that you are a valuable asset.

Believe in Yourself

Eleanor Roosevelt once said, "No one can make you feel inferior without your consent."[22] The chronology of Abraham Lincoln's career shows the importance of belief in yourself and determined effort:

- In 1831, he failed in business.
- In 1832, he was defeated for the legislature.
- In 1833, he again failed in business.
- In 1836, he had a nervous breakdown.
- In 1843, he was defeated for Congress.
- In 1855, he was defeated for the Senate.
- In 1856, he lost the race for the vice presidency.
- In 1858, he was defeated for the Senate.
- In 1860, he was elected president of the United States.

Be Willing to Take Risks

Entrepreneurship requires courage, which is not the absence of fear, but the ability to overcome fear. Fear of failure can paralyze a person to the extent that opportunities are missed and achievement is reduced. As the following poem illustrates, courage is necessary to overcome self-doubt and achieve success:

The Doubter

Edgar Guest

He had his doubts when he began;
The task had stopped another man;
And he had heard it whispered low,
How rough the road was he must go;
But now on him the charge was laid,
And of himself he was afraid.

He wished he knew how it would end;
He longed to see around the bend;
He had his doubts that he had strength,
Enough to go so far a length;
And all the time the notion grew,
That this was more than he could do.

Of course, he failed. Whoever lives with doubt,
Soon finds his courage giving out;
They only win who face a task,
And say the chance is all I ask;
They only rise who dare the grade,
And of themselves are not afraid.

There are no ogres up the slope;
It is only with human beings that man must cope;
Whoever fears the blow before it's struck,
Loses the fight for lack of pluck;
And only he the goal achieves,
Who truly in himself believes.[23]

Innovation

Innovation is the ability to generate new and usable ideas. The innovator is not satisfied with the status quo, and therefore explores, questions, and studies new ways of doing things. Innovation accounts for advances in all fields of work, from agriculture to architecture. Important products we take for granted today are the result of yesterday's inventions—Thomas Edison's electric light, the Wright brothers' airplane, and Alexander Graham Bell's telephone are but a few examples. In the field of agriculture, George Washington Carver created more than 300 synthetic products from the peanut, more than 100 from the sweet potato, and more than 75 from the pecan.

The following behaviors represent a high level of creativity:

- You continually search for better ways to do things.
- You have changed the whole approach to your work.
- You are well known for your creativity.
- Your ideas are almost always used.
- You are innovative in your ideas and approach to work.

How do you develop creativity and increase innovation? **Keep an open mind, have a questioning attitude,** and **use a new-ideas system.**

Keep an Open Mind

An essential quality of the innovator is openness to change and to new experience. Charles F. Kettering, the famous inventor, emphasized the importance of keeping an open mind when he wrote:

The experienced man is always saying why something can't be done. The fellow who has not had any experience doesn't know a thing can't be done—and goes ahead and does it. . . . There exist limitless opportunities in any industry. Where there is an open mind, there will always be a frontier.[24]

Do any of the following innovation blocks prevent you from being as creative as you could be?

- *Excessive need for order.* It is possible to be too orderly. When everything happens according to plan, innovation is ordered out of existence. As the Hungarians say, "To make an omelet, you have to break a few eggs." For creativity, order should be viewed as a tool, not a goal.

- *Reluctance to play.* Creativity requires playfulness, daydreaming, and questioning—What if? Why? Innovative people play with things, people, and ideas. Those who are afraid to play because they think they will look silly or because they feel guilty about having fun rarely come up with creative ideas.

- *Myopic vision.* Some people pride themselves on seeing things as they are. But if you see things only as they are, you miss seeing what they could be; imagination is the essence of innovation. A shoe can be a hammer, a pillow, or something from which to drink water. The playwright George Bernard Shaw once said, "You see things that are and say, 'Why?' But I dream things that never were and say, 'Why not?' "

- *Closed-mindedness.* What if Christopher Columbus had been as certain as many people in his day that the world was flat? Research has shown that the more people feel they really know something, the less open they are to new information and ideas in that area. This tendency is called the "specialist disease."[25]

Have a Questioning Attitude

People are creatures of habit. Some habits are good because they help us survive. Good driving and hygiene habits are examples. Other habits, such as wasting time or procrastinating, are harmful and prevent success. People may have poor habits and not know it unless they ask themselves two questions: Am I doing the right thing? and Is there a better way to do it? Many people sleepwalk through their days, never stopping to ask themselves these two questions. For these individuals, creativity is never realized because it is never considered. The following poem shows the importance of having a questioning attitude:

The Calf Path—The Beaten Path of Beaten Men

Samuel Foss

One day through an old-time wood,
A calf walked home, as good calves should;
But made a trail,
A crooked trail, as all calves do.
Since then three hundred years have fled,
And I infer the calf is dead.
But still, he left behind his trail,
And thereby hangs my mortal tale.

The trail was taken up the next day,
By a lone dog that passed that way.
And then a wise sheep,
Pursued the trail, over the steep,
And drew the flocks behind him too,
As all good sheep do.
And from that day, over hill and glade,
Through those old woods, a path was made.

This forest path became a lane,
That bent, and turned, and turned again.
This crooked lane became a road,
Where many a poor horse with his load,
Toiled on beneath the burning sun.
And thus a century and a half,
They followed the footsteps of that calf.

The years passed on in swiftness fleet,
And the road became a village street.
And this became a city's thoroughfare.
And soon the central street was a metropolis.
And men, two centuries and a half,
Followed the footsteps of that calf.

A moral lesson this tale might teach,
Were I ordained, and called to preach.
For men are prone to go it blind,
Along the calf paths of the mind;
And work away from sun to sun,
To do just what other men have done.
They follow in the beaten track,
And out, and in, and forth, and back;
And still their devious course pursue,
To keep the paths that others do.

They keep these paths as sacred grooves,
Along which all their lives they move.
But how the wise old wood gods laugh,
Who saw the first old-time calf.
Ah, many things this tale might teach,
But I am not ordained to preach.[26]

Use a New-Ideas System

Being open to change, avoiding innovation blocks, and having a questioning attitude are three ingredients of creativity; but a fourth element is necessary—a system is needed to generate new and usable ideas. One good system comes from the English writer Rudyard Kipling. Kipling, who was known for his creativity, was asked how he could come up with so many good ideas—what was the secret of his success? His famous answer was:

I keep six honest serving-men;
They taught me all I knew;
Their names are What and Where and When,
And How and Why and Who.
I send them over land and sea;
I send them east and west;
But after they have worked for me,
I give them all a rest.
I let them rest from nine till five,
For I am busy then,
As well as breakfast, lunch, and tea,
For they are hungry men:
But different folk have different views:
I know a person small—
She keeps ten million serving-men,
Who get no rest at all.
She sends 'em abroad on her own affairs,
From the second she opens her eyes—
One million Hows, two million Wheres,
And seven million Whys.[27]

By asking six simple questions—who, what, why, when, where, and how—and by constructively answering these, you can usually find new and workable solutions to any problem.

You Can Improve If You Want To

It is possible to improve performance, and the rewards can be great. Consider the following story:

When Gene Malusko first went to work for his company, he was hired as a laborer. Before long, it was apparent that he would become either a union steward or a work group supervisor. Gene had the ability to work with and through other people. Gene could talk people into things; he was a statesman. Gene chose supervision because he had a family to raise and needed the money. For the next year, he was a successful foreman—he had good relations with his subordinates, and he had a good production record.

Then Gene became interested in advancement. As he considered those who had been promoted in the past, he realized that they had each excelled at obtaining results. The quality and efficiency of their production had stood out over that of the other supervisors. This convinced him to set forth on a self-improvement program to improve entrepreneurship, the delivery of results.

Thereafter, when Gene arrived at work, he began working immediately, and he worked diligently until the job was done. He developed a reputation for making his production quota each day, and he could be counted on to help out in emergencies. Gene was also willing to stick his neck out and take risks when the situation warranted it. He overcame self-doubt with the attitude "nothing ventured, nothing gained." With confidence in himself and good work habits, Gene developed a superb record of achievement. Gene exhibited entrepreneurship, and within two years, he was promoted to general foreman.

Gene performed well as a general foreman on the strength of his ability to work with people (statesmanship) and his ability to obtain results (entrepreneurship). After a mere three years in this capacity, he was selected as the youngest superintendent in the history of the company.

Two years later, Gene was talking with a friend about future plans when he stated that his goal was to be a general manager. He wondered aloud, "What do those people have that I don't?" The answer was creativity. A good general manager must work with and through others, which Gene did; must achieve results regardless of obstacles, which Gene did; and must come up with new and usable ideas, which Gene almost never did.

Gene's friend told him about the ideas of Charles Kettering and the importance of keeping an open mind; he pointed out the six common blocks to innovation; he gave him "The Calf Path—The Beaten Path of Beaten Men," emphasizing the need to question things; and finally, he told him about Rudyard Kipling's six honest serving-men, a system of constructive questioning.

Until this time, Gene had not thought much about why things were as they were; he had rarely questioned whether there was a better way to do something and he had never been given a system for generating new ideas. For Gene, a new dimension of work performance was unveiled, and he set about to improve his creativity.

Each day, Gene would go into his work area and ask six important questions—who, what, why, when, where, and how—to analyze the production bottlenecks and employee problems he encountered. He would ask: Who should do this work, the machine operator or the material handler? What work should be done, milling or planing? Why should this work be done, production or politics? Where should the work be done, in the office or the field? When should the work be done, on the first shift or the second? And how should the work be done, by person or by machine? And, like Kipling, Gene always found a better way.

Gene worked at constructive questioning until it became a habit, and he gained a reputation as a creative person. He added innovation to the qualities of statesmanship and entrepreneurship that he had already developed, and two years later, Gene Malusko was promoted to general manager.[28]

Gene's story is one of professionalism. He learned what was required to perform his job well; he performed good work; yet he constantly tried to improve. He was not complacent. As a result of professional development, Gene Malusko improved the performance of his company and achieved personal rewards as well.

Performance Success Story—A Case in Point

Sam Walton, founder of Wal-Mart, was America's richest person, a multibillionaire, when he died, and he was beloved by all who knew him. His prescription for success, as detailed in *Sam Walton: Made in America, My Story,* has three key elements: statesmanship, entrepreneurship, and innovation. Walton wrote that success came only through building a team, only after hard work, and only by breaking old rules.

Statesmanship—share the rewards. "If you treat people as your partners, they will perform beyond your wildest dreams." (In the effort to treat others as partners, Sam's reading of people wasn't always 100 percent. Once he attempted to thank big-city investors by taking them camping on the banks of Sugar Creek. A coyote started howling and a hoot owl hooted. Half the Back-East investors stayed up all night around the campfire because they couldn't sleep.)

Entrepreneurship—commit to your business. "I think I overcame every single one of my personal shortcomings by the sheer passion I brought to my work." (Hard work and risk have a price, as revealed by Sam's youngest child, Alice, when she once confided to a friend, "I don't know what we are going to do. My daddy owes so much money, and he won't quit opening stores.")

Innovation—be creative. "If everybody else is doing it one way, there's a good chance you can find your niche by going in a new direction. I guess in all of my years, what I heard more than anything else was: a town of less than 50,000 can't support a decent store." (Of course, some say this strategy stemmed from Sam's wife, Helen, who insisted on raising the Walton family in a town with fewer than 10,000 people.)[29]

Five Levels of Performance Excellence

There are many models of performance excellence, none more interesting than the five-level hierarchy proposed by management author James Collins in his book *Good to Great.* Level 1 refers to highly capable individuals. Level 2 refers to contributing team members. Level 3 refers to competent managers. Level 4 refers to effective senior leaders. And Level 5 refers to the exceptional executive. See Figure 27–3.

The Level 5 leader sits on top of a hierarchy of capabilities necessary for transforming an organization from good to great. What lies beneath are four other layers, each one appropriate in its own right, but none with the power of Level 5. Individuals do not need to proceed sequentially through each level of the hierarchy to reach the top, but to be a full-fledged Level 5 leader requires the capabilities of all the lower levels, plus the special characteristics of Level 5.

Exceptional leaders are masters of paradox. They are expert at managing the "and." The combination of **personal humility** and **professional will** make a potent formula for the highest level of leadership success. Humility refers to consideration and service to others, and should not be confused with either submissiveness or introversion. Professional will refers to conviction and fierce resolve, and should not be confused with either blind ambition or ruthlessness. See Table 27–1.

Collins concludes that the most effective executives possess a mixture of personal humility and professional will. They are both timid and ferocious. They are shy and fearless. They are rare and unstoppable. The triumph of humility and fierce resolve in the leader is instrumental in catapulting an organization from merely good to truly great.

**Figure 27–3
The Five-Level Hierarchy[30]**

Level 5: Exceptional Executive
Builds enduring greatness
through a paradoxical combination
of personal humility plus professional will

Level 4: Effective Senior Leader
Catalyzes commitment to and vigorous pursuit
of a clear and compelling vision; stimulates
group to high performance standards

Level 3: Competent Manager
Organizes people and resources toward the effective
and efficient pursuit of predetermined objectives

Level 2: Contributing Team Member
Contributes to the achievement of group
objectives; works effectively with others in a group setting

Level 1: Highly Capable Individual
Makes productive contributions through talent, knowledge,
skills, and good work habits

**Table 27–1
The Paradox of Level Five
Leadership[31]**

Personal Humility	**Professional Will**
The Leader	**The Leader**
Demonstrates a compelling modesty, shunning public adulation; is never boastful.	Creates superb results; is a clear catalyst in the transition from good to great.
Acts with deliberation and determination; relies principally on inspired standards to motivate.	Demonstrates an unwavering resolve to do whatever must be done to produce the best long-term results, no matter how difficult.
Channels ambition into group success, not the self; sets up successors for even more greatness in the next generation.	Sets the standard of building an enduring and great organization; will settle for nothing less.
Looks in the mirror to assign responsibility for poor results, never blaming other people, external factors, or bad luck.	Looks out the window to assign credit for success to other people, external factors, and good luck.

Collins's good-to-great research is based on the business performance of private-sector organizations, but the case of Abraham Lincoln can be used to illustrate the Level 5 leader. Modest and willful, shy and determined, Lincoln never let his personal ego get in the way of his ambition to preserve an enduring nation. Described as a quiet, peaceful, and shy figure, Lincoln had a resolve that was unshakeable—to the scale of 258,000 Confederate and 364,511 Union lives, including Lincoln's own.

Organizational Performance

The tasks of leadership are to interpret conditions, establish direction, mobilize followers, and develop people—all for the purpose of achieving organizational success. The leader who wants to improve the performance of his or her work group or organization can use **benchmarking** as a job aid in the leadership process.[32]

Benchmarking is a careful search for excellence—taking the absolute best as a standard and trying to surpass that standard. Great leaders are constantly in search of excellence both personally and organizationally. Benchmarking begins with an objective evaluation of the organization against the very best. The goal is to determine what winners are doing, and then take steps to meet or exceed that high standard. To personalize the concept, complete Exercise 27–2, Benchmarking the Best.

**Exercise 27–2
Benchmarking
the Best**[33]

Plot your organization (company, institution, etc.) on the performance graph below. Where are you today? Then plot your best competitors. Where are they? If your organization is not in the upper right corner, you are at risk. Your current performance is not satisfactory to the people who care about the work you do—customers, employees, owners, governing boards, and the like. What you must do is take action to improve your performance record. An interesting variation is to have others who know and care about your organization provide this evaluation. Note that product quality includes elements such as fit, finish, beauty, reliability and most important, functionality. Service quality includes timely delivery, response to questions and problems, courteous treatment, and consideration of customer's needs.

An interesting example of performance excellence is Toyota at its best. A philosophy of excellence is described in Toyota's *Basic Management Handbook:* "The only acceptable quality percentage is 100%. Every car must be manufactured exactly according to specifications. No Toyota vehicle should ever leave the factory without passing every quality test perfectly." One can see the positive attitude, high standards, and uncompromising commitment of a business winner in Toyota's mandate to leaders. Toyota believes the success of the company will be determined by constant adherence to this high standard of work performance.[34]

Improving Performance through Behavior Modification

Behavior modification, established in the 1950s by B. F. Skinner, is a practical and effective way to improve human performance. Behavior modification today is based on the conceptual premises of classical behaviorists John Watson and Ivan Pavlov, reinforcement theorists C. B. Ferster and B. F. Skinner, and applied behaviorists Albert Bandura and Fred Luthans.[35] The application of behavior modification principles has been shown to have a positive impact on performance in a wide range of sales, service, manufacturing, and not-for-profit organizations in both Western and non-Western cultures.[36]

The following example shows how three elements of behavior modification—**goal setting, feedback on performance,** and **positive reinforcement**—can be used to improve employee performance.[37]

Improving Employee Performance in the Transportation Industry

The purpose of a mass transit organization is to provide safe, dependable, efficient, and courteous transportation to the public. The performance of the operator is critical in meeting this mission because this is the person who deals directly with the passenger. To improve driver performance, one organization sponsored a six-hour passenger relations program. Participants learned human relations principles and were asked, "What are the day-to-day actions a driver should perform to provide the best possible service to the public?" Table 27–2 lists the performance objectives developed by the 250 participants.

For a period of three months after attending the training session, each operator completed a self-evaluation based on the list of performance objectives. At the end of each work shift, drivers checked off the behaviors they had performed and left blank those they had not. This paper-and-pencil checklist provided personal feedback on performance. At the end of every month for three months, each driver also met privately with the supervisor, who had been a fellow participant in the passenger relations program. The supervisor held these meetings to review performance

Table 27–2 Operator Performance Objectives

A coach operator should:

1. Start and stop smoothly.

2. Avoid smoking when carrying passengers.

3. Clean up trash around driver's quarters when leaving the bus.

4. Address adults by name if known and by "Sir" or "Ma'am" if name is not known. Never call a youngster by a nickname—Junior, Sonny, Peanut, Sister, and the like—unless requested.

5. Have exact working tools—transfers, punch, change, ticket refunds, and so on—when starting the job.

6. Greet all passengers in a friendly manner.

7. Try to solve problems that arise in carrying out the job. Do not complain to passengers about other employees.

8. Wave recognition to police officers, firefighters, school guards, and other uniformed public workers.

9. Always use hand and arm signals in traffic; say thank you in this manner whenever possible.

10. Wait for slow arrivers, making sure that all who want rides get them.

11. Never run ahead of schedule.

12. Pull to the curb if possible; avoid puddles.

13. Give clear, friendly, and sensible answers to the public.

checklists, discuss job problems, and express appreciation for employee participation in the program. These meetings emphasized the positive and ignored the negative. If a driver had a good performance record, this accomplishment was praised; if a driver had a poor record, he was thanked for keeping the checklist and encouraged to continue trying to implement the agreed upon performance objectives; if a driver failed to keep records, this fact was ignored and a discussion was held reviewing and reaffirming the importance of the performance objectives.

The following were the results of the employee development program:

- Safety records showed substantial improvement, and there were significant financial savings.
- Passenger complaints decreased, and the organization's public image improved.
- The company set a national record for increased ridership.
- Employee morale and pride increased.
- Relations between managers and employees improved.

UNIT

28

Sustaining Discipline

George Washington wrote, "Discipline is the soul of an army. It makes small numbers formidable, procures success to the weak, and esteem to all." Three elements are important for effective **discipline:** (1) defined roles and responsibilities so that employees know what is expected; (2) clear rules and guidelines so that employees understand acceptable behavior; and (3) effective methods and procedures for taking corrective action. Discipline problems include **permissiveness, rigidity,** and **inconsistency.**[38]

Permissiveness results in an untrained, poorly organized, and unproductive workforce. People need to know that they are responsible for their actions. Performance problems that go unaddressed can reduce the morale of good employees and lower the performance of the entire work group.

Rigidity, on the other hand, may cause employees to fear or hate authority and to feel anxious or overly guilty about making mistakes. If people feel that conditions are too restrictive, counterproductive measures such as slowdowns, sabotage, and strikes may result.

Inconsistency should be avoided because it makes it difficult for employees to understand what behavior is appropriate and what is not allowed. When people are punished one time and ignored or even rewarded the next time for doing the same thing, they become confused. Inevitably, this confusion results in resentment, lowered morale, and reduced productivity.

Taking Corrective Action

The two central elements of caring leadership—caring about the work and caring about people—come together in the corrective action process. The effective leader knows that performance and behavior problems must be addressed. Taking corrective action can be unpleasant and unpopular, but it is necessary because people may make mistakes that should not be condoned. Examples include theft, equipment abuse, and safety violations. Use of the following principles will help provide effective discipline and corrective action.[39]

■ *Establish just and reasonable rules based on core values.* Think of civil rules that are just, reasonable, and necessary, such as not driving through a red light or not stealing. Employees need similar guidelines for behavior on the job. If corrective action is necessary, it should take the form of a **caring confrontation** based on core values of the organization.

Work rules should be established in such areas as attendance, safety, security, language, dress, and personal conduct. When possible, employees should be involved in establishing rules based on the core values of the organization—honesty, respect for others, and the like. Committees on safety and quality of work life help serve this purpose.

- *Communicate rules to all employees.* Rules should be thoroughly explained to new employees during orientation and should also be published in an employee handbook or posted on a bulletin board. As few rules as possible should be made, and these should be reviewed annually. Changes in rules should be communicated in writing, since people can be held responsible only for rules they know about.

- *Provide immediate corrective action.* Some leaders postpone corrective action because carrying it out is uncomfortable or distasteful. The practice of storing up observations and complaints and then unloading on an employee in one angry session only alienates the subordinate. Immediate correction and penalties (if appropriate) are more acceptable to the offender, and thus more effective. If there is an association between misconduct and swift corrective action, repetition of the offense is less likely to occur.

- *Create a system of progressive corrective measures for violation of rules.* Fairness requires a progression of penalties—oral warning, written warning, suspension from the job, and discharge. The leader should be sure that a final warning has been issued prior to actual discharge. This progression gives the leader a chance to help the employee improve. If a penalty is necessary, severity should depend on the offense, the employee's previous record, and the corrective value of the penalty. Theft may justify immediate suspension; tardiness may not.

- *Provide an appeal process for corrective action.* An appeal process helps ensure fair treatment for employees. If a mistake is made during the corrective process, a procedure for review can help correct a wrongful disciplinary action.

- *Preserve human dignity.* Corrective action should take place in private. This approach reduces defensiveness and the likelihood that other employees may become involved and create an even bigger problem. Meeting privately provides a better opportunity to discuss the problem and prevent it from happening again. *Never* reprimand an employee in public.

  When meeting with an employee, allow time to explain fully. Be a good listener. Ask questions that help the employee clarify actions. Allow for honest mistakes. Everybody makes a mistake sometime. Strike a balance between correcting the problem and developing the employee. Criticize the act, not the employee as a person. Be sure to look at all sides of the problem. If you are in error, admit it. It is possible that the employee is innocent of intentional wrongdoing. If this is so, do not take punitive action, but provide training if appropriate. End corrective action on a positive note. Emphasize cooperation and optimism for future performance.

- *Do not charge a rule violation without first knowing the facts.* In any situation involving disciplinary action, the burden of proof and fairness is on the accuser. Be sure that (1) the rule is enforced consistently and that this incident is not an isolated case; (2) the employee was informed of the rule; (3) the employee broke the rule; (4) it can be proved that the employee broke the rule; and (5) corrective measures are fair.

  There is no substitute for good preparation prior to a meeting on discipline. However, even in cases where you think you have all the facts, you might find otherwise once you begin discussion with the employee. If something new comes to light that should be investigated, suspend the meeting so that the facts can be determined. On those occasions when something new is presented, take time to confirm the facts before acting. Some leaders think, "Well, I've come this far. I don't like doing this anyway. I am just going to do what I planned from the beginning, regardless of these new facts." This approach is a mistake. Aside from taking action that may be wrong, you lose credibility with the employee and everyone else who knows the facts.

- *Obtain agreement that a problem exists.* If you cannot get agreement that a problem exists, the answer is to inform the employee that it is not likely that the employment arrangement will continue. If the employee will not acknowledge that a problem exists, how can steps be taken to correct it? If the problem is not corrected, the employee must be reassigned or terminated.

- *Avoid negative emotions.* Relax before meeting with your employee; remain calm. *Never* confront an employee in anger. It is difficult to think and to communicate clearly when you are upset or arguing. Never scold or talk down to the employee, and do not curse or strike the person. Once you have taken corrective action, start over with a clean slate. Do not hold grudges or stereotype the employee as a troublemaker.

- *Remember the purpose of corrective action.* The purpose is to prevent future problems, not to punish or obtain revenge. Be sure the employee understands what is wrong and why it is wrong. Be sure the employee understands the rules and the reasons they exist. Be clear. Also be fair. Ask yourself, Is this disciplinary action too severe? If a lesser measure will accomplish the same purpose, use it. Also ask, Did I clarify the problem, or did I blame the employee? Finally, ask, Does this corrective action provide a way to avoid the same situation in the future?

- *Avoid double standards.* Rules and standards of conduct should be the same for all people in the same occupation and organization, and they should be enforced equally. If this is not the case, disciplinary action is unfair, and when higher management, union arbitrators, or governmental agencies review the decision, the action taken probably will be reversed. Consider the following case:

  > Sure, I had a crescent wrench in my lunch box, but I'm no thief. Everybody does it. I could give you dozens of examples, but I won't. One thing I will say is that taking company property is not restricted to hourly employees. Look at the way management uses company cars and gasoline for personal trips. And in the shops, we're always fixing something for management—using company labor, tools, and parts. I'm always hearing stories from the front office about how managers combine vacations and company-paid business trips, or use their expense accounts for personal entertainment. I'm willing to live by the same rules everybody else does, but I won't sit still for being singled out. Let's face it: the way most employees think is that as long as you don't overdo it, taking company property is a form of employee benefits—like vacations and insurance.[40]

- *Enforce rules consistently and firmly.* Disciplinary measures should be taken only when they are fair, necessary, procedurally correct, immediate, and constructive. Once these conditions are met, if disciplinary action is in order, the leader should proceed with confidence and firmness and should stick to the decision. When a leader backs down on a rule violation, employees either think the rule is unimportant or is being applied unfairly. The only time backing down is advised is when a wrong decision has been made. If a mistake is made, the leader must correct the mistake.

- *Follow the four-step method for solving performance problems.* See Figure 28–1. Note that step 4 accomplishes two important purposes: (1) ensuring the correction is made and (2) building goodwill by recognizing improvement.

**Figure 28–1
Four-Step Method for
Solving Performance
Problems**[41]

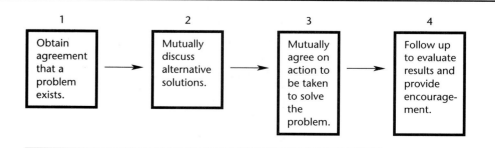

1	2	3	4
Obtain agreement that a problem exists.	Mutually discuss alternative solutions.	Mutually agree on action to be taken to solve the problem.	Follow up to evaluate results and provide encouragement.

In summary, employee discipline is an important ingredient for organizational success. Discipline in the form of a caring confrontation can be an effective leadership tool that helps employee development, keeps work morale high, and results in the best job performance.

Part Nine Summary

After reading Part Nine, you should know the following key concepts principles, and terms. Fill in the blanks from memory, or copy the answers listed below.

Performance management skills include (a) _____, _____, and _____. Management performance is important in three areas: (b) _____, the ability to work with and through other people; (c) _____, the ability to achieve results regardless of obstacles; and (d) _____, the ability to generate new and usable ideas. Statesmanship involves good (e) _____ skills and using _____. Entrepreneurship requires (f) _____, _____, and _____. Developing creativity and increasing innovation is helped by (g) _____, _____, and _____. Level 5 leadership is required to help an organization go from good to great. The Level 5 leader builds enduring greatness through a combination of (h) _____ and _____. (i) _____ is a careful search for excellence—taking the absolute best as a standard and striving to surpass it. Behavior modification, a method of improving the performance of individuals and groups, involves three elements: (j) _____, _____, and _____. George Washington thought that (k) _____ is the soul of an army, making small numbers formidable, procuring success to the weak, and esteem to all. The three enemies of effective discipline are (l) _____, _____, and _____. Corrective action taken to support core values or principles can be termed a (m) _____.

Answer Key for Part Nine Summary

a. **performance planning, performance coaching, correcting poor performance,** page 302

b. **statesmanship,** page 313

c. **entrepreneurship,** page 313

d. **innovation,** page 313

e. **good human relations skills, the four-step method to solve problems,** page 320

f. **good work habits, belief in oneself, courage to take risks,** page 322

g. **keeping an open mind, having a questioning attitude, using a new-ideas system,** page 323

h. **personal humility, professional will,** page 328

i. **benchmarking,** page 327

j. **goal setting, feedback on performance, positive reinforcement,** page 331

k. **discipline,** page 333

l. **permissiveness, rigidity, inconsistency,** page 333

m. **caring confrontation,** page 333

Reflection Points—personal thoughts on managing performance, professional performance, and sustaining discipline

Complete the following questions and activities to personalize the content of Part Nine. Space is provided for writing your thoughts.

- Discuss the importance of setting goals and establishing objectives. Apply the concept of performance planning to your own job or career.

  _____

  _____

- Discuss the merits of performance appraisal. Cite true-life examples in which performance reviews helped or hurt job performance. What do's and don'ts can you recommend for evaluating employees?

  _____

  _____

- Discuss the idea of rating leaders. If you were a supervisor, a manager, or an executive, would you want to be evaluated by your employees? Explain.

  _____

  _____

- Discuss your performance in the areas of statesmanship, entrepreneurship, and innovation. What are your strengths? What areas do you need to improve? What actions will you take to improve?

  _____

  _____

- Discuss a Level 5 leader on the basis of personal humility and professional will. How can a leader demonstrate consideration and service as well as conviction and resolve at the same time?

  _____

  _____

- Evaluate an organization you know on the basis of product quality and service quality. Compare the results against those of its best competitors. Develop an action plan to stay excellent or improve.

  _____

  _____

- Develop a behavior modification program to improve performance in an existing group: (a) Identify a group with critical performance behaviors (examples—teachers, machine operators, police officers, food service employees, salespeople, nurses); (b) meet with members of the group to help them agree on critical performance behaviors; (c) prepare a checklist of critical performance behaviors (typically, 10 to 15 points); (d) enlist the cooperation of group members in monitoring their own performance and using the checklist to document behaviors exhibited (typically, daily); (e) review progress with group members (typically, weekly); (f) reward participation and progress (provide recognition and reinforcement). Discuss results.

  _____

  _____

- Discuss the concept of the caring confrontation in the context of effective discipline, employee development, work group morale, and job performance. Have you ever experienced a caring confrontation, either as a leader or a subordinate? Describe the situation and outcome.

_____

_____

Action Assignment

As a bridge between learning and doing, complete the following action assignment.

1. What is the most important idea you have learned in Part Nine?

2. How can you apply what you have learned? What will you do, with whom, where, when, and, most important, why?

Conclusion: Challenge and Charge

UPON THE PLAINS OF HESITATION bleach the bones of countless millions, who on the threshold of victory sat down to wait; and awaiting they died.

—Winston Churchill

The Road Ahead

Leadership has become an increasingly important and popular subject. The U.S. Library of Congress contains more than 9155 books with the word *leadership* in the title. There are currently 6290 English language journals being published on the subject of leadership, and today almost every university in the United States (2100) is teaching leadership in its curriculum.[1]

Books, articles, seminars, and courses are flourishing. Instead of older models of command and control, newer models of commitment and consideration are needed to deal effectively with changing organizations, changing work, changing people, and a changing society. Instead of leadership by a few hierarchical, position-based leaders, leadership today is shared at all levels and in all walks of the organization.

It is no longer just "the boss" who leads; individuals up and down a far flatter organization provide leadership based on the task to be performed and the skills required to perform it. An individual may be a leader one day, a follower the next, and a co-leader the third. The trend toward team-based projects, virtual communities, and personal responsibility will only accelerate the move toward shared leadership and the need for leadership education.[2]

Bright new leaders of the future can draw on teachers from the past. In the first quarter of the past century, management author and business advisor Mary Parker Follett identified the challenge of leadership:

The leader must have an eye for change and a steadying hand to provide both vision and reassurance that change can be mastered, a voice that articulates the will of the group and shapes it to constructive ends, and an ability to inspire by force of personality while making others feel capable to increase and use their own abilities.[3]

The century ahead will be an exciting time, requiring leaders in the best sense of the word—people who care about others and who want to make a difference. It will be a time requiring leaders whose ideas and deeds will light the path, encourage the heart, and make the world a better place. It will be a time requiring *caring leadership*.

Nine Key Areas of Leadership

We have defined leadership, emphasized the need for caring leadership, and discussed the concepts, principles, and techniques of nine key areas of leadership success, which correspond to the nine parts of this book. The example of Abraham Lincoln, one of America's greatest leaders, shows the importance of leadership and the critical role of each of these areas:[4]

- *Part 1—Leadership variables.* Lincoln's character (honesty and courage), the ability of his followers (Grant's determination and persistence), and the nature of the situation (the North's economic strength) combined, a civil war was waged, and America endured as one nation.

- *Part 2—The power of vision.* With compassion for all people and dedication to preserving the Union, Lincoln delivered the Gettysburg Address, considered by historians the most powerful speech since the Sermon on the Mount. In so doing, Lincoln articulated a vision of a united America that would inspire and sustain his country through bitter civil war.

- *Part 3—The importance of ethics.* To his vision of a united country and his concern for all people, Lincoln applied the bedrock character elements of honesty, courage, and hard work. He was devoted to goodness as he understood it to be, regardless of self-interest or the dictates of public opinion.

- *Part 4—The empowerment of people.* Lincoln was a servant leader who used the office of president in an empowering way, saying, "Am I not helping people when I make friends of them? A drop of honey that catches a man's heart is the high road to his reason."

- *Part 5—Leadership principles.* Lincoln's great competence as a leader was seen in his knowledge of history, law, and current conditions, which he used in addition to common sense and practical judgment in dealing with people.

- *Part 6—Understanding people.* It was common to hear it said that Lincoln understood the American people better than they understood themselves, and he would tap the great fountains of humor and wit to make his points without rancor.

- *Part 7—Multiplying effectiveness.* This ability was seen best in the selection and support of Ulysses S. Grant as commander of the Union army. Lincoln was effective at achieving his goals through delegation, support, and encouragement of others.

- *Part 8—Developing others.* Lincoln was by nature a teacher—patient and encouraging in the development of others. Almost no situation could occur in which Lincoln could not apply the techniques of metaphor and example to instruct his audience and inspire them.

- *Part 9—Performance management.* Lincoln held the bar high for his war generals. He expected results and if they were not forthcoming, he replaced the generals, no matter how uncomfortable he personally felt. To victorious performers—Grant, Sherman, and Sheridan—he was grateful, and he credited the preservation of the Union to them.

These nine key areas of leadership can be used to diagnose past leadership events, as well as predict future leadership effectiveness. The ideas and deeds of one person or group will influence the behavior of others to the degree that the nine dimensions of leadership are present and in force. Deficiency in these areas leads to inaction, confusion, ethical drift, stagnation, low morale, poor communication, inefficiency, underachievement, and failure; whereas mastery in these areas leads to movement, focus, moral strength, commitment, high morale, motivation, effectiveness, fulfillment of potential, and performance excellence.

For a personal evaluation of the nine key areas of leadership, complete Exercise C–1.

**Exercise C–1
Personal Analysis
of Leadership**

Step 1:

Identify a true-life situation requiring leadership in your work, personal, or community life. Examples include creating a business, raising a family, and leading a task force or team.

Step 2:

Answer the following questions.

Leadership Variables:

Describe your leadership traits, qualities, and style. Describe the characteristics of your followers. Describe the situation in terms of time and circumstances. Are the people and conditions right for you to provide leadership?

_____

_____

_____

The Power of Vision:

What is your vision—what do you want to accomplish? Why would you provide leadership in this situation—for power, achievement, or affiliation? How strong is your interest in providing leadership?

_____

_____

_____

The Importance of Ethics:

Do you base your actions on moral principles, regardless of personal loss or gain, and without regard to social influence? Describe your values in terms of honesty, respect, concern for others, and the like. Do you have conviction and courage so that others will follow you?

_____

_____

_____

The Empowerment of People:

What authority do you have? Do you possess the power of position? Do you view leadership as the opportunity to serve others? What will you do to empower people? What steps will you take to develop a high-performance workplace?

_____

_____

_____

Leadership Principles:

What principles of leadership will you practice that will help your followers be effective? What will you do to keep work morale high? What will you do to develop communication, teamwork, and a one-team attitude?

_____

_____

_____

Understanding People:

Do you understand the nature and needs of the people you lead? What are their motivations? What are your own reasons for doing what you do? What will you say or do to persuade others to take action?

_____

_____

_____

Multiplying Effectiveness:

How will you increase your leadership effectiveness? Are you willing to delegate duties and authority to others? Who will you assign to do what by when? Are you effective in meeting the needs of and achieving results with the different personalities reporting to you?

_____

_____

_____

Developing Others:

What will you do to attract and keep good people? Do you have the ability to train and develop others? Do you have the ability to help people through change? Do you maintain a positive attitude of exploration, responsibility, and commitment?

_____

_____

_____

Performance Management:

Do you set high goals, reinforce good performance, and correct performance problems? What are your strengths and weaknesses in the areas of statesmanship, entrepreneurship, and innovation? Do you have, or are you developing, the paradoxical qualities of personal humility and strong resolve?

_____

_____

_____

Step 3:

What is your prediction of the outcome? To what extent are the nine key dimensions of leadership present in this situation? Whether you would be hero, teacher, or ruler as a leader, how successful will you be in lighting the path and encouraging others to follow? Will your ideas and actions show the way and influence the behavior of others? Explain.

_____

_____

_____

Leaders Who Care

There are two principal aspects of successful leadership—commitment to a task and concern for others. Both are necessary for leadership success. The effective leader cares not only about the work but about people as well.[5] By caring so much, the leader focuses, energizes, and empowers others. In this sense, caring leadership is the universal key that unlocks success. The caring leader (1) aims higher than others think is practical; (2) gives more than others think is prudent; and (3) achieves more than others think is possible.

A concept in literature states: "No tears in the writer, no tears in the reader." The same concept can be applied to leadership—"No passion in the leader, no passion in the people." If the leader doesn't care, the people won't either. As Lee Iacocca said when he was the leader of Chrysler Corporation during a period of great uncertainty and struggle for survival, "The speed of the leader is the speed of the team." People will never care more or perform better than their leaders do.[6]

To understand the importance of leadership passion, consider the words of author and educator Price Pritchett.[7]

People always look at the leader when they want to take the pulse of an organization. Example says a lot. Do they see a person they can believe in? Can they have faith in whom they follow? Does the fire inside the leader burn hot enough for them to warm from the heart of that flame?

Commitment climbs when people see passion in the person out front. They catch the feeling. Commitment, after all, is a highly contagious thing. It is a spirit that stirs others, that touches their souls, that inspires them to action. It carries a mental magnetism that captures the attention and enlists the energies of all who watch.

The more consuming your commitment, the more you will draw your people toward you, and toward the task to be done. Your intensity—your focus, drive, and dedication—carries maximum influence over the level of commitment you can expect from others.

Like it or not, you set the climate. People always take a reading on the person in charge. So when it comes to building commitment, you must lead by example, just as commanders must show courage if they want soldiers showing bravery on the battlefield.

If you provide lukewarm leadership, you will see the passion cool among your people. Commitment can't survive when the leader doesn't seem to care. So be obvious. Turn up the burner inside yourself. Let the heat of your commitment be strong enough to glow in the dark.

To personalize the subject, consider how you rate on leadership commitment. Do you have self-drive and determination that ignites and energizes others? Does your intensity burn bright enough to glow in the dark? Does your passion stir others and inspire them to action?

The leader also must care about people. To understand the importance of concern for others, consider the words of leader and businessman Clarence Francis:

> You can buy a person's time. You can buy a person's presence at a given place. You can buy a measured number of skilled muscular motions per hour or day. But you cannot buy enthusiasm. You cannot buy initiative. You cannot buy loyalty. You cannot buy the devotion of hearts, minds, and souls. You have to earn these things. To do this the leader must believe that the greatest assets are human assets, and that the improvement of their value is both a matter of material advantage and moral obligation. The leader must believe that workers must be treated as honorable individuals, justly rewarded, encouraged in their own progress, fully informed, and properly assigned, and that their lives and work must be given meaning and dignity on and off the job. If a leader has supervision of so much as one person, the leader must honor these principles in practice.[8]

To personalize the subject, consider how you rate on concern for people. Do you care about the well-being of others? Do they know it? Does your consideration for others create support and loyalty to you and your goals?

Learning from Lincoln

Leaders are not either–or people; they are masters of paradox. They care about the mission, and they care about people. They focus on doing the right things and doing things right, not one without the other. They think and feel and act for the benefit of others, and, in so doing, are true to themselves. They pursue the large and attend the small, knowing that both of these matter. This is the kind of leader the world needs and the kind of leader that Abraham Lincoln was.

> The people were divided and the nation was at war. Prejudice, cruelty, sickness, and death all waited at the door. In this hour, Abraham Lincoln called to Washington a soldier from the field. He wanted to talk with him about something important. The soldier was a good hearted man, but he had neglected his mother. He had not written her for two years, and she believed him killed. She had asked the President if he could locate his grave.
>
> Lincoln talked with the young man sternly, but not unkindly. He told him that he must write his mother every week beginning now, or be court martialed for a crime worse than treason: ingratitude. The record shows that one hour later, the young man left. About the time spent, Lincoln said, "It needed doing."[9]

Lincoln thought the nation should not be divided and he thought the slaves should be freed. He was committed to these great goals. He also thought a mother should be spared unnecessary sorrow and grief, and that a son should be grateful and kind. He thought all these things needed doing and he did them because he cared. There may be no such thing as a perfect leader, but Lincoln was close. Those who would be effective leaders can learn from his good example.

Going Forward

The *knowing–doing gap* is an important concept that explains a great deal about human behavior. On the one hand, we are curious and we want to improve both our public and private lives, so we study and learn. On the other hand, we often fail to apply what we discover and fail to fulfill our potential. The solution is to close the gap between knowing and doing.

As you develop the characteristics of a caring leader and apply the nine keys to success, we hope you will keep this book handy and refer to it often in your leadership role. What are the elements of caring leadership? See pages 10–11, 343–345. What are the qualities of effective leaders? See pages 26–29. What is the role of leadership style? See pages 45–50. Why would you want to be a leader? See pages 67–71. What is the importance of leadership character? See pages 92–101. How do you use and not abuse leadership authority? See pages 121–126, 129–132. What are the principles of effective leadership? See pages 148–154. How do you build a high-performance team? See pages 165–187. How do you motivate people? See pages 199–208. How do you assign work effectively? See pages 157–158, 239–240. What are the rules for effective delegation? See pages 232–238. How do you deal with different personalities? See pages 248–260. How do you help people develop and grow? See pages 272–274. How do you help people through change? See pages 278–285. How do you deal with employee problems? See pages 333–335. How do you develop and sustain organizational success? See pages 55–66, 73–78, 276–277, 327–332. We encourage you to use this book as a reference and learning guide.

Leadership is an important subject with enormous potential to help or harm. Consider your own experiences with the leaders you have known, and think how they have affected you. Now consider your own work and life and the occasions you may have to provide leadership to others, the opportunities you will have to light the way and influence others to action. During these times, remember to display the commitment to task and the support of people characteristic of caring leadership. Always keep in mind the nine key dimensions of leadership, and apply the concepts, principles, and techniques you have learned to *be the leader you have always wanted to have.*

In appreciation of leaders both past and present, we end this book with a poem by James Autry, whose wise and wonderful book *Love and Profit* inspired this one.

Retirement

It is early—6:30. The building is quiet.
Soon the place will come to life as it always
does with the rush of people working.
These days, though, it's the smaller, slower things I notice;
the droning of the fans and compressors keeping us warm or cool,
the buzz of fluorescent lights, the burble of the big percolator and
the smell of coffee.
As the time here grows shorter, I find myself thinking of other
times when I could not wait for the day or the week to be over—
The times I strained for Christmas or vacation; I think of
meetings that would never end, of hours stuck on a taxi-way,
airliners lined up as far as I could see;
of those eternal minutes right before someone was to come into my
office to be fired.
I understand now why every writer who ever lived wrote about time
and its paradoxes, and everything they ever said about
how fast time passes is true.
But, they never told us how many slow days we would have
to endure before we realized
how fast they had gone.[10]

Endnotes

INTRODUCTION

1. Samuel Deep and Lyle Sussman, *What to Ask When You Don't Know What to Say* (New York: M.J.F. Books, 1997); Richard L. Hughes, Robert C. Ginnett, and Gordon J. Curphy, *Leadership: Enhancing the Lessons of Experience* (New York: McGraw-Hill, 1999); and David Giber, Louis Carter, and Marshall Goldsmith, *Linkage Inc.'s Best Practices in Organization and Human Resource Development Handbook: Case Studies, Instruments, Models, and Research* (San Francisco: Jossey-Bass/Pfieffer, 2000).

2. J. Thomas Wren, *The Leader's Companion: Insights on Leadership through the Ages* (New York: Free Press, 1995); and Eugene E. Jennings, *An Anatomy of Leadership: Princes, Heroes, and Supermen* (New York: McGraw-Hill, 1960), 30.

3. Geoffry Ashe, *Camelot and the Vision of Albion* (London: Hinemann, 1977), 134.

4. Rex Warner, *Greeks and Trojans* (London: MacGibbon & Kee, 1951), 136.

5. Donald T. Phillips, *The Founding Fathers on Leadership: Classic Teamwork in Changing Times* (Collingdale, PA: Diane, 2000).

6. Charles Oman, *The Dark Ages: 476–918* (London: Rivingstons, 1962), 512.

7. Katherine Anthony, *Susan B. Anthony* (Garden City, NY: Doubleday, 1954), vi, viii.

8. Ulrich Wikken, *Alexander the Great* (New York: Norton, 1967), 3.

9. Karl Britton, *Philosophy and Meaning of Life* (London: Cambridge University Press, 1969), 93; and Robert L. Heilbroner, *The Worldly Philosophers: The Lives, Times, and Ideas of the Great Economic Thinkers* (London: Penguin, 2000).

10. John Allen, *100 Great Lives* (New York: World, 1945); Jennings, *An Anatomy of Leadership,* 1; Joseph Campbell, *The Hero with a Thousand Faces* (Princeton, NJ: Princeton University Press, 1972); and Michael H. Hart, *The One Hundred* (New York: Beaufort Books, 1985).

11. R. N. Osborn, J. L. Hunt, and L. R. Jauch, *Organizational Theory: An Integrated Approach* (New York: Wiley, 1980); and Geoffrey Bellman, *Getting Things Done When You Are Not in Charge* (San Francisco: Berrett-Koehler, 2001).

12. Camilla J. Wilson, *Rosa Parks: From the Back of the Bus to the Front of a Movement* (New York: Scholastic, 2001).

13. James MacGregor Burns, *Leadership* (New York: Harper & Row, 1978); and, *Rethinking Leadership: Kellogg Leadership Studies Project 1994–1997* (College Park, MD: James MacGregor Burns Academy of Leadership, 1998).

14. Jennings, *An Anatomy of Leadership,* 71; Thomas Carlyle, *On Heroes, Hero Worship and the Heroic in History* (London: Chapman and Hall, 1870); and Wren, *The Leader's Companion.*

15. Ralph M. Stogdill, *Handbook of Leadership,* rev. and exp. Bernard M. Bass (New York: Free Press, 1981), 81.

16. Richard Neustadt, *Presidential Power and the Modern Presidents: The Politics of Leadership from Roosevelt to Reagan* (New York: Free Press, 1990); and Fred Fiedler and Joseph Garcia, *New Approaches to Effective Leadership: Cognitive Resources and Organizational Performance* (New York: Wiley, 1987).

17. Stogdill, *Handbook of Leadership,* 5; see also Bernard M. Bass and Ralph Stogdill, *Bass and Stogdill's Handbook of Leadership: A Survey of Theory and Research* (New York: Free Press, 1990).

18. Stogdill, *Handbook of Leadership,* 5.

19. Harry Levinson, *Executive* (Cambridge, MA: Harvard University Press, 1981); and Dava Sobel, "Findings," *Harvard Magazine* 81, no. 3 (January–February 1979): 15.

20. James Kouzes and Barry Posner, *The Leadership Challenge: How to Get Extraordinary Things Done in Organizations* (San Francisco: Jossey-Bass, 1987).

21. Kouzes and Posner, *The Leadership Challenge.*

22. Andrew DuBrin, *Leadership Research Findings, Practices, and Skills* (Boston: Houghton Mifflin, 1998).

23. DuBrin, *Leadership Research Findings.*

24. Theodore Roosevelt, *The Strenuous Life* (New York: Bartleby. Com: Great Books Online, 1999; http://www.bartleby.com/index.html).

25. Gilbert W. Fairholm, *Capturing the Heart of Leadership: Spirituality and Community in the New American Workplace* (Westport, CT: Praeger, 1997); Hyler Bracey, *Managing from the Heart* (New York: Delacorte Press, 1990); Milton Mayeroff, *On Caring* (New York: Harper Perennial, 1990); and Jane Dutton, Peter Frost, Monica Worline, Jacoba Lilius, and Jason Kanov, "Leading in Times of Trauma," *Harvard Business Review* (January 2002): 55–61.

26. Robert H. Rosen and Lisa Burger, *The Healthy Company: Eight Strategies to Develop People, Productivity, and Profits* (New York: Putnam, 1992); and Jan Carlzon, *Moments of Truth* (Cambridge, MA: Ballinger, 1987).

27. The poem, "Threads," is excerpted from the book *Love & Profit: The Art of Caring Leadership* (Avon Books, 1991) by James A. Autry and is reprinted by permission of the author.

28. John Kotter, *The Leadership Factor* (New York: Free Press, 1987); John Kotter, "What Leaders Really Do," *Harvard Business Review* 1, no. 3 (May–June 1990): 103–111; John W. Gardner, *On Leadership* (New York: McGraw-Hill, 1990); John W. Gardner, *Self-Renewal: The Individual and the Innovative Society* (New York: Norton, 1995); and Abraham Zaleznik, *The Managerial Mystique: Restoring Leadership in Business* (New York: Harper & Row, 1989).

29. Henry Mintzberg, *The Nature of Managerial Work* (New York: Harper & Row, 1973); Ernest Dale, *Management Theory and Practice* (New York: McGraw-Hill, 1973); Peter Drucker, *Management: Tasks, Practices, Responsibility* (New York: Morrow, 1982); P. G. Northouse, *Leadership: Theory and Practice,* 2nd ed. (Thousand Oaks, CA: Sage, 2001); John P. Kotter, *A Force for Change: How Leadership Differs from Management* (New York: Free Press, 1990); and Abraham

Zaleznik, "Managers and Leaders: Are They Different?" *Harvard Business Review* 70, no. 2 (March–April 1992): 126–135.

PART 1

1. Francis Galton, *Hereditary Genius: An Inquiry into Its Laws and Consequences* (Bristol, UK: Thoemmes, 1869).

2. Peter Guy Northouse, *Leadership: Theory and Practice* (London: Sage, 2000); Warren Wilhelm, "Learning from Past Leaders," in Frances Hesselbein, Marshall Goldsmith, Richard Beckhard, eds., *The Leader of the Future* (San Francisco: Jossey-Bass, 1996); Kenneth E. Clark and Miriam Clark, *Measures of Leadership* (West Orange, NJ: Leadership Library of America, 1990); Marshal Sashkin, *The Visionary Leader: Leader Behavior Questionnaire Trainer Guide* (King of Prussia, PA: Organization Design and Development, Inc. 1990); J. P. Campbell, M. D. Dunette, E. E. Lawler III, and K. E. Weik, Jr., *Managerial Behavior, Performance, and Effectiveness* (New York: McGraw-Hill, 1971); and Gary A. Yukl, *Leadership in Organizations* (Englewood Cliffs, NJ: Prentice-Hall, 1981).

3. Edwin Ghiselli, "Traits Differentiating Management Personnel," *Personnel Psychology* 12 (1959): 535–544; Edwin Gheselli, "Managerial Talent," *American Psychologist* 18 (1963): 631–642; and Edwin Ghiselli, *Explorations in Management Talent* (Santa Monica, CA: Goodyear, 1971).

4. Kurt Lewin, Ronald Lippitt, and Ralph K. White, "Patterns of Aggressive Behavior in Experimentally Created Social Climates," *Journal of Social Psychology* 10 (1939): 271–299.

5. Ralph M. Stogdill, "Personal Factors Associated with Leadership: A Survey of the Literature," *Journal of Psychology* 25 (1948): 35–71; Ralph Stogdill and Alvin E. Coons, eds., *Leader Behavior: Its Description and Measurement* (Columbus: Ohio State University, Bureau of Business Research, 1957); Andrew DuBrin, *Leadership: Research Findings, Practices, and Skills* (Boston: Houghton Mifflin, 1998), 80–84; and Bernard Bass, *Stogdill's Handbook of Leadership,* rev. ed. (New York: Free Press, 1981). See also R. F. Bales, *Task Roles and Social Roles in Problem-Solving Groups,* in E. E. Macoby, T. M. Newcomb, and E. L. Hartly, eds., *Readings in Social Psychology* (New York: Holt, Rinehart & Winston, 1958), 437–447.

6. Rensis Likert, *New Patterns of Management* (New York: McGraw-Hill, 1961).

7. Jeffrey Pfeffer, *Managing with Power* (Boston: Harvard Business School Press, 1992); Paul Hersey and Kenneth Blanchard, *Management of Organizational Behavior* (Englewood Cliffs, NJ: Prentice-Hall, 1988); Fred E. Fiedler, "When to Lead, When to Stand Back," *Psychology Today* 21, no. 9 (September 1987): 26; Fred E. Fiedler, *A Theory of Leadership Effectiveness* (New York: McGraw-Hill, 1967); Paul Hersey and Kenneth Blanchard, "Life Cycle Theory of Leadership," *Training and Development Journal* (June 1979): 94–100; Richard E. Neustadt, *Presidential Power and the Modern Presidents* (New York: Macmillan, 1990); Fred E. Fiedler and Joseph E. Garcia, *New Approaches to Effective Leadership* (New York: Wiley, 1987); and Daniel Goleman, "Leadership That Gets Results," *Harvard Business Review* 78, no. 2 (March–April 2000): 78–79.

8. Eugene E. Jennings, *An Anatomy of Leadership: Princes, Heroes, and Supermen* (New York: McGraw-Hill, 1960), 13.

9. Northouse, *Leadership;* Paul Hersey, *The Situational Leader* (New York: Warner Books, 1985); Kenneth H. Blanchard and Paul Hersey, "Great Ideas Revisited," *Training and Development* 50, no. 1 (January 1996): 42–47; Edwin P. Hollander, "Leadership, Followership, Self and Others," *Leadership Quarterly* 3, no. 1 (1992): 43–54; and American Management Association, "How Situational Leadership Fits in Today's Organizations," *Supervisory Management* 41, no. 2 (February 1996): 1–3.

10. David C. McClelland, *Power: The Inner Experience* (New York: Irvington/Halstead Press, 1975); David C. McClelland, "Business Drive and National Achievement," *Harvard Business Review* 40 (July 1962): 99–111; and David C. McClelland, "That Urge to Achieve," *Think* (1966): 32.

11. Jerry Kramer, ed., *Lombardi: Winning Is the Only Thing* (New York: Crowell, 1976), 158, 160, 162.

12. James MacGregor Burns, *Leadership* (New York: Harper & Row, 1978), 9.

13. Noel Tichy and Mary Anne Devanna, *The Transformational Leader* (New York: Wiley, 1990); Burns, *Leadership,* Prologue; Beverly Alimo-Metcalfe and Robert J. Albon-Metcalf, "The Development of a New Transformational Leadership Questionnaire," *Journal of Occupational and Organizational Psychology* 74, no.1 (March 2001): 1–27; and Max Weber, *The Theory of Social and Economic Organization,* trans. A. M. Henderson and T. Parsons, ed. T. Parsons (New York: Free Press, 1947; original work published 1924).

14. James G. Hunt and Jay A. Conger, "From Where We Sit: An Assessment of Transformational and Charismatic Leadership Research," *Leadership Quarterly* 10, no. 3 (Fall 1999): 335–343; R. J. House, J. Woycke, and E. M. Foler, "Charismatic and Uncharismatic Leaders: Differences in Behavior and Effectiveness," in J. A. Conger and R. N. Kanungo, eds., *Charismatic Leadership: The Elusive Factor in Organizational Effectiveness* (San Francisco: Jossey-Bass, 1988), 98–121; and Alimo-Metcalfe and Albon-Metcalfe, "The Development of a New Transformational Leadership Questionnaire," 1–27.

15. Margot Morrell and Stephanie Capparell, *Shackleton's Way: Leadership Lessons from the Great Antarctic Explorer* (New York: Viking Penguin, 2001); Burns, *Leadership;* John P. Kotter, *The Leadership Factor* (New York: Free Press, 1988); Alan Axelrod, *Elizabeth I CEO: Strategic Lessons from the Leader Who Built an Empire* (Paramus, NJ: Prentice-Hall, 2000); William Edmondson, Island Creek Coal Company Leadership Conference, "Leadership in the Air Force," Maxwell Air Force Base, AL: October 1974; Shelly A. Kirkpatrick and Edwin A. Locke, "Leadership: Do Traits Matter?" *Academy of Management Executive* 5 (1991): 48–60; Stogdill, "Personal Factors Associated with Leadership"; and G. A. Yukl, *Leadership in Organizations* (Englewood Cliffs, NJ: Prentice-Hall, 1989).

16. Adlai E. Stevenson, in Will Forpe and John McCollister, eds., *The Sunshine Book: Expressions of Love, Hope and Inspiration* (Middle Village, NY: Jonathan David, 1979), 19.

17. http://www.brainyquote.com/

18. Howard Ferguson, *The Edge* (Fairview Park, OH: Ferguson, 1983), section 2, p. 16.

19. Ferguson, *The Edge,* section 4, p. 18.

20. Niccolò Machiavelli, *The Prince,* trans. George A. Bull (New York: Penguin, 1961).

21. Piers Brendon, *Winston Churchill: A Biography* (London: Pimlico, 2001).

22. Korn/Ferry International Consulting Firm, with University of California–Los Angeles, School of Management, "Leadership Study of Success," 2000.

23. See John F. Schroeder, Benson J. Lossing, and E. C. Towne, *Life and Times of Washington* (Albany, NY: Washington Press, 1903).

24. Francis Fukuyama, *Trust: The Social Virtues and the Creation of Prosperity* (New York: Free Press, 1995).

25. William C. Menninger and Harry Levinson, *Human Understanding in Industry* (Chicago: Science Research Associates, 1956), 6–7.

26. Joseph Jaworski, *Synchronicity: The Inner Path of Leadership* (San Francisco: Berrett-Koehler, 1996); Dale E. Zand, *The Leadership Triad: Knowledge, Trust, and Power* (New York: Oxford University Press, 1997); Joseph Rost, *Leadership for the Twenty-First Century* (New York: Praeger, 1991); and Edward J. Walsh, "Leadership in an Age of Distrust," *Industry Week* 246, no. 13 (July 7, 1997): 78–83.

27. Stuart R. Levine and Michael Crom, *The Leader in You: How to Win* (New York: Pocket Books, 1995); and Jane Dutton, Peter Frost, Monica Worline, Jacoba Lilius, and Jason Kanov, "Leading in Times of Trauma," *Harvard Business Review* 80, no. 1 (January 2002): 55–61.

28. "A Test: Are You a Machiavellian?" in Richard Christie, "The Machiavellians among Us," *Psychology Today* (November 1970): 82–83, 85–86; and Amos M. Drory and Ury M. Gluskinos, "Machiavellianism and Leadership," *Journal of Applied Psychology* 65 (1980): 81–86.

29. Paul Hersey, *Situational Leadership: Some Aspects of Its Influence on Organizational Development* (Doctoral dissertation, University of Massachusetts, 1976); Paul Hersey and Ken Blanchard, *Situational Leadership Simulator: A Simulation for Learning Behavioral Science* (San Diego, CA: Leaders Studies, Inc.; dist. by Pfeiffer & Co., 1988), visual material; and Itheil de Sola Pool, "The Head of the Company: Conceptions of Role and Identity," *Behavioral Science* 9, no. 2 (April 1964): 147–155.

30. Jennings, *An Anatomy of Leadership,* 13, 131–134.

31. Peter Drucker, *Managing in a Time of Great Change* (New York: Truman Talley Books, 1995); and Charles Handy, *The Age of Unreason* (London: Arrow Business Books, 1995).

32. Joan Biaoni, based on Andrew D. Szilagyi and Marc J. Wallace, *Organizational Behavior and Performance* (Santa Monica, CA: Goodyear, 1977); Lionel Stapley, *The Personality of the Organisation: A Psycho-Dynamic Explanation of Culture and Change* (London: Free Association Books, 1996); Burt Nanus, *The Leader's Edge: The Seven Keys to Leadership in a Turbulent World* (Chicago: Contemporary Books, 1989); and Hersey and Blanchard, *Situational Leadership.*

33. Adapted from J. Keith Rogers, "The Rogers Indicator of Multiple Intelligences (RIMI)," Brigham Young University, Provo, UT, 1995; Howard Gardner, *Frames of Mind: The Theory of Multiple Intelligences* (New York: Basic Books, 1983), 338; Howard Gardner, *Creating Minds* (New York: Basic Books, 1993), 338; Robert J. Sternberg, ed., *Advances in the Psychology of Human Intelligence* 5 (Hillsdale, NJ: Erlbaum, 1989); and R. J. Sternberg and Douglas K. Detterman, *What Is Intelligence:*

Contemporary Viewpoints on Its Nature and Definition (Norwood, NJ: Able X Publishing, 1986); and Teacher's Curriculum Institute (Mountain View, CA: 2001).

34. Naomi Miller, Northern Kentucky University, 1981, based on Auren Uris, "Techniques of Leading—Techniques of Following," in Auren Uris, *Techniques of Leadership* (New York: McGraw-Hill, 1953), 49–52, 78–89; Lewin, Lippitt, and White, "Patterns of Aggressive Behavior"; Olga Epitropaki and Robin Martin, "The Impact of Relational Demography on the Quality of Leader-Member Exchanges and Employees' Work Attitudes and Well-Being," *Journal of Occupational and Organizational Psychology* 72 (1999): 237–240; R. Basu and S. G. Green, "Subordinate Performance, Leader-Subordinate Compatibility, and Exchange Quality in Leader-Member Dyads: A Field Study," *Journal of Applied Social Psychology* 25 (1995): 77–92; and R. M. Dienesch and R. C. Liden, "Leader-Member Exchange Model of Leadership: A Critique and Further Development," *Academy of Management Review* 11 (1986): 618–634.

35. Based on Robert Tannenbaum and Warren H. Schmidt, "How to Choose a Leadership Pattern," *Harvard Business Review* 36, no. 2 (March–April 1958): 96, rev. 1999.

36. Based on John W. Newstrom and Keith Davis, *Organizational Behavior: Human Behavior at Work,* 11th ed. (Boston: McGraw-Hill/Irwin, 2002).

37. Hersey, *Situational Leadership;* W. H. Schmidt and R. Tannenbaum, "Management of Differences," *Harvard Business Review* 38 (November–December 1965): 107–115; K. E. Runyon, "Some Interaction Between Personality Variables and Management Styles," *Journal of Applied Psychology* 57 (1973): 288–294; Victor H. Vroom and Philip W. Yetton, *Leadership and Decision Making* (Pittsburgh, PA: University of Pittsburgh Press, 1975); Raymond T. Sparrowe and Robert C. Liden, "Process and Structure in Leader-Member Exchange," *Academy of Management Review* 22, no. 2 (April 1997): 522–552; Goleman, "Leadership That Gets Results"; and E. P. Hollander, *Leadership Dynamics: A Practical Guide to Effective Relationships* (New York: Free Press/Macmillan, 1978).

38. Ned Herrman Group, Leadership Kentucky, 1998, rev. 1999.

39. Robert Townsend, *Up the Organization* (New York: Knopf, 1970); and Robert Townsend, *Further Up the Organization* (New York: Knopf, 1984).

40. Douglas McGregor, in John R. Sargent, *What Every Executive Should Know About the Art of Leadership* (Chicago: Dartnell Corp., 1964), 13; and "Douglas McGregor: Theory X and Theory Y," *Workforce* 81, no. 1 (January 2002): 32–35.

PART 2

1. James C. Collins and William Lazier, *Beyond Entrepreneurship* (Englewood Cliffs, NJ: Prentice-Hall, 1992), 4; and Thomas A. Stewart, Alex Taylor, Peter Petre, and Brent Schlender, "The Businessman of the Century," *Fortune* 140, no. 10 (November 22, 1999): 108–128.

2. Stewart, Taylor, Petre, and Schlender, "The Businessman of the Century," 108–128.

3. Collins and Lazier, *Beyond Entrepreneurship,* 91; Warren G. Bennis and Burt Nanus, *Leaders: Strategies for Taking Charge* (New York: Harper & Row, 1997); and Richard S. Tedlow, "What Titans Can Teach Us," *Harvard Business Review* 79, no. 11 (December 2001): 70–79.

4. The Johnson & Johnson credo was written in 1943 by General Robert Wood Johnson. See also Laurence G. Foster, *The Life and Times of Robert Wood Johnson: The Gentleman Rebel* (State College, PA: Lillian Press, 1999).

5. William Stavropolus, Marion Merrell Dow Chemical Co., 1993; Richard Beckhard and Wendy Pritchard, *Changing the Essence: The Art of Creating and Leading Fundamental Change in Organizations* (San Francisco: Jossey-Bass, 1992); Rosabeth Moss Kanter, *The Change Masters* (New York: Touchstone Books, 1983); and John P. Kotter, *Leading Change* (Cambridge, MA: Harvard Business School Press, 1996).

6. Excerpted from Martin Luther King, Jr.,'s speech at the Lincoln Memorial, Washington, DC, August 28, 1963.

7. Warren Bennis, *On Becoming a Leader* (Reading, MA: Addison-Wesley, 1989); Charles M. Farkas and Philippe De Backer, *Maximum Leadership: The World's Leading CEOs Share Their Five Strategies for Success* (New York: Holt, 1996), and Joseph Jaworski and Betty S. Flowers, *Synchronicity: The Inner Path of Leadership* (San Francisco: Berrett-Koehler, 1998).

8. Adapted from John Humphrey, "Leadership: A Forum Issues Special Report," Forum Corporation, 1998; and "All in a Day's Work," *Harvard Business Review* 79, no. 11(December 2001): 55–66.

9. Adapted from Humphrey, "Leadership."

10. Adapted from Humphrey, "Leadership."

11. Marvin Ross Weisbord, *Productive Workplaces: Organizing and Managing for Dignity, Meaning, and Community* (San Francisco: Jossey-Bass, 1991); and Wendell French and Cecil H. Bell, Jr., *Organization Development*, 6th ed. (Englewood Cliffs, NJ: Prentice-Hall, 1999).

12. Robert S. Kaplan and David P. Norton, *The Strategy-Focused Organization; How Balanced Companies Thrive in New Business Environment* (Cambridge, MA: Harvard Business School Press, 2000); J. William Pfeiffer, *Strategic Planning: Selected Readings* (San Diego: University Associates, 1986); and Stephen Covey and K. A. Gulledge, "Principle-Centered Leadership," *Journal for Quality and Participation,* 17, no. 3 (March 1994): 12.

13. Pfeiffer, *Strategic Planning;* Kaplan and Norton, *The Strategy-Focused Organization;* and Covey and Gulledge, "Principle-Centered Leadership."

14. Based on John Schermerhorn, *Management,* 6th ed. (New York: Wiley, 1999), 162; Kaplan and Norton, *The Strategy-Focused Organization;* Pfeiffer, *Strategic Planning;* and Covey and Gulledge, "Principle-Centered Leadership."

15. Covey and Gulledge, "Principle-Centered Leadership"; Pfeiffer, *Strategic Planning;* and Schermerhorn, *Management.*

16. Adapted from Peter Drucker, "The New Society of Organizations," *Harvard Business Review* 70, no. 5 (September–October 1992): 95–104.

17. Chris Lee, "The Vision Thing," *Training* 30, no. 2 (February 1993): 25–33; and 37; James C. Collins and Jerry I. Porras, *Built to Last: Successful Habits of Visionary Companies* (London: Random House Business, 2000).

18. Joel Barker, *Paradigms: The Business of Discovering the Future* (New York: Harper Business, 1993); Joel Barker, *Future Edge: Discovering the New Paradigms of Success* (New York: Morrow, 1992); Loren Eiseley, *The Immense Journey: An Imaginative Naturalist Explores the Mysteries of Man and Nature* (New York: Random House, 1957); Loren Eiseley, *The Unexpected Universe* (San Diego: Harcourt, Brace, Jovanovich, 1985); and Joel Barker, "Discovering the Future: The Power of Vision" and "The Business of Paradigms," videos from "Discovering the Future" series from ChartHouse Learning Corp.

19. Frederick Polak, *The Image of the Future,* trans. from the Dutch and abridged by Elise Boulding (Amsterdam: Elsevier Scientific Publishing, 1973); Barker, *Future Edge;* and Barker, "Discovering the Future."

20. Benjamin Singer, *The Future-Focused Role Image,* in Alvin Toffler, ed. *Learning for Tomorrow* (New York: Random House, 1974); Barker, *Future Edge;* and Barker, "Discovering the Future."

21. Marian Wright Edelman, *The Measure of Our Success: A Letter to My Children and Yours* (Boston: Beacon Press, 1992).

22. Viktor Frankl, *Man's Search for Meaning* (New York: Pocket Books, 1985); and "Viktor Frankl and the Search for Meaning," *Notable Contributors to the Psychology of Personality Series* (University of Pennsylvania Audio-Visual Department, 1986).

23. Barker, *Future Edge;* Barker, "Discovering the Future"; and Barker, *Paradigms.*

24. Charles A. Garfield, *Peak Performers: The New Heroes of American Business* (New York: Morrow, 1986); J. Walker McSpadden, *How They Blazed the Way: Men Who Have Advanced Civilization* (New York: Dodd, Mead, 1939); and Leslie Kossoff, *Executive Thinking: The Dream, the Vision, the Mission Achieved* (Palo Alto, CA: Davies-Black, 1999).

25. Barker, *Future Edge;* Barker, "Discovering the Future"; and Burt Nanus, *Visionary Leadership: Creating a Compelling Sense of Direction for Your Organization* (San Francisco: Jossey-Bass, 1992).

26. Barker, *Future Edge;* Barker, "Discovering the Future"; Nanus, *Visionary Leadership;* and Brian L. Davis, *Successful Manager's Handbook: Development Suggestions for Today's Managers* (Minneapolis, MN: Personal Decisions International, 1996).

27. Frankl, *Man's Search for Meaning;* Barker, *Future Edge;* and Barker, "Discovering the Future."

28. Duane Schultz, *Theories of Personality,* 2nd ed. (Monterey, CA: Brooks/Cole, 1981); and see also Abraham Maslow, *Toward a Psychology of Being,* 3rd ed. (New York: Wiley, 1998).

29. Stanley Schacter, *The Psychology of Affiliation: Experimental Studies of the Sources of Gregariousness* (Stanford, CA: Stanford University Press, 1965); David McClellend, *Power: The Inner Experiment* (New York: Irvington, 1975); John William Atkinson and Joel O. Raynor, *Motivation and Achievement* (New York: Wiley, 1974); R. W. White, "Motivation Reconsidered: The Concept of Competence," *Psychological Review* 66, no. 5 (September 1959): 297–333; Jack E. Burleson, Northern Kentucky University (1977, rev. 1999), based on David Kolb, Irwin Rubin, and James McIntyre, *Organizational Psychology,* 2nd ed. (Englewood Cliffs, NJ: Prentice-Hall, 1974), 53, 68–69; and Kenneth E. Clark and Miriam B. Clark, *Choosing to Lead: A Center for Creative Leadership Book* (Charlotte, NC: Northgate Press, 1994).

30. Rensis Likert, *New Patterns of Management* (New York: McGraw-Hill, 1961); Rensis Likert, *The Human Organization* (New York: McGraw-Hill, 1967); P. R. Lawrence and J. W. Lorsch, *Organization and Environment* (Homewood, IL: Irwin, 1969); and

George H. Litwin and Robert A. Stringer, *Motivation and Organizational Climate* (Boston: Division of Research, Graduate School of Business Administration, Harvard University, 1968).

31. Based on Likert, *New Patterns of Management;* and Likert, *The Human Organization.*

32. Likert, *New Patterns of Management,* 222–236.

33. Likert, *New Patterns of Management,* 99, 197–211.

34. Likert, *New Patterns of Management,* 197–211.

35. Likert, *New Patterns of Management;* and Rensis Likert and Jane Gibson Likert, *New Ways of Managing Conflict* (New York: McGraw-Hill, 1976), 52, 98.

36. Likert, *New Patterns of Management;* Jaworski and Flowers, *Synchronicity;* Robert Rosen, *The Healthy Company: Eight Strategies to Develop People, Productivity, and Profits* (Los Angeles: Tarcher, 1991); and James O'Toole, *Leadership A to Z: A Guide for the Appropriately Ambitious* (San Francisco: Jossey-Bass, 1999).

37. John Hoerr, "The Payoff from Teamwork," *Business Week* (July 10, 1989): 56–62.

38. John W. Gardner, "Building Community"—prepared for the Leadership Studies Program of Independent Sector (Washington, DC: American Institutes for Research, 1991).

39. Marvin R. Weisbord, *Productive Workplaces* (San Francisco: Jossey-Bass, 1990).

40. M. Scott Peck, *A World Waiting to Be Born: Civility Rediscovered* (New York: Bantam Press, 1993), 271–298.

41. Jay A. Conger, "The Brave New World of Leadership Training," *Organizational Dynamics* (Winter 1993): 56.

PART 3

1. Harold Titus and Morton Keeton, *Ethics for Today,* 5th ed. (New York: Van Nostrand, 1976).

2. Miguel de Cervantes Saavedra, *The History of Don Quixote de la Mancha,* trans. Samuel Putnam (Chicago: Encyclopedia Britannica, 1990).

3. Titus and Keeton, *Ethics for Today.*

4. N. J. Berrill, *Man's Emerging Mind: Man's Progress Through Time* (London: Oldburne, 1962); and Edmund Sinnott, *The Biology of the Spirit* (New York: Viking Press, 1955).

5. William M. Lindsay and Joseph A. Petrick, *Total Quality and Organizational Development* (Delray Beach, FL: St. Lucie Press, 1997).

6. Titus and Keeton, *Ethics for Today,* 192–193; and Aristotle, *The Nicomachean Ethics,* book 10, chap. 5. trans. Hippocrates G. Apostle (Dordrecht, Netherlands: Reidel, 1975).

7. Vernon T. Bourke, ed., *The Essential Augustine* (Indianapolis, IN: Hackett, 1964); David Knowles, *The Evolution of Medieval Thought* (New York: Vintage Press, 1962); and Augustine, *Confessions* and *City of God.*

8. Bertrand Russell, *Bertrand Russssell's Philosophy* (New York: Barnes & Noble Books, 1974); and Bertrand Russell, *The Autobiography of Bertrand Russell: 1872–1914* (Boston: Little, Brown, 1967), 3–4.

9. Titus and Keeton, *Ethics for Today,* 194–195; and Daniel J. Kennedy, *St. Thomas Aquinas and Medieval Philosophy* (New York: Encyclopedia Press, 1919).

10. Titus and Keeton, *Ethics for Today,* 39.

11. Charles Darwin, *The Origin of Species by Means of Natural Selection* (New York: Modern Library, 1936), 471.

12. John Locke, *An Essay Concerning Human Understanding,* 1690.

13. Benjamin Franklin, *Poor Richard's Almanac: The Almanacs for the Years 1733–1758* (New York: Ballantine Books, 1977).

14. Jean Piaget, *The Moral Judgment of the Child* (New York: Free Press, 1997); and Ronald Duska and Mariellen Whelan, *Moral Development: A Guide to Piaget and Kohlberg* (New York: Paulist Press, 1975), 13.

15. Lawrence Kohlberg, "The Development of Children's Orientations toward a Moral Order: Sequence in the Development of Moral Thought," *Vita Humana* 6 (1963): 11–33; Duska and Whelan, *Moral Development,* 42–79; Lawrence Kohlberg, "Moral Stages and Moralization: The Cognitive-Development Approach," in Thomas Lickona, ed., *Moral Development and Behavior* (New York: Holt, Rinehart & Winston, 1976); and Lawrence Kohlberg, *The Philosophy of Moral Development* (New York: Harper & Row, 1984).

16. Duska and Whelan, *Moral Development,* 42–49; Lawrence Kohlberg, "Cognitive-Development Approach to Moral Education," *The Humanist* (November–December 1972): 113–116; Lawrence Kohlberg, "Stages of Moral Development as a Basis for Moral Education," in Clive M. Beck, Brian S. Crittenden, and Edmund V. Sullivan, eds., *Moral Education: Interdisciplinary Approaches* (Toronto: University of Toronto Press, 1971), 86–88; C. Gilligan, "In a Different Voice: Women's Conceptions of Self and Morality," *Harvard Educational Review* 47 (1982): 481–517; Stanley Milgram, "Behavioral Study of Obedience," *Journal of Abnormal and Social Psychology* 63 (1963): 371–378; Lawrence Kohlberg, "The Cognitive-Developmental Approach to Socialization," in D. A. Goslin ed., *Handbook of Socialization Theory and Research* (Chicago: Rand McNally, 1969); and Richard Mervin Hare, *Moral Thinking: Its Levels, Method, and Point* (New York: Oxford Press, 1981).

17. Kohlberg, "The Development of Children's Orientation toward a Moral Order: 1., 18–19.

18. Kohlberg, "Cognitive-Development Approach to Moral Education," 13–16; Kohlberg, *Moral Education,* 86–88; Kohlberg, "The Cognitive-Developmental Approach to Socialization"; and Victor Grassian, *Moral Reasoning* (Englewood Cliffs, NJ: Prentice-Hall, 1981).

19. Adapted from Zick Rubin and Elton B. McNeil, *The Psychology of Being Human,* 3rd ed. (New York: Harper & Row, 1981), 321–324.

20. Testimony of Adolf Eichmann (April 1961) at the Nuremberg War Trials, in Kohlberg, "The Cognitive-Developmental Approach to Socialization."

21. Mohandas Gandhi in his defense against a charge of sedition, March 23, 1922, in Bartlett, *Famous Quotations, http://www. bartleby.com/99/index.html/.*

22. Titus and Keeton, *Ethics for Today,* 42.

23. Hermann Hesse, *Siddhartha* (New York: Macmillan, 1962), 33–34.

24. Lou Marinoff, *Plato, Not Prozac!* (New York: HarperCollins, 1999), 162–163; and Michael D. Bayles, *Professional Ethics* (Belmont, CA: Wadsworth, 1981).

25. Charles E. Watson, *Managing with Integrity: Insights from America's CEOs* (New York: Praeger, 1991), 30, 100.

26. Rosabeth Moss Kanter, "Values and Economics," Notes from the Editor, *Harvard Business Review* 68, no. 3 (May–June 1990): 4.

27. Kanter, "Values and Economics" 4; Kenneth H. Blanchard and Michael O'Connor, *Managing by Values: Becoming a Fortune 500 Organization* (San Francisco: Berrett-Koehler, 1997); and Dave Francis and Mike Woodcock, *Unblocking Organizational Values* (Glenview, IL: Scott, Foresman, 1990).

28. Leon Wieseltier, "Total Quality Meaning," *The New Republic* (July 19, 1993): 16–18, 20–22, 24–26.

29. Gerald V. Cavanaugh, *American Business Values,* 2nd ed. (Englewood Cliffs, NJ: Prentice-Hall, 1984); and Peter Drucker, "The New Society of Organizations," *Harvard Business Review* 70, no. 5 (September–October 1992): 98.

30. Thomas Watson, *A Business and Its Beliefs: The Ideas That Helped Build IBM* (New York: McGraw-Hill, 1986).

31. Rollo May, *The Courage to Create* (New York: Norton, 1975), 3–5.

32. *The Holy Bible,* King James Version, John 8:32.

33. William Shakespeare, *Hamlet,* Act 3, Scene 1.

34. Terry Brock, "Weather Any Storm with a Little Flexibility," *CyberSense,* June 26, 2000, (http://bizjournals.bcentral.com/extraedge/consultants/cybersense/2000/06/26/column205.html; Joseph L. Badaracco, Jr. and Richard R. Ellsworth, *Leadership and the Quest for Integrity* (Boston: Harvard Business School Press, 1989); Robert W. Terry, *Authentic Leadership: Courage in Action* (San Francisco: Jossey-Bass, 1993); Judith M. Bardwick, "Peacetime Management and Wartime Leadership," in Frances Hessebein, Marshall Goldsmith, and Richard Beckhard, *The Leader of the Future: New Visions, Strategies, and Practices for the Next Era* (San Francisco: Jossey-Bass, 1996)*;* and Kevin R. Murphy, *Honesty* (Pacific Grove, CA: Brooks/Cole, 1983).

35. Joseph A. Petrick and John F. Quinn, *Management Ethics: Integrity at Work* (Thousand Oaks, CA: Sage, 1997).

36. Louis E. Raths, Merrill Harmin, and Sidney Simon, *Values and Teaching* (Columbus, OH: Merrill, 1966), 27–36; and Petrick and Quinn, *Management Ethics.*

37. Plato, *The Republic,* trans. A. Bloom (New York: Basic Books, 1968); Marinoff, *Plato, Not Prozac!;* Petrick and Quinn, *Management Ethics;* O. C. Ferrell, D. Leclair, and L. Ferrell, "The Federal Sentencing Guidelines for Organizations: A Framework for Ethical Compliance," *Journal of Business Ethics* 17, no. 4 (1998): 353–363; Stuart J. Wells, *From Sage to Artisan: The Nine Rules of the Value Driven Leader* (Palo Alto, CA: Davies-Black, 1997); and Thomas J. Peters, "Leadership: Sad Facts and Silver Linings," *Harvard Business Review* 79, no. 11 (December 2001): 121–128.

38. Karl Albrecht, *The Northbound Train* (New York: AMACOM, 1994); David G. Bowers, *Systems of Organizations: Management of the Human Resource* (Ann Arbor: University of Michigan Press, 1976), 3; James Kouzes and Barry Posner, *Credibility: How Leaders Gain and Lose It, Why People Demand It* (San Francisco: Jossey-Bass, 1993); and W. W. Manley, *Executive's Handbook of Model Business Conduct Codes* (Englewood Cliffs, NJ: Prentice-Hall, 1991).

39. Marianne Bailey and Doreen Winters, Northern Kentucky University, 1982.

40. Charles Schwab, *The Ten Commandments of Success, Carnegie Steel Company—1897* (Montgomery, AL: Copy Center, 1991).

41. Eduard Spranger, *Types of Men: The Psychology and Ethics of Personality* (New York: Johnson Reprint, 1966); and Jim McCue and Marianne Bailey, Northern Kentucky University, 1983 (rev. 1997), based on Gordon W. Allport, Vincent P. Ewart, and Gardner Lindzey, *The Study of Values: A Scale for Measuring the Dominant Interests in Personality, Grade 10–Adult,* 3rd ed. (Boston: Houghton Mifflin, 1970).

42. Morris Massey, *The People Puzzle: Understanding Yourself and Others* (Reston, VA: Reston, 1979).

43. Frederick Guy Stevens and Bruce Rogers, trans., *The Reflections and Maxims of Vauvenargues* (London: Humphrey Milford, 1940).

44. Peter Drucker, *Management Tasks, Responsibilities, Practices* (New York: Harper & Row, 1973), 645.

45. James O'Toole, *Vanguard Management: Redesigning the Corporate Future* (New York: Doubleday, 1985).

46. Rotary International, Evanston, IL.

47. Robert Hay and Ed Gray, "Social Responsibilities of Business Managers," *Academy of Management Journal* 18, no. 1 (March 1974): 135–143.

48. Charles S. McCoy, *Management of Values: The Ethical Difference in Corporate Policy* (Marshfield, MA: Pitman, 1985); Hal Morgan and Kerry Tucker, *Companies That Care: The Most Family-Friendly Companies in America, What They Offer, and How They Got That Way* (New York: Simon & Schuster/Fireside, 1991); Terrence E. Deal and Allen A. Kennedy, *Corporate Culture: The Rites and Rituals of Corporate Life* (Reading, MA: Addison-Wesley, 1985); and Hay and Gray, "Social Responsibilities of Business Managers," 142.

49. Petrick and Quinn, *Management Ethics;* Craig Hickman and Michael A. Silva, *Creating Excellence* (New York: New American Library, 1984); H. J. Leavitt, *Corporate Pathfinders* (Homewood, IL: Dow Jones–Irwin, 1986); O'Toole, *Vanguard Management;* J. Greenberg, "Organizational Justice: Yesterday, Today, and Tomorrow," *Journal of Management* 16 (1990): 606–613; and Hay Associates, *Linking Employee Attitudes and Corporate Culture to Corporate Growth and Profitability* (Philadelphia: Hay, 1984).

PART 4

1. Arthur G. Bedeian, *Management,* 3rd ed. (Dryden, 1993), 267.

2. Chester I. Barnard, in Bedeian, *Management,* 267; and Chester I. Barnard, *The Functions of the Executive* (Cambridge, MA: Harvard University Press, 1938), 161–184.

3. Bedeian, *Management,* 267.

4. Bedeian, *Management,* 268; and Douglas McGregor, *The Human Side of Enterprise* (New York: McGraw-Hill, 1960), 23.

5. Bedeian, *Management,* 268.

6. Robert K. Greenleaf, *On Becoming a Servant-Leader* (San Francisco: Jossey-Bass, 1996); and Robert K. Greenleaf, *Servant Leadership: A Journey into the Nature of Legitimate Power and Greatness* (New York: Paulist Press, 1997).

7. Greenleaf, *On Becoming a Servant-Leader;* and Larry C. Spears, *Insights on Leadership: Service, Stewardship, Spirit, and Servant-Leadership* (New York: Wiley, 1998).

8. Hermann Hesse, *The Journey to the East* (New York: Noonday, 1968); Gilbert Fairholm, *Leadership and the Culture of Trust*

(Westport, CT: Praeger, 1994); David H. Maister, *True Profession-alism: The Courage to Care About Your People, Your Clients, and Your Career* (New York: Free Press, 1997); and Greenleaf, *Servant Leadership.*

9. Harry Levinson and Cynthia Lang, *Executive* (Cambridge, MA: Harvard University Press, 1981), 187–189.

10. Levinson and Lang, *Executive;* 187–189; Margaret J. Wheatley, *Leadership and the New Science: Learning About Organization from an Orderly Universe* (San Francisco: Berrett-Koehler, 1992); and Edward M. Hallowell, "The Human Moment at Work," *Harvard Business Review* 77, no. 1 (January–February 1999): 58–65.

11. John Schermerhorn, *Management,* 6th ed. (New York: Wiley, 1999), 11; James A. Belasco and Ralph C. Stayer, *Flight of the Buffalo: Soaring to Excellence, Learning to Let Employees Lead* (New York: Warner Books, 1994); and Margaret Wheatley, *Leadership and the New Science: Discovering Order in a Chaotic World* (San Francisco: Berrett-Koehler, 1999).

12. Max DePree, *Leadership Is an Art* (New York: Doubleday, 1989), 45–53.

13. Paula Underwood, *Who Speaks for Wolf: A Native American Learning Story* (Austin, TX: The Meredith Fund, 1983).

14. Masaaki Imai, *Kaizen (Ky'zen): The Key to Japan's Competitive Success* (New York: Random House, 1986); and Henry R. Neave, *The Deming Dimension* (Knoxville, TN: SPC Press, 1990); Donald L. Dewar, *The Facilitator's Handbook for Employee Involvement Teams* (Red Bluff, CA: QCI International, 1991), F 2.2–F 2.8.

15. Jack Welch, *Jack: Straight from the Gut* (New York: Warner Books, 2001); and Philip E. Slater and Warren Bennis, "Democracy Is Inevitable," *Harvard Business Review* (March–April 1964): 51–53.

16. William Lindsay, Kent Curtis, and George Manning, "A Participative Management Primer," *Journal for Quality and Participation* (June 1989): 78–84; Joe D. Batten, *Total Quality Culture* (Los Altos, CA: Crisp Publications, 1989); James H. Harrington, *Business Process Improvement* (New York: McGraw-Hill, 1991); Kenneth Kaiser and Marshall Sashkin, *Putting Total Quality Management to Work* (San Francisco: Berrett-Koehler, 1993); and J. M. Juran, *Managerial Break-through: A New Concept of the Manager's Job* (New York: McGraw-Hill, 1984).

17. Marvin Weisbord, *Productive Workplaces* (San Francisco: Jossey-Bass, 1990), 97.

18. Herb Kelleher, as quoted in Katrina Brooker, "The Chairman of the Board Looks Back," *Fortune* (May 28, 2001): 62–70.

19. *Forum Issues Special Report,* 1996.

20. Laozi and Raymond B. Blakney, *The Way of Life: Tao Te ching* (New York: New American Library, 2001); and Laozi and Wing-Tsit Chan, *The Way of Lao Tzu (Tao-Te ching)* (Indianapolis, IN: Bobbs-Merrill, 1963, originally written 6th century B.C.).

21. Adapted from John R. P. French, Jr., and Bertram Raven, "The Basis of Social Power," in Darwin Cartwright, ed., *Group Dynamics: Research and Theory* (Evanston, IL: Row, Peterson, 1962), 607–613; and Gary A. Yukl and Tom Taber, "The Effective Use of Managerial Power," *Personnel* 60 (1983): 37–49; Robert C. Benfari, Harry E. Wilkinson, and Charles D. Orth, "The Effective Use of Power," *Business Horizons* 29 (1986): 12–16; Jeffrey Pfeffer, *Managing with Power: Politics and Influence in Organi-zations* (Boston: Harvard Business School Press, 1994); Jeffrey Pfeffer, *Power in Organizations* (Marshfield, MA: Pitman, 1981); and A. Zaleznik and M. R. R. Kets de Vries, *Power and the Corporate Mind* (Boston: Houghton Mifflin, 1975).

22. Adapted from T. R. Hinkin and C. A. Schreisheim, "Development and Application of New Scales to Measure the French and Raven (1959) Basis of Social Power," *Journal of Applied Psychology* 74 (1989): 74, 561–567.

23. Henry Mintzberg, *Power In and Around Organizations* (Englewood Cliffs, NJ: Prentice-Hall, 1983); John P. Kotter, *Power and Influence: Beyond Formal Authority* (New York: Free Press, 1985); John P. Kotter, "Power, Dependence, and Effective Management," *Harvard Business Review* 55 (1977): 125–136; and Levinson and Lang, *Executive,* 44–46.

24. George E. Reedy, *The Twilight of the Presidency* (New York: World, 1970), 11–15, 76–83.

25. Albert Mehrabian, *Silent Messages: Implicit Communication of Emotions and Attitudes* (Belmont, CA: Wadsworth, 1981); John W. Newstrom and Keith Davis, *Organizational Behavior: Human Behavior at Work* (Boston: McGraw-Hill/Irwin, 2002); William Byham and Jeff Cox, *Zapp! The Lightning of Empowerment: How to Improve Productivity, Quality, and Employee Satisfaction* (New York: Fawcett Columbine, 1992); Kathleen Ryan and Daniel Oestreich, *Driving Fear Out of the Workplace: How to Overcome the Invisible Barriers to Quality, Productivity, and Innovation* (San Francisco: Jossey-Bass, 1991); Reuel L. Howe, *The Miracle of Dialogue* (New York: Seabury Press, 1968); Judith L. Brownell, *Building Active Listening Skills* (Englewood Cliffs, NJ: Prentice-Hall, 1986); and Ralph G. Nichols and Leonard A. Stevens, *Are You Listening?* (New York: McGraw-Hill, 1957).

26. *Hamlet* 1. 3. 68; Charles DeLoach, *The Quotable Shake-speare: A Topical Dictionary, Hamlet* (Jefferson, NC: McFarland, 1988) 1, 3, 68.

27. DeLoach, *The Quotable Shakespeare,* 1, 3, 59.

28. Keshavan Nair, *A Higher Standard of Leadership, Lessons from the Life of Gandhi* (San Francisco: Berrett-Koehler, 1997).

29. John Hoerr, "The Payoff from Teamwork," *Business Weekly* (July 10, 1989): 60; Edward E. Lawler, *The Ultimate Advantage: Creating the High Involvement Organization* (San Francisco: Jossey-Bass, 1992); and J. A. Conger, "Leadership: The Art of Empowering Others," *Academy of Executive Management* 3 (1989): 17–24.

30. Schoichi Suzawa, "How the Japanese Achieve Excellence," *Training and Development Journal* (May 1985): 114.

31. Welch, *Jack: Straight from the Gut;* Joseph Cosco, "General Electric Works It All Out," *Journal of Business Strategy* 15, no. 3 (May–June 1994): 48–50; and Marshall Loeb "Where Leaders Come From," *Fortune* 130, no. 6 (September 19, 1994): 241–242.

32. Robert Slater, *The G. E Way Fieldbook: Jack Welch's Battle Plan for Corporate Revolution* (New York: McGraw-Hill, 2000); and Robert Slater, *Jack Welch and the G. E. Way: Management Insights and Leadership Secrets of the Legendary CEO* (New York: McGraw-Hill, 1998).

33. Robert E. Cole, Director, Center for Japanese Studies, University of Michigan, Ann Arbor, "Employee Involvement in Japan: Implications for Ford Motor Company."

34. Michael Conner, Tastemaker International, Cincinnati, OH, 1997; Robert H. Rosen and Paul B. Brown, *Leading People:*

Transforming Business from the Inside Out (New York: Viking, 1996); and Judith F. Vogt and Kenneth L. Murrell, *Empowerment in Organizations* (San Diego: University Associates, 1990).

35. Gloria Boone and Richard P. Kropp, *Communicating in the Business Environment* (Amherst, MA: Human Resource Development Press, 1991); and Selma Friedman, "Where Employees Go for Information (Some Surprises!)," *Administrative Management* (September 1981): 72–73.

36. Eric Harvey and Alexander Lucia, *144 Ways to Walk the Talk* (Dallas: Performance Publishing, 1997).

37. Michael Treacy and Frederik D. Wierseman, *The Discipline of Market Leaders: Choose Your Customers, Narrow Your Focus, Dominate Your Market* (Reading, MA: Addison-Wesley, 1997), 52–58; and *Forum Corporation Special Report on Leadership.*

38. Thomas Peters and Robert Waterman Jr., *In Search of Excellence* (New York: Harper & Row, 1983), 16.

39. Greenleaf, *Servant Leadership;* and Joseph Petrick and D. Furi, *Total Quality in Managing Human Resources* (Delray Beach, FL: St. Lucie Press, 1995); Dorothy Marcic, *Managing with the Wisdom of Love: Uncovering Virtue in People and Organizations* (San Francisco: Jossey-Bass, 1997); William W. Arnold and Jeanne M. Plas, *The Human Touch: Today's Most Unusual Program for Productivity and Profit* (New York: Wiley, 1993); and Margaret J. Wheatley and Myron Kellner-Rogers, *A Simpler Way* (San Francisco: Berrett-Koehler, 1996).

40. Joseph Jablonski, *Implementing Total Quality Management: An Overview* (San Diego: Pfeiffer, 1991), 41; Joseph R. Jablonski, *Implementing Total Quality Management—Competing in the 1990's* (Albuquerque, NM: Technical Management Consortium, 1991); and Thomas Choi and Orlando Behling, "Top Managers and TQM Success: One More Look Over After All These Years," *Academy of Management Executive* 11, no. 1 (February 1997): 37–47.

41. Peters and Waterman, *In Search of Excellence,* 249–250.

42. A. Ichikawa, *Practical Strategic TQM for Middle Management* (Tokyo: Diamond, 1986); David Halberstam, *The Reckoning* (New York: Avon Books, 1987); and Christopher Byron, "How Japan Does It," *Time* (March 30, 1981): 57.

43. Halberstam, *The Reckoning;* Lloyd Dobyns, "Ed Deming Wants Big Changes and He Wants Them Fast," *Smithsonian* 21, no. 5 (August 1990): 77; and Lloyd Dobyns, "If Japan Can Do It, Why Can't We?" *NBC News.*

44. William W. Scherkenbach, *The Deming Route to Quality and Productivity: Road Maps and Roadblocks* (Washington, DC: CEEPress Books; 1994); Dobyns, "Ed Deming Wants Big Changes and He Wants Them Fast," 76; and Dobyns, "If Japan Can Do It, Why Can't We?"

45. Ronald Yates, "Game Plan," *Chicago Tribune Magazine* (February 16, 1992): 20; and W. Edwards Deming, "Experiment to Show Fault in System," *Quality, Productivity, and Competitive Position* (Cambridge: Massachusetts Institute of Technology—Center for Advanced Engineering Study, 1982), 138–146.

46. Henry Neave, *The Deming Dimension* (Knoxville, TN, SPC Press, 1990).

47. David Pauly with Joseph Contreras and William Marbach, "How to Do It Better," *Newsweek* (September 8, 1980): 59; and Del Jones, "Teamwork Speeds Boeing Along," *USA Today* (November 18, 1998).

48. Mary Walton, *The Deming Management Method* (New York: Putnam, 1986); and W. Edwards Deming, *On the Management of*

Statistical Techniques for Quality and Productivity (Washington, DC: Continuing Engineering Education, George Washington University, 1981) 2: 16–17.

49. Frederick Taylor, *Principles of Scientific Management* (New York: Harper, 1911).

50. Weisbord, *Productive Workplaces,* 69.

51. Fritz Roethlisberger, *Management and the Worker* (Cambridge, MA: Harvard University Press, 1939).

52. Sud Ingle, *Quality Circle Master Guide: Increasing Productivity with People Power* (Englewood Cliffs, NJ: Prentice-Hall, 1982), 170–181.

53. Ingle, *Quality Circle Master Guide,* 12; and Keith Davis, "The Case for Participative Management," *Business Horizons* 6 (Fall 1963): 55–60.

54. Ingle, *Quality Circle Master Guide,* 12; Davis, "The Case for Participative Management," 55–60; and Edward E. Lawler, Susan A. Mohrman, and Gerald E. Ledford, *Employee Involvement and Total Quality Management: Practices and Results in Fortune 100 Companies* (San Francisco: Jossey-Bass, 1992).

55. *Management Practices: US Companies Improve Performance Through Quality Efforts* (Washington, DC: U.S. General Accounting Office, May 1991).

56. Otis Port, "Innovations" *Business Week* no. 3594 (September 7, 1998): 111–116.

57. Wendy Leebov, *The Quality Quest* (Chicago: American Hospital Publishing, 1991), 1; John Guaspari, *I Know It When I See It: A Modern Fable About Quality* (New York: AMACOM, 1985); and Dennis C. Kinlaw, *Continuous Improvement and Measurement for Total Quality: A Team-Based Approach* (Homewood, IL: Business One Irwin, 1992).

PART 5

1. Warren Bennis and Burt Nanus, *Leaders* (New York: Harper & Row, 1985); Warren Bennis, *On Becoming a Leader* (Reading, MA: Addison-Wesley, 1989); and Marshall Loeb, "How's Business," *Fortune* 130, no. 6 (September 19, 1994): 241.

2. Max DePree, *Leadership Jazz* (New York: Doubleday, 1997); Andy Grove, *One on One with Andy Grove* (New York: Putnam, 1987); Ed Oakley and Doug Krug, *Enlightened Leadership* (New York: Simon & Schuster, 1991); John E. Flaherty and Peter Drucker, *Shaping the Managerial Mind* (San Francisco: Jossey-Bass, 1999); and Peter Drucker, *The Practice of Management* (New York: Harper & Row, 1954).

3. David H. Freedman, *Corps Business: The 30 Management Principles of the U.S. Marines* (New York: Harper Business, 2000); Steve McMillen and Steve Martin, Northern Kentucky University, 1984, rev. 2000; and John C. Maxwell, *The 21 Irrefutable Laws of Leadership: Follow Them and People Will Follow You* (Nashville, TN: Thomas Nelson, 1998).

4. Ralph Waldo Emerson, *Journals,* in Burton Stevenson, ed., *Home Book of Quotations* (New York: Dodd, Mead, 1967), 338.

5. *Plutarch's Lives,* trans. John Dryden and Arthur Clough (New York: Modern Library, 2001); and Robert M. Strozier, *Epicurius and Hellenistic Philosophy* (Lanham, MD; University Press of America, 1985).

6. Karl Menninger, as found in W. Steven Brown, *13 Fatal Errors Managers Make and How to Avoid Them* (New York: Berkley Books, 1985).

7. Marvin G. Gregory, ed., *Bits and Pieces* (Fairfield, NJ: Economics Press, 1980), 16–17.

8. Merle Miller, *Plain Speaking: An Oral Biography of Harry S. Truman* (New York: Berkley Books, 1984).

9. Ben Jonson, *Explorata: Consilia,* in Burton Stevenson, *Home Book of Quotations: Classical and Modern* (New York: Dodd Mead, 1967).

10. Based on T. G. Cummings's "Analysis of Job Satisfaction Studies," Case Western Reserve University, Cleveland, OH, 1988; and F. E. Emery, "Characteristics of Socio-Technical Systems" (London: Tavistock Documents no. 527) abridged in F. E. Emery, *The Emergence of a New Paradigm of Work* (Canberra: Centre for Continuing Education, Australian National University, 1978).

11. Robert Levering and Milton Moskowitz, "The Best Companies List—Employees at Hundreds of Companies Cast Their Votes—and Southwest Airlines Came Up No. 1," *Fortune* 137, no. 1 (January 12, 1998): 84–95.

12. Levering and Moskowitz, "The Best Companies List"; and Herb Kelleher, "Flying His Own Course," *Industry Week* 244, no. 21 (1995): 22–24; Kevin Freiberg and Jackie Freiberg, *Nuts! Southwest Airlines' Crazy Recipe for Business and Personal Success* (New York: Broadway Books, 1998).

13. Katrina Brooker and Alynda Wheat, "The Chairman of the Board Looks Back," *Fortune* 143, no. 11 (May 28, 2001): 62–70.

14. Robert Levering, *A Great Place to Work: What Makes Some Employers So Good (and Most So Bad)* (New York: Random House, 1988); Kenneth H. Blanchard and Sheldon Bowles, *Gung Ho! Turn On the People in Any Organization* (New York: Morrow, 1997); George Dixon, *What Works at Work: Lessons from the Masters: Personal Profiles of 27 Workplace Experts and the 10 Most Important Lessons They've Learned About People, Performance, and Productivity* (Minneapolis, MN: Lakewood Books, 1988); Joanne B. Ciulla, *The Working Life: The Promise and Betrayal of Modern Work* (New York: Times Books, 2000); and Linda Grant, "Happy Workers, High Returns," 137 no. 1 (January 12, 1998): 81.

15. John S. McClenahen, "On the Job: Lean and Mean," *Industry Week* (November 2, 1992): 30.

16. Harry Levinson, *Executive* (Cambridge, MA: Harvard University Press, 1981), 28.

17. Mihaly Csikszentmihalyi and Isabella Selga Csikszentmihalyi, *Optimal Experience: Psychological Studies of Flow in Consciousness* (New York: Cambridge University Press, 1992); and Joseph Campbell and Bill Moyers, *The Power of Myth* (New York: Doubleday, 1989).

18. Mihaly Csikszentmihalyi, *The Evolving Self: A Psychology for the Third Millenium* (New York: HarperCollins, 1993).

19. Emery, "Characteristics of Socio-Technical Systems"; J. Richard Hackman, Greg R. Oldham, R. Janson, and K. Purdy, "A New Strategy for Job Enrichment," *California Management Review* 17 (1975): 57–71; J. Richard Hackman and Greg R. Oldham, *Work Design* (Reading, MA: Addison-Wesley, 1980); and R. E. Kopelman, "Job Redesign and Productivity: A Review of Evidence," *National Productivity Review* (Summer 1985): 237–255.

20. John Donne and William Blake, *The Complete Poetry and Select Prose of John Donne and the Complete Poetry of William Blake* (New York: Random House, 1941), 332.

21. M. Scott Peck, *The Different Drum* (New York: Simon & Schuster, 1987), 288.

22. For a more detailed explanation of this concept, see William Menninger and Harry Levinson, *Human Understanding in Industry* (Chicago: Science Research Associates, 1956).

23. Elton Mayo, *The Human Problems of an Industrial Organization* (New York: Macmillan, 1946), 56–59, 129–130; and Fritz Roethlisberger and William Dickson, *Management and the Worker* (Cambridge, MA: Harvard University Press, 1939).

24. Mayo, *The Human Problems of an Industrial Organization;* and Roethlisberger and Dickson, *Management and the Worker.*

25. Adapted from John E. Jones and Johanna J. Jones, in J. William Pfeiffer and John E. Jones, ed., *A Handbook of Structured Experiences for Human Relations Training* (San Diego: Jossey-Bass/Pfeiffer, 1985).

26. Warren Bennis, *Professional Trainer,* McGraw-Hill Training System 5 (Winter 1985); W. Ouchi, *Theory Z: How American Business Can Meet the Japanese Challenge* (Reading, MA: Addison-Wesley, 1981); and Douglas McGregor, *The Human Side of Enterprise* (New York: McGraw-Hill, 1960).

27. McGregor, *The Human Side of Enterprise;* and Douglas McGregor, "The Human Side of Enterprise," *SOL Journal* 2, no. 1 (Fall 2000): 6–19.

28. McGregor, *The Human Side of Enterprise;* and McGregor, "The Human Side of Enterprise."

29. Bennis, *Professional Trainer.*

30. W. Steven Brown, *13 Fatal Errors Managers Make and How You Can Avoid Them* (Old Tappan, NJ: Revell, 1985).

31. Steve Martin, Northern Kentucky University, rev. 2001, based on McGregor, *The Human Side of Enterprise,* 232–235.

32. William Stattler and N. Edd Miller, *Discussion and Conference,* 2nd ed. (Englewood Cliffs, NJ: Prentice-Hall, 1968), 297–301, 303–305, 309–312, 331–334; and John Hasling, *Group Discussion and Decision-Making* (New York: Thomas Crowell/Harper & Row, 1975), 33–42.

33. Stattler and Miller, *Discussion and Conference,* 476–488; and Hasling, *Group Discussion and Decision-Making,* 33–42.

34. Billie Stockton, Anita Bullock, and Anne Locke, Northern Kentucky University, 1981, based on "Learning and Problem-Solving," in David A. Kolb, Irwin A. Rubin, and James M. McIntyre, *Organizational Psychology: An Experiential Approach,* 3rd ed. (Englewood Cliffs, NJ: Prentice-Hall, 1979), 37–53; and David Kolb, *Learning Style Inventory* (Boston: Hay/McBer Training Resources Group, 1999).

35. Charles Darwin, *On the Origin of Species* (London: J. Murray, 1859); and Charles Darwin, *The Descent of Man and Selection in Relation to Sex* (New York: Burt, 1874).

36. John Allen, *100 Great Lives* (New York: Journal of Living, 1944), 20–22, 25.

37. Upton Sinclair, *The Flivver King* (New York: Phaedra, 1969).

38. Team building story from the authors' files.

39. Allan B. Drexler, David Sibbet, and Russell H. Forrester, "The Team Performance Model," NTL Institute for Applied Behavioral Science, 1988.

40. Michael Jordan, *I Can't Accept Not Trying* (San Francisco: Harper, 1994), 20.

41. Bradford D. Smart, *Topgrading: How Leading Companies Win by Hiring, Coaching and Keeping the Best People* (Paramus, NJ: Prentice-Hall Press, 1999), 1.

42. "Achieving Results Through Teamwork," *Forum Corporation Issues Report;* Glenn H. Varney, *Building Productive Teams: An Active Guide and Resource Book* (San Francisco: Jossey-Bass, 1989); and Jon R. Katzenbach and Douglas K. Smith, *The Wisdom of Teams: Creating the High-Performance Organization* (New York: Harper Business, 1999).

43. Carl E. Larson and Frank M. J. Lafasto, *Teamwork: What Must Go Right, What Can Go Wrong* (Newbury Park, CA: Sage, 1989); and J. Richard Hackman, *Groups That Work (and Those That Don't)* (San Francisco: Jossey-Bass, 1990).

44. Based on Glenn M. Parker, *Team Players and Teamwork* (San Francisco: Jossey-Bass, 1990); and Roy B. Lacoursiere, *The Life Cycle of Groups: Group Development Stage Theory* (New York: Human Sciences Press, 1980).

45. B. W. Tuckman and M. A. C. Jensen, "Stages of Small-Group Development Revisited," *Group and Organizational Studies* 2, no. 4 (1977): 419–427.

46. Jerry B. Harvey, *The Abilene Paradox and Other Meditations on Management* (San Francisco: Jossey-Bass, 1996); and Irving L. Janis, "Groupthink," *Psychology Today* 5, no. 6 (1971): 43–46, 74–76.

47. Janis, "Groupthink"; Irving L. Janis, *The Anatomy of Power* (New York: Houghton Mifflin, 1982); "Groupthink: The Challenger Disaster" and "Organization Dynamics: Groupthink," videos from CRM Educational Films, Del Mar, CA; and Irving L. Janis, *Victims of Groupthink* (Boston: Houghton Mifflin, 1972).

48. Janis, "Groupthink"; Janis, *The Anatomy of Power;* "Groupthink: The Challenger Disaster" and "Organization Dynamics: Groupthink"; and Janis, *Victims of Groupthink.*

49. Ibid.

50. Joseph Jaworski, *Sychronicity: The Inner Path of Leadership* (San Francisco: Berrett-Koehler, 1996); David Bohm, Lee Nichol, eds., *On Dialogue* (New York: Routledge, 1996).

51. Wendell L. French and Cecil H. Bell, Jr., *Organization Development: Behavioral Science Interventions for Organization Improvement* (Upper Saddle River, NJ: Prentice-Hall, 1999); and W. Brendan Reddy and Kaleel Jamison, *Team Building: Blueprints for Productivity and Satisfaction* (Alexandria, VA, and San Diego, CA: National Institute for Applied Behavioral Science; University Associates, 1988), 3.

52. Richard Harris, "What Makes Teams Work," Forum Corporation (1995).

53. Harris, "What Makes Teams Work."

54. Ibid.

PART 6

1. B. J. Cummings, Organizational Psychology, Northern Kentucky University, 1978.

2. Lee Iacocca, *Iacocca* (New York: Bantam Books, 1985)—see Chapter 5, "The Key to Management"; and Mark McCormack, *What They Don't Teach You at Harvard Business School* (New York: Bantam Books, 1986), XIV.

3. Abraham Maslow and Robert Frager, *Motivation and Personality* (New York: Addison Wesley Longman, 1987).

4. Viktor Frankl, *Man's Search for Meaning* (New York: Pocket Books, 1963), 44–45.

5. Muzafer Sherif and Hadley Cantril, *The Psychology of Ego-Involvements* (New York: Wiley, 1947).

6. R. A. Spitz, "The Psychoanalytic Diseases in Infancy: An Attempt at Etiologic Classification," *Psychoanalytic Study of the Child* 6 (1951): 255–275.

7. Ashley Montagu and Floyd Matson, *The Human Connection* (New York: McGraw-Hill, 1979), 114, 116, 118.

8. William James, *Principles of Psychology* (New York: Dover, 1950), 293–294. Original work published 1890.

9. Abraham Maslow, *Toward a Psychology of Being* (New York: Wiley, 1998); Abraham Maslow, *Motivation and Personality,* 2nd ed. (New York: Harper & Row, 1970) and adapted from James F. Calhoun and Joan Ross Acocella, *Psychology of Adjustment and Human Relationships* (New York: Random House, 1978), 35.

10. Julian Huxley, *Evolution in Action* (New York: Harper & Row, 1953), 162–163.

11. John Simpson and E. S. C. Weiner, eds., *The Oxford English Dictionary,* 2nd ed, vol. 9 (Oxford: Clarendon Press, 1989), 1131.

12. Richard L. Hughes, Gordon S. Curphy, and Robert C. Ginnett, *Leadership: Enhancing the Lessons of Experience* (London: McGraw-Hill, 1999).

13. Questionnaire based on concepts presented by Maslow, *Motivation and Personality;* Frederick Herzberg, *Work and the Nature of Man* (New York: Crowell, 1966); and Frederick Herzberg, "One More Time: How Do You Motivate Employees?" *Harvard Business Review* 46, no. 1 (January–February 1968): 53–62. Interpretation based on Jay Hall, *Understanding Motivation at Work According to Types of Needs.*

14. John Steinbeck, *The Grapes of Wrath* (New York: Viking Press, 1939), 124.

15. Studs Terkel, *Working* (New York: Pantheon Books, 1974), xi.

16. Maslow, *Motivation and Personality*; and Herzberg, "One More Time."

17. Jeffrey Pfeffer, *The Human Equation* (Cambridge, MA: Harvard Business School Press, 1998); and Andy Cohen, "The Best Motivators," *Sales and Marketing Management* 151, no. 11 (November 1999): 14–19.

18. Gustave Flaubert and Geoffrey Wall, *Madame Bovary* (London: Penguin, 2001; original work published 1924).

19. Barbara Engler, *Personality Theories: An Introduction* (Boston: Houghton-Mifflin, 1999), 338–341; M. Scott Peck, *The Road Less Traveled* (New York: Walker, 1978); and Sheldon B. Kopp, *If You Meet the Buddha on the Road, Kill Him!* (New York: Bantam Books, 1976).

20. Daniel Yankelovich, "Who Gets Ahead in America?" *Psychology Today* 13 (July 1979): 43.

21. Saul W. Gellerman, *Motivation and Productivity* (New York: American Management Association, 1963); Herzberg, *Work and the Nature of Man;* and Stephen C. Schoonover, *Managing to Relate: Interpersonal Skills at Work* (Reading, MA: Addison-Wesley, 1988).

22. Chris Argyris, *Integrating the Individual and the Organization* (New York: Wiley, 1964).

23. Tracy Goss, *The Last Word on Power* (New York: Currency Doubleday, 1996); Robert B. Cialdini, *Influence: Science and Practice* (New York: HarperCollins, 1988); Fred E. Fiedler, *A Theory of Leadership Effectiveness* (New York: McGraw-Hill, 1967); and Richard Neustadt, *Presidential Power: The Politics of Leadership* (New York: New American Library, 1964).

24. Daniel Goleman, *Working with Emotional Intelligence* (New York: Bantam Books, 1998); and Daniel Goleman, "What Makes a Leader?" *Harvard Business Review* 76, no. 6 (November–December 1998): 92–105.

25. Dale Carnegie, Dorothy Carnegie, and Arthur R. Pell, *How to Win Friends and Influence People* (New York: Pocket Books, 1998); Goleman, *Working with Emotional Intelligence;* Goleman, "What Makes a Leader?"; and Warren Bennis, *Managing People Is Like Herding Cats* (Provo, UT: Executive Excellence Publishing, 1997).

26. Michael Michalko, *Thinkertoys: A Handbook of Business Creativity for the 90's* (Berkeley, CA: Ten Speed Press, 1991).

27. Andrew J. DuBrin, *Leadership: Research Findings, Practices, and Skills* (Boston: Houghton Mifflin, 1998); Goleman, *Working with Emotional Intelligence*; and Goleman, "What Makes a Leader?"

28. DuBrin, *Leadership.*

29. Daniel Goleman, "Leadership That Gets Results," *Harvard Business Review* 78, no. 2 (March–April 2000): 78–89; and Goleman, *Working with Emotional Intelligence.*

30. Anne Fisher, *Fortune* 138, no. 8 (October 26, 1998): 293. © 1998 Time Inc. All rights reserved.

31. *Bits & Pieces,* Lawrence Ragan Communications, Inc., 316 N. Michigan Ave., Chicago, IL 60601.

32. Lyman K. Steil, Larry Lee Barker, and Kittie W. Watson, *Effective Listening: Key to Your Success* (McGraw-Hill; New York, 1993).

33. Winston S. Churchill and Guy Boas, *Winston S. Churchill: Selections from His Writings and Speeches* (London: Macmillan, 1952).

34. Churchill and Boas, *Winston S. Churchill.*

35. Ibid.

36. Speech by Patrick Henry, delivered at St. John's Church, Richmond, Virginia, March 23, 1775.

37. Michael Z. Hackman and Craig E. Johnson, *Leadership: A Communication Perspective* (Prospect Heights, IL: Waveland, 1996); and John W. Gardner, "Building Community," paper prepared for the Leadership Studies Program of the Independent Sector (Washington, DC: American Institutes for Research, 1991).

38. Robert Lussier, *Human Relations in Organizations: Applications and Skill Building* (Boston: McGraw-Hill, 2002); Afzalur Rahim, Jan Edward Garrett, and Gabriel F. Buntzman, "Ethics of Managing Interpersonal Conflict in Organizations," *Journal of Business Ethics* 11 (1992): 423–432; Sun Tzu, *The Art of War,* trans. Thomas Cleary (New York: Shambhala, 1991); and Roger Fisher, William Ury, and Bruce Patton, *Getting to Yes: Negotiating Agreement Without Giving In* (Boston: Houghton Mifflin, 1991).

39. Joyce L. Hocker and William W. Wilmot, *Interpersonal Conflict* (Boston: McGraw-Hill, 2001); and E. S. Browning, "Computer Chip Project Brings Rivals Together, but Cultures Clash," *The Wall Street Journal-Eastern Edition* (May 3, 1994), A1–A2.

40. Based on Alan C. Filley, *Interpersonal Conflict Resolution* (Glenview, IL: Scott, Foresman, 1975); and Vincent L. Ferraro and Shelia A. Adams, "Interdepartmental Conflict: Practical Ways to Prevent and Reduce It," *Personnel* (1984): 12–23; and John R. Schermerhorn, *Management,* 6th ed. (New York: Wiley, 1999), 341–342.

41. Based on Schermerhorn, *Management,* 342.

42. Based on Filley, *Interpersonal Conflict Resolution*; and Ferraro and Adams, "Interdepartmental Conflict."

43. Adapted from Thomas Kilmann, *Conflict Mode Instrument* (Tuxedo, NY: Xicom, 1974); and Schermerhorn, *Management.*

44. Deborah Borisoff and David A. Victor, *Conflict Management: A Communication Skills Approach* (Englewood Cliffs, NJ: Prentice-Hall, 1989); and John D. Arnold, *When the Sparks Fly: Resolving Conflicts in Our Organization* (New York: McGraw-Hill, 1993).

45. Perry Pascarella, "Thinking Globally Is 'Sacred' Management Duty," *Management Review* 86, no. 4 (1997): 58–59; Arvind V. Phatak, *International Dimensions of Management* (Cincinnati, OH: South-Western, 1995); R. Roosevelt Thomas, Jr., and Marjorie I. Woodruff, *Building a House for Diversity: How a Fable About a Giraffe and an Elephant Offers New Strategies for Today's Workforce* (New York: AMACOM, 1999); Geert Hofstede, "Motivation, Leadership, and Organization: Do American Theories Apply Abroad?" *Organizational Dynamics* (Summer 1980): 42–63; and Cherlyn S. Granrose and Stuart Oskamp, eds., "Cross-Cultural Workgroups," Claremont Symposium on Applied Psychology, 1996 (Thousand Oaks, CA: Sage, 1997).

46. Dorothy Manning, of International Business Protocol, in Heidi J. LaFleche, "When Rome Burns," *TWA Ambassador* (October 1990): 69; William Pantalon III, "Kodak Author: Asia or Gold Mine," *Rochester Democrat and Chronicle* (September 25, 1995), 5B; Carla Johnson, "Cultural Sensitivity Adds Up to Good Business Sense," *HR Magazine* (November 1995): 82–83; DuBrin, *Leadership,* 373; and Gary Fontaine, *Managing International Assignments* (Englewood Cliffs, NJ: Prentice-Hall, 1989).

47. William Gudykunst, Stella Ting-Toomey, and Tsukasa Nishida, *Communication in Personal Relationships Across Cultures* (Thousand Oaks, CA: Sage, 1996); Sondra Thiederman, *Bridging Cultural Barriers for Corporate Success: How to Manage the Multicultural Work Force* (Lexington, MA: Lexington Books, 1991); and R. Roosevelt Thomas, *Beyond Race and Gender: Unleashing the Power of Your Workforce by Managing Diversity* (New York: AMACOM, 1991), 25.

48. Lennie Copeland, "Learning to Manage a Multicultural Workforce," *Training* (May 1988): 48–49, 51, 55–56.

49. Martin Marger, *Race and Ethnic Relations: American and Global Perspectives,* 5th ed. (Belmont, CA: Wadsworth Thomson Learning, 2000); Taylor H. Cox, *Cultural Diversity in Organizations: Theory, Research and Practice* (San Francisco: Berrett-Koehler, 1994); Clifton L. Taulbert, *Eight Habits of the Heart: The Timeless Values That Build Strong Communities Within Our Homes and Our Lives* (New York: Viking/Dial Books, 1997); and Copeland, "Learning to Manage a Multicultural Workforce," 48–49, 51, 55–56.

50. Copeland, "Learning to Manage a Multicultural Workforce."

51. Copeland, "Learning to Manage a Multicultural Workforce," 48–49, 51, 55–56.

52. Copeland, "Learning to Manage a Multicultural Workforce"; and Phillip R. Harris and Robert T. Moran, *Managing Cultural Differences* (Houston: Gulf, 1986).

53. Ann Morrison, *The New Leaders: Guidelines on Leadership Diversity in America* (San Francisco: Jossey-Bass, 1992), 292.

54. Marilyn Loden and Judy B. Rosener, *Workforce America! Managing Employee Diversity as a Vital Resource* (New York: McGraw-Hill, 1991); David Jamieson and Julie O'Mara, *Managing Workforce 2000: Gaining the Diversity Advantage* (San Francisco: Jossey-Bass, 1991); John P. Fernandez, *Managing a Diverse Work Force: Regaining the Competitive Edge* (Lexington, MA: Lexington Books, 1991); Jeff Walter, "Managing Differences: Critical Skills for Supervision," *Great American Insurance Companies,* 2001; and Taylor H. Cox and S. Blake, "Managing Cultural Diversity: Implications for Organizational Competitiveness," *Academy of Management Executive* 5, no. 3 (1991): 45–46.

55. John W. Newstrom and Keith Davis, *Organizational Behavior: Human Behavior at Work* (Boston: McGraw-Hill, 2002); Lussier, *Human Relations in Organizations;* Thomas, *Beyond Race and Gender;* Granrose and Oskamp, *Cross Cultural Workgroups;* and Gudykunst, Ting-Toomey, and Nishida, *Communication in Personal Relationships Across Cultures.*

56. Alvin Poussaint, "A Negro Psychiatrist Explains the Negro Psyche," in *Confrontation: Issues of the 70's,* Part 3 (New York: Random House, 1971), 183–184.

57. James Henslin, *Sociology: A Down to Earth Approach,* 4th ed. (Boston: Allyn & Bacon, 1999).

58. Deborah Tannen, *You Just Don't Understand: Women and Men in Conversation* (New York: Quill, 2001), 216–221; and Rodney W. Napier and Matti K. Gershenfeld, *Groups: Theory and Experience,* 6th ed. (Boston: Houghton Mifflin, 1999).

59. Tannen, *You Just Don't Understand;* and Napier and Gershenfeld, *Groups.*

60. Ibid.

61. Ibid.

62. Ibid; and Ellen Van Velsor and Martha W. Hughes, *Gender Differences in the Development of Managers: How Women Managers Learn from Experience* (Greensboro, NC: Center for Creative Leadership, 1990).

63. "Catalyst Census of Women Corporate Officers and Top Earners, 2000," report in Matthew S. Scott, "For Women, the Glass Ceiling Persists," *Black Enterprise* 32, no. 1 (August 2001): 30; Karen S. Koziara, Michael H. Moskow, and Lucretia D. Tanner, *Working Women: Past, Present and Future* (Washington, DC: Bureau of National Affairs, 1987); A. M. Morrison, R. P. White, and E. Van Velsor, *Breaking the Glass Ceiling* (Reading, MA: Addison-Wesley, 1987); Nancy Kline, *Women and Power: How Far Can We Go?* (London: BBC Books, 1993); Kathleen H. Jamieson, *Beyond the Double Bind: Women and Leadership* (New York: Oxford University Press, 1997); S. Helgesen, *The Female Advantage: Women's Ways of Leadership* (New York: Doubleday, 1995); Joseph F. Coates, Jennifer Jarratt, and John B. Mahaffie, *Future Work: Seven Critical Forces Reshaping Works and the Workforce in North America* (San Francisco: Jossey-Bass, 1990), 62; and David Bender, *Working Women* (San Diego: Greenhaven Press, 1994).

64. Coates, Jarratt, and Mahaffie, *Future Work;* and Morrison, White, and Van Velsor, *Breaking the Glass Ceiling;* and "Catalyst Census of Women Corporate Officers and Top Earners, 2000."

65. "Catalyst Census of Women Corporate Officers and Top Earners, 2000."

66. Margaret Price, "Women Reaching the Top," *Industry Week* (May 16, 1987): 39.

67. Catalyst report, "Women of Color in Corporate Offices: A Statistical Picture, 1997"; Marilyn Loden, "Disillusion at the Corporate Top," *New York Times* (February 9, 1986), F2; Catalyst report, "Women of Color in Corporate Offices: A Statistical Picture, 1997"; and U.S. Census Data, 1994–95.

68. Loden, "Disillusion at the Corporate Top."

69. "Why Women Execs Stop before the Top," *US News & World Report* (December 29, 1986): 72.

70. Robert M. Fulmer, *Practical Human Relations* (Homewood, IL: Irwin, 1983).

71. Jay A. Conger, "The Brave New World of Leadership Training," *Organizational Dynamics* 21, no. 3 (Winter 1993): 46–58.

72. Marian Wright Edelman, *The Measure of Our Success: A Letter to My Children and Yours* (Boston: Beacon Press, 1992).

PART 7

1. Bill Gates, Michael Dean, and Stephen Bryant, *Business @ the Speed of Thought* (Harlow, England: Pearson Education, 2001).

2. Laurie Beth Jones, *Jesus CEO: Using Ancient Wisdom for Visionary Leadership* (New York: Hyperion, 1995).

3. W. Steven Brown, *13 Fatal Errors Managers Make and How You Can Avoid Them* (New York: Berkley, 1985).

4. Brown, *13 Fatal Errors Managers Make.*

5. Katrina Brooker, "The Chairman of the Board Looks Back," *Fortune* (May 28, 2001): 62–70.

6. Peter Drucker, *Effective Executive* (New York: Harper & Row, 1985); and Ronald A. Heifetz, *Leadership Without Easy Answers* (Cambridge, MA: Belknap Press of Harvard University Press, 1995).

7. Gene Archbold and Steve McMillen, based on *Delegation Concepts* (Grandville, MI: Time Management Center, 1977); and John McKinney, *Time Management* (New York: Penton Learning, 1977, rev. 1999).

8. Archbold and McMillen; Lyndall F. Urwick, *Elements of Administration* (London: Pitman, 1951); Leonard Sayles, *Leadership: What Effective Managers Really Do . . . And How They Do It* (New York: McGraw-Hill, 1981); C. H. Vroom and A. G. Jago, "Decision Making as Social Process: Normative and Descriptive Models of Leader Behavior," *Decision Sciences* 5 (1974): 743–769; Auren Uris, *The Executive Deskbook* (Florence, KY: Van Nostrand Reinhold, 1979); and G. P. Huber, *Managerial Decision-Making* (Glenview, IL: Scott, Foresman, 1980).

9. Norman R. R. Maier, *Psychology in Industrial Organizations,* 4th ed. (Boston: Houghton Mifflin, 1973), 437–438.

10. Urwick, *Elements of Administration;* John Lawrie, *You Can Lead! Essential Skills for the New or Prospective Manager* (New York: AMACOM, 1989); John Sargent, *What Every Executive Should Know About the Art of Leadership* (Chicago: Dartnell Corp., 1964); and Ernest Dale, *Management Theory and Practice,* 3rd ed. (New York: McGraw-Hill, 1973).

11. Edgar H. Schein, "The Individual, the Organization, and the Career," *Journal of Applied Behavioral Science* 7, no. 4 (1971): 401–426; D. T. Hall and M. Morgan, "Career Development and Planning," in W. C. Hammer and F. Schmidt, eds., *Contemporary Problems in Personnel,* rev. ed. (Chicago: St. Clair Press, 1977);

and G. W. Dalton, P. H. Thompson, and R. L. Price, "The Four Stages of Professional Careers," *Organizational Dynamics* 6, no. 1 (Summer 1977): 19–42.

12. Adapted from Robert L. Katz, "Skills of an Effective Administrator," *Harvard Business Review* 52, no. 5 (September–October 1974): 90–102; John R. Schermerhorn, Jr., *Management,* 6th ed. (New York: Wiley, 1999), 15, 90–102; and Leslie W. Rue and Lloyd L. Byars, *Management: Skills and Applications,* 9th ed. (Boston: Irwin/McGraw-Hill, 2000).

13. Henry Mintzberg, *The Nature of Managerial Work* (Englewood Cliffs, NJ: Prentice-Hall, 1980).

14. Jennifer Stafford, Special Topics Class Project, Psychology 495/595, Northern Kentucky University, 2000.

15. Martin M. Broadwell and Carol Broadwell Ditrich, "Culture Clash," *Training* 437, no. 3 (March 2000): 34–36.

16. Laurence J. Peter and Raymond Hull, *The Peter Principle: Why Things Always Go Wrong* (Mattituck, NY: American House, 2000).

17. Adapted from Lawrence L. Steinmetz, *The Art and Skill of Delegation* (Reading, MA: Addison-Wesley, 1976), 46–63.

18. Adapted from Thomas E. Bier, "Contemporary Youth: Implications of the Personalistic Life Style for Organizations," doctoral dissertation, Case Western Reserve University, 1967, Cleveland, Ohio.

19. Cecil Woodham-Smith, *Queen Victoria, from Her Birth to the Death of the Prince Consort* (New York: Knopf, 1972).

20. Joan Hoff-Wilson and Marjorie Lightman, *Without Precedent: The Life and Career of Eleanor Roosevelt* (Bloomington: Indiana University Press, 1984).

21. Frederic A. Birmingham, "The Infinite Riches of Ben Franklin," *Saturday Evening Post* (January–February 1982): 50; and Ronald William Clark, *Benjamin Franklin: A Biography* (New York: Random House, 1983).

22. Henry David Thoreau, *Walden* (Chicago: Lakeside Press, 1930), 285–286; and Walter R. Harding, *The Days of Henry Thoreau* (Princeton, NJ: Princeton University Press, 1992).

23. Regine Pernoud, *Joan of Arc: By Herself and Her Witnesses* (New York: Stein & Day, 1969).

24. C. Kagitcibasi and J. W. Berry, "Cross-Cultural Psychology: Current Research and Trends," *Annual Review of Psychology* 40 (1989): 493–531.

25. Geert Hofstede, *Culture's Consequences: Comparing Values, Behaviors, Institutions, and Organizations Across Nations* (Thousand Oaks, CA: Sage, 2001).

26. Ibid.

27. C. H. Hui and M. J. Villareal, "Individualism-Collectivism and Psychological Needs," *Journal of Cross-Cultural Psychology* 20 (1989): 310–323; C. Kagitcibasi, "Diversity of Socialization and Social Change," in P. R. Dasen, John W. Berry, and N. Sartorius, eds., *Health and Cross-Cultural Psychology: Toward Application* (Newberry Park, CA: Sage, 1988): and H. Triandis, "Collectivism vs. Individualism: A Reconceptualization of a Basic Concept in Cross-Cultural Social Psychology," in Christopher Bagley and Gajendra R. Verman, eds., *Personality, Cognition, and Values* (Calgary, Alberta, Canada: University of Calgary Press, 1986).

28. B. Schwartz, "The Creation and Destruction of Value," *American Psychologist* 45 (1990): 7–15.

29. Stephen M. Joseph, *The Me Nobody Knows* (New York: Avon, 1969).

30. Emanual Hertz, *Lincoln Talks—A Biography in Anecdotes* (New York: Viking Press, 1939), 367.

31. Robert Frost, *The Road Not Taken: A Selection of Robert Frost's Poems* (New York: Holt, Rinehart & Winston, 1985), St. 4.

32. Edwin Markham, in Raymond F. Gale, *Developmental Behavior* (New York: Macmillan, 1969), 192.

PART 8

1. Max DePree, *Leadership Is an Art* (New York: Doubleday, 1989).

2. William Stewart, "Developing Others," Department of Adult Technical Education, University of Cincinnati, 1980.

3. Robert K. Merton, "The Self-Fulfilling Prophecy," *Antioch Review* 8 (1948): 193–210; Robert Rosenthal, *Pygmalion in the Classroom: Teacher Expectation and Pupil's Intellectual Development* (New York: Irvington, 1992); and R. Rosenthal and L. Jacobson, "Teacher's Expectancies: Determinates of Pupils' I. Q. Gains," *Psychological Reports* 19 (1966): 115–118.

4. John W. Gardner, *On Leadership* (New York: Free Press, 1990).

5. W. Steven Brown, *13 Fatal Errors Managers Make and How You Can Avoid Them* (New York: Berkley Books, 1985); and Dennis C. Kinlaw, *Coaching for Commitment: Managerial Strategies for Obtaining Superior Performance* (San Diego, CA: Pfeiffer, 1989).

6. Philip S. Wosley and Bruce Rogers, eds., *The Odyssey of Homer* (Edinburgh, Scotland: Blackwood, 1868); Michael C. Lang and Jerry Kelly, *Homer: Printed Editions of the Iliad and Odyssey in Greek and in Translation, and Landmarks in Homeric Scholarship* (New York: Grolier Society, 2001); and Mitchell Malachowski, "The Mentoring Role in Undergraduate Research Projects," *Council on Undergraduate Research Quarterly* (December 1996): 91–93.

7. Harry Levinson, *Executive* (Cambridge, MA: Harvard University Press, 1981), 150.

8. R. M. Gagne, *Conditions of Learning* (New York: Holt, Rinehart & Winston, 1985); James C. Coleman, *Personality Dynamics and Effective Behavior* (Chicago: Scott, Foresman, 1960), 97–98; John Dewey, *Democracy and Education: An Introduction to the Philosophy of Education* (New York: MacMillan, 1961); and Edward L. Thorndike, *Human Learning* (New York: Century, 1931).

9. Thorndike, *Human Learning*; Peter M. Senge, *The Fifth Discipline: The Art and Practice of the Learning Organization* (New York: Currency/Doubleday, 1990); and Charles Ehin, *Unleashing Intellectual Capital* (Woburn, MA: Butterworth-Heinemann, 2000).

10. Alan Zimmerman, Commun-Care, Prior Lake, MN, 1992.

11. Thomas A. Stewart, "The Businessman of the Century," *Fortune* 140 (November 22, 1999): 64–79.

12. Mike Hils and Kenny Shields, Leadership Behavior Course, Northern Kentucky University, 2000; and Kathy E. Kram, *Mentoring at Work: Developmental Relationships in Organizational Life* (Lanham, MD: University Press of America, 1988).

13. *The Sayings of Confucius,* trans. James R. Ware, (New York: New American Library, 1955).

14. Henry Mintzberg, *The Manager's Job: Folklore and Fact* (Boston: Harvard Business Review Reprint Service, 1990); and Jeffrey Pfeffer and Robert I. Sutton, *The Knowing-Doing Gap: How Smart Companies Turn Knowledge into Action* (Cambridge, MA: Harvard Business School Press, 2000).

15. Robert and Judith Waterman, "Toward a Career Resilient Workforce," *Harvard Business Review* 72, no. 4 (July 1994): 87; and "Training Pays," *The Wall Street Journal,* May 7, 1996.

16. Anthony Carnevale, *Put Quality to Work: Train America's Workforce* (Alexandria, VA: American Society of Training and Development and the U.S. Department of Labor, 1990).

17. Ibid.

18. "Eleven Characteristics of Highly Effective Training."

19. Phil Jackson and Hugh Delehanty, *Sacred Hoops: Spiritual Lessons of a Hardwood Warrior* (New York: Hyperion, 1995).

20. Robert Katz, *Skills of an Effective Administrator* (Boston: Harvard Business Review Reprint Service, 1974); and "Networking Guide to Fifty Corporate Universities," *Benchmarking Best Practices Among Corporate Universities* (New York: Corporate University Xchange, Fifth Annual Benchmarking Report, 2002).

21. Yogi Berra, *When You Come to a Fork in the Road, Take It: Inspiration and Wisdom from One of Baseball's Greatest Heroes* (Waterville, ME: Thorndike Press, 2001); and Jay A. Conger and Beth Benjamin, *Building Leaders: How Successful Companies Develop the Next Generation* (San Francisco: Jossey-Bass, 1999).

22. Morgan McCall, Jr., M. M. Lombardo, and A. Morrison, *The Lessons of Experience* (Lexington, MA: Lexington Books, 1988).

23. Noel M. Tichy, *The Leadership Engine: Building Leaders at Every Level* (Dallas, TX: Pritchett, 1998).

24. Daniel Goleman, *Working with Emotional Intelligence* (New York: Bantam Books, 2000); Anthony P. Carnevale, Leila J. Gainer, and Ann S. Meltzer, *Workplace Basics: The Skills Employers Want* (San Francisco: Jossey-Bass, 1991); and Gene Dalton and Paul H. Thompson, *Innovations: Strategies for Career Management* (New York: Scott, Foresman, 1986).

25. RoAnne Barnett Marrett, Employee Retention Systems, "The Turmoil of Employee Turnover," *Kentucky Index* (October 1999).

26. John Byrne, Andy Reinhardt, and Robert D. Hof, "The Search for the Young and Gifted," *Business Week* (October 4, 1999): 108–112.

27. Marcus Buckingham, *First Break All the Rules: What the World's Greatest Managers Do Differently* (New York: Simon & Schuster, 1999); Marcus Buckingham and Donald Clifton, *Now Discover Your Strengths* (New York: Free Press, 2001); and Marcus Buckingham and Curt Coffman, "How Great Managers Develop Top People," *Workforce* (June 1999): 102–105.

28. Daryl R. Conner, *Managing at the Speed of Change* (New York: Villand Books, 1993), 38.

29. Harold J. Leavitt, *Corporate Pathfinders* (Homewood, IL: Dow Jones–Irwin, 1986); and Harold J. Leavitt, *Managerial Psychology* (Chicago: University of Chicago Press, 1964).

30. Price Pritchett, *Business as Unusual: The Handbook for Managing and Supervising Organizational Change* (Dallas: Pritchett, 1994).

31. Bob Filipczak, "Weathering Change: Enough Already," *Training* 31, no. 9 (September 1994): 23; and Richard S. DeFrank and John M. Ivancevich, "Stress on the Job: An Executive Update," *Academy of Management Executive* 12, no. 3 (August 1998): 55–66.

32. Cynthia D. Scott and Dennis T. Jaffe, *Managing Organizational Change: A Practical Guide for Managers* (Los Altos, CA: Crisp Publications, 1989).

33. Kurt Lewin, *A Dynamic Theory of Personality* (New York: McGraw-Hill, 1935).

34. John P. Kotter, *Leading Change* (Boston: Harvard Business School Press, 1996), 21.

35. Ibid. 16.

36. Ibid. 115.

37. Price Pritchett, *Team Reconstruction* (Dallas: Pritchett, 1992); and Pritchett and Associates, *High-Velocity Culture Change: Creating a Change-Adaptive Culture (Participant's Guide)* (Dallas: Pritchett, 1994); see also R. Kanter, *The Change Masters* (New York: Simon & Schuster, 1983).

38. Charles Darwin, *On the Origin of Species by Means of Natural Selection* (London: J. Murray, 1859).

39. Scott and Jaffe, *Managing Organizational Change;* and Cynthia D. Scott and Dennis T. Jaffe, *Managing Personal Change: Self-Management Skills for Work and Life Transitions* (Los Altos, CA: Crisp Publications, 1989).

40. Brian L. Davis, *Successful Manager's Handbook: Development Suggestions for Today's Managers* (Minneapolis, MN: Personnel Decisions International, 1996), 426–427.

41. Jack Canfield and Mark Hansen, *Chicken Soup for the Soul: 101 Stories to Open the Heart and Rekindle the Spirit* (Deerfield Beach, FL: Health Communications, 1993), 72.

42. Adapted from Patti Nickell, *Burnout: Could It Happen to You?* (East Jefferson, MA: East Jefferson General Hospital, 1983), 6–8, 24; and Herbert J. Freudenberger, "Burn-Out: The Organizational Menace," *Training and Development* 31, no. 7 (July 1977): 26–27.

43. Nickell, *Burnout;* and Freudenberger, "Burn-Out."

44. Freudenberger, "Staff Burnout," *Journal of Social Issues* 30 (1974): 159–165; Herbert J. Freudenberger, *Burnout: The High Cost of Achievement* (Garden City, NY: Doubleday, 1980); Christina Maslach, "Burned Out," *Human Behavior* 5 (1976): 16–22; and Christina Maslach, *Burnout: The Cost of Caring* (Englewood Cliffs, NJ: Prentice-Hall, 1980).

45. *Minneapolis Star,* July 23, 1979.

46. Murray H. Rosenthal, "How to Win the Burn-Out Game," *USA Today Magazine* (January 1991): 70–72. Reprinted from *USA Today Magazine,* January 1991 by SAE.

47. Adapted from Carol Krucoff, "Careers: Confronting On-the-Job Burnout," *The Washington Post,* August 5, 1980, health section, p. 5.

48. Donald Tubesing, *Manage It! Skill Building Guide* (Duluth, MN: Whole Person Associates, 1992).

49. S. L. Sauter, L. R. Murphy, and J. Hurrell, Jr., "A National Strategy for the Prevention of Work Related Psychological Disorders," *American Psychologist* 45 (1990): 1146–1158; A. J. Elkin and R. J. Rosch, "Promoting Mental Health at the Workplace: The Prevention Side of Stress Management," *Occupational Medicine: State of the Art Review* 5, no. 4 (1990): 739–754; and David Lewin and Steven Schecter, "Four Factors in Lower Disability Rates," *Personnel Journal* 74, no. 11 (November 1995): 14–15.

50. Merrill R. Raber and George Dyck, *Managing Stress for Mental Fitness* (Los Altos, CA: Crisp Publications, 1993).

51. Michael Losey, "Managing Stress in the Workplace," *Managing Office Technology* (February 1991).

52. "Breaking Point," *Newsweek* (March 6, 1995): 56–61; and Juliet Schor, *The Overworked American: The Unexpected Decline of Leisure* (New York: Basic Books, 1993).

53. Barbara Garson, *The Electronic Sweatshop* (New York: Simon & Schuster, 1988); Shoshana Zuboff, *In the Age of the Smart Machine: The Future of Work and Power* (New York: Basic Books, 1988).

54. Wayne F. Cascio, "Whither Industrial and Organizational Psychology in a Changing World of Work," *American Psychologist* 50, no. 11 (November 1995): 928–939.

55. "Using Technology to Improve our Management of Labour Market or Trends," *Journal of Organizational Change Management* 3, no. 2 (1990): 44–57.

56. Richard E. Walton, *Innovating to Compete* (San Francisco: Jossey-Bass, 1987).

57. S. C. Gwynne, "The Long Haul," *Time* (September 28, 1992): 34–38.

58. P. R. Lawrence and D. Ryer, *Renewing American Industry* (New York: Free Press, 1983).

59. Wayne F. Cascio, "What Do We Know? What Have We Learned?" *Academy of Management Executive* 7, no. I (February 1993): 95–104.

60. Cascio, "Whither Industrial and Organizational Psychology in a Changing World of Work"; and S. M. Dray, "From Tier to Peer: Organizational Adaptation to New Computing Architectures," *Ergonomics* 31, no. 5 (1988): 721–725.

61. E. Carroll Curtis, Panel comments, "Surveillance of Psychological Disorders in the Workplace," in Gwendolyn Puryear Keita and Steven L. Sauter, eds., *Work and Well-Being: An Agenda for the 1990s* (Washington, DC: American Psychological Association, 1992), 97–99.

62. Steven L. Sauter, "Introduction to the NIOSH National Strategy," in Keita and Sauter, *Work and Well-Being.*

63. Arlie R. Hochschild, *The Second Shift: Working Parents and the Revolution at Home* (New York: Viking, 1989).

64. Joseph V. Brady, "Ulcers in Executive Monkeys," *Scientific American* 199, no. 4 (October 1958): 95–100.

65. Jay M. Weiss, "Psychological Factors in Stress and Disease," *Scientific American* 226 (June 1972): 104–113.

66. Robert Karasek and Töres Theorell, *Healthy Work: Stress, Productivity, and the Reconstruction of Working Life* (New York: Basic Books, 1990); Geoffrey Cowley and Mary Hager, "Dialing the Stress-Meter Down," *Newsweek* (March 6, 1995): 62; and Claudia Wallis, Ruth Mehrtens Galvin, and Dick Thompson, "Stress: Can We Cope?" *Time* (June 1983): 52.

67. Thomas J. Peters and Robert H. Waterman, Jr., *In Search of Excellence* (New York: Harper & Row, 1982), xxiii, xxiv.

PART 9

1. W. Steven Brown, *13 Fatal Errors Managers Make* (Old Tappan, NJ: Revell, 1985); Peter Drucker, *Managing for Results* (New York: Harper & Row, 1964); Peter Drucker, *People and Performance: The Best of Peter Drucker on Management* (New York: Harper's College Press, 1977); and Dave Ulric, Jack Zenger, and Norm Smallwood, *Results-Based Leadership* (Boston: Harvard Business School Press, 1999).

2. Kenneth H. Blanchard and Spencer Johnson, *The One Minute Manager* (New York: Berkley Books, 1982); Kenneth H. Blanchard, *Putting the One Minute Manager to Work* (New York: Morrow, 1984); and Kenneth H. Blanchard, Patricia Zigarmi, and Drea Zigarmi, *Leadership and the One Minute Manager* (New York: Morrow, 1985).

3. Paul L. Brown, *Managing Behavior on the Job* (Boston: Houghton Mifflin, 1982).

4. Norman R. Maier and Gertrude C. Verser, *Psychology in Industrial Organizations,* 5th ed. (Boston: Houghton Mifflin, 1982).

5. *Bits and Pieces,* Lawrence Ragan Communications Inc., 316 N. Michigan Ave., Chicago, IL 60601.

6. Peter Drucker, *The Practice of Management* (New York: Harper & Row, 1954), 126–129.

7. Brown, *13 Fatal Errors Managers Make.*

8. Patti Holmes, "Productive Performance Appraisals," Information from our Professional Colleague's class presentation at Northern Kentucky University, 2001; Richard A. Fear, *The Evaluation Interview* (New York: McGraw-Hill, 1972); Peggy Simonsen, "Give Positive Feedback," *CPA Journal* 68, no. 5 (May 1998); and Steve Martin, "Performance Appraisal—Employee Interview Checklist," Cincinnati, OH, 1988, rev. 2000.

9. Leanne Atwater and David Waldman, "Accountability in 360 Degrees Feedback," *HR Magazine* 43, no. 6 (1998): 96–105; and John E. Jones and William L. Bearley, *360° Feedback: Strategies, Tactics, and Techniques for Developing Leaders* (Amherst, MA: HRD Press, 1996).

10. Martin, "Performance Appraisal."

11. Norman R. F. Maier, "Three Types of Appraisal Interviews," *Personnel* (March–April 1958): 39.

12. Barry Montgomery and Jackie Meeke, "Organizational Psychology" class report, Northern Kentucky University, 1982, rev. 2000; Bernard M. Bass, *Leadership and Performance Beyond Expectations* (New York: Free Press, 1985); Bernard M. Bass, *Bass and Stogdill's Handbook of Leadership,* 3rd ed. (New York: Free Press, 1990); and Kenneth E. Clark and Miriam Clark, *Measures of Leadership* (Greensboro, NC: Center for Creative Leadership, 1990).

13. Source unknown.

14. Adapted from Phillip Marvin, *The Right Man for the Right Job: The Executive's Guide to Tapping Top Talent* (Homewood, IL: Dow Jones–Irwin, 1973); James M. Kouzes and Barry Z. Posner, *The Leadership Challenge: How to Get Extraordinary Things Done in Organizations* (San Francisco: Jossey-Bass, 1987); and Phillip Marvin, *Management Goals: Guidelines and Accountability* (Homewood, IL: Dow Jones–Irwin, 1980), 95–113.

15. Marvin, *Management Goals.*

16. Will Forpe and John C. McCollister, *The Sunshine Book: Expressions of Love, Hope and Inspiration* (Middle Village, NY: Jonathan David, 1979).

17. Gordon W. Allport, "The Ego in Contemporary Psychology," *Psychological Review* 50 (1943): 466.

18. William James, as quoted in John M. Cohen and Mark J. Cohen, *The Penguin Dictionary of Quotations* (London: Claremont Books, 1995).

19. Katrina Brooker, "The Chairman of the Board Looks Back," *Fortune* (May 28, 2001): 62–70.

20. Upton Sinclair, *The Flivver King* (New York: Phaedra, 1969), 6, 7, 19, 69, 70, 78.

21. R. Marshall and Edgar A. Guest, *Edgar A. Guest: A Biographical Sketch* (Chicago: Reilly & Lee, 1920); and Edgar Guest, as quoted in Forpe and McCollister, *The Sunshine Book,* 5.

22. Eleanor Roosevelt, *This Is My Story* (New York: Harper, 1936).

23. Marshall and Guest, *Edgar A. Guest;* and "The Doubter," Edgar Guest, from the course training materials of William J. Stewart, University of Cincinnati, 1970.

24. *The Reader's Digest Great Encyclopedic Dictionary* (Pleasantville, NY: Reader's Digest Association, 1966), 2039.

25. Robert P. Levoy, "Getting Your Money's Worth from Courses," Professional Practice Consultants; J. P. Guilford, "Creativity: Its Measurement and Development," in Sidney J. Parnes and Harold F. Harding, eds., *A Sourcebook for Creative Thinking* (New York: Scribner, 1962); and Robert J. Sternberg and Todd I. Lubart, *Defying the Crowd: Cultivating Creativity in a Culture of Conformity* (New York: Free Press, 1995).

26. Samuel Foss, "The Calf Path," as found in Peter J. Frost, Vance F. Mitchell, and Walter R. Nord, *Organizational Reality: Reports from the Firing Line,* 3rd ed. (Glenview, IL: Scott, Foresman, 1986), 486–487.

27. John Beecroft, *Kipling: A Selection of His Stories and Poems* (Garden City, NY: Doubleday, 1956), 383–384.

28. Case from the authors' files.

29. Sam Walton, *Sam Walton, Made in America: My Story* (New York: Doubleday, 1992).

30. Jim Collins, "Level 5 Leadership," *Harvard Business Review* 79, no. 1 (January 2001): 66–76.

31. Ibid.

32. Kouzes and Posner, *The Leadership Challenge;* Michael J. Spendolini, *The Benchmarking Book* (New York: AMACOM, 1992); Robert C. Camp, *Benchmarking: The Search for Industry Best Practices That Lead to Superior Performance* (Milwaukee: ASQC Quality Press, 1989); and Carol J. McNair and Kathleen H. J. Leibried, *Benchmarking: Adding Distinctive Value to Every Aspect of Your Business* (New York: Harper Business, 1992).

33. Richard Whiteley, *The Customer Driven Company: Moving from Talk to Action* (Reading, MA: Addison-Wesley, 1993); Theodore B. Kinni, *America's Best* (New York: Wiley, 1996); and Andrew S. Grove, *Only the Paranoid Survive: How to Exploit the Crisis Points That Challenge Every Company* (New York: Currency Doubleday, 1999).

34. *Board Room Reports,* October 15, 1986, rev. 2001.

35. John B. Watson, "Psychology as the Behaviorist Views It," *Psychological Review* 20 (1913): 158–177; Ivan P. Pavlov, *Conditioned Reflexes: An Investigation of the Physiological Activity of the Cerebral Cortex* (London: Oxford University Press, 1927); Burrhus Frederic Skinner, *Science and Human Behavior* (New York: Free Press, 1953); Charles B. Ferster and B. F. Skinner, *Schedules of Reinforcement* (New York: Appleton-Century-Crofts, 1957); Albert Bandura, *Principles of Behavior Modification* (New York: Holt, Rinehart & Winston, 1969); F. Luthans and J. Schweizer, "How Behavior Modification Techniques Can Improve Total Organizational Performance," *Management Review* (September 1979): 43–50; and Albert Bandura, *A Social Learning Theory* (Englewood Cliffs, NJ: Prentice-Hall, 1977).

36. Alexander D. Stajkovic and Fred Luthans, "A Meta-Analysis of the Effects of Organizational Behavior Modification on TASK Performance, 1975–95," *Academy of Management Journal* 40, no. 5 (October 1997): 1122–1149.

37. Authors' files, Transit Authority of Northern Kentucky (TANK), King Kwik Convenient Stores, and Health Alliance of Cincinnati; and Edward E. Lawler, *High-Involvement Management: Participative Strategies for Improving Organizational Performance* (San Francisco: Jossey-Bass, 1986).

38. James C. Coleman, *Personality Dynamics and Effective Behavior* (Chicago: Scott, Foresman, 1960), 102.

39. Ibid; Robert DeBoard, *Counselling People at Work* (Brookfield, VT: Gower, 1983); and K. Thomas, "Conflict and Conflict Management," in Marvin D. Dunnette, ed., *Handbook of Industrial and Organizational Psychology* (New York: Wiley, 1983).

40. J. Clifton Williams, *Human Behavior in Organizations* (Cincinnati; OH: South-Western, 1986).

41. Mike Hils and Ken Shields, "Behavior Problem Flow Chart," "Organizational Behavior" class presentation, Northern Kentucky University, 1999.

CONCLUSION ENDNOTES

1. Library of Congress online catalog, http://catalog.loc.gov/; General Education Online, http://www.findaschool.org; and *Peterson's Four Year Colleges* (Princeton, NJ: Peterson's, 2001).

2. Peter Drucker, *Managing the Future: The 1990s and Beyond* (New York: HarperCollins, 1992); and Frances Hesselbein, Marshall Goldsmith, and Richard Beckhard, *The Leader of the Future: New Visions, Strategies, and Practices for the Next Era* (San Francisco: Jossey-Bass, 1996).

3. Mary Parker Follett, *Dynamic Administration: The Collected Papers of Mary Parker Follett* (New York: Harper, 1949); and Mary Parker Follett and Pauline Graham, *Prophet of Management: A Celebration of Writings from the 1920s* (Boston: Harvard Business School Press, 1996).

4. Donald T. Phillips, *Lincoln on Leadership: Executive Strategies for Tough Times* (New York: Warner, 1992); and David H. Donald, *Lincoln* (New York: Touchstone Books, 1996).

5. Milton Mayeroff, *On Caring* (New York: Harper & Row, 1971).

6. Patricia Pitcher, *The Drama of Leadership* (New York: Wiley, 1997); Barbara Kellerman and Larraine R. Matusak, *Cutting Edge: Leadership 2000* (College Park, MD: James MacGregor Burns Academy of Leadership, 2000); Jim Shaffer, *The Leadership Solution* (New York: McGraw-Hill, 2000); and Lee Iacocca, *Iacocca* (New York: Bantam Books, 1986).

7. Ellen Romano, "Leadership," *Journal of Property Management* 64, no. 4 (July–August 1999): 22–26; Price Pritchett, *The Employee Handbook of New Work Habits for the Next Millennium: Ten Ground Rules for Job Success* (Dallas, TX: Pritchett and Associates, 1999); and Price Pritchett, *Firing Up Commitment During Organizational Change: A Handbook for Managers* (Dallas, TX: Pritchett and Associates, 1996).

8. Clarence Francis, "Hippocratic Oath for Executives," in John Sargent, *What Every Executive Should Know about the Art of Leadership* (Chicago: Dartnell Corp., 1964), 24.

9. Phillips, *Lincoln on Leadership;* and Donald, *Lincoln.*

10. The poem "Retirement" is excerpted from the book *Life & Work: A Manager's Search for Meaning* (Avon Books, 1994) by James A. Autry and is reprinted by permission of the author.

Glossary

A

ability innate and learned competency; talent required to perform a task; one's level of achievement based on skill, motivation, and expectation that one will succeed. The greater the ability, the greater the potential for leadership effectiveness. See *job knowledge.*

access a means of approach and interaction, both electronic as well as personal; an important commitment of the servant leader who satisfies the human need for face-to-face contact.

achievement accomplishment of a task; fulfillment; a social motive for assuming leadership responsibility.

action the doing of something or a thing done; the criterion used to judge one's values. The leader gives time, attention, and resources to support what he or she values.

aesthetic sensitive to art and beauty; pleasing to senses of sight, hearing, smell, taste, and touch; pertaining to a value orientation advancing form, harmony, and beauty as ideals.

affiliation the joining of people for mutual support; membership; a social motive for assuming leadership responsibility.

alignment the arrangement and adjustment of parts, such as the alignment of people and resources to accomplish a goal; an essential leadership function.

art a skill acquired by experience or study; an endeavor requiring special knowledge and ability, such as the art of leadership.

assigning work effectively deploying personnel, designating duties, and giving orders, following such proven principles as the following: know what you want to communicate before giving an order; ask rather than tell, but leave no doubt that you expect compliance; be considerate but never apologetic for asking someone to do a job; take responsibility for the orders you give; give people the opportunity to ask questions and express opinions; follow up to make sure assignments are being accomplished.

associations the company one keeps, as in family, friends, and other role models who help shape one's life; important determinants of individual character.

attitude a disposition or mood; the combination of thought and feeling that predisposes one to take action. Positive attitudes focus and energize people whereas negative attitudes depress people.

authority the power or right to command, create, change, or otherwise act. The successful leader uses both formal and informal authority to accomplish goals.

autocratic pertaining to a form or style of leadership that is directive and leader-centered, and in which power is exercised by a dominant and dictatorial individual.

axiological arrest reduced level of morality that occurs if one fails to know, cherish, declare, act, and act habitually according to one's values. Axiology is the branch of philosophy concerned with the study of values.

B

behavior one's bearing, demeanor, and conduct. Behavior theory in leadership focuses on leadership style, such as autocratic, democratic, and laissez-faire, as well as leadership dimensions, such as initiating structure and showing consideration.

behavior modification an effective way to improve human performance, established in the 1950s and used in a wide variety of business, government, and nonprofit organizations. Elements include goal setting, feedback on performance, and positive reinforcement.

benchmarking in a search for excellence, taking the absolute best as a standard and trying to surpass it; objectively evaluating what an organization does compared with what its best competitors do and then taking steps to meet or exceed that high standard. Fundamental benchmark measures are product quality (what is produced) and service quality (how one deals with customers).

book a literary work, record, or account entailing many forms, such as volume, scroll, treatise, pamphlet, script; an important determinant of human character and leadership development.

burnout physical, psychological, and spiritual fatigue; inability to cope. Symptoms include lack of energy, low vitality, depression, loss of sharpness in thinking and feeling, lack of interest and meaning in life. Types of burnout victims include workaholics, burned-out Samaritans, mismatched people, and midcareer coasters. The formula for burnout is: Too many demands on strengths and resources, plus high expectations and deep personal involvement, plus too few actions taken to replenish the energy consumed, equals burnout.

burnout prevention strategies for dealing with inability to cope, including emergency aid, such as positive self-talk and physical retreat; short-term actions, such as reducing workload and setting priorities; and long-term solutions, such as clarifying values and making lifestyle changes.

C

care concern for the well-being of others and commitment to the accomplishment of a task. Caring is the emotional element required for successful leadership. See *concern* and *commitment.*

career success rules guidelines for succeeding in one's work, including exceeding expectations, delivering results, being considerate of others, being creative, and having integrity.

caring confrontation a corrective action that is taken to support core values, such as truth, trust, and respect, while simultaneously preserving human dignity.

caring leadership leadership marked by two principle aspects—commitment to a task and concern for people. The component of caring is the underlying requirement for successful leadership. See *commitment, concern,* and *Level 5 leadership.*

change alteration and transformation; paradoxically, a constant in nature and life. Types of change in the workplace include structure, tasks, technology, and people. Effective responses in dealing with change include exploration, responsibility and commitment, versus denial, resistance, or an attitude trough characterized by resentment, anger, and worry.

charisma a special charm or allure that inspires allegiance; an amalgam of inspirational traits or qualities of the leader, such as optimism, sense of adventure, and commitment to a cause. See *transformational leadership.*

code of conduct a listing of rules to live by; the basis for determining whether an action is ethical. An example is the Rotary International code of conduct, which requires asking these questions: Is it the truth, is it fair to all concerned, will it build good will and better relationships, will it be beneficial to all concerned?

commitment a pledge or promise; an agreement that binds one with others or to a cause; the sense of duty one has to accomplish a task; an essential element of caring leadership. See *care* and *caring leadership.*

communication   the giving and receiving of information; the basis of constructive relationships; the essential requirement for both a humanistic and productive workplace. Types of communication ranked in order of importance to employees include immediate supervisor, small group meetings, information from top executives, policy handbooks, orientation programs, and member newsletters.

concern   consideration; regard for others; a demonstration of respect; the sense of responsibility one has for the well-being of others; an essential element of caring leadership. See *care* and *caring leadership.*

conditions conducive to growth   favorable conditions for personal development, including a felt need or desire to learn, encouragement by someone who is respected, movement from general goals to specific actions, movement from a state of lower to higher self-esteem, and movement from external to internal commitment.

contingency   dependence on chance. Contingency theory holds that multiple leadership variables determine the probability that leadership will occur, including qualities of leaders, characteristics of followers, and the nature of a situation.

courage   the ability to overcome fear and live (or die) by one's convictions, even in ambiguous, uncertain, and dangerous situations; the virtue that underlies and gives reality to all other values; the basis for moral worth and dignity.

creativity   innovation; the ability to use imagination and insight to produce new ideas, products, and processes; an important ability that can be enhanced by keeping an open mind, having a questioning attitude, and using a new-ideas system.

cultural sensitivity   an awareness of and willingness to understand why people of another culture act as they do; a leadership quality requiring patience, willingness to learn, and flexibility, resulting in a bond of trust and respect among diverse people.

D

deed   an act accomplished; a means of influence. A leader's deeds may inspire and mobilize people.

delegation   the act of assigning to another; authorization and entrustment of tasks; enlistment of the energy and talents of others to accomplish more than would be possible working alone; a leadership skill required for multiplying effectiveness, including the following rules: Don't delegate the bad jobs, saving the good ones for oneself; use delegation as a development tool; delegate work fairly among all employees; insist on clear communications; and learn to live with work styles that are not like your own.

democratic   pertaining to a form or style of leadership based on equality, shared power, group decision making, and the greatest good for the greatest number.

dilemma   any situation requiring a choice between alternatives; any serious problem or quandary, such as making difficult moral decisions.

direction   the point, objective, or targeted goal; the establishment of purpose as an essential leadership function. See *vision, commitment,* and *initiating structure.*

discipline   action that develops self-control, efficiency, and orderly conduct; regulation, training, and enforcement. Discipline problems include permissiveness, rigidity, and inconsistency. Elements of effective discipline include defined roles and responsibilities, clear rules and guidelines, and methods for taking corrective action.

diversity challenge   the task of dealing with a wide variety of people and customs, including different genders, races, ages, religions, nationalities, and personalities; the goal of behaving in a way that creates mutual trust and interpersonal respect among people and gains benefits from their differences.

diversity practices   actions that can result in increased knowledge, skill, and creativity; better products and services provided to diverse populations; and the ability to recruit excellent talent from the entire labor pool. Such practices include top management's personal involvement, targeted recruitment, diversity education, network and support groups, and work and family policies that support diversity.

E

economic   pertaining to the production, distribution, and consumption of products and services; the management of income and expenditures; a value system based on the satisfaction of material needs and the accumulation of wealth.

effective group   a work group with the following characteristics: a clear mission, an informal atmosphere, lots of discussion, active listening, trust and openness, acceptance of disagreement, issue-oriented (never personal) criticism, consensus as the norm, effective leadership, clarity of assignments, shared values and norms of behavior, and commitment.

effective leadership   leadership that is the result of getting the facts, creating a vision, motivating people, and empowering others. Effective leadership requires being oneself, hiring good people, treating others fairly, focusing on key objectives, listening well, calling the play, and encouraging others, as well as being enthusiastic, setting the example, showing support, and keeping promises. See *leadership.*

emotional intelligence (EI)   the ability to understand and deal effectively with people; a type of intelligence possessed by successful leaders. Elements include self-awareness, impulse control, persistence, confidence, self-motivation, empathy, and social deftness, resulting in an overall characteristic of persuasiveness. See *persuasion.*

empowerment   authorization and enablement; the awakening, liberation, and inspiration of people. Principles of empowerment include trust in people, investment in people, recognition of accomplishment, and decentralized decision making. Empowerment is closely associated with the concepts of democratic and participative leadership. See *democratic* and *participative leadership.*

energize   to activate and mobilize, as in empowering people to accomplish results, an essential leadership function. See *empowerment* and *motivation.*

energy   force of expression and capacity for action; vitality and stamina to initiate tasks and see them to completion; an important trait or quality for leadership success. See *vitality* and *stamina.*

enlightened leadership   highly effective leadership resulting from viewing human resources as an organization's greatest asset; treating every individual with dignity, warmth, and support; tapping the constructive power of groups through visioning and team building; and setting high performance goals at every level of the organization.

enthusiasm   intensity of interest; the passion one has for a purpose or task; a leadership quality that ignites the interest and energy of others. See *commitment.*

entrepreneurship   the ability to achieve results, based on demonstrating good work habits, believing in oneself, and having the courage to take risks; an important element of leadership performance.

environment   surroundings; conditions and circumstances including physical and social factors; climate, geography, habitat, and social custom.

equation   a statement that matches, links, or relates objects or quantities. A leadership equation relates qualities of leaders, characteristics of followers, and the nature of a situation to explain the occurrence of leadership.

ethics   the branch of philosophy concerned with the intent, means, and consequences of moral behavior; derived from the Greek word *ethos,* referring to a person's fundamental orientation toward life or inner character. See *moral.*

example   a case, prototype, or illustration; a representative model or ideal, as in one who leads by personal example.

excellence   a state of exceptional merit or goodness; a performance ideal. See *quality.*

experience   the act of living through an event; that which is known through personal exposure or involvement, such as leadership skills learned through experience.

F

flow   a satisfying psychological state resulting from the confluence of high challenge and high skill, in contrast to states of apathy, anxiety, and boredom. Dimensions of flow include a clear and present purpose, immediate feedback, supreme concentration, a sense of growth, and an altered sense of time.

full-swing values   a concept used to describe the strength of one's values; full-swing values are known, cherished, declared, acted upon, and acted upon habitually. See *values* and *axiological arrest*.

G

glass ceiling   a term used to describe the impediments women face as they seek top leadership positions, including lack of encouragement, closed corporate culture, and double standards of conduct and performance.

goals   enduring intentions to act; process or functional accomplishments that are targets of effort; the ends one strives to attain.

groupthink   a mode of thinking that people engage in when they are deeply involved in a cohesive group, and when members striving for unanimity override their motivation to realistically appraise alternative courses of action; in contrast to group strength, groupthink results in mistakes and failure. Causes of groupthink include the illusion of invulnerability, belief in the inherent morality of the group, rationalization, stereotyping of out-groups, self-censorship, direct pressure, mindguards, and the illusion of unanimity.

H

headache   a cause of worry, annoyance, or trouble; a source of vexation.

heart   that which is vital; the center or core of a person or thing. Expressing one's innermost thoughts and feelings is termed "speaking from the heart," and it is the basis of credibility and trust.

hero   one who inspires through manners and actions; an individual who leads through personal example and accomplishments requiring bravery, skill, determination, and other admirable qualities.

honesty   truthfulness; a quality of character necessary for trust, respect, and honor; a foundation value and fundamental requirement for successful leadership.

human side of enterprise   all aspects of an organization relating to people, including relationships, performance, morale, and leadership. *The Human Side of Enterprise* is the title of a book by Douglas McGregor emphasizing the human potential for growth, the importance of the individual in the organization, and enlightened leadership practices. See *enlightened leadership*.

I

idea   a thought, mental conception, or image; a means of influence, as when the leader's ideas influence the behavior of the people.

imperative   a necessary, urgent, and important command, such as a quality imperative dictated by customers in the marketplace.

income   earnings; material rewards received (usually money), such as in wages, rent, interest, dividends, commissions, royalties, profits.

individualistic   pertaining to a style of interpersonal relations characterized by a need for freedom. Individualists generate new ideas and creativity, challenge the system, and accentuate possibilities. Leadership needs of individualists include being treated as separate individuals and avoiding rigid controls and close supervision.

initiating structure   the process of defining relationships, assigning tasks, making decisions, and holding performance to schedules and standards; job-centered leadership; concern for production. See *direction* and *vision*.

innovation   generation of new and usable ideas; an important element of leadership performance. See *creativity*.

integrative   pertaining to an approach to leadership that brings different people together and develops a whole that is greater than the sum of its parts; a building-up versus a melting-down process that preserves the identity of the individual while this identity is simultaneously transcended and made greater.

integrity   completion, wholeness, and soundness; a quality of character requiring honesty and courage; a virtue necessary for trust; the most important quality desired in a leader. See *values, honesty,* and *courage.*

intelligence   the ability to understand and solve problems; an important leadership trait or quality involving discernment, comprehension, and judgment; capacity to understand information, formulate strategies, and make good decisions.

interpersonal   between persons; for example, interpersonal trust and respect.

interpersonal styles   a construct of personality that helps explain why people do what they do. Although no trait or concept can capture the full richness and uniqueness of a single human being, styles of interpersonal relations reflect general patterns of behavior and needs.

J

job knowledge   mastery of essential theory and practical skills necessary to perform a function or task; a quality of leadership admired and deemed important by followers. See *ability*.

K

knowing–doing gap   knowing what to do, but failing to do it; a tendency to study and learn a concept, principle, practice, or skill, but neglect to use it in a practical way.

L

laissez-faire   pertaining to a free-rein form or style of leadership characterized by minimum control and maximum individual freedom.

leadership   social influence; showing the way or course of action; causing to follow by ideas and deeds; influencing through instruction, heroic feats, and force of will, magnified by the component of caring about the task to be done and the welfare of others; the functions or processes of establishing direction, aligning people and resources, and energizing people to accomplish results. See *effective leadership*.

learning   acquisition of knowledge, skills, and attitudes; growth and development enhanced by attention, pace, relevance, value, participation, repetition, and application; developed through study and experience.

level 5 leadership   the paradoxical combination of personal humility and professional will that makes a potent formula for the highest level of leadership success. Personal humility refers to consideration and service to others; professional will refers to conviction and fierce resolve. Together, these define the caring leader who is able to catapult a group or an organization from merely good to truly great. See *caring leadership.*

listening   hearing and paying attention to another as an expression of respect; an effective means of raising the psychological size of others, liberating their energies, and leading them to higher levels of achievement.

loneliness   a state of detachment, separation, and isolation; a feeling of being friendless and forlorn.

M

management   the performance of four functions or processes—planning, including charting a direction, determining strategies to succeed, and making policy decisions; organizing, including aligning structure, people, and resources to achieve goals; directing, including supervising, facilitating, coaching, and developing people; and controlling, including tracking progress against plans and making corrections; an endeavor requiring technical, relational, and conceptual skills.

managing change   helping people through change. Leaders should be guided by these seven rules: Have a good reason for making a change; personalize change; implement change thoughtfully; put a respected person in charge of coordinating change; tell the truth; wait patiently for results; acknowledge and reward people.

managing conflict   dealing effectively with conflicting purposes and personalities, and achieving solutions that benefit all parties; a social skill of the effective leader, involving a collaborative style, versus avoidance, accommodation, domination, and compromise.

methods of learning   approaches to learning, including classroom instruction, performance coaching, action learning, field assignments, and studying the masters.

mission   central purpose or reason for existence; a clear, compelling statement that provides focus and direction; an organization's answer to the question, Why do we exist?

moral   referring to what is right and wrong, good and bad, with emphasis on overt behavior—acts, habits, and customs. Levels of moral reasoning include preconventional morality, based on avoiding punishment and striving for pleasure; conventional morality, based on pleasing others and doing one's duty as prescribed by authorities; and postconventional morality, based on mutual consent and personal conviction. See *ethics.*

morale   mental and emotional condition with respect to satisfaction, confidence, and resolve; the attitude or spirit of an individual or group resulting in courage, dedication, and discipline; the level of satisfaction one has with intrinsic job factors, such as variety and challenge, feedback and learning, wholeness and meaning, and room to grow, as well as extrinsic conditions of employment, such as fair and adequate pay, job security, and health and safety. See *raising morale.*

motivation   stimulation and inspiration to move; the leadership task of mobilizing people with different ideas, skills, and values to achieve a common mission; the experience of physical and emotional needs, progressing from basic needs for survival and security, to social needs for belonging and respect, to the complex need for fulfillment. See *energize* and *empowerment.*

motivation principles   principles for understanding human behavior in the workplace, including the following: A satisfied need is not a motivator, employee motivation and company success are related, leadership is important in meeting employee needs, and the ideal is to align individual needs with organizational goals.

multiple intelligences   different kinds of ability required to understand and solve problems; innate and learned competencies, including verbal–linguistic, musical–rhythmic, logical–mathematical, visual–spatial, bodily–kinesthetic, intrapersonal, and interpersonal.

N

negative group member roles   group member roles that reduce effectiveness, including ego tripper, negative artist, above it all, aggressor, jokester, and avoider. See *effective group.*

O

organization   any group or aggregation of individuals into a purposeful entity, such as those found in business and industry, government, and the social community; also, the process of aligning people and resources to accomplish tasks (visions, goals, initiatives, and the like).

organizational climate   the social and psychological work atmosphere, including reward systems, organizational clarity, standards of performance, warmth and support, and leadership practices; a range of organizational health from exploitation to enlightenment that influences both employee morale and organizational effectiveness.

P

participative   pertaining to a style of interpersonal relations characterized by a need for human interaction and warm relationships. Participatives provide peace and harmony, give encouragement to others, and instill team spirit. Leadership needs include keeping human relations smooth and considering personal feelings.

participative leadership   a philosophy of and approach to leadership that taps the constructive power of people, resulting in both a humanistic and productive workplace. The participative leader begins by involving people, which is necessary to achieve understanding, which is necessary to achieve commitment. See *democratic* and *empowerment.*

people-building skills   the ability to teach, counsel, and otherwise develop others to higher levels of performance; a quality of leadership desired by followers. Developing others is a leadership function viewed by many leaders as the most rewarding of their tasks.

people, products, profit   the focus of concern for effective business leaders; a formula for success identified by business leader Lee Iacocca.

performance management   the heart and essence of leadership success; the process of performance planning, establishing direction and clarity of assignment; performance coaching, developing and encouraging others; and correcting poor performance, modifying and improving performance when mistakes are made.

performance review   evaluation and discussion of work behavior, such as dependability, initiative, and cooperation, as well as achievement of results in the areas of quantity, quality, timeliness, and cost. Performance reviews are used to capitalize on strengths and improve weaknesses. The process includes preparation, implementation, and follow-up. Types of performance reviews include tell and sell, tell and listen, problem-solving, and multisource assessment from supervisors, employees, peers, and customers.

persistence   constancy of purpose and unrelenting determination; a leadership quality required to persevere and prevail, even when others lose their strength and will.

personality   the sum total of an individual's character, resulting from biological, cultural, and psychological factors. Personality differences can account for frustrations and conflicts that lower performance and reduce opportunities, as well as satisfactions and accomplishments that enrich the human experience.

personality differences   conflict that occurs when personalities clash. Four steps should be used for solving personality differences: Talk it out in private when people are fresh, making sure every word spoken is true, necessary, and kind; be understanding and look at things from the other person's view; be flexible and willing to compromise to meet the other person's needs; be tolerant, recognizing that differences in personality are inevitable, because no two people are exactly alike.

persuasion   the act of influencing; the ability to get buy-in based on an understanding of people, the effective use of words, and the ability to manage conflict.

Peter principle   a term coined by author Lawrence J. Peter describing the tendency to promote individuals to their levels of incompetence. The overpromotion syndrome harms the individual and the organization because it inevitably results in lowered morale and job performance.

political   of or concerned with governance and the expression of power; a value orientation prizing social influence and the exercise of authority.

positive group member roles   group member roles that enhance effectiveness, including encourager, clarifier, harmonizer, idea generator, ignition key, standard setter, and detail specialist. See *effective group.*

power   vigor and strength; the force necessary to exert one's will. A social motive for assuming leadership responsibility. A leader with power has the ability to dominate and control people and events. Sources of power used by leaders include rewards, coercion, legitimacy, and information; types of power include expertise, reference, rational, and charisma.

prestige   renown and influence; reputation based on position, achievement, and character.

principles   standards of ethical conduct; fundamental truths and proven rules, such as the principles of effective leadership. See *values* and *ethics.*

problem-solving styles   distinct approaches to problem solving resulting from different emphases in having experiences, reflecting on results, building theories, and taking action. Identifiable styles include those of Charles Darwin, Albert Einstein, Socrates, and Henry Ford, each with special strengths and potential weaknesses.

psychological size   the perceived power one person has over another; the ability to make others feel weak and dependent; the ability to determine careers, decide wages, and make job assignments; an important concept for people in authority positions. The abuse of psychological size results in resentment and rebellion, or apathy and dependence, whereas the effective use of psychological size results in maximum morale and productivity.

Q

qualities   characteristic elements that make things what they are; attributes deemed desirable, such as the leadership qualities of integrity, job knowledge, and people-building skills.

quality   the degree of excellence of a thing; a virtue resulting from superior form, function, beauty, utility, fit, and other valuable attributes; the character of a person or thing that makes it desirable. See *excellence.*

quality movement   the synthesis of "hard" efforts to improve work performance, such as scientific management and quantitative methods, with "soft" efforts, such as improving morale and building community. The quality movement, most associated with the work of W. Edwards Deming, typically involves participative leadership, continuous process improvement, and the use of groups.

R

raising morale   taking actions that have a positive impact on employee satisfaction and work performance, including introducing a group bonus, allowing job autonomy, providing training, assigning whole tasks, gaining direct feedback from users, and increasing group interaction. See *morale.*

relational skill   the ability to work effectively with people, including the ability to motivate, coordinate, and advise other people; an important skill required at all levels of leadership—frontline supervisor, mid-level manager, and senior executive.

religious   pertaining to the belief in and worship of a god or gods, a specific system of belief and worship involving a code of ethics, a value orientation emphasizing spiritual peace.

respect   honor and esteem for another; regard for others as demonstrated through listening and being responsive to their beliefs and needs whenever possible.

retention   avoidance of turnover and ability to keep good people, which requires knowing what makes them stay. Factors that are particularly important to talented and productive employees include letting people know what is expected of them, giving them materials and equipment to do their jobs right, giving them the chance to do what they do best every day, providing recognition and praise for good work, showing that you care about them as people, and encouraging their development.

rich job   a job that contains optimum variety and challenge, opportunity for decision making, feedback and learning; maximum support and respect, wholeness and meaning, and room to grow; as well as fair and adequate pay, job security, benefits, safety, health, and due process.

ruler   one who governs, determining policy and making decisions; a commander, such as a chief, king, or other authority figure, who leads through power and enforcement.

S

school   a place or process of learning with many varieties, including elementary, secondary, and high school; technical, professional, community college, and university; continuing education and graduate studies; an important factor in the development of character and leadership.

secular   not religious; not connected with a church, synagogue, mosque, pagoda, temple, or other religious institution.

self-actualization   a state of psychological fulfillment, including acceptance of self and others, accurate perception of reality, close relationships, personal autonomy, goal directedness, naturalness, need for privacy, orientation toward growth, sense of unity with nature, sense of brotherhood with all people, democratic character, sense of justice, sense of humor, creativity, and personal integrity.

self-concept   a unifying construct of personality; the most important determinant of human behavior; the basis of present identity and future conduct; the primary factor in character formation.

self-confidence   a belief in oneself that gives inner strength to overcome difficult tasks; a leadership quality that raises the trust and confidence of followers and increases their ability to perform.

servant leader   a person devoted to others or to a cause or creed. A servant leader advances the interest of others, often at personal sacrifice. The essential component of servant leadership is the element of caring. See *concern, commitment,* and *care.*

service   aid and assistance provided to others; concern for the well-being and the best interest of another person or group.

showing consideration   developing relationships, providing support, and demonstrating kindness toward others; exhibiting employee-centered leadership, concern for people. See *concern* and *servant leader.*

situational factors   factors that influence the leadership process, including size of the organization, social and psychological climate, patterns of employment, and type, place, and purpose of the work performed.

social   of or having to do with other beings of one's kind; genial and companionable; a value orientation concerned with the well-being of others, typified by kindness, understanding, and helpfulness.

social motive   cause of human interaction. Social motives for assuming leadership include power, the goal to influence people and events; achievement, the need to discover, create, and build; and affiliation, concern for others and their welfare.

stability   steadiness and firmness of purpose; a leadership quality required for making good judgments and generating the trust and confidence of others.

stages in the life of a group   the natural sequence of conditions in the life of a group, including forming, the start-up stage; storming, a period of polarization and conflict; norming, a shift to affiliation and agreement; and performing, a state of focus, energy, and high performance.

stakeholders   individuals and groups who may be affected by what an organization does or does not do. Stakeholders include owners, employees, customers, suppliers, and the general public.

stamina   resistance to fatigue and illness; vigor, strength, and endurance to continue even in the face of difficult and trying conditions; a leadership quality required to create, advance, and sustain a vision. See *energy* and *vitality.*

statesmanship   the ability to work with and through other people, based on mastery of human relations skills and use of the four-step method to solve problems; an important element of leadership performance.

strategy   the science of planning; the process of giving definition to a vision, of focusing people and resources on specific objectives that can be measured; analysis of conditions and determination of initiatives; a requirement for successful leadership.

stress   physical and emotional wear and tear resulting from pressures, conflicts, and frustrations. Stress can be caused by self or others, work-related or personal, short-term or continuous. Sources of job stress for increasing numbers of people include new technology, workforce diversity, global competition, organizational restructure, and changing work systems.

support   care, encouragement, and help. The servant leader provides support to others through constructive feedback to reinforce and/or improve performance.

SWOT   an acronym standing for *s*trengths, *w*eaknesses, *o*pportunities, and *t*hreats. A SWOT analysis is a thorough and objective study of an organization's internal strengths and weaknesses and external opportunities and threats.

T

tactical   pertaining to the science of maneuvering, methods and techniques to achieve an end, projects and activities designed to implement strategy, the plays that drive the game to success.

teacher   one who provides knowledge, skill, and attitude development; a master or mentor who leads through insight, modeling, and the encouragement of others.

team concept   belief in the principle that together everyone can accomplish more than each could do working alone; tapping the constructive power of the group by having clear and elevating goals, a results-driven structure, competent team members, unified commitment, a collaborative climate, standards of excellence, external support and recognition, and principled leadership.

theoretical   that which is based on speculative thought and abstract reasoning; pertaining to a value orientation seeking universal principles and the discovery of truth.

tolerance of differences   openmindedness; understanding, appreciation, and patience with different kinds of people, such as those with different styles of interpersonal relations, types of intelligences, value orientations, and problem-solving styles.

top grading   the staffing process of selecting and developing high-quality (A and B) performers, and reassigning lower-quality (C, D, and F) performers to more appropriate functions; a difficult but necessary task of the successful leader in a competitive environment.

traditional   pertaining to a style of interpersonal relations characterized by a need for structure, order, and consistency. Traditionals provide stability and discipline, give attention to detail, and adhere to high standards. Leadership needs include respecting traditions and being clear and logical when giving orders.

trait   a distinguishing characteristic, such as a habit, manner, or peculiarity. Trait theory in leadership focuses on qualities that mark a leader, such as intelligence, integrity, and energy.

transformational leadership   the elevation of the potential of followers beyond previous expectations; the ability to raise aspirations and achievements to new levels of performance primarily as a result of the intelligence, charm, and talents of a charismatic leader. See *charisma.*

trust   a firm belief in the honesty and reliability of another; confidence developed by dealing openly with others, considering all points of view, keeping promises, and caring about people.

V

value   the estimated worth of something. To be most valued, a person, object, or principle must be known, cherished, declared, supported, and supported habitually, even at personal sacrifice. The value-based leader demonstrates courage of conviction, an important leadership trait or quality. See *integrity* and *full-swing values.*

vision   a positive and future-focused image of what could and should be that focuses and energizes people; an essential requirement for effective leadership. A successful vision is leader-initiated, shared and supported by followers, comprehensive and detailed, and uplifting and inspiring.

vitality   the strength to live; a basic requirement for successful leaders who, through personal energy and stamina, breathe life into their visions and followers. See *energy* and *stamina.*

vital shift   a change in work responsibilities when one moves from doer to coordinator to thinker; a transition period requiring adjustment to different job demands.

W

work   a thing made or done; a creation requiring effort; an endeavor that can be positive and ennobling or negative and unpleasant, depending on one's attitude.

Z

Zeigarnik effect   deterioration of morale and performance when tasks begun are not completed, which can be prevented by assigning whole tasks and allowing sufficient time for completion.

zeitgeist   trend of thought and feeling in a period of history, such as individual freedom, social responsibility, and love as an ideal—the spirit of a time.

Index